Hurlbut/Noonan

**Also by Seth Mnookin**

*Hard News: The Scandals at* The New York Times
*and Their Meaning for the American Media*

# Feeding

## How Money, Smarts,

*Simon & Schuster*

# the Monster

## and Nerve Took a Team to the Top

### Seth Mnookin

NEW YORK · LONDON · TORONTO · SYDNEY

SIMON & SCHUSTER
Rockefeller Center
1230 Avenue of the Americas
New York, NY 10020

For information about special discounts for bulk purchases,
please contact Simon & Schuster Special Sales at
1-800-456-6798 or business@simonandschuster.com

Designed by Paul Dippolito

Manufactured in the United States of America

10  9  8  7  6  5  4  3  2  1

The Library of Congress Cataloging-in-Publication Data is available.

ISBN-13: 978-0-7432-8681-7
ISBN-10:     0-7432-8681-2

A portion of Chapter 34, "Can You Believe It?" appeared in a different form
in *Vanity Fair* magazine.

*To my sister and brother, Abigail and Jacob;*
*and my grandparents, Marjorie, Seymour,*
*Marion, I.J., and Richard.*

# Contents

*Contents*

## PART V: THE WORLD CHAMPION
## BOSTON RED SOX: 2004

## PART VI: FEEDING THE MONSTER: 2005

# Feeding the
# Monster

# *Introduction*

**IT WAS JUST AFTER SEVEN THIRTY** on the evening of October 7, 2005, when Boston shortstop Edgar Renteria grounded out to second base to end the game, and although telephone operators at Fenway Park would continue to greet callers to the "home of the World Champion Boston Red Sox" for another couple of weeks, the Red Sox's magical run—the one that began in February 2002, when John Henry, Tom Werner, and Larry Lucchino took control of one of the most iconic sports teams in America—was over. The Red Sox, after winning the 2004 World Series to cap what will go down as the most famous postseason run in history, had been swept in the first round of the playoffs by the Chicago White Sox.

The immediate postmortems would center on that bases-loaded, no-outs jam the White Sox had wriggled out of in the sixth inning, but the air had been let out of the Red Sox's game, and their season, an inning earlier. In the bottom of the fifth, designated hitter David Ortiz came up with two men on and two men out. As he lumbered toward the plate at Fenway, Ortiz was busy mulling over his previous at-bat, when he had finally put the Red Sox on the board with a towering home run to straightaway center field. Now, with the score tied 2–2, the Fenway crowd began to scream in unison as Ortiz made his deliberate, heaving journey to the batter's box: "M-V-P! M-V-P!" It was as if the crowd felt it could will the country's sportswriters into granting Ortiz the award if its cheers were loud enough.

Ortiz, who bears a passing resemblance to the cartoon movie monster Shrek, contorts his face into a menacing snarl when he's hitting; it makes him look as if he's preparing to eat the opposing pitcher for dinner. With Johnny Damon, the team's matinee idol of a center fielder, dancing off second base, his wild mane of hair flapping below his batting helmet, and Renteria edging off first, Ortiz uncoiled his mammoth arms and chased after Chicago starter Freddy Garcia's first offering. The bat hit the ball sharply—*thwack!*—and, at first, it seemed to mirror perfectly the trajectory of Ortiz's fourth inning shot. The crowd leapt to its feet with a roar. But as strong and powerful as Ortiz is, not even he can push a ball out of the deepest part of the park when he doesn't connect dead on, and his bat had gotten just under this ball. As he dashed for first, and Damon rounded third, the ball arced through the crisp Boston air and fell, finally, into Aaron Rowand's glove in center field. Inning over.

Ortiz stopped about 20 feet from first base and froze, staring blankly at the spot where his blast had died. He stayed there as the White Sox jogged off the field. He stayed there as his teammates began taking their defensive positions around him. It was as if he couldn't believe that this time, in this at-bat, he hadn't been able to come through. The Red Sox had to win this game . . . didn't they? They had all the trappings of a championship team, including a $127 million payroll, the second highest in baseball. (The Yankees, the perennial bullies down the block, led the field at $208 million.) They had a roster full of All-Stars: Manny Ramirez, the slugging left fielder who was often described as the best right-handed hitter in the American League; Jason Varitek, the unassuming catcher who was known as one of the premier pitch-callers in baseball; and, of course, Damon and Ortiz. They had what was commonly described as the smartest front office in the business and an ownership group that seemed as devoted to fielding a winning team and giving back to the community as it was to making money. It was a recipe that was supposed to all but ensure success.

Indeed, since Henry, Werner, and Lucchino had taken over, being a Boston Red Sox fan, once a pastime best suited to masochists and depressives, had become fun, exciting, even trendy. Henry, the shy commodities trader, brought the same faith in statistical analysis to his baseball team that he did to his work in the markets. Werner, the television executive responsible for hits like *The Cosby Show* and *Roseanne,* helped ensure that the Red Sox's regional sports network, the New England Sports Network (NESN), raked in revenue. And Lucchino, the hard-charging former litigator, was an uncommonly creative chief executive known for never resting on his laurels and having a keen eye for emerging front-office talent. He delighted in fostering and developing smart, young leaders, most notably Theo Epstein, the 31-year-old Bostonian who became a folk hero when he was named the team's general manager before the 2003 season.

Together, Henry, Werner, and Lucchino had taken an organization known primarily for its heartbreaking losses and perennial runner-up status and transformed it into a world champion. Gone were the days when the team failed to sign Jackie Robinson or Willie Mays because its owner and its general manager were racists. Gone were the days when Carlton Fisk, a New England native and one of the best catchers ever to play the game, was lost to free agency because the Red Sox front office neglected to mail him his contract on time. Gone were the days of owners not speaking to management, of management not speaking to the coaching staff, of the coaching staff not speaking to the players. Gone was the Curse of the Bambino, the specter of Bucky F-ing Dent and Billy Buckner. Even the notoriously combative Boston media seemed to have been pacified by the team's press-friendly policies and winning ways. The Red Sox of old might have fielded a team of whining, overpaid misfits who got swept in the first round, and in the old days, that sort of failure would be followed by a course of inevitable finger-pointing and recriminations, whether deserved or not. But that wouldn't happen now. These days, things were different.

Weren't they?

It had been just five years earlier, on October 6, 2000, that John Harrington, then chief executive officer of the Red Sox, announced that, for the first time in a generation, the team was up for sale. Harrington was the last direct link to Tom Yawkey, the millionaire playboy who bought the Red Sox in 1933, and whose name now graced Yawkey Way, the street on which the entrance to Fenway Park's offices were located. Yawkey died in 1976; his wife, Jean, helped run the team until her death in 1992, at which point Harrington, one of Jean Yawkey's closest confidants, took control of the Jean R. Yawkey Trust, which by 1994 owned a majority stake in the team.

At first, the timing of Harrington's announcement seemed odd. The Red Sox had just emerged victorious from a grueling legislative battle that all but guaranteed the construction of a new, modern ballpark to replace Fenway, the oldest, smallest, and least comfortable place to watch a ball game in the whole country. But Jean Yawkey's will had compelled the trust to put the team up for sale eventually (the profits would be used to endow the charitable Yawkey Foundations), and the Red Sox's value was at an all-time high. Attendance was up, baseball had recovered from the labor dispute that had led to the strike that canceled the 1994 World Series, and the Red Sox were stocked with exciting, top-tier talent, including pitching great Pedro Martinez and homegrown superstar shortstop Nomar Garciaparra. In the press conference announcing the sale, Harrington said that, above all else, he hoped the team would go to a local bidder. "God willing," Harrington said, "my last act will be to turn this incredible team over to a die-hard Red Sox fan from New England who knows how important the team is to this town and the fabric of this community." In an article the next day, *The Boston Globe* noted that Harrington would, of course, be willing to listen to bids from outsiders.

The journey that began that day would continue for another 14 months. The sale of Major League Baseball teams is a notoriously Byzantine and time-consuming process; after the seller finds a buyer and the two agree on a price, the new owner still must be approved by three-fourths of MLB's 30 owners. Baseball commissioner Allan H. "Bud" Selig is perpetually rumored to fix this or that deal to help his cronies or allies end up with the winning bid. In Boston's case, the sale was even weirder than usual: The intense emotional hold the Red Sox have over the New England populace meant the entire region, from sportswriters to politicians, was strongly predisposed to a local group buying the team, whether or not it was willing to put up the money to do so. For much of 2001, the *Boston Herald* (and to a lesser extent, the *Globe*), unabashedly promoted the bid of Joe O'Donnell and Steve Karp, a pair of local businessmen who seemed to be friends or business associates with virtually every power broker in the city. Tom Werner, who had teamed up with Les Otten, a controversial New England ski entrepreneur, was seen as a long shot. And John Henry, who spent much of 2001 trying to get a new stadium built for the Florida Marlins, the Miami-based team he had bought in 1998, didn't even enter the fray until November, just weeks before final bids for the Red Sox were due.

Yet, on December 20, 2001, Henry, Werner, and Lucchino were awarded the team. Within days, word had it that the sale had been a fix, a bag job, orchestrated by Selig and perpetrated by Harrington and Red Sox lawyers. Advanced by Massachusetts attorney general Tom Reilly and rabidly propagated by the *Herald* (as well as *Globe* sports columnists Dan Shaughnessy and Will McDonough), the notion spread. For years, any discussion of the Henry ownership group would include some sort of caveat about the rigged sale of the team. Over time, this notion began to calcify—the transformation of myth into accepted reality is an essential motif in the Red Sox's history*—and eventually the new owners more or less stopped trying to correct the record.

The unconcealed bitterness and acrimony that greeted Henry and Werner when they arrived in Boston was only part of the problem the new owners faced. In the years leading up to the sale, the internal workings of the Red Sox organization had almost totally broken down. General manager Dan Duquette's pathological distrust of the media had fostered a paranoid culture in which team

---

* Try, for instance, telling your average Red Sox fan that former owner Harry Frazee didn't sell Babe Ruth to the Yankees to finance the Broadway production of *No, No, Nanette*. It's true that Frazee sold Ruth—in 1919. It's also true that he produced *No, No, Nanette* on Broadway—in 1925. By that time, Frazee was already two years removed from his ownership of the team. Still, the myth, and the attendant outrage, endures.

employees had to request explicit permission before answering the most basic of questions. (At one point, a team spokesman refused to give ESPN's Rob Neyer a list of people who had sung the national anthem at Fenway during the 2000 season, despite the fact that the information was broadcast on the park's JumboTron before every game.) Duquette's open feuding with his managers and the infighting among the players had only heightened the natural claustrophobia of Fenway Park, which had a tiny clubhouse to begin with.

Still, after the sale of the team became official, Henry and his partners were ecstatic. The Red Sox, they believed, were not only one of baseball's marquee franchises, they were also one of its most neglected. Fan outreach was nonexistent, creative revenue enhancement unheard of, marketing diffident to the point of being almost immaterial. With Boston's fan base, and the Red Sox's rich history, the new owners felt they were in a position not only to field consistently winning teams but also to explore previously untapped ways to bring in more money to what was already, in spite of everything, one of baseball's more successful organizations.

Upon taking over the team, Henry was, at first, greeted enthusiastically by many of its stars. He was known for being close to some of his former Marlins players, and word of his collegial, even paternal, relationship with players traveled quickly through Major League Baseball, with its close and chatty fraternity of multimillionaire athletes. Even Garciaparra, who had recently spoken out about how frustrating it was to play in Boston, told Henry he was excited about the future. But for all the hope and optimism he generated, Henry soon discovered just how odd a team he'd bought. On the first day of spring training in 2002, Manny Ramirez, who'd signed an eight-year, $160 million contract with the Sox before the 2001 season, approached the new owner. "Look, man, you gotta get me out of here," Ramirez told Henry. "I hate the pressure, I hate the manager. Please. I've heard you're a good guy. Please—you need to trade me." Henry was stunned. Just weeks earlier, he was giggling in amazement over the fact that he now owned a team that could afford stars like Ramirez, who hit the first pitch he saw at Fenway as a member of the Red Sox into the netting above the Green Monster, the park's fabled left field wall, and finished his first year with the team with 41 home runs. We can, Henry told Ramirez, do something about the manager—the Red Sox were already planning on firing Joe Kerrigan, who had taken over after Dan Duquette had axed Jimy Williams the previous August. And, per his request, the Red Sox did briefly explore trading Ramirez, but ultimately, Henry decided there was no way the team was going to part with one of the most potent offensive forces in all of baseball.

Over the next four seasons, these dramas cropped up again and again. Ramirez's annual trade demands would have been farcical if they weren't so distracting. (Despite his professed unhappiness, Ramirez averaged 40 home runs and 122 runs batted in from 2001 through 2005.) Before the 2004 season, Garciaparra was felled by a mysterious Achilles injury, and that July, the most popular Red Sox player since Carl Yastrzemski was traded to the Chicago Cubs. Pedro Martinez, even when he was earning $17.5 million a year, was obsessed with the perceived amount of respect he received from team executives. After becoming a free agent before the 2005 season, he signed a four-year deal with the New York Mets.

If the never-ending clubhouse turmoil—and the ensuing, usually overwrought coverage by the Boston media—seemed reminiscent of the Red Sox of old, the on-field results and front-office approach were starkly different. In 2003, Epstein's first year as general manager, the Red Sox led all of baseball in virtually every offensive category. After trailing the Oakland Athletics two games to none in their first round, best-of-five playoff series, they came back in thrilling fashion to advance to the American League Championship Series against the Yankees. That seven-game set featured on-field fights, off-field sniping, and a heartbreaking, extra-innings loss in the deciding Game 7. The next year, the Sox kept most of their offense intact while adding perennial All-Star starter Curt Schilling and bulldog closer Keith Foulke. After playing .500 ball for much of the year, the team ripped off a dominating stretch of victories late in the season and then clawed back from a three-game deficit to embarrass the Yankees in the 2004 ALCS, becoming the first team in baseball history to fall behind 3-0 and go on to win a seven-game series.* The World Series sweep of the St. Louis Cardinals, which secured Boston's first championship since 1918, almost seemed anticlimactic in comparison, like the 1980 U.S. Olympic hockey team's gold-medal–winning victory over Finland after it had upset the Soviet Union in the semifinals. Lucchino, meanwhile, helped craft an aggressively creative business approach that led to everything from the formation of a group that outsourced the team's marketing expertise to a string of consecutive sellouts that threatens to break baseball's all-time record.

When the Red Sox won baseball's ultimate prize that chilly night in St. Louis, Henry, Werner, and Lucchino embraced in the stands. They could not have helped being optimistic about the future of the organization. During the offseason, they planned to refurbish the team's clubhouse, adding a new upper level that would be off-limits to the prying eyes of the press; that way, they hoped, they could continue the Red Sox's transformation into the type of organization that would attract the game's biggest—and pickiest—stars. Epstein and his baseball operations crew, it seemed, would only grow stronger. Within days, the team embarked on a World Series trophy tour that eventually reached every single city in the state of Massachusetts, creating good will while simultaneously helping to attract new fans. The Red Sox's victory even quieted talk of the supposed Selig-orchestrated bag job. For a few months, it seemed as if all their dreams were coming true.

Five days after the end of the Red Sox's 2005 season, on the morning of Wednesday, October 12, the team's senior staff gathered for one of its regular strategy sessions. One of the quirks of Fenway is its lack of readily available conference spaces. Often, these management meetings were held in one of the luxury suites that ring the

---

*Before the 2004 Red Sox, none of the 25 Major League Baseball teams that had fallen behind 3-0 even forced a seventh game, and in the four major North American sports leagues, only two out of 239 teams had won a seven-game series after losing the first three games: the National Hockey League's New York Islanders in 1975 and Toronto Maple Leafs in 1942.

upper level of the stands. On this day, it was held in Fenway's Crown Royal Club, a street-level room decorated with wall-mounted flat-screen televisions and framed black-and-white photographs of Red Sox heroes from years past. The club, directly accessible from Brookline Avenue and available for rental for private functions and parties, is just one of the many money-raising additions the new owners had made to Fenway since they had bought the team four seasons earlier.

Larry Lucchino was the first to speak. Although Werner first pursued the Red Sox and Henry actually put up most of the money to buy the team, the 60-year-old Lucchino was usually the public voice of the organization, as well as the man responsible for day-to-day operations. Lucchino had been a standout high-school athlete —he was an all-city basketball player in Pittsburgh as well as a varsity second baseman. He went to Princeton, then Yale Law School, and in the early 1970s, found a mentor in Edward Bennett Williams, who had started the Washington, D.C.–based law firm Williams & Connolly. Williams steered Lucchino toward the sports world, and Lucchino served as general counsel of the Washington Redskins in the late 1970s before becoming general counsel of the Baltimore Orioles when Williams purchased the team in 1979. In the 1980s and 1990s, Lucchino gained a reputation as a swaggering, fierce competitor and a brilliant executive: As the CEO of the Orioles and the San Diego Padres, he oversaw vast improvements in each team's record (the Padres even went to the World Series in 1998), and was often credited as the driving force behind the successful new stadiums that were built in both cities.

Lucchino, who sat at the head of the rectangular table, is not a fan of small talk or fussing around. As soon as everyone was seated, he quieted the banter and asked people to identify the pros and cons of the previous season. "The fact that we won 95 games obviously goes on the positive side of the ledger," Lucchino said, starting things off. Indeed, the 2003, 2004, and 2005 seasons marked the first time in the team's history that the Red Sox had made the playoffs three years in a row; since 2002, only the Yankees had won more games in the American League. Still, Lucchino's opening statement seemed more like a carefully planned reminder than an acknowledgment of an actual accomplishment, for after the heady roller-coaster rides of the previous two years, many of the team's employees—to say nothing of its fans—seemed to feel that the 2005 campaign had been, in the end, a disappointment. Just a week earlier, the entire organization had been preparing for what it expected would be another long postseason run.

Mike Dee, a Lucchino disciple and, as the team's chief operating officer, the man in charge of wringing every last dollar of revenue out of the Red Sox experience, nodded to the improved atmosphere at the ballpark. Dee, who looks a little bit like Mr. Clean—tall and bald with a round face—noted that an increased security presence and stricter rules governing in-stand behavior meant many fewer drunken, cursing fans. Fenway, Dee said, was more hospitable to children and families than ever before, and this was accomplished during a season in which the team was publicly criticized for the addition of new beer stands and a huge increase in the amount of alcohol sold at the park. Meg Vaillancourt, the eccentric former *Boston Globe* reporter now in charge of the team's charitable operations, talked about how successful the paid tours of Fenway Park had become. They were, Vaillancourt said, a way to keep fans emotionally connected to the team even if they couldn't always afford to come to actual games. (At $44.56, the Red Sox, for the eighth straight season, had baseball's highest average ticket price; the Chicago Cubs, at $32, were second. At $12 a pop, these hour-long tours of Fenway cost as much as bleacher seats in many of the country's other ballparks.)

Finally, it was Theo Epstein's turn. Epstein looked much older than he had on the day in 2002 when he had become, at 28, the youngest general manager in baseball history. His hair had begun to thin, and his face had been shorn of its soft edges. Epstein is a workaholic—he had been in his basement office working early on Saturday, about fifteen hours after the Red Sox had been eliminated—and John Henry, worried about Epstein's stress level and his workload, had recently begun urging him to take some time off.

Two-thousand five had been an arduous and trying year for Epstein. After the Red Sox won the World Series in 2004, he'd become a local celebrity on par with, and perhaps even above, the team's players. He'd stopped watching games from his seat about a dozen rows behind home plate because he found it impossible to walk through the stands without being poked at and mobbed. He'd started having his hair cut in the basement of Fenway; not only would he save time but he could also avoid the endless gawking he endured whenever he was spotted on the street. Eating out had become a chore, as had running errands or trying to catch a movie with his girlfriend. While many thirtysomethings would have enjoyed the endless adulation and attention—the gifts of women's underwear, the marriage proposals—Epstein found it stifling. Over the course of the year, several of his closest colleagues said that he'd seemed sluggish or hesitant for the first time since he began working for the Red Sox. His interactions with the media, once friendly and frequent, became rare and combative. He seemed increasingly affected by fans' expectations for the team and the harsh glare of the Boston media.

There was also the fact that, although he'd been the architect of the team that had won Boston its first World Series in 86 years, Epstein still had to contend with grumbling from both inside and outside the organization that he had made a series of missteps in the past year. Several of the team's 15 minority partners had complained about everything from Epstein's signing of Renteria to a four-year, $40 million contract to the precipitous decline of left-handed reliever Alan Embree, who, after an ineffective half-season, was cut by the Red Sox only to sign with the Yankees. (At one point, one of the team's partners mistakenly hit "reply all" to send an email in which he groused about Epstein's personnel decisions and said he didn't think the Red Sox deserved even to make the playoffs.) Toward the end of the year, as the Sox's thin pitching staff struggled to stay afloat, even Lucchino had taken to humming Simon & Garfunkel's "Mrs. Robinson" in Fenway's corridors, replacing the song's famous refrain with the words, "Where have you gone, Pedro Martinez? / A nation turns its lonely eyes to you." Everyone from the team's executives to its most casual fans now seemed to expect the Sox to win 100 games and play deep into the playoffs every year.

That, Epstein knew, was not going to be possible. And he was dismayed—offended, even—by the fact that the organization, instead of tempering the unrealistic expectations for the team, had been adding more fuel to the fire, always agitating for more coverage in the local media, always promising that the team could and would get bigger, better, stronger. His pride in his accomplishments was being overwhelmed by the resentment he felt at the direction of the club. Part of the perfectionism that led him to study obsessively anything that could affect the team's on-field performance had also caused him to grow frustrated when other parts of the organization were not functioning in a way that he thought was most effective. His agitation had only increased as the season progressed. Finally, at the October 12 meeting, he spoke up.

"In general, we've had a lot of success in player development," Epstein said, starting off with an unqualified positive. After years of being known as an organization that traded away its best up-and-coming players in dubious—or just plain stupid—deals,* the Red Sox, under Epstein's leadership, had hoarded draft picks and jealously guarded the team's minor league prospects. One of the brightest spots of the second half of the 2005 season was the emergence of Jonathan Papelbon, a flame-throwing right-hander whom Epstein envisioned as the type of hard-working, no-nonsense player the Red Sox would be defined by in the years to come. In 2005, Epstein told everyone at the table, the Red Sox had been able to integrate some of the team's most promising young pitchers into the bullpen. Still, he felt compelled to warn his colleagues of what the future would likely bring: "We're going to need a lot of patience, because there's going to be a lot of failure." He reminded the group that most young hitters will look lost at the plate for their first half-season or so, and

---

* Right before the trade deadline in 1990, the Red Sox traded minor leaguer Jeff Bagwell, who had just been named the Eastern League MVP, to the Houston Astros for relief pitcher Larry Andersen. (Houston originally requested minor leaguer Scott Cooper, but the Red Sox offered Bagwell instead.) Andersen pitched in a total of 15 games for Boston. In his seven-season career, Cooper hit a total of 33 home runs and averaged .265. Bagwell, meanwhile, was the 1991 National League Rookie of the Year, the 1994 N.L. MVP, hit 449 home runs through the 2005 season, and is a likely first-ballot Hall of Famer.

most young pitchers will struggle with their confidence and command before settling into a groove.

"It could get rough," he said. "Right now, there's a lot of hope [about the team's young talent]. But remember, the most popular player on the football team is always the backup quarterback. When [second base prospect Dustin] Pedroia gets up here and he hits a buck-fifty, discovers he can't reach the wall and can't find his stroke because it's freezing out—well, that will happen. The rest of the organization really needs to realize this."

Epstein, who can appear reserved in public, began to speak more quickly. "We sat here in April and talked about building an über-team. That's dangerous. That's very dangerous. We need to be aware of the potential that the bubble could burst. Yes, it's a pro that, on the business side, we continued to grow. But on the con side is the amount of hype as we move toward superpower status. Yes, we won 95 games this year, but this approach isn't really sustainable over the long run. Sooner or later we might need to take half a step backward in return for a step forward. . . . I warned about this in April. What if we win 85 games [in 2006]? We're bringing up some young players that are going to be better in '07 than they will be next year. And they'll probably be even better than that in '08."

Lucchino, who'd been running the Orioles when Epstein was hired as a summer intern 13 years earlier, jumped in. Epstein and Lucchino had a complicated relationship, one that was undergoing a tense transition from mentor–protégé to peer–peer. After having broached with Lucchino the subject of his contract, which was set to expire at midnight on October 31, back before the season began, Epstein, who made around $350,000 a year—roughly what the lowest-paid players in baseball earned—still didn't have a deal in place for next season. Unbeknownst to almost everyone in the organization, the two men had each, over the previous year, become convinced the other was trying to undermine him. "Theo is talking about a slightly different approach that would need to be reflected in the PR of the organization as a whole," Lucchino said. "But frankly, I'm not sure how you would project that."

Epstein had some ideas. Though he'd never say it publicly, Epstein wished Lucchino would cool some of his public pronouncements: labeling the Yankees the Evil Empire, for instance, or, as he did two years ago, taking swipes at the players union just as the Red Sox were on the verge of completing a trade for Alex Rodriguez, who was at the time the Texas Rangers shortstop and the American League's reigning MVP. And he wasn't sure whether to laugh or cry at the efforts of Charles Steinberg, the team's executive vice president of public affairs and Lucchino's right-hand man. (Steinberg had actually hired Epstein while with the Orioles and had followed Lucchino to San Diego and then to Boston.) Steinberg frequently bragged about the fact that the Red Sox had been prominently featured in the Boston media every single day of 2004. He was especially proud of the fact that the team had waited until Christmas Eve to announce that catcher Jason Varitek had been signed to a four-year, $40 million contract and was being named the team's third captain since 1923, a move that guaranteed plenty of coverage on Christmas, normally a slow news day in the baseball world. That kind of continuous press was, Steinberg often said, a great accomplishment. Epstein disagreed. It was just this approach, he thought, that increased the pressure on a team already operating under intense scrutiny. After all, every seat in Fenway Park had been sold out for several years running. What was one more front-page story going to accomplish?

"It's a subtle thing," Epstein said that day. "We can't always make ourselves out to be a superpower. For our part, on the baseball operations side, we know that's not an effective strategy in the long haul." Epstein only had to look a couple of hundred miles to the south to realize this: The Yankees, after building a dynasty in the 1990s by developing their own stars, had spent the first years of the new millennium trading away their farm system and signing high-priced free agents whose peak performances were likely in the past. "That has to be reinforced on the public level," he said. "We may be reaching a saturation point. We keep asking for more, more, more. But there will be a point where we don't do more [one year] because we need to do things for the long run."

Epstein took pleasure in talking about, and planning for, the days when the team's emerging talent took center stage, but he worried that the transition to the team's up-and-coming stars would be hindered by the too-bright glare of unrealistic expectations. The previous year had been a good reminder of how an overabundance of media could become suffocating.

"Somehow, we still get involved in these weekly soap operas," Epstein told the table. "A lot of it's because the veteran players who have a forum because they always have a mic in their face become blowhards. Certain people have too much influence—the older, louder veteran players. They need to get a little more professional about presenting themselves. . . . That's one element of becoming an über-organization. We build the brand so big that it becomes hard to manage." Epstein was trying to remain calm, but he was clearly distressed by much of what he was describing.

Soon, as happens with many conversations involving the Red Sox, this one evolved into a discussion of money. The Red Sox had been very successful, but were constrained by baseball's revenue-sharing system and had to compete in their division with the Yankees, the richest team in the sport. One of the team's financial advisors warned that a single 85-win season could cost the organization as much as $20 to $30 million in lost ticket and advertising revenue. Lucchino raised the haunting legacies of teams like Baltimore, Colorado, Cleveland, and Toronto, all clubs that had enviable runs of high attendance followed by years of mediocre on-field performances and prolonged periods of fan apathy.

"We have the long-term solution to that problem," Epstein repeated. "We can be both a large revenue club [that can afford to sign high-priced free agents] and have a strong farm system. But it's probably not going to be a seamless transition. This year we had a great year. We will probably be worse next year."

An old Red Sox hand who worked in Fenway Park operations spoke up. "We'll just tell [the fans] different, we'll just tell them we'll be better."

Finally, Epstein lost his cool. "No!" he barked. "No!" Struggling to control himself, he said, "We can't just tell them we'll be better. That's the whole point! That's what I'm trying to say!" Epstein, already flustered, let the topic drop, and Lucchino steered the conversation toward other issues before breaking for lunch.

Later that afternoon, Epstein paced among the cubicles outside of his basement office. "What a joke: 'Just tell them we'll be better,' " he said to no one in particular. "Two more weeks. Two more weeks and I might be a free man."

And so he was. Epstein's season-long frustration, coupled with some last-minute leaks regarding his contract negotiations, resulted in the biggest bombshell to hit Red Sox Nation since Henry and Werner had bought the team four years earlier. On October 31, the same day the *Globe* reported Epstein would be signing a three-year deal worth $4.5 million, Epstein announced his resignation. An apparently irreparable break in his relationship with Lucchino, compounded by his frustration over what he felt was not-so-subtle backstabbing by his old boss Charles Steinberg, convinced him to walk away from one of the most lucrative general manager contracts in all of baseball.*

Over the next several months, the Red Sox were roiled by the kind of drama and controversy fans had associated with the Yawkey era. John Henry, in an emotional press conference, said Epstein's departure had forced him to question whether he was fit to be the principal owner of the Red Sox. Larry Lucchino was accused of being everything from an egomaniacal cowboy to an insecure bully. The normally loquacious Steinberg all but disappeared from view. Suddenly there was, Boston reporters agreed, a level of dysfunction not seen since the waning days of the Dan Duquette–John Harrington era.

---

* Most baseball general managers, despite often working seven days a week close to year-round, make under $1 million annually. The game's best-paid GMs are Atlanta's John Schuerholz, whose Braves have won 14 consecutive division titles, at $1.6 million per year; the Yankees' Brian Cashman, who signed a three-year deal for around $5.5 million after the 2005 season; Detroit's Dave Dombrowski, who was reported to have earned $2 million in 2005 while serving as the Tigers GM and club president; and Oakland's Billy Beane, who makes over $1 million annually and whose contract includes an ownership stake in the A's. When the Red Sox tried to hire Beane after the 2002 season, they offered him $13 million over five years.

The John Henry era was supposed to be about finally realizing the squandered potential of a team that had been so miserably mismanaged for so much of its existence. Within three years, the Sox seemed to have accomplished everything they could have ever hoped to achieve. One year later, it looked like it was all falling apart.

# PART I

# A Century of Boston Baseball

## CHAPTER 1

# From the Beaneaters to the Babe

**IF IT'S TRUE THAT BASEBALL,** along with jazz, is one of the great indigenous American art forms, then certainly the story of baseball in Boston has been, for most of its history, one of America's most compelling tragedies. As John Cheever famously said, "All literary men are Red Sox fans—to be a Yankee fan in literate society is to endanger your life." The Yankees play on the biggest stage, they've fielded the biggest superstars, and, of course, they've won the most championships. But it's the Red Sox who truly represent the trials, tribulations, and triumphs of man as he struggles to transcend the limits of his essential nature.

The saga of the Red Sox has it all, a rich intertwining of biblical leitmotivs and uniquely American morality tales. There's the myth of the Original Sin—the supposedly greed-driven sale of Babe Ruth to the Yankees in 1919—which drove the team from the Garden of Eden, or, in the Red Sox's case, its standing as the best team in baseball. There's a mirroring of the country's conflicted relationship with money and power, and an eerily perfect reflection of the damaging effects of the nation's racist past. There are the cautionary tales about the dangers of hero worship, the always ambiguous relationship between the press and both its subjects and the public, and the specter of political corruption and nefarious back-room dealings. Finally, there's the Moses-like trip to the Promised Land, a trip that can only be completed when the father figure is banished and an outsider comes in to lead the tribe on the final, triumphant leg of its journey. Since the start of the new century, the Red Sox have been the most enthralling story in all of sports. To truly understand why that is, one needs to go back more than a hundred years, almost to the beginnings of baseball in America.

The history of professional baseball in Boston can be traced to 1871, when manager Harry Wright and several players from the Cincinnati Red Stockings, baseball's first professional team, joined up with a new semipro National Association team in Boston that, in time, also came to be known as the Red Stockings. In 1876, the disbanding of the National Association led to the birth of the first true professional baseball league, named the National League. The Boston team—usually called the Beaneaters*—was far and away baseball's dominant force, and over the next 25 years the team won eight pennants, including three straight from 1891 to 1893.

At the time, Boston was known for having some of the most rabid fans in the country. The city's white immigrant neighborhoods passionately embraced the city's rugged ballplayers, many of whom came from the same backgrounds as their fans. The Beaneaters' most ardent supporters were known collectively as the Royal Rooters, and they, along with many of the city's sportswriters and the similarly working-class players themselves, gathered every evening in Michael "Nuf Ced" McGreevey's Roxbury saloon, Third Base. (It was so named because McGreevey said it was the last stop on the way home. McGreevy's own nickname came from his signature exhortations, invoked whenever he felt a debate had reached its natural conclusion.) Politicians and city leaders also assembled at Third Base, including ardent baseball fan John F. "Honey Fitz" Fitzgerald, the future mayor of Boston and grandfather of John F. Kennedy. When

---

* In the late-nineteenth and early-twentieth centuries, team names, or nicknames, were not as important or as immutable as they are today.

they weren't debating this or that strategy decision or drinking rounds of toasts to the city's best hitters, the Rooters would sympathize with the plight of the Beaneaters, who played for Boston's famously parsimonious owner, Arthur Soden. Soden, in addition to forcing his players to pay for their own uniforms, charged fans an outrageous 50 cents for admission at a time when many of the other parks around the country charged only a quarter. Soon, Soden would have competition for the hearts—and dollars—of the Royal Rooters.

In 1901, Byron "Ban" Johnson renamed his amateur baseball league the American League and took aim at the National League, telling owners he didn't intend to honor their reserve clause, which essentially tied a player to the same team for the duration of his career.* Johnson had already started teams in Cleveland and in Chicago's South Side, and had moved others to Baltimore, Washington, and Philadelphia. On January 28, 1901, Johnson announced he intended to open an American League club in Boston, which came to be known as both the Boston Americans and the Boston Somersets. The Somersets signed some of baseball's biggest names, including hard-nosed third baseman Jimmy Collins and Denton True "Cy" Young, already renowned as the best pitcher ever to grace a baseball diamond.

In 1903, the Boston team, by now more generally known as the Pilgrims, inaugurated what remains the greatest rivalry in sports. That year, on May 7, the American League team from Boston met the American League team from New York, then called the Highlanders, for the first time. Even before a pitch was thrown, the two teams had reason to dislike each other. The cities themselves already had a natural rivalry: New York had been steadily eclipsing Boston as the country's seat of culture and business for decades. What's more, the Highlanders were born from the ashes of

---

* At the time, baseball players had almost no control over where they played. Once a contract expired, the rights to that player were retained by the team that had initially signed him. If the player didn't want to re-up for what his club was offering him, he could choose to sit out and not play; he did not, however, have the right to sign with another team. Teams, of course, had the right to trade players—they could even trade or sell the rights to players they no longer had under contract but still controlled.

Boston's National League team's former rivals, the old Baltimore Orioles.* Boston won two out of the first three games, which, in what would become commonplace in Boston–New York contests, featured plenty of offensive fireworks, a bench-clearing argument, and a pitcher being knocked nearly unconscious after being run over while covering first base.

For the rest of the 1903 season, the New York Highlanders, to say nothing of the other American League teams, were no match for the Pilgrims, who ran away with the pennant. That fall, after the National League's owners finally resigned themselves to the fact that the American League was around to stay, the American and National Leagues brokered a peace, and Boston's owners and the owners of Pittsburgh's pennant-winning National League team agreed to meet for a best-of-nine-games world championship series, which Boston won, 5-3.

A year later, in 1904, General Charles Taylor, already a legendary newspaperman and the owner and publisher of *The Boston Globe,* bought the Pilgrims for around $150,000. Taylor gave the team to his ne'er-do-well son, John I. Taylor, so the boy would have something to occupy his time. John Taylor's tumultuous reign as owner of the team was, for the most part, a disaster. Still, Taylor did leave an indelible mark on the team's history. In 1907, Taylor decided his players would start wearing red socks and trim, and beginning with the 1908 season, the Pilgrims became known as the Red Sox. Taylor was also responsible for building what has become associated with the Red Sox above all else: Fenway Park. Taylor broke ground in the winter of 1911, and by 1912, the Sox had a new home.†

At the time, Fenway bore only a passing resemblance to the park nestled in Boston's Kenmore Square area today. There was only a single-deck grandstand, with wooden bleachers in left and way out in right and center fields. The left- and right-field fences were just over 300 feet away from home plate—in those days, at the height of

---

* The Orioles were reborn as an American League team when the St. Louis Browns moved to Baltimore after the 1953 season.
† The Red Sox beat the Highlanders, 7–6, in Fenway's major league opener.

the dead ball era, batters rarely hit balls out of the park—and the center-field fence was 390 feet away. There was a 10-foot embankment built out in left; that way, overflow spectators could be seated in the outfield and still see the action. It wouldn't be for another two decades that the Fenway spectators know today would take shape.

Fenway's first years saw the appearance of another of the Sox's most enduring icons, a loud-mouthed young player with questionable work habits named George Herman "Babe" Ruth. The 19-year-old Ruth was acquired from Baltimore in the middle of the 1914 season, and for the first several years of his career, he was used almost exclusively as a left-handed starting pitcher. Within days of his arrival on the club, he rubbed some of the Red Sox veterans the wrong way. "He had never been anywhere, didn't know anything about manners or how to behave among people," said Sox outfielder Harry Hooper. "[He was] just a big, overgrown ape." Referring to Ruth's transformation into the best baseball player in the history of the game, Hooper said, "If somebody had predicted that back on the Boston Red Sox in 1914, he would have been thrown in a lunatic asylum."

Ruth was clearly a talented pitcher, and for a while, seemed destined to go down as one of the game's better southpaw hurlers. That changed with America's involvement in World War I. Suddenly, teams had barely enough players to suit up a full team, and the 23-year-old Ruth began taking turns in the field. Nineteen-eighteen marked Ruth's emergence as an offensive talent, as he batted .300 and smacked 11 home runs in an era when players frequently led the league with fewer than 10.

Red Sox owner Harry Frazee, meanwhile, was engaged in a feud with American League president Ban Johnson that would eventually help drive both men from baseball. Frazee had purchased the Red Sox for $400,000 in 1917, and began squabbling with Johnson over power and control almost immediately. The feud deepened when Frazee fought Johnson's plans to stop play during the war. In 1918, Johnson threatened to terminate the Red Sox's membership in the league due to gambling in Fenway's stands, despite the fact that Boston's gambling problem was no worse than any other city's.

In 1919, when Frazee sold pitcher Carl Mays to the Yankees, Johnson attempted to void the deal. Frazee responded by calling the league president's actions "a joke."

In 1919, as the Red Sox returned to mediocrity due to an abundance of aging players, virtually the only exciting thing about the team was the unprecedented emergence of Ruth, who clouted 29 home runs that year, setting an all-time record. All the while, the already burly slugger continued to pack on more weight. When the season ended, Ruth, less than one year after threatening to walk out on the team during negotiations for a three-year deal, once again announced his intention to walk out unless his salary was doubled to $20,000 a year. Soon, other Boston players began grumbling as well.

While facing Ruth's threats, Frazee was also preparing for what he feared could be a lengthy—and costly—battle with Ban Johnson. Looking to shore up his cash reserves and tired of Ruth's behavior, on December 26, 1919, Frazee sold Ruth to the New York Yankees for $100,000, at the time the most lucrative deal in the history of the game. Frazee, knowing he'd be criticized for selling one of Boston's most popular players, released a statement as soon as the deal hit the papers. Ruth, Frazee wrote, "had become impossible and the Boston club could no longer put up with his eccentricities." He was "one of the most inconsiderate men that ever wore a baseball uniform" and was "taking on weight tremendously" and "doesn't care to keep himself in shape." Fair-minded parties, Frazee concluded, "will agree with me that Ruth could not remain in Boston under existing conditions." There was an outcry, to be sure, but Boston's regard for Ruth was by no means unanimous. In any case, the Yankees didn't seem to be much of a threat; in the seven years since they'd changed their name from the Highlanders, they'd averaged a fifth-place finish, while the Sox had won three championships.

Harry Frazee held on to the Red Sox until 1923, and his remaining years with the team were notable mostly for his colorful squabbles with Johnson. But at the time that Frazee sold Ruth, he did not, contrary to what's become accepted as fact, face serious financial difficulties, nor did he need the money he got from the sale to finance *No, No, Nanette*. Frazee's mistake—and the cause of the fossilization of his legacy as the man responsible for the media-constructed Curse of the Bambino—had everything to do with his failure to ally himself more strongly with the local press. Many of Boston's sportswriters were already friendly with Ban Johnson, and Frazee, in taking away some of the perks (like free booze and food) the writers had grown used to receiving at Fenway, gave the city's scribes further reason to line up against him. There was also the lingering suspicion that Frazee was Jewish (he wasn't), a definite black mark in early-twentieth-century, heavily Irish-Catholic Boston. This wouldn't be the first time the members of Boston's sporting press would take it upon themselves to decide the proper way to run the Red Sox.* That had been going on since the days when the Royal Rooters and the city's sportswriters took on Arthur Soden.

After Ruth's sale to the Yankees, the Babe, of course, went on to hit 665 more home runs, cementing his place as the sport's most famous player of all time. The Red Sox, meanwhile, were about to begin an epically barren stretch. After winning more World Series than any other team in its first two decades, the Red Sox and their fans would soon learn what it was like to truly suffer.

---

* So deeply rooted was the press's antipathy toward Frazee that they continued to slander him in death. As Glenn Stout and Richard Johnson write in *Red Sox Century*, "Paul Shannon's obituary of Frazee in the [Boston] *Post* is most notorious for its inaccuracies, and he again raised questions over Frazee's religion. . . . The [New York] *Times* made a particularly egregious error, reporting that Frazee died nearly broke." The *Times* corrected its obituary shortly thereafter, but the first, inaccurate one was usually used for reference.

## CHAPTER 2

# Tom Yawkey's Team, Ted Williams's Town

IN 1923, Bob Quinn, a Ban Johnson ally, led a consortium that bought the Red Sox for $1.15 million. By the end of the decade, the Red Sox had become the biggest joke in baseball, and Fenway, devoid of fans and sorely in need of upkeep, took on the appearance of a haunted house. In 1932, the Red Sox finished the year at 43-111, drawing fewer than 200,000 fans. The Yankees, meanwhile, were well on their way to building a reputation as one of the twentieth century's greatest dynasties. In 1932, powered by Ruth and Lou Gehrig's combined 75 home runs (the entire Red Sox team had only 53), the Bronx Bombers went 107-47, swept the Cubs in the World Series, and drew almost a million fans, tops in the league.

During the nine full seasons in which he owned the Red Sox, Quinn led the team to a 483-897 record, one of the worst stretches in baseball history.* Before the 1933 season, despondent and desperate to sell, Quinn finally found a suitable buyer. New York millionaire Tom Yawkey had been casting about to buy a baseball club, and,

* In those nine seasons, the Red Sox compiled a .350 winning percentage over 1380 games. From 1998 to 2005, in the hapless Tampa Bay Devil Rays' first eight years in baseball, the team amassed a record of 518-775, for a .401 winning percentage over its first 1293 games.

when one of Yawkey's confidants, former Philadelphia A's star Eddie Collins, introduced Quinn and Yawkey, the two men struck a deal. In February 1933, just days after his thirtieth birthday, Yawkey bought the Red Sox and Fenway Park for $1.2 million.* Since Yawkey had no experience running a baseball organization, he named Collins the team's vice president and general manager.

Yawkey was born Thomas Austin in 1903. His mother, Augusta Yawkey, was an heir to the Yawkey lumber and mining fortune; his father, also named Thomas Austin, was an insurance executive. The elder Thomas Austin died of pneumonia when his son was less than a year old, and the young Tom Austin was brought into the household of Augusta's brother Bill Yawkey, who had used some of his share of the family fortune to purchase the Detroit Tigers. When Tom was 15, his mother died, and he was formally adopted by Bill Yawkey; when Bill died a year later, Tom, who had by then changed his last name, had an inheritance that was estimated at around $20 million. Growing up, Yawkey constantly tried to prove himself on the athletic fields, where he often fell just short. By the time he reached his twenties, Tom Yawkey had grown into a young man who both jealously guarded his privacy and desperately wanted to make his mark in the world. In 1924, he met a young dancer, Elise Sparrow; the two married a year later.

Yawkey wasted little time before making it clear that he intended to use his money to make the Red Sox relevant—and victorious—once again. When a fire wiped out Fenway's new left-field bleachers in 1934, Yawkey took the opportunity to give the park a major renovation, adding new grandstands and a second deck and covering the 37-foot wooden wall that rose over left field with sheet metal. In 1935, desperate to land the league's best player, Yawkey purchased Washington Senators shortstop Joe Cronin, who became the Red Sox player-manager. Cronin, a slick-fielding, two-time All-Star, was, to be sure, a good ballplayer, but he was far from the most powerful or talented player in the game. For the next quarter cen-

---

* One of Yawkey's other main business interests during the years he owned the Red Sox was the Sunset Lodge, a South Carolina whorehouse he ran until authorities closed it down in 1969. A one-time patron recently described the Sunset as "the Wal-Mart of fast, fast relief."

tury, Cronin, for better and worse, would come to define Red Sox baseball in his various stints as a player, manager, and member of the team's front office. For years, he selfishly insisted on forcing other, better players out of position so he could remain at shortstop. In 1939, a year in which he made 32 errors in the field, Cronin told Yawkey to sell a highly touted shortstop prospect in the Sox's farm system named Pee Wee Reese. Yawkey did. Reese, of course, would play on 10 All-Star teams and seven pennant winners as a member of the Brooklyn Dodgers.

Yawkey, meanwhile, was growing estranged from his wife, Elise, and slowly succumbing to the drinking that would mark much of his life. He has been described during this time as an isolated, pathetic figure. Still, desperate to prove his mettle on the playing fields, he'd pay the team's batboys to throw him batting practice so he could try to smack a ball over Fenway's left field wall. (He never did.) During games he'd sit sullenly in his private suite next to Fenway's press box, drinking alone or with Eddie Collins; afterward, he'd retire to his room at the Ritz, where he took his meals by himself. By the mid-1930s he'd met Jean Hiller, a young divorcée who sometimes modeled clothes for Elise Yawkey at exclusive New York stores. By 1944, both Tom and Elise were having affairs. The couple divorced, and Yawkey married the 35-year-old Jean Hiller on Christmas Day.

If Tom Yawkey is the man who has had the single biggest impact on the Boston Red Sox, Ted Williams is the player with whom the team will likely always be most intimately connected. To this day, a red 9, signifying the number Williams wore throughout his career, is all that's needed to identify the Splendid Splinter in much of New England.

The lithe, left-handed hitting Williams joined the team in 1939, when he was 20 years old. An indifferent fielder possessing a cantankerous personality, Williams would, for the next two decades, prove himself to be one of the best hitters the game has ever known. In his first season in the bigs, Williams hit .327 and led the league with 145 runs batted in; the next year, at age 21, he hit .344. Forty-five years later, while attending the Red Sox's spring training, he told *The New Yorker*'s Roger Angell the reason for his success. "I didn't get laid for the first time until the All-Star Game break of my second year in the majors," Williams said. "I was thinking about hitting."* Whether or not he was having sex, Williams continued to put up eye-popping numbers. In 1942, at age 23, he hit .356 with 36 home runs; by that point, he'd already hit 127 home runs. Williams lost the next three years to World War II, during which he served as a pilot in the Navy Air Corps. When he returned to the Red Sox in 1946, he picked up right where he had left off, hitting .342 with 38 home runs. Williams also lost much of the 1952 and 1953 seasons to the Korean War, where, as a Marine fighter pilot, he flew some of his missions as a wingman to John Glenn.† He is the only person in the last 75 years to hit above .400—he hit .406 in 1941—and, at .482, he has the highest career on base percentage in history.‡

---

* Williams similarly ascribed the problems today's young players have to too much sex. "They're fucking their brains out," he told Angell. "They're just kids but they're all married, and the ones that aren't have got somebody living in with them, so it's like they're married. They're just thinking of that one thing."

† Williams averaged 32 home runs during his first 12 complete seasons of play, spanning 1939 to 1955, and he finished his career with 521 home runs. If you assume he would have at least reached that average during the years he lost to his military service—and, since those were what should have been Williams's peak years as a hitter, he likely would have been even more pro-lific—Williams would have hit 667 home runs in his career, placing him fourth on today's all-time list behind Hank Aaron, Babe Ruth, and Barry Bonds. As it is, he's tied for 15th.

‡ Batting average is computed by dividing a player's number of hits by his number of at-bats. (Walks, instances where a batter was hit by a pitch, and times when a batter sacrifices himself in order to move a base runner up a base, do not count as at-bats.) On base percentage is obtained by adding up a batter's hits with his walks and the times he was hit by a pitch and dividing that by his at-bats plus his walks, the times he was hit by a pitch, and his sac-rifices. So, for instance, a batter who comes up to plate ten times and gets two hits, is walked twice, and has one sacrifice would have a batting average of .285 (two hits divided by seven at-bats) and an on base percentage, or OBP, of .400 (two hits plus two walks, for a total of four, divided by seven at-bats plus two walks and one sacrifice, for a total of ten).

It is one of the tragedies of Ted Williams's tenure with the Red Sox that he was rarely surrounded with the talent needed to make his team a winner. For most of his career, the Sox languished somewhere in the middle of the American League. During the Red Sox's best four-year run of Williams's career, from 1946 to 1949, lousy managing did in the team.

Take 1946, Williams's first year back after the war. He was typically dominant, with an on base percentage of almost .500 and a slugging percentage of .667.* The Sox cut a swath through the league, and won the pennant handily. Despite being the heavy favorite in that year's World Series, they were defeated in seven games by the St. Louis Cardinals. In typical Red Sox fashion, shortstop Johnny Pesky was later blamed for the loss; he is said to have hesitated for a split-second before throwing a relay to home plate in the deciding game of the series. Historical accounts of the game differ; many observers felt Pesky wouldn't have been able to nail the Cardinals' Enos Slaughter even if he'd come up throwing and had a rifle for a right arm. What's unquestionable is that a staggering number of bone-headed moves by manager Joe Cronin preceded that throw. Cronin didn't take advantage of favorable pitching matchups, didn't sacrifice hitters in order to move runners into scoring positions, and left crucial role players on the bench. Pesky's throw should have been unnecessary because the Red Sox should have already won the championship.

Nineteen forty-eight and 1949 offered more heartbreaking defeats. In '48, the Sox lost a one-game playoff with the Cleveland Indians, and in '49, Boston blew the final two games of the season

---

* Slugging percentage is the average number of bases per at-bat, and is derived by adding the number of singles with two times the number of doubles (because each double is worth two bases), three times the number of triples, and four times the number of home runs. That number is then divided by the total number of at-bats. A .667 slugging percentage means that a player averages about two-thirds of a base every time he comes to bat and reaches base due to a hit, as opposed to a walk, an error, or being hit by a pitch. In 2005, the American League's highest slugging percentage belonged to Alex Rodriguez, at .610; Derek Lee led the National League at .662. At .634, Williams has the second-highest career slugging percentage in history, behind Babe Ruth's .690.

against the Yankees, handing their rivals the pennant. (The Yankees went on to win their first of five straight World Series that year.) For the last decade of Williams's career, while the Yankees were busy winning eight pennants and five World Series titles, the Red Sox never finished better than third.

In 1959, at age 40, Williams played most of the year with a pinched nerve in his neck. It was the only year in his career during which he hit below .300. After insisting on a pay cut from $125,000 to $90,000, he came back to play one more season in Boston, and at age 41, batted .316 with 29 home runs. For his last game, fewer than 11,000 fans showed up at Fenway. Williams, who wanted to keep his retirement low-key, nevertheless agreed to say a few words before the game. He began by complaining about the city's sportswriters, who had increasingly turned their attention from the Sox's moribund record to Williams himself, often in the form of printed taunts and heckles. "Despite the fact of the disagreeable things that have been said about me," he said, pointing to Fenway's press box, "by the Knights of the Keyboard out there, baseball has been the most wonderful thing in my life. If I were starting over again and someone asked me where is the one place I would like to play, I would want it to be Boston, with the greatest owner in baseball and the greatest fans in America. Thank you."

In the last at-bat of his career, Williams hit a home run. The few fans that did show up screamed and stomped for a curtain call, a tip of the cap, some acknowledgment from the man who embodied baseball for Boston. John Updike famously chronicled the scene for *The New Yorker* in his article, "Hub Fans Bid Kid Adieu." "Our noise for some seconds passed beyond excitement into a kind of immense open anguish, a wailing, a cry to be saved," Updike wrote. "But immortality is nontransferable. The papers said that the other players, and even the umpires on the field, begged him to come out and acknowledge us in some way, but he never had and did not now. Gods do not answer letters."

When Ted Williams called Tom Yawkey "the greatest owner in baseball," it was partially the hyperbolic musings of an employee acknowledging his boss, but it was also a sincere tribute. For Williams, Yawkey was, for the most part, a positive force. Yawkey always paid his stars well, and frequently treated them more like members of his family than a workforce.

By 1961, however, it was clear to any impartial observer that, far from being a great owner, Tom Yawkey often exhibited a destructive force on both the Red Sox and on baseball. He larded his organization with sycophants and drinking buddies and blowhard ex-players like Eddie Collins and Joe Cronin, who together would make virtually every baseball-related decision affecting the team from 1933 through the late 1950s.

Over the years, the bigotry of many of the team's employees—including, some historians and baseball scholars have argued, that of Yawkey himself—meant the Red Sox lost out on some of baseball's brightest talents. In the mid-1940s, though Boston was still a de facto segregated city, a city councilman, Isadore Muchnick, threatened to revoke the Red Sox's permit to play baseball on Sunday unless they auditioned black ballplayers. And so, on April 14, 1945, an ally of Muchnick's brought three Negro League stars, Jackie Robinson, Marv Williams, and Sam Jethroe, for a tryout at Fenway. For two days, the three players weren't allowed entrance to the field; the delay, ostensibly, was because of Franklin Roosevelt's death on April 12. Finally, on April 16, they were permitted to take part in a brief workout. It was the first time Robinson would perform for a major league club.

The Red Sox, however, would not take advantage of their opportunity. While the Negro League stars were going through their paces, a voice from Fenway's stands shouted, "Get those niggers off the field." At least one newspaper reporter who attended the tryout thought it was Tom Yawkey who shouted the racial epithet, although nothing has been established conclusively. Whatever the case, the Brooklyn Dodgers signed Robinson later that year. The Sox also had the first chance to sign another future Hall of Famer, the transcendent outfielder Willie Mays. In 1948, the 17-year-old Mays joined the Negro League's Black Barons, a team that shared an Alabama field with the Birmingham Barons, a minor league Red Sox affiliate. Because of the playing field arrangement, the Sox got first crack at Birmingham players, but the team passed on Mays. More than half a century later, Mays still sounded surprised he didn't end up patrolling the Fenway Park outfield with Ted Williams. "There's no telling what I would have been able to do in Boston. To be honest, I really thought I was going [there]," Mays told Howard Bryant for *Shut Out,* his 2002 book about the intersection of race and baseball in Boston. "But for that Yawkey. Everyone knew he was racist. He didn't want me."

By 1959, 12 years after Robinson broke baseball's color barrier, the Red Sox were the only team in baseball to remain segregated. When a reporter asked general manager Pinky Higgins why none of the Red Sox's black minor leaguers were being given a chance to make it with the club, Higgins responded by calling the writer a "nigger lover." But even the Red Sox had to succumb to the inevitable, and a few months later, the Sox brought up infielder Elijah "Pumpsie" Green and pitcher Earl Wilson. (Ted Williams, in his second-to-last season, made it a point to warm up with Green before every game as a signal to his teammates and Red Sox fans alike to accept the new player.) The Red Sox would have many black superstars in the decades to come, from Luis Tiant to Jim Rice to Ellis Burks to Mo Vaughn, but it would take almost 40 years for the team to finally shed its reputation as an organization in which it was difficult for minorities to thrive. As recently as 2004, Barry Bonds said he would never consider playing for the Red Sox. "Boston is too racist for me," Bonds, who is Willie Mays's grandson, said. "That's been going on ever since my dad [Bobby Bonds] was playing baseball [in the 1960s and 1970s]. . . . It ain't changing."*

---

* Bonds has a reputation for inflammatory racial rhetoric. In *Game of Shadows,* a 2006 book that offers extensive documentation of Bonds's steroid use, Bonds is quoted as saying in 1998 that Major League Baseball officials were not investigating Mark McGwire's increased muscle mass "because he's a white boy."

CHAPTER 3

# The Impossible Dream and the Sixth Game

**BY THE 1960s,** Tom Yawkey had become largely uninterested in the Red Sox and periodically considered selling the team. Many players still liked to play for the Sox—besides paying well, Yawkey, unlike Yankees management, didn't expect much in return. The city was more divorced from the Red Sox than it had been since the team's lowly days in the 1920s, before Yawkey came on board. Young left fielder Carl Yastrzemski—who soon came to be known by the nickname "Yaz"—was an exciting player to watch, and Fenway's sparse crowds certainly cheered for the new left-handed slugger who seemed destined to take Williams's spot as the team leader. Still, the Red Sox, the once-proud franchise that helped inaugurate the American League, were not only bad, they were boring.

Only Yawkey's complete disengagement from the team allowed this to change. In 1965, Dick O'Connell replaced Pinky Higgins as the team's general manager. He was, perhaps, the first man to actually deserve the job. At the end of the 1966 season, O'Connell hired minor league manager Dick Williams to run the club. The baseball establishment wasn't impressed, and the Sox opened the 1967 season as 100–1 longshots to win the pennant. On Opening Day, only 8,324 fans showed up at Fenway.

That was arguably the last boring day of the season. By the end of April, the Sox were flirting with first place, with right fielder Tony Conigliaro and hurler Jim Lonborg complementing Yaz. On June 15, Conigliaro—known now by the heartthrob nickname Tony C.*—won a game with an 11th-inning, two-run blast over Fenway's left field wall. The next day, a *Boston Globe* headline, referring to a song from the hit musical *Man of La Mancha,* wrote of the Sox's "Impossible Dream" of winning the American League pennant.

For the next three-and-a-half months, Dick Williams's Red Sox made baseball relevant in Boston once again. The team was full of young, charming, good-looking players, and the Sox appealed to the city's college students and old-time fans alike. After a 10-game winning streak in July, almost twice as many fans as had come to Opening Day were waiting for the team when they returned to Boston's Logan Airport. Yawkey, suddenly interested in the team again,† started showing up at Fenway. After treading water for the first two weeks of September, the Red Sox surged in the last half of the month, powered by the clutch hitting of Yastrzemski, who batted .523 during the season's final two weeks, with five home runs and 16 runs batted in. Entering the season's final weekend, the Minnesota Twins, Detroit Tigers, Chicago White Sox, and Red Sox were all within two games of each other. The Red Sox and the Twins had a two-game series at Fenway, and the Twins, at 91-69, were a game ahead of the 90-70 Sox. A single Twins win would end the year for Boston. On the last day of the season, backed by a 4-for-4 effort by Yaz, Lonborg capped his 22-9, 246-strikeout, Cy Young–winning season with a win over the Twins, putting the Red Sox into first

---

* On August 18, Conigliaro was hit in the face with a pitch. His cheekbone was shattered, and his left eye and eye socket were severely damaged. Robbed of the 20-15 vision with which he had been blessed, Conigliaro was forced to sit out the remainder of the season and the entire 1968 season.

† Dick Williams, for one, wasn't so thrilled about Yawkey's renewed interest in the Red Sox. In his autobiography, Williams wrote, "You'd have thought he was one of the damn players. He was in the clubhouse, around the batting cage, on the field until the last possible minute, chatting and kibitzing and being about as fake as an owner can be. . . . Where had he been when we got our asses kicked earlier in the season?"

place. A couple of hours later, when the Tigers fell to the California Angels, it was official: the Red Sox had won the pennant.

In the Series, the Red Sox once again faced the St. Louis Cardinals, who, with Lou Brock and Bob Gibson, were the overwhelming favorites. After Boston lost Game 1, Lonborg, pitching four days after he helped clinch the pennant, threw a complete-game, one-hit shutout as the Sox evened the Series. Lonborg came back on three days' rest for Game 5, with the Sox now trailing three games to one. He was masterful once again, throwing another complete game, and the Sox won 3–1. Boston evened the Series after winning Game 6, 8–4, and Williams decided to send Lonborg to the hill once again, this time on only two days' rest, to face Gibson, the Cardinals ace, for the Series' deciding game. It was the fourth time Lonborg had been asked to save the Red Sox's season in less than two weeks. He gutted it out through six innings, but left with the Sox on the losing end of a 7–1 score. Tears streamed down Lonborg's face as he came off the mound.

For Dick Williams and the Red Sox players, losing the World Series was a disappointment, but 1967 was the year the Red Sox helped create magic in Boston. The country was being torn apart by the Vietnam War and the burgeoning youth movement, and the boyish, happy-go-lucky Red Sox, who hadn't been expected to do much of anything before the season began, seemed to embody both the younger generation's sense of possibility as well as an older generation's nostalgia for a simpler, more innocent era. After the Impossible Dream season, the Sox won a fan base that would forge an almost religious connection with the team, awarding them a loyalty whose intensity and durability would prove astonishing.

The Sox wasted no time testing that loyalty. The next seven seasons were a return to the Red Sox's modus operandi of inefficiency and lost opportunity. Almost every year, the Sox fell short of expectations. Paradoxically, it was during these fallow years that the lure of the Red Sox began to reach a national audience, largely due to the emergence of a young sportswriter who approached the game with a fan's passion and fervor. Peter Gammons was a Massachusetts native who joined the *Globe*'s sports staff soon after graduating from the University of North Carolina in 1969. By the mid-1970s, his

Sunday "Baseball Notes" columns were known for featuring the most important baseball reporting in the country. Unlike so many Boston writers, Gammons didn't seem primarily interested in finding ways to tear down the local team. He was critical, to be sure, but his criticism was usually couched in his obvious love of both the game and the Red Sox. Gammons's wonderfully evocative stories and detailed analyses helped form and then cement the notion of the Red Sox as the quintessentially American team. *The New Yorker*'s Roger Angell, one of the best-known baseball writers of all time, has said that Gammons is "as important to New England baseball as a Yastrzemski or a [Carlton] Fisk."

During Gammons's first years on the beat, the team was slowly remaking itself. In 1972, Fisk, a Vermont native, excelled as the team's catcher, winning the league's Rookie of the Year award. In 1975, the Sox again won the pennant, and were matched up against Cincinnati's "Big Red Machine" in the World Series. The Reds, like the Cardinals in 1967, were perhaps baseball's most dominant team, and they won the National League West by an astounding 20 games. The Red Sox, meanwhile, were underdogs once again, and most people were surprised they had managed to beat the defending champion Oakland A's in the American League playoffs. In the Series, the Red Sox's Cuban maestro, Luis Tiant, won Game 1 with a 6–0 shutout, and he won again in Game 4. As the Series moved back to Boston for its final two games, Cincinnati was leading, three games to two. Game 6 was delayed for three days, as biblical rains drenched the Northeast.

The game, which was finally played on October 21, is still remembered as one of the best ever postseason baseball contests. With Tiant again on the mound and center fielder Fred Lynn hitting an early three-run home run, things looked good for Boston. By the eighth, the Reds had fought back and led, 6–3. In the bottom half of that inning, Boston's Bernie Carbo hit a pinch-hit, three-run homer, and after the Red Sox left the bases loaded in the ninth, the game went into extra innings. The next two innings featured missed calls and defensive gems, but no scoring. Even the players seemed to realize they were part of something special; as Cincinnati's Pete Rose stepped into the batter's box in the 10th inning, he looked back at Fisk as the Red Sox catcher settled into his crouch. "This is some kind of game, isn't it?" Rose asked rhetorically.

Two innings later, Fisk made Rose's words seem prescient. In the bottom of the 12th inning, with the score still tied 6–6, Fisk launched a shot toward Fenway's left field wall. The ball clearly had enough distance to be a game-winning home run; the only question was whether it would go foul, and as Fisk began to move down the line toward first base, he jumped up and down, waving his arms as if he could will the ball to stay fair. As the ball arced out of the park, it glanced off of the foul pole.* The Red Sox had won.

After such a heart-stopping contest, it almost seemed fated that the Red Sox would lose the deciding Game 7 as they, of course, did. The 1975 World Series is often referred to as one of baseball's best. As Gammons wrote, "The Sixth Game was an abridgment of the entire splendid series in which Boston led in all seven games and lost the lead in five of them, in which five games were decided by one run, two were decided in extra innings, and two others in the ninth inning." Playing in a historic match was little consolation for the Red Sox, or for the people of Boston.

On July 9, 1976, Tom Yawkey died of leukemia. At the time of his death, Yawkey was estimated to be worth $57 million, most of which he left to his wife. Julia, his adopted daughter from his first marriage, got just $10,000. Yawkey and the Red Sox organization he had bought 43 years earlier would be forever linked; in time, Yawkey came to be seen as the kind of rich benefactor baseball purists yearned for when they harkened back to the sport's supposedly gentler past.† In typical Boston fashion, this myth became an accepted

---

* The famous television footage of Fisk trying to will the ball fair was said to be the result of a cameraman's being frightened by a rat and therefore failing to track the ball as it came off Fisk's bat. Before that moment, cameramen were trained to follow the path of the ball; after that, they kept their lenses trained on the players themselves. In 1998, *TV Guide* ranked that moment as the single greatest in the history of televised sports.

† In 1980, Yawkey became the first owner to be inducted into baseball's Hall of Fame. His plaque at Cooperstown lauds him as "one of sport's finest benefactors."

reality, and soon obscured Yawkey's surly alcohol-fueled rants, his unwillingness to break down baseball's color barrier, his occasional indifference to the Red Sox, and even his threats to move the team out of town. Tom Yawkey, the person most responsible for the Red Sox's decades of futility, became Tom Yawkey, the gentlemanly, sporting owner more interested in winning than turning a profit. It's a portrait that remains largely intact to this day.

## CHAPTER 4

# The Gerbil, the Spaceman, the Rocket, and the Curse

**IN MAY 1978,** Tom Yawkey's estate sold the Red Sox for $20.5 million to a partnership consisting of Jean Yawkey; Haywood Sullivan, a Sox executive who was often likened to an adopted son for the childless Yawkeys; and Buddy LeRoux, a former Red Sox trainer. At the time, it was thought to be the largest amount ever paid for a baseball team. Sullivan, LeRoux, and Yawkey would be the team's three general partners; nine limited partners also bought in, at $500,000 a share.

Although this was the first change in the team's ownership since the 1930s, 1978 wouldn't be remembered for the sale of the team. Just as the Impossible Dream season of 1967 had established the Red Sox as the darlings of New England, the events of 1978 helped solidify the Sox's reputation as an organization that inevitably broke its fans' hearts. With Sullivan running the show and Don Zimmer managing the team, the Red Sox surged early in the year. The Red Sox's outfield—Jim Rice, Fred Lynn, and Dwight Evans— seemed destined to go down as one of baseball's best. Fisk was still manning the plate, and Yaz, at 38, was still a feared hitter. Even the pitching staff, which included Dennis Eckersley, Mike Torrez, Luis Tiant, and Bill "Spaceman" Lee, was strong. By July 20, the Red Sox led their closest pursuers, the Milwaukee Brewers, by nine games, while the Yankees were a staggering 14 games back. A division title seemed all but assured.

Once again, poor management hurt the Red Sox's chances. Zimmer, who didn't have a contract beyond the season, kept playing injured starters such as third baseman Butch Hobson* rather than take a chance with the team's reserves. By September, Boston's lead over New York was down to six-and-a-half games. It had dwindled to four when the Yankees came to Fenway early in the month for a four-game set. Those four days are still referred to as the Boston Massacre. The Yankees swept the Sox, outscoring the home team by a combined 42–9, including 15–3 and 13–2 spankings in the first two games. In the last game of the series, Zimmer refused to start Bill Lee because the flamboyant pitcher had referred to the manager as a "gerbil," instead sending Bobby Sprowl to the mound for his second major league appearance. Sprowl didn't make it through the first inning, and pitched only once more for Boston in his career.

If that had been the end of it, if the Sox had folded and the Yankees had run away with the division, the memories of '78 would be difficult but not gut-wrenching. Boston battled back, however, winning its final eight games, and at the end of the season the two teams had identical 99-63 records. The Red Sox, just as they had done 30 years earlier against the Cleveland Indians, would play a sudden-death playoff game to decide the division.

The game was at Fenway. By the seventh inning, Red Sox fans were, for the first time in weeks, allowing themselves to think they might actually pull it off: Mike Torrez seemed to be cruising, and the Sox led, 2–0. There were two men on and two men out when Bucky Dent, the Yankees shortstop, came to the plate. In his two years with New York, Dent had not hit above .250, and he had only

---

* Hobson played most of the 1978 season with bone chips in his throwing elbow. He made 43 errors that year.

four home runs on the season. Torrez got him to loft a lazy ball into left field, an easy pop fly. At least it would have been at any other park in baseball; in Boston, it was a Green Monster–aided home run. The Yankees had the lead, 3–2. "We talk about loving Fenway Park so much," Yastrzemski would say later. "That's probably the one time I hated Fenway Park." Still, Boston crawled back, and in the bottom of the ninth, Yaz was at the plate with two outs, a runner on third, and New York leading 5–4. He popped out, and the Yankees went on to win the American League pennant and their second consecutive World Series.

In the wake of 1978's heartache, Haywood Sullivan quickly proved he was a worthy heir to almost every Red Sox general manager who'd come before him. He let Luis Tiant sign with the Yankees and traded Bill Lee to Montreal. In 1980, he sent out Fred Lynn's and Carlton Fisk's contracts two days later than was mandated, with the result that Lynn forced a trade to the California Angels and Fisk became a free agent and signed with the White Sox. By the early 1980s, bumper stickers reading "Haywood and Buddy Are Killing the Sox" began to appear on cars around Fenway.

By the mid-1980s, almost in spite of the team's management and ownership, the Red Sox were exciting again. "Rocket" Roger Clemens, who came up as a rookie in 1984, dominated baseball in 1986, going 24-4, with a 2.48 earned run average* and 238 strikeouts. On April 29, with Fenway Park about one-third full, he set a new major league record, striking out 20 batters in a game against the Seattle Mariners. Clemens won the American League's Most Valuable Player award that year, and he helped lead the Red Sox to

---

* Earned run average is the average number of runs a pitcher lets up in a nine-inning game, and does not include runs that score due to an error or any runs that score after an inning-prolonging error. If a pitcher pitches for six innings and the opposing team scores three runs, one of which was due to an error, his ERA for that game would be 3.00: He allowed two earned runs in six innings, for an average of one run every three innings, which works out to 3.00 over nine innings.

the postseason, where they beat the California Angels in the American League playoffs.

In the World Series, the Sox faced the New York Mets, whose 1986 squad was arguably the decade's best team. Veterans like catcher Gary Carter and first baseman Keith Hernandez anchored the team, and 24-year-old right fielder Darryl Strawberry and 21-year-old pitching phenom Dwight Gooden provided excitement. The Red Sox won the first two games in New York, beating Gooden in Game 2, giving Boston five more chances to win two games, and the championship. After the Mets clawed back to win Games 3 and 4 in Boston, the Red Sox, behind lefty hurler Bruce Hurst, again beat Gooden in Game 5. They now had two chances to clinch the Series, and Clemens took the mound to start Game 6.

Clemens left after seven innings with a 3–2 lead. Calvin Schiraldi was brought in to finish the job, but he let the Mets back in it. After nine innings, the game was tied, 3–3. In the 10th, outfielder Dave Henderson hit a home run, and a Wade Boggs double followed by a Marty Barrett single scored another run. Going in to the bottom of the 10th, the Red Sox were winning, 5–3.

Schiraldi, in his third inning of work, retired the first two Mets batters, and as champagne was wheeled into Shea Stadium's visiting clubhouse, the park's scoreboard congratulated Bruce Hurst for winning the World Series MVP award. A pair of singles put men on first and second, but the Sox still appeared to be safe. Schiraldi brought the next batter, Ray Knight, to an 0-2 count. The Red Sox were one strike away. Knight tapped at Schiraldi's third offering, and his single drove in a Mets run and left runners on first and third. All was not yet lost. Boston still led, 5–4, and the Red Sox still needed only one more out.

Finally, Sox manager John McNamara brought in Bob Stanley, the Sox veteran, to face Mookie Wilson. Stanley must have cherished the moment. In April, after getting heckled at Fenway, he said, "Those fans who are booing me now will be cheering for me when I record the final out in the World Series." Now he'd get a chance to prove himself right. With the count 2-1, Wilson fouled off three straight pitches. Catcher Rich Gedman wasn't able to handle

Stanley's seventh pitch, and another Mets run scored, tying the game at five and moving the Mets' Ray Knight to second base. Three pitches (and two more foul balls) later, Wilson finally hit the ball fair. It was a slow roller toward first base.

For each of the Red Sox's World Series victories that year, McNamara had, late in the game, replaced Bill Buckner, his regular first baseman, with Dave Stapleton, who was a nimbler, better, defensive player. The whole world knew about Buckner's painfully arthritic knees, and the Mets, obeying one of the chivalric, unspoken rules that still dictates how the game is played, didn't bunt on Buckner once the entire series. But McNamara wanted Buckner to be on the field when the Sox finally won it all. And so it was Buckner, not Stapleton, who was manning first base as Wilson's grounder rolled up the line. Buckner shuffled over and bent down to pick up the ball. He was too late. The ball went through his legs, and the Mets won the game.

In his recap of the game in *The New York Times*, columnist George Vecsey referred tangentially to "the Curse of Babe Ruth," incurred when Red Sox owner Harry Frazee "[sold] the slugging pitcher to the Yankees early in 1920." (The sale actually occurred in December 1919.) With Game 7 still to come, not much attention was paid to Vecsey's column at the time, but after the Red Sox lost that game, and the Series, Vecsey returned to the theme in a column titled "Babe Ruth Curse Strikes Again." In that piece, Vecsey picked up on a theme that had been floating around the press for years, but had rarely, if ever, made its way into print. "[T]he Boston Red Sox have been playing under a cloud ever since their owner, Harry Frazee, sold off Babe Ruth early in 1920, and that cloud settled over them in this Series. All the leads they had, all the chances, went down the drain, just as they had in 1946 and 1949 and 1967 and 1975 and 1978." Finally, Vecsey repeated what the *Times*'s Fox Butterfield had written a week earlier, when Butterfield echoed the urban legend that Frazee had sold Ruth so he could finance *No, No, Nanette.* Ever since Frazee sold Ruth "to the lowly New York Yankees to finance one of his Broadway shows," Vecsey wrote, "it has never been the same."

Vecsey helped introduce the idea of Ruth's curse, and the power and prestige of the *Times* helped cement the notion that Frazee's sale of the team's star was tied to his theatrical aspirations. But it wouldn't be until 1990, when *Boston Globe* columnist Dan Shaughnessy appropriated "Curse of the Bambino" for the title of his book on the history of the Red Sox, that the phrase—and the sentiment—really entered the popular lexicon and mythology.

Shaughnessy was raised in Groton, Massachusetts, about 40 miles outside Boston. Six years younger than fellow Grotonite Peter Gammons, Shaughnessy went to Baltimore to cover the Orioles for *The Sun* after graduating from Holy Cross. After a stint with the now-defunct *Washington Star,* Shaughnessy was hired by the *Globe* in 1981. In 1982, he replaced the formidable Bob Ryan as the paper's Celtics beat reporter, and he covered the Larry Bird–led championship team of 1984 before moving over to cover the Red Sox in time for their first pennant-winning season since 1975.

Shaughnessy's book focused almost exclusively—some might say masochistically—on the Red Sox's misery, as he repeated many of the inaccuracies that had hardened into perceived fact. Failing to acknowledge that some contemporary articles and editorial cartoons had argued it was better for the team that Ruth had been sold, Shaughnessy wrote how the sale of the slugger was almost universally seen as a horrible move at the time it occurred. He quoted the *Times* obituary that said that Frazee's estate "did not exceed $50,000" when he died, but left out what followed in the *Times*'s account—that "it may be much larger after Mr. Frazee's interests in Boston and Chicago are appraised." (Frazee owned or controlled theaters in both cities.) Shaughnessy also reprinted the most incendiary quote in Frederick Lieb's widely discredited 1947 history of the Red Sox: After Frazee had died and could no longer defend himself, Lieb claimed that the former Sox owner had told him that "the Ruth deal was the only way I could retain the Red Sox." (There is no evidence that this was ever the case, or that Frazee ever said those words.) In order to support his strained hypothesis that all of the team's misfortunes could be traced to an event that had occurred six decades earlier, Shaughnessy ignored the many problems of Tom Yawkey's ownership of the team, even going so far as to whitewash Yawkey's troubled history with black ballplayers.

His book, Shaughnessy wrote, was the story of "baseball's original sin" and the "subsequent seventy years of sorrow for New England's baseball fans." In fact, *The Curse of the Bambino* served as an unintentional primer on the ways in which the Boston press was able to inflict itself on players and fans alike. Forever after, every Red Sox fumble, misstep, or mistake would be attributed to a curse that had been popularized, if not largely invented, by a cantankerous sports columnist.

## CHAPTER 5

# The Yawkey Trust

BY 1987, Jean Yawkey had tired of Haywood Sullivan and "adopted" a new surrogate son: John Harrington. Harrington was born and raised in Boston, the son of Irish immigrants; his father was a bus mechanic and his mother a domestic. His career in baseball had begun in 1970, when the 33-year-old Boston College accounting professor took a call from former Sox player, manager, and executive Joe Cronin. Cronin was by this time the American League president, and was looking for a new league treasurer. A neighbor of Harrington's, Cronin said, had recommended him for the job. Within a couple of years, Cronin had introduced Harrington to Tom Yawkey, and in 1973 Harrington was named the treasurer of the Red Sox. Harrington grew close to Tom Yawkey, but from early on, it was clear his strongest bond was with Yawkey's childless wife. When Tom Yawkey died in 1976, Harrington helped Jean Yawkey with the ownership transition, but by 1978 he was burned out and left the team.

Soon, Jean Yawkey had succeeded in luring Harrington back by promising him a small stake in the Red Sox. There was, however, a catch: It vested only when Yawkey died, thereby guaranteeing that one of the people she was closest to never left her employ. Before long, Harrington was named Yawkey's legal proxy for all matters relating to the Red Sox.

In February 1992, Jean Yawkey passed away. She was 83 years old, and most local observers assumed Harrington would sell Yawkey's two-thirds controlling stake in the team to Sullivan, who still owned the other third. Instead, in 1993, the Yawkey Trust bought out Sullivan's share and Harrington embarked on an eight-year stewardship of the team. With Sullivan gone, Harrington bumped general manager Lou Gorman upstairs and hired Dan Duquette, Montreal's 35-year-old general manager, who, in 1991, had been made the youngest GM in baseball.

Together, Harrington and Duquette led the team to some memorable successes. In 1995, the first year of baseball's new three-division playoff format,* the Red Sox, led by eventual MVP Mo Vaughn, won the American League East. In 1997, Duquette traded pitching prospects Carl Pavano and Tony Armas Jr. to his old team for Pedro Martinez, who blossomed into one of the best right-handed pitchers in the history of the game. Nineteen ninety-seven Rookie of the Year Nomar Garciaparra flourished into a perennial All-Star, and his .372 batting average in 2000 was the highest for a Red Sox player since Ted Williams had hit .388 in 1957.

The high point of Harrington's and Duquette's tenure atop the Sox was likely 1999, when the All-Star game was played at Fenway Park for the first time since 1961. Billed by Major League Baseball as the last All-Star contest of the twentieth century, candidates for an All-Century team were introduced on Fenway's field before the game. Fisk and Yastrzemski were both there, along with Dennis Eckersley, Bob Gibson, Hank Aaron, and Willie Mays. After the '99 squad had been introduced, the Fenway PA announced the arrival of "The Greatest Hitter Who Ever Lived." With that, the 80-year-old Ted Williams emerged in a golf cart and slowly rode to the Fenway mound. Fenway Park seemed to pulse with adoration, as the 34,000 fans joined some of the greatest ballplayers ever to step onto a diamond as they bathed Williams with applause. Williams moved his hand to his head, and, finally acknowledging the cheers that had started with his career-ending home run 39 years earlier, tipped his

---

* The three-division system debuted in 1994, but the players strike canceled the playoffs.

cap to the crowd.* After struggling to stand and squinting to make out the plate, Williams threw the game's first pitch to Fisk. And then, for several long minutes, the best players in baseball milled around the Splendid Splinter like a bunch of awe-struck schoolboys until Fenway's announcer had to beg everyone to retire to their respective dugouts so the game could begin.

Unlike many All-Star games, the 1999 contest would not be a mere exhibition. Martinez, who already had a 15-3 record on the year, made sure of that. He began the game by becoming the first All-Star pitcher to strike out the game's first three batters, making Barry Larkin, Larry Walker, and Sammy Sosa all look foolish. Then, to begin the second, he fanned Mark McGwire. After Matt Williams reached on an error, Martinez struck out Jeff Bagwell, and Williams was thrown out trying to steal second. Martinez had struck out five of the game's first six hitters,† and he was named the game's MVP.

Nineteen ninety-nine was a transcendent, magical season for Martinez. He finished with gaudy numbers: a 23-4 record, a 2.07 earned run average,‡ 313 strikeouts. A better indicator of his sheer dominance is the extent to which he outclassed the competition. He allowed an average of 8.31 base runners per nine innings, or fewer than one base runner per inning of work. The next best average in the league belonged to the Minnesota Twins' Eric Milton, who allowed 11.04 base runners per nine innings. No one in the twentieth century had ever led the league by so large a gap. Martinez was the American League's unanimous choice for the Cy Young Award, and he received more first-place votes than any other player for the

---

* Unlike the other retired ballplayers on the field, Williams was not wearing the hat of his former team; instead, his cap advertised Hitter.net, a now defunct business started by Williams's son, John Henry Williams.

† In baseball's second All-Star game, in 1934, New York Giants pitcher Carl Hubbell struck out five American League batters in a row after allowing the first two American League hitters to reach base. Hubbell's victims were Babe Ruth, Lou Gehrig, Jimmie Foxx, Al Simmons, and Joe Cronin. All five are now in the Hall of Fame.

‡ After the 2005 season, Martinez had a career ERA of 2.72; he is the only active player with at least 1,000 innings pitched who has a career ERA under 3.00.

league's MVP. He lost out on that award to Ivan Rodriguez only after two voters refused to put Martinez on their ballots at all. (One of the voters who snubbed Martinez, the *New York Post*'s George King, initially claimed he didn't believe pitchers deserved to win the award. It was soon revealed that in 1998, King had cast votes for two pitchers—the Yankees' David Wells and the Texas Rangers' Rick Helling. In 1999, King was the only voter in the country to cast his first-place vote for Yankees shortstop Derek Jeter.)

In 1999, for the third time in five years, the Red Sox won the wild card, and for the third time, they'd face the Cleveland Indians, who'd beaten the Sox in 1995 and 1998 in the first round of the playoffs. Martinez was on the hill to start the best-of-five series, but the spindly pitcher had to leave the game after four shutout innings with a strained muscle in his back. The Red Sox lost Game 1, 3–2, and dropped Game 2, 11–1, leaving them one game from elimination, with Martinez likely out for the rest of the playoffs.

The Sox bounced back, winning Games 3 and 4 by a combined score of 32–10. But for Game 5, Sox manager Jimy Williams was forced to call on Bret Saberhagen, the old Kansas City Royals star who'd gutted out a late-career revival in Boston. Saberhagen surrendered three runs in the first before allowing two more without retiring a batter in the second. Derek Lowe, Williams's next choice, wasn't much better, and by the end of the third inning, Cleveland had scored eight runs. Boston, behind a grand slam Troy O'Leary hit following an intentional walk to Nomar Garciaparra, managed to crawl back into the game. The only problem was, there didn't seem to be any pitchers left, and Williams had already ruled out letting Martinez pitch, saying, "We can't hurt the kid."

Martinez, however, thought differently, and convinced Williams to let him take the mound to start the fourth. Just days after his injured back and shoulder caused him to fight back tears, Martinez no-hit the powerful Indians* lineup for six innings, finessing his eight strikeouts on guile and guts rather than brute force. In the sev-

---

* The Indians, with Manny Ramirez, Jim Thome, Roberto Alomar, Omar Vizquel, David Justice, and Kenny Lofton, had by far the most potent lineup in the league. They led all of baseball with a .372 on base percentage, and were the first team to score more than 1,000 runs since the 1950 Red Sox.

enth, O'Leary once again hit a homer after the Indians had intentionally walked Garciaparra, and the Red Sox won, 12–8, only to then lose, four games to one, to their archrivals, the Yankees, in the American League Championship Series. (Martinez, not surprisingly, helped provide the only highlight of the Yankees series, winning 13–1 in Game 3, in which he bested Roger Clemens, who had left the Red Sox after the 1996 season. That would be the only game the Yankees would lose in the entire postseason.)

Despite the Red Sox's string of playoff appearances, Duquette and Harrington had by this time become increasingly controversial figures in Boston. They were already known for facilitating—some would say forcing—the acrimonious departures of some of Boston's biggest stars, such as Clemens and Mo Vaughn, who left after the 1998 season. Duquette had famously called Fenway "economically obsolete," a characterization many Boston fans found insulting, and had helped spearhead a campaign to shut down the independent sausage vendors that had been a feature of the pregame scene outside of Fenway since the park opened in 1912.

Harrington and Duquette also brought the dysfunction of Boston's front office to new levels. Both men despised Boston's press corps, and under their leadership the organization became cripplingly secretive and paranoid. Oakland A's manager Ken Macha, who spent four years in the 1990s working as a manager for Boston's minor league teams, complained to Howard Bryant, then with the *Boston Herald,* about the situation: "What was I supposed to do? A reporter would call me up and ask about a prospect and I wasn't allowed to speak about a player I was watching every day. I mean, I felt like an idiot."

PART II

# For Sale

## CHAPTER 6

# Selling Boston's Salvation

**LES OTTEN IS A GRAY-HAIRED,** exuberant man who is always coming up with fantastical, half-baked ideas. It can be hard to take him seriously: He's the type of guy who'll spend 20 minutes talking in excruciating detail about how he's looking for someone to ghostwrite a novel he's plotted before acknowledging that the storyline is essentially the same as the Bernard Malamud book *The Natural,* which was made into a hit Robert Redford movie in 1984. ("I know they're similar," Otten says. "But I had thought of this *before* the movie came out.")

But just often enough, Otten comes up with an idea that, when combined with his certitude, leads to considerable success. Take his career in the ski resort industry. Beginning in 1972, when he took a job at Maine's Sunday River Mountain as a 22-year-old assistant general manager, Otten devoted nearly three decades to building the largest ski resort operation in the country. In 1980, he bought Sunday River from the Sherburne Corporation, and over the next 13 years, he transformed it into an East Coast destination, proving that superlative snowmaking and aggressive marketing really could make all the difference. In 1994, Otten began snapping up other New England mountains, and over the next three years, he bought up more than half of the skiable terrain in Vermont, including Sugarbush, Killington, and Mount Snow. By 1997, Otten's American Skiing Company owned property not only in New England, but in Colorado, Utah, and California as well. That November, Otten took ASC public. The IPO netted the company $244 million, and Otten retained majority ownership. He seemed to be at the peak of his power and influence. *Ski Magazine* named Otten one of the 100 most influential people of the century, and he was perhaps the ski industry's most effective evangelist during the 1980s and much of the 1990s.

Unfortunately for Otten, the story of the American Skiing Company did not end there, and within three years, much of his personal fortune and prescient acquisitions were undone by his pie-in-the-sky expansion plans. *Vermont Magazine* compared Otten's company's accumulation of debt to a "college student with a Visa." Instead of focusing on skiing, Otten wanted all the money consumers spent on ski vacations—for lodging, meals, or entertainment—to be funneled through his company. Despite the fact that the ASC was recording millions of dollars of losses a year, Otten continued to snatch up resorts and dump money into hotels, condos, and on-mountain services, simultaneously endangering his company and fostering the resentment of truculent New Englanders not eager to see their once-pristine mountains transformed into high-end destinations. ("More Snow, Less Otten," a popular bumper sticker from Otten's expansion years, can still be seen decorating cars in some northern New England towns.)

By 1999, consecutive bad ski seasons had left the American Skiing Company in danger of collapsing. The business Otten had built up from scratch was sagging under $400 million in debt; ASC's stock, which initially traded at $18, had fallen to just over $1 per share. A Merrill Lynch analyst summed up the company's problems succinctly: "management arrogance." That year, Otten ceded majority control of the company to the Texas-based Oak Hill Capital Partners in return for a $150 million investment. By fall 2000,

Otten, while still nominally connected with the company he built, had begun to cast around for his next adventure.*

It was at virtually that moment, on October 6, 2000, that John Harrington announced that he had finally decided to put the Yawkey Trust's 53 percent stake in the Red Sox up for sale. At first, Boston's power brokers were stunned. While it was widely known that Jean Yawkey's will compelled her charitable trust to sell the team at some point, Harrington didn't appear to observers to be a man who was about to walk away from his position at the head of the Red Sox's chain of command. "This announcement is obviously a bittersweet moment for me," Harrington said that day. "I have said in the past that every kid under 15 wants to be Nomar [Garciaparra] and every kid over 40 wants to be me."

Harrington, who'd been accused of loving the limelight too much ever to sell the Yawkey Trust's stake in the team, explained why he had waited almost a decade after Jean Yawkey's death before putting the team on the block. "When I first took over the club in the early '90s," Harrington told the media that day, "baseball was in terrible shape. Teams were being sold on a regular basis. The economics of the game were lousy. [The Red Sox's] television contract was terrible. That wasn't the time to sell. Now all of that has changed. You don't see teams being sold or up for sale." Harrington did allow that he was saddened by the fact that it appeared the Red Sox would not win a championship while being formally associated with the family that had shaped and guided the team for much of the twentieth century. "It would have been great to win the World Series at least once with the Yawkey name still on the team," he said. Publicly, Harrington said he hoped the sale could be completed by the start of spring training in 2001. Privately, he suspected the sale wouldn't be completed until the end of the 2001 season, and he let himself hope that he might get one last chance to win it all for the Yawkeys.

---

*Otten resigned as the American Skiing Company's CEO in 2001; press reports at the time implied that he'd been pushed out. ASC shareholders eventually lost more than $250 million.

In either case, whether the sale took a couple of months or more than a year, John Harrington wasn't walking off the stage just yet. He would, he announced, personally handle the negotiations for the sale with the help of Justin Morreale and Daniel Goldberg, the Red Sox's and Yawkey Trust's lawyers and partners at the venerable Boston law firm Bingham, Dana & Gould. Harrington, Morreale, and Goldberg would begin by doing background checks on prospective bidders to see if they had the financial heft and the moral character to own the team. Bidders who made it through their initial screening—and who plunked down a nonrefundable $25,000 fee required for the bid—would then be allowed to examine the team's books.

Like virtually everything connected with the Red Sox, the sale would not be a straightforward process. Unlike normal team sales, which are conducted through private negotiations, Harrington and his lawyers decided to conduct what was essentially an auction, with the highest qualified bidder winning the team. Even then, though, Harrington would not have the final say. Although the Yawkey Trust owned a majority of the Red Sox, it had, in a weird through-the-looking-glass arrangement, very little ultimate control over who would buy its stake in the team. That was to be decided by the seven limited partners who owned the other 47 percent of the Sox. Under the terms of the agreement governing the team, "the limiteds," as they were called, had functional veto power over any new owner, who had to win 12 out of the 23 total votes controlled by these minority partners. After that, the sale, like the sale of any ball club, had to be approved by three-quarters of Major League Baseball's 30 owners, and this, too, was far from a rubber-stamp process. In 1998, the charitable trust that took control of the Kansas City Royals following Ewing Kauffman's death in 1993 agreed to sell the team to New York–based lawyer Miles Prentice for $75 million; the next year, baseball's owners rejected Prentice's bid because they were concerned he had too many partners and not enough money. Finally, because the Yawkey Trust's proceeds from the sale would be used as seed money for The Yawkey Foundation, which would become one of the state's largest private charities, Tom Reilly, the

Massachusetts attorney general, would have to sign off on the sale as well.

The sale of any sports team is almost guaranteed to be a big local story. Interest in the Red Sox's sale was greatly enhanced by both the team's unique place in New England's collective unconscious and an escalating sense of anxiety about Boston's national identity. By 2001, Boston, which for much of the nineteenth century had thought of itself as the most important city in the country, had been almost entirely transformed into a second-tier metropolis. As recently as the 1980s and 1990s, there were still a number of prominent national companies based in the area, including Continental Cablevision, which at one point in the mid-1990s was the third-largest cable operator in the country; Gillette, which was founded in Boston in 1901; and Wang Laboratories, which, at its peak in the 1980s, employed more than 30,000 people. But the Denver-based US West acquired Continental Cablevision in 1996, and Wang filed for bankruptcy in 1992 and was bought up by the Netherlands' Getronics N.V. in 1999. Even Jordan Marsh, the venerable Boston department store that had been founded in the mid-nineteenth century, was acquired by (and eventually rebranded as) the New York–based Macy's. Paul Grogan, the president and CEO of The Boston Foundation, a community group dedicated to "building and sustaining a vital, prosperous city and region," acknowledged what was becoming the unavoidable truth when he said, "You find yourself in more and more conversations where people are referring to Boston as a branch office town." Such a designation was devastating for Bostonians, who prided themselves on their sophistication and urbanity and desperately wanted to think of their hometown as an international attraction on par with London, Paris, or Rome. Boston, the branch office town? It was an embarrassing thought.

By the new millennium, it was becoming more and more of a reality. In October 2000, Boston's homegrown corporate base was basically limited to Gillette, the bank FleetBoston (the result of a takeover of BankBoston by the Providence-based Fleet Bank), the insurance company John Hancock, and the city's daily tabloid, the

*Boston Herald.*★ The city's once-thriving newspaper culture had withered away, and in 1993, the city's proud broadsheet, the *Globe,* had been bought by The New York Times Company. The region still had a robust bio-tech industry and the most impressive collection of universities in the country—Harvard, MIT, Brandeis, Wellesley, Boston University, Boston College, Northeastern, U-Mass Boston, and Tufts, among many others, are all located within a few miles of each other—but compared to the glitz and glamour of Los Angeles, the power of Washington, the sheer breadth of Chicago, and, of course, the omnipotence of New York City, Boston had a hard time stacking up.

But none of those other cities could boast the Red Sox. The Sox weren't baseball's most storied or successful franchise, but they were its most interesting, and certainly had the most intimate and intense connection with their fans. Beginning with the Impossible Dream season of 1967 and escalating in the mid-1970s, they'd grown into America's most popular baseball team. The Yankees' dominance stretched through the years—they'd been baseball's best team for at least several years during every decade since the 1920s except the 1980s—and for much of their history were either beloved or grudgingly admired in the rest of the country. That began to change on January 3, 1973, when Cleveland shipbuilder George Steinbrenner led a group of investors in buying the Yankees from CBS for $8.7 million. Soon, Steinbrenner began to throw unheard-of amounts of money at players, even as his temper tantrums and capricious hiring and firing of front-office personnel generated overheated tabloid headlines. In 1974, he paid former A's pitcher Catfish Hunter, who'd been released from his contract, around $3.5 million for five years. (At the time, baseball's highest-paid player was making $250,000 a year, and Tom Seaver, the game's

---

★ This trend continued in the first years of the new millennium: In October 2003, the North Carolina–based Bank of America acquired FleetBoston. In April 2004, the Canadian company Manulife Financial acquired John Hancock. In January 2005, Cincinnati-based Procter & Gamble acquired Gillette. In April 2005, one of Boston's last remaining nationally circulating magazines, *The Atlantic,* announced that it was moving to Washington. For the last year, the struggling *Herald* has been the subject of persistent sale rumors.

highest paid pitcher, was making $175,000.) Two years later, when players and owners agreed to put an end to the reserve clause that had been in effect since the nineteenth century by negotiating a system of free agency,* it was Steinbrenner who bid exorbitant amounts for newly available stars such as Reggie Jackson.

Steinbrenner's spending sprees brought the Yankees success, but it also turned the team into an emblem of all that was wrong with baseball, and for that matter, America. In an era in which fans were just getting used to players being allowed to switch teams freely, the Yankees were seen as being all too willing to use their money to create an unfair advantage. The Red Sox, as New York's perennially struggling rivals, became the team the rest of the country could root for. They were steeped in romance and tradition, and their losses were proof of life's tragic nature. When the *Globe*'s Peter Gammons ascended to a national stage, first at *Sports Illustrated* and then on ESPN, where he became the country's best-known baseball analyst, he helped bring the gospel of the Sox to an even wider, and ever-more receptive, audience.

By the end of the century, Boston might not have been a world-class city, but the Red Sox were considered a world-class team, and one that was discussed in sacrosanct terms. (As Boston personality Mike Barnicle once said, "Baseball is not a life and death matter, but the Red Sox are.") When John Harrington announced he was putting the team up for sale, hopeful speculation on who the buyer might be immediately coalesced around a number of well-heeled— and exceedingly well-connected—local businessmen. Harrington had barely made his announcement before David Mugar, an heir to the Star Market supermarket fortune and the man who produced Boston's legendary Fourth of July celebrations on the banks of the Charles River, all but proclaimed his interest in purchasing the

---

* The 1976 collective bargaining agreement dictated that players would be controlled by the clubs that initially signed them for their first six years of major league play. After six years, players not under contract became free agents and were allowed to sign with whichever club they chose. In 1978, the salary arbitration system was effected, whereby players with three to six years of service, plus the most senior 17 percent of players with two to three years of service, can elect to have their salaries decided by an arbitrator.

team. "Like all Red Sox fans," he said in a statement, "I have a passion for the team and their place in this city. I am willing to do whatever I can to help ensure the team will flourish in the coming years and someday soon reward its loyal fans with a world championship." Joe O'Donnell, a Boston concessionaire, and Steve Karp, a local developer, were also mentioned publicly, along with a whole host of national figures ranging from Nebraska-based investment guru Warren Buffett and media magnate Sumner Redstone to Cablevision's Charles Dolan and bestselling author (and lifelong Red Sox fan) Stephen King.

For the incendiary Boston sports media, the prospect of a sale represented a bonanza. Immediately, they began questioning whether a new owner, especially one not born and raised in New England, would be tempted to move the team out of town, despite the fact that virtually no one seemed to think this was a realistic worry. Before any bids had even been entered—indeed, before the specifics of what was for sale had even been discussed—some of the heaviest hitters in the Boston media began advocating for the prospective local suitors with the most connections. "I'm in favor of Steve Karp, David Mugar, and Joe O'Donnell," Dan Shaughnessy announced in his October 7 *Boston Globe* column, completely ignoring the fact that the three men hadn't formed any kind of coalition, or even said whether they were interested in the team. No worries: Karp, Mugar, and O'Donnell, Shaughnessy assured his readers, were "three guys who love Boston, love baseball, and have money."

Shaughnessy had, by this time, become one of the best-known sports columnists in the city. His tight, red curls and ever-present half-smile were recognizable in much of the state, and if he wasn't as well known as Peter Gammons, he was a close second in New England. Ever since the success of *The Curse of the Bambino,* he'd been associated with the relentless negativism that defined so much of the local press's relationship with the Red Sox, and was known as being a reporter who wasn't afraid to get into it with ballplayers.* In many

*The Red Sox's Carl Everett had once yelled at the *Globe*'s Gordon Edes to leave the Red Sox clubhouse and told Edes to take Shaughnessy, whom Everett referred to as Edes's "curly haired boyfriend," with him. While Everett was a known loose cannon, other Red Sox stars, from Nomar Garcia-

ways, Shaughnessy seemed like a replica of a Boston archetype that had been set more than a century earlier, when the city's sportswriters had decided that they, in alliance with the Royal Rooters, represented the best interests of the Boston Beaneaters. Shaughnessy's fluid writing style, his perch at the *Globe,* and his ability to define a story made him a force to be reckoned with, and if he was coming out for Karp, Mugar, and O'Donnell, it was safe to assume they'd be front-runners should they decide to enter the bidding.

Les Otten, needless to say, didn't have the backing of any local columnists. To the extent he was a subject of discussion in Boston business circles, it was because he had become an object of derision or scorn. However, Otten has never been someone who doubted his own ability to get things done, and he had had his eye on the Red Sox for several years. Dan Duquette was a personal friend; in fact, Otten had asked Duquette to serve on the American Skiing Company's board of directors several years earlier. Otten knew John Harrington as well, and had indicated to Harrington almost a year earlier that, if and when the team eventually was put up for sale, he would be interested. Soon after Harrington's announcement, Les Otten put $50,000 in a bank account, $25,000 of which went to the application fee, and filed papers to incorporate Longball LLC.

"Out of everyone in the mix, I had to be the furthest out there," says Otten. "I was up against Joe O'Donnell, Charles Dolan, these kind of guys, and we launched forward without a real plan as to where the money was going to come from." Speculation on the value of the Yawkey Trust's 53 percent stake in the team ran anywhere from $250 million to close to $500 million. Even at the low end of that scale, Otten didn't have access to anywhere close to that amount of money. What's more, the new stadium that everyone seemed to agree the team needed would cost another $350 million or so, to augment more than $300 million in public funds that Harrington had secured.

Desperate for an angle, Otten decided to center his bid on the

---

parra to Curt Schilling, have complained about Shaughnessy's columns, and in 2005, Terry Francona loudly berated Shaughnessy in view of other reporters, saying, "After reading what you wrote, I lost all respect for you."

emotional appeal of Fenway Park, John Updike's "lyric little band-box of a ballpark." It was a smart move: Fenway has a deeply romantic hold on baseball fans. To be sure, Fenway offered plenty to complain about. It seated only 34,218 at a time when most stadiums seated a minimum of 40,000, and some, like New York's Yankee Stadium, had room for more than 57,000. The corridors that snaked through the stands were woefully narrow, and the bottlenecks that occurred before games could send a claustrophobe into a panic attack. Shockingly, many of Fenway's seats didn't even face home plate; fans along the first and third baselines found themselves aimed more or less at the outfield, and the steel trusses that supported the upper deck meant that a handful of seats in baseball's smallest ballpark wouldn't be able to see much of anything at all.* Since Harrington and Duquette had been arguing that the team desperately needed a new stadium, necessary improvements—everything from new paint to mark the seating sections to better drainage so the team's dugout didn't flood every time it rained—had been ignored.

Indeed, Fenway Park in 2001 looked much the same as it did after Tom Yawkey's renovations following the fire of 1934. In 1936, a 23.5 foot tall screen was added to the top of the left field wall in order to protect the windows on adjoining Lansdowne Street from balls hit out of the park, and in 1947, the Wall's advertisements were covered with green paint, giving it a new nickname: the Green Monster. There were some other changes made over the years—in 1940, the Sox built bullpens in front of the right-field bleachers in order to create a more hospitable hitting environment for the left-handed-hitting Ted Williams—but not much else had changed in the old park. At the time it was built, Fenway was seen as an ultra-modern marvel, with comfortable seats and the nicest press box in the country. Almost 90 years later, Fenway's narrow seats proved far too small for most patrons, and the absence of legroom all but necessitated a day at the chiropractor following a night at the ballpark.

* In all, around 1,000 seats at Fenway have some obstructed view because of the park's steel trusses.

Despite all that, Fenway Park was, inarguably, a gorgeous monument to American baseball. It still used a manual scoreboard, and scoreboard operators could sometimes be glimpsed peeking out from behind the numbers to catch the action on the field. The very same steel beams that blocked some patrons' views allowed the second deck to be built almost directly on top of the infield grandstand, creating an intensely intimate setting. Unlike most stadiums, Fenway didn't have an upper deck, and first-time visitors could not help but be struck by how Fenway allowed fans to gaze out onto the Boston skyline, with the Prudential and the John Hancock buildings rising behind right-center field and the famous Citgo sign blinking over the Wall in left. The odd triangle of grass that was delineated by the end of the Red Sox bullpen and Fenway's center-field wall was an inexplicable a patch of outfield territory as exists in baseball, and a point of stubborn pride. The Green Monster rose majestically over the outfield grass, where it turned screaming line drive shots into harmless singles and transformed breezy pop flies into home runs. It was here that Carlton Fisk had willed his walk-off home run in the sixth game of the 1975 World Series. It was this field that Babe Ruth and Ted Williams once roamed. "The ballpark is the star," *Globe* columnist Marty Nolan wrote in 1999, trying to explain the Red Sox's—and Fenway's—sway over New England. "A crazy-quilt violation of city planning principles, an irregular pile of architecture, a menace to marketing consultants, Fenway Park works. It works as a symbol of New England's pride, as a repository of evergreen hopes, as a tabernacle of lost innocence." Baseball commissioner Bart Giamatti compared Fenway to "Mount Olympus, the Pyramid at Giza, the nation's Capitol, the czar's Winter Palace, and the Louvre—except, of course, that it was better than all those inconsequential places." Pitching great Tom Seaver said simply, "Fenway is the essence of baseball."

That, Otten decided, was a sentiment he could use. "We needed to have a hook," he says. "For me, the most important part of the Boston Red Sox, other than the fact that they hadn't won the World Series in 82 years, was Fenway Park. Fenway Park is bigger than the Statue of Liberty; it's bigger than the Empire State Building. People would put their parents' ashes in the outfield. When I began to understand how important Fenway Park is to the people of New England, I realized that if I had a way to keep Fenway, then maybe I might have something special that no one else had."

At first, Otten's plan to keep the Red Sox in Fenway seemed like the same sort of hare-brained idea that led to the collapse of his ski empire. The team had already paid for an engineering study that concluded that Fenway was in danger of falling apart; the oldest park in the game had, after all, been built on swampland. When Otten tried to hire his own engineering team to conduct a study, Harrington denied him access to the stadium. "Nobody wanted to be told they could stay at Fenway," Otten says. "But I was determined to find a way."

## CHAPTER 7

# *The Producer*

**THE PATH THAT LED** to that way first presented itself on a cold night in January 2001, when Otten was relaxing after a day on the slopes at his house in Greenwood, Maine, with Tom Werner and Werner's then girlfriend, the *Today* show's Katie Couric. Werner, whose father was a lawyer, grew up on the Upper West Side of Manhattan. He was educated at Connecticut's tony Hotchkiss School and Harvard, where he joined the Harvard Lampoon, a semisecret social organization that occasionally published a purported humor magazine. He'd lived for most of his adult life in Southern California, where he'd moved soon after beginning his professional career as a researcher at ABC television in New York. When he finally left ABC in 1981, he was a senior vice president for prime-time programming, a high-ranking and well-paying position that all but ensured Werner a comfortable life. Instead of continuing to climb his way up the corporate ladder, Werner set off with his former boss, Marcy Carsey, and formed Carsey-Werner Productions, whose first headquarters was in an unair-conditioned office space above a sneaker store. The duo hit it big in 1984 with *The Cosby Show*, and later produced *Roseanne*, *3rd Rock from the Sun*, and *That '70s Show*.

That night, after a day on the slopes, the conversation turned to what Otten was planning to do next. (In a typical Otten yarn, Otten remembers the trio being on their second or third bottle of wine at this point of the conversation. Werner says he's pretty sure there wasn't a lot, if any, wine consumed that night.) "I'm going to try to buy the Boston Red Sox," Otten said. "Whattaya think?"

Werner was intrigued. As a student at Harvard in the 1960s, he'd made a documentary about Fenway Park, and fondly remembered skipping science classes to buy bleacher seats for day games. But Werner's more recent memories of baseball were considerably more painful. From 1990 until 1994, Werner was the principal owner of the San Diego Padres, a period that was marked by fan disgust and on-field failure.

His tenure was controversial almost from the get-go. On July 25, 1990, several months into Werner's first season as owner, Roseanne Arnold, the star of one of Werner's biggest television shows, was tapped to sing the national anthem before a Padres home game. Her screechily off-key rendition prompted a chorus of boos from the stands. While walking off the field, Arnold grabbed at her crotch and spit on the field, an act, she said later, which was meant as an homage to ballplayers everywhere. The rest of the country, from President Bush on down, interpreted it more literally.

For the next four years, Werner was arguably the most reviled owner in Major League Baseball; *The Dallas Morning News* even referred to him as the single most-hated man in Southern California. After buying the team from McDonald's heir Joan Kroc in 1990, Werner discovered the extent to which small-market teams were hamstrung by their revenue base. Instead of losing millions of dollars each year to field a middling team that still wouldn't be able to compete with the big-market clubs like the Los Angeles Dodgers and the New York Yankees, Werner and his partners began to shed payroll, either trading or losing to free agency stars such as Gary Sheffield, Fred McGriff, Bruce Hurst, and Benito Santiago.* At one point, fan disgust had reached such high levels that San Diego's Jack Murphy Stadium was dotted with anti-Werner banners, which

---

*With these trades, Werner's Padres acquired some of the key players that led the team to its 1996 division title and 1998 World Series appearance. Gary Sheffield, for instance, was traded for an unknown pitcher named Trevor Hoffman, who went on to become one of the most dominant closers in history.

the team briefly tried to ban. (The threat of an ACLU lawsuit ended that plan.)

The physically unassuming Werner, with his somewhat nasal inflections and self-effacing manner, doesn't fit the mold of a preening television executive, or, for that matter, a swashbuckling sports team owner. He's unfailingly polite and hates confrontation. (While in San Diego, Werner used to beep his horn at a heckler holding a "Honk If You Hate Tom Werner" sign at the entrance to the Padres' stadium in order to avoid detection.) His natural instinct to be accommodating and to hear everyone out only added to his misery. Even though Werner, as the largest investor, was the team's controlling partner, he tried to operate as democratically as possible when making decisions with his 14 minority partners, many of whom were San Diego businessmen. "I tried to conduct it as an open board of directors," Werner says. "It didn't work. Some of them didn't really understand the game and they put me in a situation where there was no way to win." At one point, things got so bad that one partner suggested that the team fly to another city the morning of a night game instead of the evening before in order to save a day's hotel charges. While Werner's partners privately groused about the team's losses and refused to sink more money into the franchise, some simultaneously (and anonymously) bad-mouthed Werner to the local media. "I thought the San Diego investors would be real assets to me," Werner says. "I felt that, you know, they were my partners and they would stand up for me. But instead they ducked and ran when things got bumpy."

To this day, Werner gets emotional when talking about his time in San Diego. "It was exhausting. It was not fun. Look, I'm extremely competitive. There isn't an owner who doesn't go into this without the goal of winning a World Series for their city. . . . I came to the conclusion that without revenue sharing, the widening disparity between small- and large-market teams was such that it was going to be impossible to be that competitive without losing huge amounts of money." At the time, baseball was in a state of turmoil. In 1992, after three years of intermittent feuding with the league's owners, commissioner Fay Vincent resigned following a vote of no confidence; Milwaukee Brewers owner Bud Selig took the job on an interim basis. A year later, in August 1993, baseball's owners gathered for a conference in Kohler, Wisconsin, to have, for the first time ever, serious discussions about revenue sharing among the clubs.

It was, participants agree, one of the most contentious ownership meetings ever to occur in baseball. To this day, Selig says those sessions in Kohler were the most difficult of his baseball career. "I've never seen anger like that," Selig said later. "It wasn't just bad. It was vile." The teams were so divided that the owners refused to meet as one group; instead, the small-market teams like the Padres and Selig's Brewers got together, the medium-market teams like the St. Louis Cardinals and the Texas Rangers met separately, and the large-market teams like the Los Angeles Dodgers and the New York Yankees talked among themselves. Werner and his cohorts were arguing that, in order for the game to remain healthy, there had to be more aggressive revenue sharing; the money that teams based in major media markets could make from television and radio contracts alone meant that those clubs would always be able to afford exponentially higher payrolls than the teams playing in smaller, less affluent markets. It was in the best interests of all of baseball, the small-revenue teams argued, to have as many teams as possible be competitive instead of having the game divided into one group of teams that regularly made the playoffs and one group that rarely, if ever, had a chance. The large-market owners countered by essentially accusing the less financially lucrative clubs of looking for handouts.

After one grueling all-night session, the Kohler meetings broke up without any agreements, and the next year, major league players went on strike because they couldn't come to terms with the owners over salary caps, salary arbitration, free agency rules, or minimum salaries. In 1994, unable to see any end to the Padres' problems, Werner decided to sell the team. "It was just too difficult," he says. "Bill Cosby once said to me, '[When you own a baseball team,] people think of your money as their money.' And pretty soon, if you act like that, you won't have any money left. I've been very philanthropic in my life, and I got to a point where one day I said, 'Well, jeez, I could be, you know, losing five million dollars a year doing this or I could be giving five million dollars away to worthy causes.'

And there's no question that I'd rather do the latter." Four years after he bought the team for around $75 million, he sold it for around $85 million to software mogul John Moores and former Baltimore Orioles chief executive Larry Lucchino. Werner stayed on as an investor, but, he says, "I really never thought that I'd be back in the game again."

The Red Sox, however, were just tempting enough to cause Werner to reconsider. In addition to the baseball club, the Red Sox sale included Fenway Park, which the team owned, and the team's 80 percent stake in NESN, the regional sports network that broadcasts Red Sox and Boston Bruins hockey games. Over the previous decade, regional sports networks—or RSNs—had become increasingly profitable, and NESN was the crown jewel of the bunch.* In fact, to many of the parties interested in bidding for the Red Sox, NESN was the main draw. While the Red Sox themselves might turn a profit or a loss of a couple of million dollars in any given year, NESN, whose profits were not supposed to be subject to baseball's revenue-sharing agreements, was seen as a likely cash cow. The Red Sox had a monopoly on baseball fans in most of New England, and NESN was usually the only way those fans could watch their team play. The potential for advertising revenue was enormous.

When Otten said he was going to make a bid for the team, "it seemed like a stretch," says Werner. "But it seemed like at least it was something that I wanted to examine. Obviously, the difference between the Red Sox and the San Diego Padres is considerable. And the Red Sox, as I started to dwell on it, had some real interest for me. I had a lot of respect for John Harrington, but I was also aware that, even on the baseball side, the management of this asset was not par-

---

* Most RSNs are independently owned and pay teams a negotiated fee for the right to broadcast its games. The success of team-owned RSNs like NESN has led other teams to adopt that model. In 2002, the Yankees established the Yankees Entertainment and Sports (YES) Network; previously, Yankees games had been carried by the MSG Network. In 2006, the New York Mets began broadcasting games on their new regional network. It was partially in anticipation of this that the Mets went on an expensive free-agent acquisition spree the last several seasons, as they tried to build a fan base for their cable network.

ticularly aggressive." While Werner had to scrap and fight for every ticket sale in San Diego, the Red Sox had such a dedicated fan base that they were infamous for taking their patrons more or less for granted. "It seemed like there were a lot of possibilities for adding value to the Red Sox, including my feeling that Fenway Park could become an even bigger asset than it was. And since I actually had real expertise in the communications business I could help increase value on both sides of the equation."

Soon, Otten and Werner had formed a partnership. They must have seemed like an unlikely pair: Otten, the brash, back-slapping, attention-loving salesman, and Werner, the family-centered, affable television producer who often ends calls to his longtime business partner by saying, "I love you." By this time, it was clear the sale would not be completed before the 2001 season, which at first looked promising for the Red Sox. Pedro Martinez was coming off consecutive Cy Young Awards—in the past two seasons he'd gone a combined 41-10 and had a cumulative earned run average of less than 2.00. (In both of those years, the league's next-best ERA was between 3.40 and 3.70.) Nomar Garciaparra had won two straight batting titles, and in the offseason, the Sox added free agent Manny Ramirez, the prodigious Cleveland Indians slugger, to the lineup.

For most of the first half of 2001, as the Red Sox flirted with first place, Werner's and Otten's interest in the team seemed to be a non-factor. Joe O'Donnell and Steve Karp had, indeed, joined forces (David Mugar never did enter the bidding), and the two, with the help of some cheerleading from some *Globe*'s columnists and the *Herald*'s sports and business pages, were seen as clear front-runners. Frank McCourt, a Boston developer who owned a piece of waterfront property on which he wanted to build a new ballpark for the team, was another much-discussed candidate, as were Boston Bruins owner Jeremy Jacobs, Cablevision's Dolan, Miles Prentice (the New York lawyer who had previously failed in his bid to buy the Kansas City Royals), and the Aramark Corp., the Philadelphia-based company that already held Fenway's concessions contract.

Werner and Otten, meanwhile, didn't even know where their money would come from. "You would have had to have handi-capped us as a long shot," Werner says. "The O'Donnell group was fairly confident they'd be successful." While Otten worked on hiring an engineering firm to prepare a feasibility study regarding the renovation of the existing Fenway Park, Werner worked on remaining realistic about the improbability of their bid.

At least, that is, until that summer. In July, Werner was vacationing in Long Island when he turned on ESPN radio and heard the voice of Larry Lucchino. "There were six harmonious years," Lucchino was saying. "Last year was pretty rocky, but that doesn't alter the reality." When he heard those words, Werner realized that Lucchino was stepping down as the president and CEO of the San Diego Padres.

"I'd known Larry since 1990, when I got involved in baseball [and Lucchino was the president and chief executive officer of the Baltimore Orioles]," Werner says. "I thought he was one of the most exceptional people in the game." During the Kohler meetings, Lucchino had been coordinating the big-market teams' strategy (at the time, the Orioles were one of baseball's more financially successful franchises). "I grew to respect him as an adversary, and then, after he took over the Padres, I came to know and admire him as an ally. He is not only one of the brightest men I've ever met, but man, when the game's on the line, he's the guy you want in the trenches." Werner tracked down Lucchino's phone number and put in a call. "I'm on a quest to acquire the Boston Red Sox," he said. "You interested?"

"I don't think he was that surprised to hear from me," Werner says. "And of course, when you mention the Red Sox to anyone, well, this is not just a baseball club, this is a jewel." Lucchino wasn't available right away—he was staying on as a consultant with the Padres until after the 2001 season ended in the fall. But, Lucchino said that day, he was most definitely interested. "The Red Sox are magic words to the ears of any baseball executive," Lucchino says. "It's Mecca. It's the top of the mountain. If someone brings up the possibility of owning the Boston Red Sox . . ." Lucchino trails off. "What do you say? I said, 'Of course. Let's do it.' "

## CHAPTER 8

# *The Baseball Visionary*

**TOGETHER, LES OTTEN AND TOM WERNER** were right to think of themselves as long shots. But Larry Lucchino was commonly regarded as a genius when it came to running baseball teams. He had it all: a well-established record of both on-field success and increased team revenue (in two cities, no less), well-placed connections around the league, and the legacy of Baltimore's Camden Yards, the hugely successful retro baseball park that Lucchino had helped conceive and shepherd into existence. Known as a demanding boss and a combative foe, he inspired loyalty from his allies and enmity from those he tangled with.

Lucchino was raised modestly in Pittsburgh, Pennsylvania, and, from early in his life, he loved to do two things: compete and win. Tall, handsome, athletic, outgoing, and driven, he was the kind of golden boy who seemed capable of doing everything well. He was president of the 1963 senior class at Allderdice High School and the starting second baseman on the varsity team that won the city championship. At Princeton, Lucchino was a backup point guard on a varsity basketball team that played in the NCAA Final Four and posted a record of 23-6. After a stint teaching English in Beirut, Lucchino set off for Yale Law School, and, by the late 1970s, he had joined the Washington, D.C., law firm Williams & Connolly, where he found a mentor in Edward Bennett Williams, a legendary Washington figure and one of the firm's founders.

Lucchino has always exhibited an uncanny ability to connect with the famous or soon-to-be famous. At Princeton, he roomed with future New York Knicks star and U.S. senator Bill Bradley. After law school, he worked with the future Hillary Clinton on the Watergate impeachment committee. At one point, he even dated Maria Shriver. (Arnold Schwarzenegger wouldn't come along until later.) But it was Williams, the brash D.C. powerhouse whose clients ranged from Jimmy Hoffa to Senator Joseph McCarthy, who would have the biggest impact on Lucchino's life and career.

Williams was an intensely driven man whose own children showed no interest in the law. Perhaps because of this, he had a habit of adopting young lawyers in his firm, men like Vince Fuller, Peter Taft, and Greg Craig, as surrogate sons. But it was Larry Lucchino with whom he formed the closest bond of all. Even Williams's children remarked that Lucchino became like a member of their family. Williams's young acolytes, and particularly Lucchino, would travel with Williams, play sports with him, drink with him, even go to morning Mass with him. In 1985, when Lucchino was being treated for non-Hodgkin's lymphoma, Williams, who had been treated for lung cancer the year before, tried to buck up his protégé's sagging spirits. As Evan Thomas recounts in *The Man to See,* his biography of Williams, one afternoon Williams found Lucchino worn down and depressed from his chemotherapy treatments. "Let's go have some real chemotherapy," Williams said, dragging Lucchino out to drink gin for the remainder of the afternoon.

When Lucchino joined Williams & Connolly, Williams was the owner and the president of the Washington Redskins. In short order, he named Lucchino one of the team's vice presidents and its general counsel. In 1979, when Williams bought the Baltimore Orioles, he named Lucchino a vice president and the general counsel of that team as well. And just like that, a career that Lucchino thought would be spent working on a mixture of criminal cases and First Amendment law was forever altered.

It was during these years, while working daily with Williams, that Lucchino honed his hyperaggressive style. Williams championed a militaristic approach to life he termed "contest living," which meant relishing the daily battles that came one's way. The already competitive Lucchino responded viscerally to Williams's philosophy, and embraced it wholeheartedly, even as some associates began to complain of Lucchino's viciousness and attack-dog mentality. Over the next decade, as Lucchino and Williams grew even closer, Lucchino took an increasingly active role in the Orioles, and in the middle of the 1988 season, when Williams was struggling with a recurrence of cancer, he named Lucchino the Orioles president. When Williams died that August, Lucchino also became the team's chief executive officer.

At the time, the Orioles were suffering through one of their worst seasons ever. Five years off the team's 1983 World Series victory, the Orioles began the 1988 campaign by losing their first 21 games, as the team sagged under the weight of its over-the-hill, overpriced veterans. In the offseason, in addition to completely remaking the team, Lucchino helped orchestrate its sale to New York investor Eli Jacobs. After initially assuming that the end of Williams's ownership would conclude his involvement as well, Lucchino ended up buying 9 percent of the team and staying on as the team's president and CEO.

By the time the 1989 season began, Lucchino and the Orioles baseball operations crew had decided to surround franchise icon Cal Ripken Jr. with a crop of mainly unknown and unheralded rookies. That year, much to the surprise of the baseball intelligentsia, the team missed the playoffs by only two games, and the Orioles stayed in the playoff hunt until late in the 1992 and 1993 seasons.

Lucchino's most defining accomplishment in Baltimore was envisioning and then helping to ensure the building and success of Camden Yards, which opened in 1992. In the 14 years since it opened, Camden has been attributed with near mystical powers. It has been credited for everything from the revitalization of Baltimore's once-dangerous downtown to the resurrection of baseball itself. Camden, Lucchino has said, started out with a "simple idea": The Orioles should build a traditional, old-fashioned ballpark with modern amenities. "That was a thought of mine that came out of my childhood, in Pittsburgh," Lucchino said. "I saw a charming ball-park in Forbes Field replaced by Three Rivers Stadium. Much of the charm of baseball was lost by virtue of the utterly charmless stadium that was Three Rivers."

In the early 1990s, baseball was at the tail end of a 30-year trend that saw the quirky ballparks of the turn of the century replaced with cookie-cutter concrete monoliths. Lucchino, Eli Jacobs, and Janet Marie Smith, the architect in charge of planning and developing the new stadium, envisioned something entirely different. To start, they didn't want to use any concrete in the Orioles' new home; instead, they planned to build the park with steel trusses that could be painted to blend into the surrounding environment. They chose a location rich with baseball history, only blocks from Babe Ruth's birthplace. (Ruth's father operated his eponymous tavern at a spot now occupied by center field.) True to Lucchino's word, Camden was full of the amenities of new stadiums—bigger seats, more leg room, plenty of luxury boxes, high-end food options—while retaining the charm of parks like Fenway and the Chicago Cubs' Wrigley Field. More than a simple place to see a baseball game, Camden Yards became the much-beloved centerpiece of a revitalized neighborhood. Sodded with verdant Maryland bluegrass and constructed with a brick exterior for a more traditional appearance, the park was built bordering the old Baltimore & Ohio Railroad Warehouse, which rises over right field. The team's offices, along with a cafeteria, sports bar, gift shop, and exclusive club, are now housed in the warehouse, which has banks of lights mounted on its roof.

After the park opened, Paul Goldberger, then the architecture critic for *The New York Times,* said Camden Yards was "a building capable of wiping out in a single gesture 50 years of wretched stadium design." Those seemed to be prescient words: Over the next decade, a dozen new ballparks were built around the country, including stunning new facilities in Cleveland, Seattle, Cincinnati, and Pittsburgh. All of these would imitate the marriage of past and present that Camden had managed so brilliantly.

With Camden built, Lucchino would not stay long in Baltimore. When Eli Jacobs ran into financial trouble, he was forced to part with the team, and in August 1993, Peter Angelos led a group of investors that bought the Orioles in a bankruptcy auction for $173 million, at the time a baseball record. Lucchino found himself a rich man: His 9 percent share had earned him approximately $10 million. Although Angelos invited Lucchino to stay on in some capacity, Angelos made it clear that he himself intended to operate as the team's CEO. Instead of accepting a demotion, Lucchino decided it was time for a new challenge. He pondered assembling a coalition to buy his hometown Pittsburgh Pirates, and even talked with Angelos about joining forces in an effort to bring a National Football League franchise to Baltimore.

Eventually, though, Lucchino headed west, pairing up with software entrepreneur John Moores to buy the San Diego Padres from Tom Werner. The transition would be a stark one. The Orioles, a proud, history-laden franchise, had been baseball's winningest team since 1960. The Padres, in contrast, were a small-market expansion team that had never built a solid relationship with fans and were perhaps best known for their incomparable mascot, the San Diego Chicken, and the odd color of their uniforms, which had been at various times compared to the color of diarrhea.

Lucchino, well aware that the Padres' relationship with their fans was at a crisis point, decided to signal immediately his intention to do things differently. He imported one or two people from each department from the Orioles to the Padres in order to quickly instill a new mind-set. Among those he brought along were some of his most trusted lieutenants, men like public relations guru Charles Steinberg. The roly-poly and always upbeat Steinberg had been a 20-year-old Orioles intern about to embark on a career in dentistry when, in 1980, he first met Lucchino, the "hard-charging vice president and general counsel," as Steinberg describes him. Many Orioles employees didn't know what to make of Edward Bennett Williams's young protégé. "I had the benefit of being sufficiently young, naïve, and open-minded, so the idea of this young guy coming in wasn't a threat to me at all," Steinberg says. "We've been together ever since."

In addition to aides such as Steinberg, Lucchino brought along some associates he'd known in Baltimore who hadn't even worked for the Orioles. For example, Mike Dee, an Orioles season ticket holder, came to know Lucchino socially in the early 1990s—for a while, Lucchino had dated one of Dee's best friends—and the two frequently chewed over ideas about sports and sports marketing. Soon after taking over the Padres, Lucchino called up Dee. "It's Larry," he said. "We only have eight full-time employees out here." (Because of the 1994 strike, the Padres had all but shuttered their day-to-day operations.) "I always told you you'd be great in sports. Why don't you come out here and work with me?" Dee, who was at the time running the sales department for a family-owned business, said yes. Lucchino also hired Theo Epstein, a recent Yale graduate who had previously interned in the Orioles public relations department.

"The goal was to bring some of the experience and work ethic that came from Baltimore and replicate it [in San Diego]," Lucchino says. "We knew that there was a contrast that we had to draw right away. One of the things we did quite literally was get dozens of stickers that said 'New' on them and we stuck them over everything that said 'Padres,' so everywhere you looked, it was 'New Padres, New Padres, New Padres.'" To drive this point home, a week after taking over, Lucchino oversaw a 12-player deal that brought third baseman (and future Most Valuable Player) Ken Caminiti and center fielder Steve Finley to San Diego from Houston. "We wanted people to know right off the bat that we were going to be bold. We were going to focus on improving the quality of the team. When we got there, the Padres had the worst record, the lowest attendance, and the lowest revenue in baseball. We were determined to change all of that." Kevin Towers, who served as the general manager of the Padres under Lucchino, describes his former boss as "a very driven son of a gun, very outspoken. He's Italian: It's energy, energy, energy, go, go, go. Don't sit and think, do it."

When Lucchino moved from the large-revenue Orioles to the small-revenue Padres, he found himself on the opposite side of what had become one of baseball's most contentious labor issues. The 1994 players strike had been brought about, in part, by an inability to resolve the disparity between the league's wealthiest and poorest teams. Lucchino, whom Werner admired when he fought for financially flush teams like the Orioles at the Kohler conference in 1993, now became one of baseball's most forceful advocates for increased revenue sharing. At the time, most of the game's shared revenue came from fees paid for national, baseball-wide television contracts and income from all official baseball merchandise, which was divided equally among all the teams.* Beyond that, a small percentage of the ticket gate was shared: In the American League, the gate was split 80–20, while in the National League, the visiting club received 42 cents per admission.†

But in baseball, the real money came from contracts for local television and radio rights. If large-market teams had an easier time drawing fans, they benefited even more from the kind of concentrated, affluent fan base advertisers loved. Teams like the Yankees, with around 20 million people in their media market, obviously stood to make far more from their local contracts than teams like the Cincinnati Reds, and the explosion of cable television only added to this disparity.

In 1996, just two years after the strike that canceled the World Series, Major League Baseball worked out a difficult compromise with the players union. Instead of a salary cap—something the union threatened to strike over—the new collective bargaining agreement called for a payroll tax, which was paid when a team's total payroll rose above a set level, and a vastly increased system of revenue sharing. Teams would no longer simply share a fraction of their ticket receipts; instead, they'd pay 20 percent of their local revenues (stadium expenses were allowed as deductions) into a pool. Seventy-five percent of this pooled money would be split evenly among the teams, while the other 25 percent would be distributed to those teams with below-average local revenues.

---

* This means that teams like the Red Sox and Yankees get no more money from the sale of their hats and jerseys than the Kansas City Royals do: At the end of each year, all merchandise revenue is pooled and divided equally among all the clubs.

† Sharing of gate receipts varies widely among American sports leagues. The National Football League, widely considered to have the most parity among North American sports leagues, splits its gate receipts 60–40. In the National Basketball League, the gate is split 94–6, and in the National Hockey League, the home team retains the entire gate.

In his years with the Padres, Lucchino helped prove that small-revenue teams could be competitive. The Padres won two division titles, and in 1998, the National League pennant. (In the World Series, they were swept by the New York Yankees, who were in the midst of winning four championships in five years and 14 World Series games in a row.) He also planned, with the help of Janet Marie Smith, the architect behind Camden Yards, a new, intimate, baseball-only stadium for San Diego. Even more impressively, he convinced San Diegans to support construction of a facility for a team that had, until recently, been thought of as a public disgrace.

This was only possible because Lucchino had worked so hard to attract new fans to the Padres. "You tend to replicate in later life successes you've had earlier," Lucchino says. "We had spent years striving for a regional franchise in Baltimore. We had marketing meetings all the time where regionalization was the dominant theme. How do we market a team in and around the whole mid-Atlantic region? How do we make the Orioles the team of all of Maryland, the team of southern Pennsylvania, the team of Washington, D.C., and Northern Virginia? And we took that whole concept to California and decided we were not going to limit the Padres to San Diego County. We went to the north and tried to recruit fans from the Dodgers and the Angels by saying, 'We're a Southern California team.' We went to the east. We went into Mexico, in the south." After drawing just over a million fans in 1995, the Padres sold 2,187,886 tickets in 1996 and set a club record with 2,555,874 paying customers in 1998.

Even with on-field success, increased revenue sharing, and record fan attendance, Lucchino and Moores were finding, much as Tom Werner had before them, that making money in San Diego was no easy task. By the end of the 2000 season, although fans were flocking to the park, the team was losing around $15 million a year. Eventually, Lucchino said, the team would have to cut back on payroll. "The [monetary] losses have become intolerable for us," he said. "We aren't going to continue to absorb them. We've been spending beyond our means in an effort to keep the team competitive. We cannot continue to do that endlessly. We're tapped out and awash in red ink." At the same time, Lucchino's relationship with

John Moores, once warm, had grown strained. Lucchino's friends say this was due to some legal issues Moores was having; others at the Padres said Moores grew tired of Lucchino's combative and abrasive management style. In July 2001, after several months in which Moores and Lucchino's relationship went from bad to worse, both men agreed it made sense for Lucchino to move on.

While nominally staying on the Padres board until October, Lucchino quickly began to sort through his options. Tom Werner's invitation to join his bid to acquire the Red Sox was one of the first offers to come in. In the meantime, Lucchino had a new task in front of him. Bud Selig had asked Lucchino, who by that time had become known as an expert in convincing cities to help pay for new stadiums, to head to South Florida, where Marlins owner John Henry was thinking about selling the team or moving it elsewhere. Since buying the Marlins in 1998, Henry had spent enormous amounts of energy working to pass legislation that would help build the Marlins a baseball-only stadium. After yet another setback, he was ready to give up. Selig wanted Lucchino to find out if Henry had really exhausted all his other options.

## CHAPTER 9

# From Soybeans to Stadiums

**JOHN W. HENRY WAS BORN** on September 13, 1949, in Quincy, Illinois. In the early 1950s, his family moved to Arkansas, where his father owned a large farm. Henry was a shy and awkward child: His peers would sometimes come to the Henrys' yard to play ball and the young John Henry was too timid to ask if he could join in the fun. Increasingly, he took refuge in listening to baseball games, especially those of the St. Louis Cardinals, whose broadcasts Henry could pick up on his radio. It wasn't until he was 10 years old, in 1959, that Henry made the trip to St. Louis, and that was only because his father was hospitalized with a brain tumor. Cardinals coach Johnny Keane, who went on to manage the Yankees, was staying at the same hotel as Henry, and Keane left the young boy tickets to games. "It was really heaven and hell," Henry says. Henry's father, whom he describes as so commanding a presence that "even the insects got quiet" when he entered a room, never fully recovered.

By the time he was a teenager, Henry found that his facility for numbers made baseball even more of a potential source of wonder and escape than before. He could, he discovered, calculate a player's batting average in his head. A talented but occasionally indifferent student, Henry also devoted much of his energy to learning how to play music, which helped transport him away from his sometimes lonely reality.

After high school, Henry spent several years taking philosophy courses at various California colleges, although he never got a degree. He also traveled to Las Vegas, where for a brief period he made good money counting cards at blackjack tables. (Once he was found out, the local casino owners politely—but forcefully—asked Henry to find some other way to occupy his time.) During these years, his main focus was on his budding progressive rock band, Elysian Fields, which was named after the mythical abode of the blessed situated at the end of the world. Henry played bass in the trio, which also featured a keyboardist and a drummer. He bankrolled the group's elaborate stage shows, which for a while featured a ring of speakers arranged around auditoriums in such a way to create roiling waves of sound. (At one point, the band's live shows centered on a rock opera about aliens from the Cassiopeia solar system. During this era, the entire band shaved their eyebrows in order to get into character.) Eventually, Henry decided to break up Elysian Fields, although not without some trepidation: "I wasn't sure if I'd ever have sex again," he says, laughing. "I thought the only reasons girls liked me was because I was in a rock band."

In 1975, Henry's father died, and Henry moved back to Forrest City, Arkansas, to run the family farm. While managing a 1,000-acre soybean farm, he began to examine the commodities markets, in which contracts for agricultural products are bought and sold, and soon realized he was more interested in numbers than in working farmland. He began spending his days at a small commodities brokerage firm in town, eventually moving on to trading commodities in Memphis. What happened next is a fortuitous coincidence that forever altered his life. While in Memphis, Henry got a hunch that soybean prices were about to spike upward, and he began aggressively buying. Sure enough, up they went, from just under $7 a bushel when Henry began his buying spree to more than $13 a bushel. Henry was convinced they'd go even higher but was prevented from riding his hunch when his girlfriend became crippled by panic attacks. Henry sold his contracts and moved back to Illinois to help.

While Henry was gone, soybeans collapsed to about $4 a bushel. Henry had been saved from financial ruin by the emotional vicissitudes of a lover. Instead of simply thanking his lucky stars and moving on, Henry realized he would never again be comfortable relying on instinct; instead, he wanted to develop a systematic approach to commodities trading. He decided that, unlike so-called fundamental traders who try to predict where prices will go, he would track prices in order to identify broad market trends that were already occurring. In doing this, Henry was partially influenced by the college philosophy courses he took in California in the early 1970s, where he met the Indian philosopher Jiddu Krishnamurti and became fascinated with the work of Carl Jung. "It's the whole notion of 'what is,' not 'what should be,' " he says. Henry had also become convinced that markets, for the most part, reflect people's expectations and if he could identify market trends early on, he could invest accordingly. And so, at an age when many of his similarly music-obsessed peers were touring with rock bands or embracing the drug culture, John Henry all but moved into local libraries, pawing through microfilm printouts and fraying newsprint, studying commodities pricing all the way back to the nineteenth century. By the end of 1979, he had devised what he thought was a valuable model. With the help of little more than a hand-held calculator, he spent most of the following year testing his model against historical data, and as he had expected, found that it worked across varied eras and assorted markets. In 1981, at 31 years old, the formerly eyebrowless aspiring rock star opened John W. Henry & Co. and began offering managed futures funds.

Seven years later, JWH & Co. had experienced such fantastic success that Henry was able to hand the day-to-day running of his company over to a full-time professional staff. Though he never did make it as a rock star, he eventually built a recording studio in his home and became friends with musicians, including members of the Rolling Stones and Aerosmith. By the late 1980s, he was wealthy enough that he could actually consider fulfilling his other boyhood dream: buying a baseball team. In 1989, he debated making a bid for the Kansas City Royals. "I had lived in Southern California for two-and-a-half decades, and I was ready to live somewhere else,"

Henry says. "But I flew into Kansas City and . . . drove around during the day and thought to myself, 'I just don't think I could live in Kansas City.' I lived in Middle America. I wasn't ready to go back." Instead, he purchased a stake in the minor league Tucson Toros of the Triple-A Pacific Coast League, and then, after moving to Boca Raton, Florida, helped start the Senior Professional Baseball Association, a short-lived league of former pro players. Henry's team, the West Palm Beach Tropics, was the runaway star of the league. Dick Williams, the manager of the Impossible Dream Red Sox, ran the club, which featured former big-league stars such as Dave Kingman, Mickey Rivers, Ron Washington, and ace reliever Rollie Fingers, who was elected to the Hall of Fame in 1992. "We had an enormous amount of fun," says Henry, who ran the in-game entertainment at Tropics games. "We went 52-20. They changed the league's rules because we were so good."

By 1991, the senior league had shut down, and Henry briefly thought about trying to join a Republican group that would establish a Major League Baseball expansion franchise in Colorado. After Colorado's Democratic governor, Roy Romer, gave his blessing to a rival bidding group, Henry dropped out, angry that he had been cut out of the process before he'd even been allowed to make his pitch. "Had I known that a beauty pageant was being conducted . . . perhaps I would have chosen not to participate," Henry said in a statement at the time. "Isn't it more important to assist investors in helping to make Denver's dream of baseball a reality rather than to eliminate them?" Romer responded by calling Henry's gripes "sour grapes."

"I ended up getting into this very public thing with the governor," Henry says. "That was really my first experience with the media; it was the first time I was on the front page of a major newspaper. It wasn't that pleasant, but I learned something." Henry finally got a stake in a baseball franchise later that year, when he bought a Florida neighbor's 1 percent share of the New York Yankees. Being a part of the Yankees, Henry says, was a lot of fun. He would occasionally fly some of the partners to playoff games on his private plane (affectionately dubbed TWH, or Trans World Henry). Yankees principal owner George Steinbrenner was always solicitous of Henry's mother. "The partners were all very close, and I had a great relationship with George. I didn't have any desire to be out front. I didn't have any desire to stick my nose out. I was a small partner, and I was happy with that."

Nevertheless, when Wayne Huizenga announced in 1998 that he was going to sell the Miami-based Florida Marlins, Henry was intrigued. The Marlins were by this time his hometown team: He owned a palatial lake-front mansion in an exclusive gated community in Boca Raton and Henry wanted to ensure the team stayed in South Florida. The team had won a World Series faster than any expansion team in history: In 1997, only four years after the team's inaugural season, the Marlins beat the Cleveland Indians in an exciting seven-game series. The next year, after claiming he had lost more than $30 million during the '97 season, Huizenga completely dismantled the team,* shedding payroll and embittering fans around the region. By the middle of the '98 season, Marlins president Don Smiley was searching for wealthy backers with whom he could purchase the club.

"I had just taken delivery on my boat," Henry says, referring modestly to his 164-foot yacht, the Iroquois.† "I was in the south of France, and Smiley called and asked me if I would come and be the lead general partner." Henry, who had been vacationing with the actor Michael Douglas and Miami Heat coach Pat Riley, immediately flew back to the States. By late August, with Smiley no longer

---

* As part of his payroll reduction, Huizenga traded outfielder Moises Alou to the Houston Astros, starting pitcher Kevin Brown to the San Diego Padres, first baseman Jeff Conine to the Kansas City Royals, center fielder Devon White to the Arizona Diamondbacks, and closer Robb Nen to the San Francisco Giants. A month into the 1998 season, the Marlins traded right fielder Gary Sheffield and third baseman Bobby Bonilla to the Los Angeles Dodgers. The Marlins finished the 1998 season with 54 wins and 108 losses.

† Henry's boat was christened as a way of honoring his steadfast approach to business. In 1985, a suddenly weakened dollar caused Henry to lose as much as 10 percent of his clients' funds in a single day. One investment firm immediately fired JWH & Co. as manager of a futures fund named Iroquois. Henry didn't alter his approach, rode out the plunge, and ended up recording one of his best years ever. The Iroquois fund didn't fare as well, and soon went belly up.

part of the deal, Henry's negotiations with Huizenga had begun in earnest.

For Henry, any deal to buy the Marlins would have to include a plan to build a new stadium. The Marlins had played throughout their existence in Pro Player Stadium, the cavernous (and charmless) home to the National Football League's Miami Dolphins. Besides being located away from any urban center, Pro Player does not have a retractable roof, and the summer is Florida's rainy hurricane season. "Every afternoon all summer, at just the time people are thinking about going to a game, rains come in and soak the region," Henry says. Even though the nights were generally dry, "Of course no one's going to decide to go to a game when it looks like you'll be sitting in a rainstorm." At the time, Henry made clear the Marlins would need public support for a stadium if the team wanted to be competitive. "Anyone who purchases the Marlins has to do so with the understanding they may have to privately finance a stadium," he told the local press. "But the team would not be able to compete in the National League East for the next 30 years." Henry, whose company was continuing to do exceedingly well, also said he wouldn't buy the team with the intention of adding to his wealth. "I don't expect to make money," he said, tellingly wearing a 1996 Yankees World Series ring he'd won as a partner in the team. "My interest is in having a competitive baseball team."

The next two months were strikingly contentious. On September 1, Henry and Huizenga came to a handshake deal for $150 million. Soon, however, Huizenga was demanding another $8 million—ostensibly for stadium improvements for Pro Player Stadium, which Huizenga owned—which Henry said put the deal in jeopardy. Huizenga responded by saying Henry was "chickening out" of the deal, "just like with the ten other teams he's tried to buy." By October 21, the two men had come to terms again. And by November 4, the deal was back off. "The deal kept changing," Henry said at the time. "It's been two months of a lot of hard work and thought and expense for nothing." Adding to the carnival-like atmosphere, Huizenga announced that if he weren't able to find a buyer, he'd establish an eight-member board of directors, consisting of sports editors from local papers and county commissioners from Palm Beach, Broward, and Miami-Dade counties, to run the team. Finally, on November 6, 1998, Henry agreed to buy the Marlins for $150 million, plus the $8 million Huizenga was insisting on for stadium improvements.

Almost immediately, Henry set about trying to find some trusted lieutenants to help him run the Marlins. As soon as his purchase of the team was finalized, he approached Lucinda Treat, a 28-year-old mergers and acquisitions lawyer at New York's Shearman & Sterling, the law firm that represented Henry. Treat, along with Shearman & Sterling's Creighton Condon, had been instrumental in guiding Henry's bid for the team. At the time, she was comfortably ensconced in a brownstone in Brooklyn's Park Slope with her husband and two young children. She'd just decided to leave private practice, and had accepted a job as an in-house counsel at the media company Reuters.

"I have a better idea," Henry said. "Why don't you come down to Florida and work with me?" Within a week, Treat had told Reuters something else had come up and signed on as the Marlins director of legal affairs. "It was a once-in-a-lifetime opportunity," says Treat. "I'd gotten to know John, and I knew he had a good sense of values. It was just so unusual to be offered that kind of job—how could I say no?" Treat's whole family relocated to Florida.

"When I started out with the Marlins, I was just so thrilled," says Henry. "I was excited about the people I was working with, and I was excited to get a chance to help build up baseball in southern Florida after what had happened with the dismantling of the World Series team." The Marlins also afforded Henry a chance to explore some new aspects of his personality. After a career filled with dizzying successes, John Henry had become close friends with sports owners, rock stars, and politicians. Despite this, he had rarely been in the public eye. A naturally shy person, Henry, with his soft voice, translucent skin, and watery eyes, appeared frail to many people.

Now, he was taking over a beleaguered franchise that was regularly covered by three major metropolitan dailies—*The Miami Herald*, Fort Lauderdale's *Sun Sentinel*, and *The Palm Beach Post*. Instead of avoiding the spotlight, Henry decided to challenge himself, and made a particular point of opening up and being available to the public. He held regular meetings with the beat writers covering the team and actively sought these reporters' input on how best to manage the team, a welcome change from the openly combative relationship Huizenga had had with much of the local press. He anointed himself the Marlins fan ambassador, frequently greeting ticket holders as they walked into and out of the ballpark. During games, he would sometimes wander the stands, thanking patrons for their support. Over time, he came to know many of the team's season-ticket holders by name.

Henry's connection with and ownership of the Marlins was a stark contrast to the prevailing trend in baseball. While baseball teams were once seen as investments or vanity acquisitions for rich, swashbuckling men—witness Tom Yawkey, George Steinbrenner, and Ted Turner—clubs were increasingly being bought by corporations that were drawn to baseball's synergistic or marketing possibilities. Time Warner controlled the Braves, The Walt Disney Company ran the Anaheim Angels, and the News Corporation owned the Los Angeles Dodgers. Henry wasn't looking to the Marlins to pad his fortune, and the team's marketing or media potential certainly wasn't a draw; instead, he was propelled by his boyhood love of the game. For him, owning the Marlins was a way both to connect with his past and to explore neglected aspects of his own personality.

"I had spent my life in a very insular business," Henry says. "And I had a great reticence in public speaking, or even in being a public figure. But doing that with the Marlins seemed to give me tremendous energy and reinvigorate my life. It made my life a lot richer. I connected with the fans, I became friends with the reporters, and I went from a very insular existence to one that was very community oriented. It was one of the most unexpectedly wonderful things that ever happened to me."

Henry's early efforts to forge a connection with the community would prove crucial during the three years he owned the Marlins. Instead of concentrating solely on building up a competitive team, much of Henry's (and the entire Marlins organization's) efforts during that time were devoted to trying to find a way to build a retractable roof stadium. Within months of signing on to join Henry in Florida, Lucinda Treat found that the assorted stadium plans and negotiations would take up an enormous amount of her daily work. Jonathan Mariner, the team's executive vice president, joined Treat in working virtually around the clock on various stadium deals. When Mariner quit the team in August 2000, David Ginsberg, a former Wall Street investment banker and London portfolio manager who had known Henry through his commodities business, took over. If Henry thought owning a baseball team would transport him to the romantic relationship he had with the game as a child, he was about to discover how wrong he was.

By the end of the 1999 season, as a Marlins team still decimated by Huizenga's 1998 fire sale sputtered through their first year under Henry's stewardship, Henry, Treat, and Mariner decided to focus their energy on gaining support for a stadium in a downtown bayfront park next to the Miami Heat's new arena. The planned ballpark, to be designed by the same architectural firm that built Camden Yards, would seat approximately 38,000 people. Initially, Henry said he hoped to have the stadium completed before the 2003 season and wanted to raise approximately $300 million of the estimated $400 million needed for the park from public funds; that way, he said, he could use his own money to go after the kind of high-priced talent the team would need to be competitive. "I had no reason to think at that time that we couldn't be successful," he says.

Indeed, Henry's advisors had come up with a plan that would seemingly cost Florida taxpayers next to nothing, since the park was to be funded by a proposed tax on passengers who took luxury cruises that departed from Florida. Henry even assured both lawmakers and the public that he wouldn't personally lard his coffers with revenue from the new stadium: He promised to return 90 percent of the team's profits to the Miami area and said he'd invest a minimum of $1 million a year on community projects. "It seemed like such a slam-dunk," he says. "We'd help revitalize a part of downtown that was in dire need of attention. Coupled with the Heat, we'd create a kind of sports complex that would have brought in new business. And Florida taxpayers wouldn't have had to pay."

As Henry was about to discover, however, nothing is ever simple when it comes to Florida politics. Despite preliminary indications of support from the state legislature, Governor Jeb Bush said he'd veto a bill that did nothing more than set a date for the state's residents to vote on whether they wanted to approve the proposed cruise tax. (Bush called the proposed tax "bad public policy" and argued it would drive the cruise industry to other states' port cities.)

With the cruise tax seemingly moribund, Treat and David Ginsberg next spent the rest of 2000 hammering out a completely new funding plan with Miami-Dade County mayor Alex Penelas. Now, funding for the stadium would come from a nightly county tax on Miami's hotel visitors, a city parking surcharge, and state money from a sales tax rebate. Before long, the state pulled out, and that plan fell apart as well. Soon, so did the promise of the land next to the Heat's arena. Finally, in a last-ditch effort, Henry agreed to build a stadium on a polluted 60-acre site along the Miami River. On May 4, 2001, Florida's House of Representatives overwhelmingly approved a measure that would have allowed for public financing of the proposed $385 million stadium. That same day, the state Senate president adjourned early, without even allowing the bill to come up for a vote, essentially killing it without any debate.

Henry, defeated and frustrated, was ready to give up. "I'm not going to comment or speculate on what happens at this point," he said at the time. "We have spent the last two-and-a-half years expecting to be successful. At some point, we just can't continue. It doesn't make sense." He acknowledged that he had the money to build a new ballpark himself, but if he wanted to limit his overall losses, that would drain much needed resources from the team's payroll. "We could probably build our own ballpark, but we wouldn't be competitive," he said. "We could do that, but it would make no sense to field minor leaguers, and everybody would write about what jerks we are for the next 30 years." Baseball commissioner Bud Selig, speaking out publicly about the situation, said that without a new stadium the team would likely be forced to move or would be selected for contraction.

The memories of this period still haunt Henry. "I lost $25 million over the first two years [of owning the Marlins]," he says. "And I knew I was going to lose—I was going to have to reduce payroll in

2002 just to keep my losses to $25 million [per year]. You have to have some idea about how you're gonna eventually be able to break even. If there's no hope at the end of the day, it just becomes ridiculous, and that was the point I reached in 2001." He pauses. "You know, I really thought we were going to be successful. I was sure I would spend the rest of my life in Miami."

By the spring of 2001, even officials in Major League Baseball were urging Henry to explore other options rather than continuing to lose money in South Florida. Since buying the Marlins, Henry had, in many ways, been a model owner. He'd been active in the baseball community, he'd made efforts to connect with his team's fans, and he'd reached out to other owners around the league. The game, Bud Selig kept telling Henry, needed to keep people like him involved. In May 2001, during a trip Henry made to New York City, Selig dispatched Paul Beeston and Bob DuPuy, two of the league's top officials, to speak with Henry.

DuPuy, Beeston, and Henry met on the deck of Henry's yacht, which was docked in Manhattan's Chelsea Piers. Baseball, DuPuy said, was looking seriously at the issue of contraction. In all likelihood, two teams would be dissolved following the 2001 season, and the Marlins, with their persistently poor attendance, low revenue, and lack of prospects for improvement, would be at the top of the list. "We cannot allow you to sit down there in the rain for years losing the kind of money you would have to with no assurances on the future of a team down there," DuPuy said. Then DuPuy and Beeston began to talk about the future.

"They took the position that I had done a good job [in Florida], so they came to see me about other potential teams," Henry says. Beeston and DuPuy went over franchises that were for sale. How about the Red Sox? That sale was expected to conclude right after the season ended. No, said Henry: That was more money than he was looking to spend. Besides, he said, "I didn't want to get into a very public bidding war that had already left the docks, so to speak." Beeston and DuPuy then brought up The Walt Disney Company–owned Anaheim Angels, which were up for sale as well. That seemed more appealing, thought Henry. He'd owned a house in Orange County for years, and he thought his wife, Peggy, whom he'd met in Florida, would be amenable to living in Southern California.

Still, Henry said that he'd prefer simply moving the Marlins. Unlike many owners, Henry essentially functioned as the team's CEO, and was intimately connected with virtually every aspect of the organization. Decades after being too shy to play with his neighbors in his own yard, he'd become close to many of the Marlins players. "He was always coming in to the locker room, talking to us," says Mark Kotsay, the Oakland A's center fielder who played for the Marlins from 1997 through 2000. "To me, he's unparalleled. He treats everybody like his family. When I was in Florida, I got a chance to become his friend, and the stories he shared with me about overcoming adversity early in his ventures to be successful meant a lot to me." Kotsay and Henry's friendship was no secret in the Marlins organization; still, Henry gave his general manager permission to trade Kotsay to the San Diego Padres before the 2001 season. It was, Henry says, one of his hardest days as a baseball owner. "When I was traded, he personally called me," Kotsay says. "It made me feel great, as a person and as a player. . . . Until you talk to him, it can seem like he's very shy, but once you start to develop a relationship with him, you see what an amazing guy he is. He's like a little kid. He loves the game. And he's just as concerned with wins and losses as anybody, but he just wants you to go out there and do your best. There is one person that I would play for any time of the day and that's Mr. Henry."

DuPuy told Henry that moving a team could potentially be accomplished through the mechanisms of contraction. At the time, Steve Schott and Ken Hoffman, who owned the Oakland A's, were also looking to sell. DuPuy said he thought the owners of both the Angels and the A's might be willing simply to have their teams contracted instead of dealing with a public, and potentially messy, sale. What was even more likely, DuPuy and Beeston explained, was that one of the teams—say, the Angels—would be contracted, along with the Marlins. Henry could then buy the A's, but instead of staying in Oakland, he could move the team to Orange County, where the Angels had been based. Then, rather than moving the A's infrastructure and players, he would import the Marlins roster. It would be, in essence, a brand-new team with the history of three former major league franchises: the Marlins' players and personnel, the A's name, and the Angels' former territory. If that didn't work, there was always the somewhat more remote possibility of simply moving the Marlins somewhere else, New Jersey, say, or Charlotte, North Carolina.*

It was soon after this meeting that Henry began to come to grips with the fact that it was unlikely he'd be able to keep the Marlins in South Florida. "I am grieving over the extinction of this franchise [we] have worked so hard to have and have felt so much about," he wrote that month in an email to Lucinda Treat. "We have to work to save as much [of it] as possible." By June 2001, Henry's negotiations concerning the Angels had advanced to the point at which Henry and Treat were examining the terms of the Angels' stadium lease. Soon afterward, Larry Lucchino reported back to Selig that Henry did, indeed, seem to have exhausted all his options for staying in Florida. Not long after that, Henry asked Lucchino if he wanted to join his bid to take over the Angels, whether through an outright sale or contraction. "Let's talk," Lucchino said. "That could be interesting."

* Following the 2004 season, the Montreal Expos became the first team to relocate in more than 30 years when they moved to Washington, D.C., and renamed themselves the Nationals. Before that, the last team to move had left D.C.: In 1972, the Washington Senators relocated to Texas, becoming the Rangers.

## CHAPTER 10

# Putting Together the Team

IN OCTOBER 2000, when John Harrington announced that the Red Sox were up for sale, he became a very popular man. Throughout the fall, he received dozens and dozens of inquiries about the team; eventually, more than 100 parties indicated they'd be interested in bidding. Fewer than half that number paid the $25,000 fee required to start the process, and by the summer of 2001, that number had been whittled down to between five and 10 serious bidders.

"We basically spent most of the [2001] season revving up interest in the team," says Bingham, Dana & Gould's* Daniel Goldberg, one of the lawyers who handled the sale. "And the best way to realize the most value is to make it clear, repeatedly, that the only thing we're looking for is the most money. There wasn't going to be a local guy's discount, or anything else."

On the field, the Red Sox seemed almost determined to convince potential suitors to resist the urge to buy the team. In May, Pedro Martinez beat the Yankees, throwing eight innings of shutout ball. With a 7-1 record, he looked well positioned to make a run at his

---

* In 2002, Bingham, Dana & Gould merged with San Francisco's McCutchen, Doyle, Brown & Enersen. The new firm is known as Bingham McCutchen.

third straight Cy Young Award. After the game, Martinez got to talking. "I don't believe in damn curses," he said, referring to the by then infamous Curse of the Bambino. "Wake up the damn Bambino and have me face him. Maybe I'll drill him in the ass." Soon after, it became clear that something was physically wrong with Martinez, and by the end of June, he had been put on the disabled list, where he'd spend most of the rest of the season with a partially torn rotator cuff. Manny Ramirez, in his first season in Boston, began a pattern of confounding his teammates, his managers, and the media alike. When he arrived late at July's All-Star Game—he was Boston's only representative—he explained his tardiness by telling one group of reporters that his grandmother was "kind of sick," while telling another group she had died. Ramirez's agent, meanwhile, told the press that Ramirez was delayed because he had to attend to business in New York, while Ramirez himself said he'd flown in from Miami.

Then there was the team's manager, the inscrutable Jimy Williams. He often refused to tell players if they'd be starting before the day of the game, leading to scenes like the one that occurred when infielder Mike Lansing gave a posted lineup card the middle finger when he came to the park and discovered he wouldn't be playing that day. When asked about almost anything, Williams responded with a terse, enigmatic "Manager's decision." Duquette and Williams, who had been feuding since the close of the 2000 season, rarely spoke. In August, Williams was finally fired* and replaced by pitching coach Joe Kerrigan, under whom the team lost nine in a row and 13 out of 14. Less than a month after promoting Kerrigan, Duquette demoted John Cumberland, who'd been acting as the team's interim pitching coach, just as the media was entering the Red Sox clubhouse. Nomar Garciaparra watched the scene unfold in amazement. "That," he announced in a voice purposefully loud enough for reporters to hear, "is why nobody wants to fucking play here."

Perhaps most disturbingly, Duquette and Kerrigan let the in-

---

* Duquette, in a move typical of his tenure, implied to reporters that Williams had some answering to do after he took Martinez out of a June game against the Yankees that New York came back to win, despite the fact that Duquette knew that Martinez was nursing a sore shoulder.

jured Martinez return to the mound in late August. He pitched 13 innings in three games—all Red Sox losses—between August 26 and September 7. The stupidity of allowing an injured, already fragile, franchise pitcher to risk a career-ending injury is staggering, but Duquette was looking to burnish his credentials for the team's new owners. If Martinez gave the Red Sox even the slightest chance of advancing to the playoffs, Duquette was determined to take advantage of it.

Neither the Red Sox's late-summer slide nor the dysfunctionality of its management seemed to dull the ardor of the team's suitors, and by August, Harrington was ready to start collecting opening proffers. He asked for nonbinding bids from the most serious contenders, along with financial documents proving the interested parties could actually afford the team. Six legitimate bids came in from Cablevision's Charles Dolan; Jeremy Jacobs, the owner of the Boston Bruins; Boston real estate developer Frank McCourt; Joe O'Donnell and Steve Karp; New York lawyer Miles Prentice; and Tom Werner and Les Otten. All of the bids were for between $305 and $325 million.

"We needed these bids before we allowed anyone in to see the documents relating to the team's financials, before they could go and talk to John Harrington or kick the tires at NESN," says Justin Morreale, the Bingham, Dana & Gould lawyer who handled the sale with Daniel Goldberg. Over the next month, Harrington, Morreale, and Goldberg met with every bidding group to discuss the specifics of a potential sale.

By this point, it had become clear that NESN, the Red Sox's cable network, was a huge factor in several bidders' interest in the team. A few months before, Harrington had successfully negotiated deals with all the major cable providers in eastern Massachusetts to move NESN onto basic cable lineups; the switch, once complete, would mean the network would reach 3.6 million homes in New England, about 10 times the number of subscribers who paid to receive the channel when it was a premium-only option. The network's revenues, which would be around $3 million for 2001, were expected to rise to more than $40 million within four years, and conservative estimates put NESN's worth at around $300 million. Crucially, while the money NESN paid to the Red Sox for the right to broadcast the team's games qualified as local revenue and was therefore subject to baseball's revenue-sharing agreement, NESN's actual profits were supposed to be untouchable by Major League Baseball. The network virtually guaranteed that the new owners of the Red Sox would make money regardless of whether the team itself was profitable.

Harrington and his lawyers knew that the team's newly negotiated cable deals and industry analysts' robust projections for NESN likely meant that the team would go for more than what the six viable suitors had offered in the first round of bids. On September 10, the team gave Salomon Smith Barney, its investment banker, permission to go over its estimation of the team's value with a reporter from *The Boston Globe*. The Yawkey Trust's stake in the team, the investment firm told the *Globe,* was likely worth "upward of $400 million." With final, binding bids due on November 29, the Sox hoped this robust projection would help drive the team's price even higher.

That same afternoon, Les Otten and Tom Werner had a meeting scheduled with John Harrington and the Red Sox's lawyers at Bingham, Dana & Gould's downtown Boston offices. The meeting was called for two o'clock. Not knowing how long it would last, Werner had booked the first flight from Boston to Los Angeles the next morning: American Airlines Flight 11.

The meeting that afternoon went well; Werner remembers thinking that Harrington seemed to feel that Werner and Otten would be good caretakers for the team. By four thirty, Werner was done for the day. Instead of spending the night wandering around Boston, he called his girlfriend, Katie Couric, who was in Washington interviewing Vermont senator Jim Jeffords.

"I'm out of my meeting early," Werner said. "If you're okay with it, I'll fly out to New York and have dinner with you tonight and leave tomorrow morning for L.A." Couric was almost done with her work in D.C., and the two agreed to meet around seven. Racing to the airport, Werner caught the 5:30 P.M. Delta Shuttle to New York City. The next morning he left on the day's first flight from JFK Airport to Los Angeles.

"I remember so vividly what a clear day it was," Werner says. "The plane had a stunning view of the World Trade Center over the Hudson River. It was beautiful." Less than an hour later, the pilot on Werner's plane made an announcement. There was a systemwide grounding, the pilot said, and all the planes in the air had been directed to the nearest airport. Werner wondered if someone had called American Airlines with a bomb threat. It was only after landing in Kansas City that he learned about the terrorist attacks on New York City and Washington, D.C.

"Now there's something like 300 people in the airport lounge, and American is telling everyone we're all going to take off and continue to go to our destinations in a couple of hours," Werner says. "My instinct was I wanted to be with my kids. I had spoken to one of them the night before, but one still thought I was on Flight 11 [one of the planes that had crashed into the World Trade Center]. And also there was the assumption that there might be terrorists on other planes. So until I landed and could reach them, there was a lot of concern that I was dead." Werner decided it was unlikely his flight would be taking off anytime soon. Instead of waiting at the airport, he rented a car and made the three-day trek to California.

"It was a very sobering experience," says Werner. "And obviously, it makes you think about what's important in life." During the drive back to California, Werner kept thinking about how unpleasant his tenure with the Padres had been. If he was successful in his attempt to purchase the Red Sox, he vowed that the experience would be one that would bring him joy.

Immediately after the September 11 attacks, Major League Baseball shut down operations. Planes around the country were grounded and there was great anxiety about the potential for violence or suicide attacks at large public gatherings. Ballparks hadn't been built with bomb threats or renegade terrorists in mind; in fact, most stadiums made an effort to get as many people as possible into the park with minimum hassle. Throughout the game, owners were concerned about how the attacks would affect fan attendance. Even after the 2001 season resumed, with attendance more or less equal to what it had been previously, baseball executives were worried about how the long-term repercussions of a post-9/11 world could affect the game.

The Red Sox were particularly worried. If baseball, which had experienced an enormous boom in the previous five years, was seen to be on shaky footing, the interest in the team could crumble. "We had no idea how this was going to affect the economy, how it'd affect fans, how it'd affect efforts to build a new stadium," says Daniel Goldberg. "We'd spent all these months driving up the price. And now we were worried the bottom could fall out."

Even without worrying about a drop-off in fan support—the Marlins rarely had enough paying customers to make the threat of low attendance much of a concern—John Henry's situation in Florida was rapidly changing as well. The September 11 attacks had hurt Florida's tourism industry, thereby ending any possibility the Marlins would get public money for a stadium. What's more, the collective bargaining agreement that governed the players' relationship with the league was up for renewal, and the threat of a protracted labor dispute seemed at least to delay, and possibly squelch, baseball's contraction plans. After a year of telling Henry that he wouldn't need to continue losing money in Florida, Bud Selig gave him a "put" for his team, guaranteeing that Major League Baseball would buy the franchise from Henry for $158 million—the price he paid in 1999—if Henry had an opportunity to purchase another team and couldn't find a suitable buyer for the Marlins.* At last, Henry entered into serious negotiations with the Angels to buy the team outright. He asked Larry Lucchino—"by far and away the smartest man in baseball," Henry says—to join his effort as the Angels CEO should Henry win the team.

"That might be a problem," Lucchino said. "Tom Werner called

---

* Selig's put, or promise to buy the Marlins, was likely related to his desire to get Montreal Expos owner Jeffrey Loria out of his hair. The Expos were still considered a prime candidate for contraction, and Loria was threatening to sue Major League Baseball. Selling the Marlins to Loria was one of the potential solutions to this problem, but to do so Henry first had to be free to pursue other clubs.

and offered me the position of president and CEO of the Red Sox. But I don't think he's going to get the team."

"Look," Henry said, "if you're in a position to run the Red Sox, you gotta go for it." And if, as Henry and Lucchino both suspected, Werner failed in his bid to get the Sox, maybe all three of them could join forces in California, with Lucchino running the team and Werner coming on board as a minority partner. "You'll love Tom," Lucchino promised. "He's an incredible guy."

"The Angels situation seemed perfect," says Henry. "I had lived there, Peggy was okay with moving back there, we could be relatively low key about the whole thing." But Disney was proving difficult to negotiate with. "They just wanted to negotiate the hell out of the deal," Henry says. "And what they wanted to do wasn't a good deal for us from the player-contract standpoint. It wasn't a good deal from the price standpoint. And it wasn't a good deal from the cable standpoint." The Angels were saddled with the prohibitively expensive contract of ex-Red Sox slugger Mo Vaughn, who had been hobbled by injuries but was still owed $40 million over the next three seasons. Henry refused to take on Vaughn's contract. "Disney was being pretty intractable, and the chances of a deal occurring seemed increasingly remote," Henry says. "I'm very intractable myself, especially because the Angels weren't a team I was wedded to. So I began to think that, you know, a deal just wasn't going to happen."

The baseball season, meanwhile, drew to a close. After a late-season run, the New York Mets, who'd become the sentimental favorites of much of the country, missed the playoffs. So, predictably, did the Red Sox, who collapsed at the end of the season, finishing 13.5 games behind the division-winning Yankees and 19.5 games behind the wild-card–winning Oakland A's. There was off-field turmoil as well, with outspoken center fielder "Caveman" Carl Everett (who once famously said, "You can't say there were dinosaurs when you never saw them") becoming a punching bag for the press as well as a clubhouse distraction. At one point, while Everett was on the injured list, Red Sox right fielder Trot Nixon said Everett was "waiting around and not rehabbing or anything." Nixon soon tried to backpedal. "I am not trying to piss off Carl by any means," he said, "because that is not my job." Even Red Sox reliever Derek Lowe commiserated with the team's angry fans: "I'd boo too," he said. Manny Ramirez, despite hitting 41 home runs and knocking in 125 runs, complained about never feeling at ease in his new home. "Manny performs best in a relaxed environment," Ramirez's agent said after the season ended. "He prefers a comfortable clubhouse. It was anything but that last season."

The Yankees, for their part, advanced to the World Series for the fifth time in six years. There they faced the Arizona Diamondbacks, who had the imposing pitching tandem of Randy Johnson, the 6-foot-10 southpaw who hurled fastballs close to 100 miles per hour, and Curt Schilling, the media-loving warrior who threw almost as hard. Schilling and Johnson started five of the seven games in the series, and Johnson came on to win Game 7 in relief. The Diamond-backs beat the Yankees four games to three, and the two pitching aces shared the 2001 World Series Most Valuable Player award.

On Friday, November 2, two days before the World Series ended, Henry took a walk around the man-made lake that borders his house in Boca Raton. By this point, Peggy Henry, who had already picked out a house in Southern California, was urging her husband to just sell the Marlins and get out of baseball. "I didn't want to do that," he says. "I still really wanted to be a part of the game." That night, after deciding he was no longer going to pursue the Angels, he began to consider making a play for the Oakland A's. Before going to sleep he asked Peggy if she'd consider moving to San Francisco. She looked at him with tears in her eyes.

"The next day, I woke up and I'm in our morning room still thinking about Oakland. They're down at the bottom of the revenue scale, too. Do I really want to do that again? Why don't I look at the opposite end of the spectrum? So I said, 'OK, what about the Yankees? Is George [Steinbrenner] going to sell?' I had a great relationship with him, and with all of the partners. What would it take to gain control of the Yankees? But I just didn't see that happening.

"So then I thought, 'OK, the Mets are next. That's $500 million, and I'd be a co-owner with Fred [Wilpon], and Fred's had a partner-ship with [Nelson] Doubleday that's been a bad partnership. And the last thing he probably wants is to be in another partnership.'

"The Red Sox were next. And I thought, 'You know, I should just call Larry and check in and see what's going on with that.' "

Larry Lucchino was spending the morning of November 3 at the Yale Bowl, in New Haven, Connecticut, watching his law-school alma mater's football team play Brown University. He was worried about Tom Werner and Les Otten's bid for the Red Sox. Joe O'Donnell and Steve Karp, Lucchino knew, were the hometown favorites. Charles Dolan's pockets seemed bottomless. Werner and Otten, meanwhile, were still struggling to raise about $200 million for their $350 million bid, all the while being brutalized in the Boston media.

Lucchino answered his phone in the Yale Bowl's stands. "How's the deal going in Boston?" Henry asked.

"Well, we're pretty much dialing for dollars right now," answered Lucchino. Just days earlier, Lucchino had met with executives from The New York Times Company in an effort to convince them to make a $50 million investment in the Werner-Otten bid.

"Well, that's what I have," Henry answered. "Maybe I could provide the missing dollars?"

"It's a lot of missing dollars," Lucchino said.

"After Larry explained the situation, it seemed fairly clear [Werner and Otten] weren't getting the team," Henry says. "They were short a lot of money." Henry told Lucchino to look into setting up a meeting with Tom Werner. "But this is the deal," Henry said. "If I'm putting up the most money, I want to have control. If I can be the control person"—the person Major League Baseball recognizes as being ultimately responsible for all decisions relating to the team—"I'll fund the thing. Whatever money we can't raise I'll put up."

Werner and Henry had never met, but both men had been told repeatedly by friends and associates how much they'd like the other. Within days, Henry flew out to California to sit down with Werner. The two met at Mr. Chow, the Beverly Hills celebrity hotspot.

"I had an immediate connection to him," Werner says. "If John were a different sort of fellow, if he weren't so cooperative, this wouldn't have worked. I could sort of tell right away that he was just a terrific, terrific individual who agreed with me that baseball was a labor of love." Henry felt a similar connection with Werner. Still, there were issues that had to be resolved. Initially, Werner and Otten saw the Red Sox as an organization so rife with inefficiencies and untapped potential that they looked at the club as a possible return-on-investment deal, where they'd stay involved with the team for a limited amount of time, say, five or ten years, and then sell it at a profit. "For me, I was in it for the long term. I was in it for the rest of my life," says Henry. "This is what I want to do, and I wanted to make sure everyone agreed with that." There was also the question of control. Werner remembered all too well from his days in San Diego that partnerships sometimes didn't work out. And Les Otten, convinced he was being marginalized, was growing increasingly agitated about the entire deal. At one point, Henry said he'd simply walk away.

"There was no bluffing on my part," says Henry. "Because I was taking all the risk, it was either, 'I'm in control or I'm not in.' " Werner ultimately agreed. Otten, however, proved to be more difficult, and since he had been the one who initially filed the team's bidding papers, he could stop the partnership from going forward. "Les was going to torpedo the whole deal," says Henry. "The clock was running on this thing, and we needed a unanimous vote [to join in a partnership]." The week of November 5, Otten and Henry met in New York. "He wasn't happy about the situation," says Henry. "And I couldn't blame him. It seemed like Tom and I were deciding what to do about what had started out as his bid." Henry explained to Otten that he was happy to extricate himself from the deal, but that he didn't think Otten would get the team without his financial backing. Finally, after being paid several million dollars for some of his plans for the team and his ideas about how to renovate Fenway, Otten agreed to a reduced role, and Henry officially became part of the bid. The shape of the Red Sox ownership was taking place: Henry would be the principal owner, Werner would be the chairman, Otten would be a vice chairman, and they'd hire Lucchino as the team's president and chief executive officer. The New York

Times Company had agreed to sign on as well. Since Henry still owned the Marlins, his involvement would have to be kept secret; for the time being, he was simply known as "Investor 11." The team now had approximately three weeks to put together its bid.*

* It was around this time that then-Disney chairman Michael Eisner called up Henry and accepted his previous bid for the Angels. "It's too late," Henry replied. "I'm joining up with Tom Werner to buy the Red Sox." About a week later, Henry agreed to sell the Marlins to Expos owner Jeffrey Loria. At that point, it seemed as if there was still a good chance that the Expos would be contracted; in the meantime, Major League Baseball bought and ran the team. Disney didn't end up selling the Angels until 2003, when Arizona businessman Arturo Moreno bought the team for $184 million.

# CHAPTER 11

# *A Surreal Process*

**JOHN HARRINGTON, DANIEL GOLDBERG,** and Justin Mor-reale awoke on the morning of November 29, the day final bids were due for the Red Sox, with a combination of anxious excitement and nervous anticipation. All three men had been extremely close to Jean Yawkey, and took their roles as caretakers of her team and her legacy extremely seriously. All three also loved the Red Sox, but each, in his own way, was looking forward to the conclusion of what had been an emotionally trying process.

That day, the six groups that had bid in August submitted binding offers for the team: Charles Dolan; Jeremy Jacobs; Frank McCourt; Joe O'Donnell and Steve Karp; Miles Prentice; and Tom Werner and Les Otten, backed by John "Investor 11" Henry. Dolan (because of his money), O'Donnell and Karp (because of their local connections), and Henry, Werner, and Otten (because of their Major League Baseball connections) all had reason to be optimistic.

After collecting the bids, Goldberg and Morreale drove out to Harrington's four-bedroom home in Westwood, a quiet suburb about 12 miles southwest of Boston. Cautiously optimistic that the September 11 attacks would not significantly affect the final bids, the three old friends were hopeful that they'd at least be able to match the nonbinding bids that had been submitted in August. Back then, the bids had ranged from Charles Dolan's $305 million offer to Miles Prentice's $325 million offer.

Before examining the offers, the men took out pictures of the three of them with Jean Yawkey. "We felt really strongly that we were carrying out Jean's wishes," says Goldberg. "And we wanted to acknowledge her presence."

"We had basically decided that if there was one blowout bid that we think is the highest qualified bidder, we're just going to go with them and negotiate a deal," says Morreale. "So we're sitting around John [Harrington]'s living room, we open up the envelopes, and there was a clear winner." With the other bidders all between $300 and $370 million, Charles Dolan had offered $405 million for the Yawkey Trust's 53 percent of the team. He hadn't attached any conditions to his bid—no financing contingencies, no sticking points. "He won," says Goldberg. "It was over." Over the next several days, Morreale and Goldberg called the team's limited partners to arrange a time when everyone could meet with Dolan and vote on his purchase of the team. They also called Dolan and, without saying definitively that he'd been selected, told him he'd need to fly to Boston sometime within the next week or two for a face-to-face talk with the limiteds.

Most of the partners were free to meet within the next few days, but Arthur Pappas, the team doctor and owner of two shares (or about five percent) of the team, had surgeries scheduled for most of the next week and wasn't available until the week of December 10. "We had it all lined up," says Morreale. "We'd scheduled a press conference [to announce the sale] for later in the day [after the meeting]. We had our PR people ready. It was done."

By Friday, December 7, the likely selection of Dolan had been leaked to the press, and that day, *The Boston Globe* ran a story that reported that the team was negotiating exclusively with the Cablevision mogul. The *Globe* story also made note of the potential problems with Dolan's bid, including his brother Larry's ownership of the Cleveland Indians (a purchase that was heavily financed by family trusts funded by Charles Dolan's wealth), and Dolan's long-standing personal feud with George Steinbrenner.* Finally, the *Globe* reported, there was the hurdle of the team's limited partners, "who are widely perceived to prefer O'Donnell and Karp." Goldberg, Morreale, and Harrington weren't worried. To them, the *Globe* article simply featured the standard caveats journalists use to hedge their bets. "He came in so much above anyone else and his bid was so much cleaner, it wasn't going to be an issue," Morreale says. "It didn't matter how much some of these guys might have liked Joe [O'Donnell]. He didn't have the cash."

Dolan's advisors, however, grew concerned, and tried to find a way to shore up support for their boss's bid. By Friday afternoon, apparently thinking that some courting of the limited partners was in order, they were telling local reporters that Dolan was willing to pay a premium for the limited partners' portion of the team as well. The next day, the Boston papers trumpeted the news. "Cablevision Systems Corp. chairman Charles Dolan is willing to spend as much as $250 million to buy out the limited partners of the Red Sox as he attempts to complete a deal to become the team's new owner, according to an advisor to his bidding group," began a front-page *Globe* story. After a year of steadfastly maintaining they weren't interested in selling their shares, the limited partners, who'd initially thought their stake in the team was worth only around $150 million, indicated they were willing to listen to Dolan's bid.

When Morreale, Goldberg, and Harrington saw Saturday's papers, their stomachs dropped. Since the first day the Sox had been up for sale, they had been explicit about the fact that, because of the limited partners' ultimate ability to select the winning bid, no one was allowed to talk to or negotiate with them prior to the sale. "If they wanted to buy some of the limited shares once the sale was complete, fine," says Morreale. "But they weren't allowed to do that before the sale. It would look like they were trying to buy their votes. So now here we had decided to sell the team to Dolan and his

---

* A Dolan-owned Red Sox team would provide the "wildest chapter [yet] in the history of the Red Sox–Yankees rivalry," wrote Peter Gammons at the time. Dolan would give "Red Sox fans an owner who hates The Boss more than any of them hate *any* Yankee."

guys are out talking to the press and announce that he's willing to pay all this money for the limiteds. Well, all of a sudden, a) he's violating the rules, b) the limiteds now have a bid they read about in the paper for their interest, and c) all the other bidders who respected the rules are saying, 'Wait a minute, what about us, we were all playing by the rules!'"

By Monday morning, Dolan's planned meeting with the limited partners had been canceled. There would be no press conference, no announcement. Instead, Harrington, Morreale, and Goldberg decided they had no choice but to go back to the five other bidders and offer them a chance to make a pitch for 100 percent of the team. They'd have a little over a week—until Thursday, December 20—to make a new bid.

Morreale reached Henry as Henry was in the back of a taxicab in New York City. "John, it's Justin. You're going to have another chance to bid for the team. But this time it's for 100 percent."

"This is a huge rule change, Justin," Henry replied. "We're going to need to come up with another $350 million in a week. How can we be expected to do that?"

"I'm sorry, John, but that's what you got. We can't give you anything more." Morreale himself was uncomfortable with the dramatic change. "It was," he says echoing a refrain that was repeated about the Red Sox's sale from many of its participants, "a bit surreal. But the [Major League Baseball] owners [annual] meeting was in January, and we needed to have the new owners in place by then to be approved. If not, we'd potentially be facing the start of the new season [without a new owner]." Since Bud Selig didn't like teams changing hands in the middle of a season, any delay would mean the sale would likely have to wait until November 2002. "Who knew what the economics of the situation was going to be by then?" Morreale says. "Who knew who would still be interested? Who knew what shape baseball would be in? We all felt we had done a great job of getting some very good bids for the team, and we definitely did not want to risk needing to wait another year."

Unlike every other sports franchise he had ever pursued, Henry had, by this point, decided he was willing to spend pretty much whatever it took to buy the Boston Red Sox. "This was a rare, unique opportunity to own one of the crown jewels of baseball," Henry says. "I had also gotten very close with Tom and Larry, and I wanted to keep on working with them." The press had reported Dolan's proposed bid for the team at $695 million—$405 for the Yawkey Trust's stake, $250 million for the limited partners' shares, and the assumption of $40 million in debt. (In fact, Dolan had initially only been willing to pay $230 million for the limiteds' shares.) Henry and Werner decided fairly quickly they'd be willing at least to match that.

Joe O'Donnell and Steve Karp had decided they'd raise their bid as well, and enormous pressure was building behind their candidacy. Craig Stapleton, who was married to a cousin of President Bush and had been a partner of Bush's when he had owned the Texas Rangers, had joined the O'Donnell-Karp bid, and the press's cheerleading was growing more intense. But O'Donnell was about to run into some problems of his own.

By December 2001, Joe O'Donnell must have felt increasingly frustrated. It often appeared as if everyone of any importance in Boston—*Globe* sports columnists Will McDonough and Dan Shaughnessy, seemingly everyone who worked at the *Boston Herald*, Boston mayor Tom Menino and Massachusetts Senate president Thomas Birmingham—were in his corner. With Stapleton's inclusion in his team, he even had the backing of the president. The bid he put together with Newton mall developer Steve Karp had been championed since the day John Harrington announced the team was up for sale more than a year earlier. So what was the holdup? The owners, the media, even the fans all kept saying that they wanted the Sox to go to a homegrown owner.

You couldn't get more homegrown than O'Donnell. As press reports kept pointing out, O'Donnell hadn't merely been raised in Boston; he'd never left the city. He was the local boy made good, a hard-working son of an Everett police detective, a schoolboy standout at Malden Catholic High School, and the popular captain of Harvard's baseball team in 1967. In 1971, after graduating from Harvard Business School, he spent a couple of years working for the university before accepting a job as the head of Drive In Concessions, then owned by Jeremy Jacobs, who went on to purchase the Boston Bruins. A year later, O'Donnell bought the company from Jacobs, and spent the next two decades building the renamed Boston Concessions Group into one of the largest concessions companies in the region.* Through the 1970s and 1980s, O'Donnell quietly amassed skiing operations, hotels, bars, restaurants, even amusement parks and movie theaters. Eventually, he bought the single largest stake of Boston's Suffolk Downs racetrack.

Over the decades, he'd come to know virtually all of the major players in Boston's stubbornly parochial political and business communities. By the time he decided to bid on the Red Sox, he knew he didn't have to be overly aggressive about making his case to the public; his many allies would do that for him. "As a kid, I was taught not to shine a spotlight on yourself, and I always thought people who did that were kind of jerks," he told the *Globe*'s Meg Vaillancourt in 2001 for a rare profile. "Even today, I still think that's true." At the time of O'Donnell's comments, Tom Werner was being chided—often anonymously—in the press for mounting what was often portrayed as a crass campaign to win over the locals.

O'Donnell's distaste for the spotlight did not dull the shine of his bid, and as the process moved closer to completion, his partisans only grew louder. On December 2, the *Globe*'s McDonough all but instructed John Harrington to sell the team to O'Donnell and Karp. If, McDonough wrote in his column, Harrington wanted to do the "right thing," he would "choose the Joe O'Donnell–Steve Karp group, because their local roots and financial stability combine the best of what [the Yawkey] tradition wanted to champion."†

"Maybe I'm old school," McDonough went on, "but the O'Donnell group has been positioning itself in a way I'm much more com-

---

* In 2004, O'Donnell rechristened his company the Boston Culinary Group.
† It's likely hard for people not from Boston to understand the power McDonough had in the city. When he died at age 67 in 2003, his body was laid out in FleetCenter, where the Boston Celtics play, so people could file by to pay their respects. Boston mayor Tom Menino, Massachusetts governor Mitt Romney, and National Football League commissioner Paul Tagliabue were among those who came.

fortable with: staying low-profile but still putting together a sub-stantive financial and business package for the Red Sox." (Just to be sure nobody missed his point, McDonough added that he was none too happy with the way Tom Werner had been brazenly making his case to the public.) Finally, McDonough quoted an anonymous "business/sports figure in town" as saying, "Check out all the groups. Only one gives a damn about the Red Sox—O'Donnell and Karp. The rest of them are all in it for some kind of business deal."

It didn't take long for Otten and Werner to figure what was going on. "We were getting raked through the coals," says Otten. "I'd been in New England doing business for thirty years and never seen any-thing like this. Every day, there was somebody trying to drop a dime on our heads." Otten and Werner eventually hired a Boston PR firm in an effort to defend themselves. "[O'Donnell and Karp] spent a lot of time and money and effort trying to discredit us," Otten says. "We needed someone who could help us go on the offensive, who could ramp up our credibility in the marketplace."

Not even a local media handler could help much with the press's invective. The same day McDonough's column appeared in the *Globe*, the *Boston Herald*'s Tony Massarotti wrote disparagingly that the Henry-Werner group had already hinted that they'd likely cut player payroll. What's more, they wanted to renovate Fenway Park, "which most everyone knows is preposterous." Eleven days later, a page one *Herald* story claimed, inaccurately, that the "Werner bid" was "losing steam" because of defecting investors. "Even as Wer-ner's group loses steam, New York cable tycoon Charles Dolan and a group of powerful [Boston] businessmen led by Joe O'Donnell and Steve Karp have emerged more clearly as bidding finalists, in-dustry sources say," the story read.*

The growing press chorus became so deafening it almost worked. "At one point, I just said [to John Harrington and Justin

---

*Throughout much of the sale process, the *Herald* was the hardest on the Werner-Otten, then the Henry-Werner, bid. Within Boston media circles, some have assumed this was because *Herald* publisher Patrick Purcell was upset about the prospect of the investment of The New York Times Company, which owns *The Boston Globe*.

Morreale], 'We should just sell it to the O'Donnell group,' " says Daniel Goldberg. Dolan's leak meant all the bidding groups knew they'd need to put up at least $695 million. "Everyone was basically at the same point [in their bids], and since the dollars were pretty much the same, we don't need to keep fighting all this relentless press. Let's just sell it to the local guys. And there was a general consensus that that made sense."

There was one problem with that plan. Contrary to what McDonough and all of O'Donnell's other cheerleaders were claiming, O'Donnell and Karp had not put together a substantial financial package for the Red Sox. In fact, according to Goldberg and Morreale, they weren't willing to put up enough money to buy the team. "As soon as we started pushing back on their financials, it became clear they were pretty much hoping to get the team and then raise the money once they had it in hand. Maybe they could have done that, but we didn't want to find out," says Goldberg. Indeed, out of all of the four most competitive bidders still left in the game—Miles Prentice, Charles Dolan, O'Donnell and Karp, and the Henry-Werner group—the O'Donnell group's bid seemed to be on the shakiest financial footing.

Henry, meanwhile, was reading the same newspaper articles that had succeeded in convincing Harrington, Goldberg, and Morreale to try to find a way to sell the team to O'Donnell and Karp. Just as it became clear to the Red Sox that O'Donnell didn't have enough commitments to submit a fully financed bid, Henry and his advisors had concluded they were unlikely to get the team unless they found a way to join forces with the local favorites. Now Henry's good relationship with Bud Selig came into play, as Henry suggested to Selig that his group and O'Donnell's group be allowed to discuss joining forces. "We didn't think we'd get the team otherwise," Henry says. "And the commissioner really liked the idea. It would solve the problem of the carpetbaggers versus the local guys. It was from [Major League Baseball's] perspective the best of all worlds, and it'd remove the controversy." Despite a previous rule that prohibited any conversations between rival bidding groups, Harrington and his lawyers, at Selig's urging, agreed to let the two sides speak. "The press, everybody, was just relentless about the 'local owners,' how could they get the team. It was constant," says Goldberg. "We knew John Henry could obviously be approved [by baseball] because he had been approved with the Marlins"—and because Selig had told them so—"and this would solve the financial issues on the Karp-O'Donnell side. So we thought we'd try to marry these two groups and see if they could work it out."

In the last weeks before the final bids were due, Joe O'Donnell, Steve Karp, John Henry, Tom Werner, and Larry Lucchino met several times to see if they could join forces. It seemed, at first, like an uphill battle. O'Donnell's advocates had been virulently disparaging the other bidding groups for months. Recently, allies of O'Donnell's had even hired private investigators to poke around in Henry's life. "I was getting these phone calls from all over the United States from people [the investigator] was trying to get stuff from about my personal life, old girlfriends, business stuff, whatever," says Henry. Beyond their personal disputes, there were disagreements about where the Red Sox would play their home games: Henry and Werner wanted to try to find a way to stay at Fenway, O'Donnell and Karp were committed to building a new stadium on the waterfront, and Lucchino wanted to run focus groups and find out what the community wanted. (Karp and Lucchino clashed frequently while discussing the ballpark issue. At one point, according to several eyewitnesses, Karp began screaming at Lucchino. "We know this town, we know Boston, this is our city," he shouted. Referring to Lucchino's proposed focus groups, he said, "We don't need to talk to anybody!")

Over a series of meetings, however, the two sides began to bridge their personal differences. Henry found that, despite everything, he liked O'Donnell and Karp. The issue, ultimately, was going to be one of control, and as he had done a month earlier with Tom Werner, Henry said that if he was going to be responsible for putting up the most money, he wanted to have the final authority over the team. With a week to go before final bids were due, the two groups assembled one last time to see if they could work things out. "At that point," Henry says, "we're all sitting there and I just figured, 'Forget it. It's not going to happen.' " Henry hadn't yet realized that O'Donnell and Karp likely weren't willing to put up the money to do the deal on their own.*

Even as the two former rival bidding groups were meeting, John Harrington was trying to firm up support among the team's seven limited partners, who collectively controlled 23 shares of the team, more than half of which would have to approve a new owner. Since Harrington himself owned one share, and the Yawkey Trust controlled three, Harrington needed the votes of partners who controlled at least eight more shares in order to sell the team to the bidding group of his choosing. He started with the Aramark Corporation, which controlled 7.5 shares; if Harrington was able to win the concessionaire's support, he'd only need to sway the owner of one more share. The week the bids were due, Harrington negotiated an eight-year extension of Aramark's food-and-beer contracts, which were set to expire after the 2003 season, and also granted the Philadelphia-based company a contract for the team's premium services, which included Fenway's luxury boxes. Harrington's lawyers would say later both that the Aramark deal was simply a good business opportunity for the team that happened to occur the week the team was going to be sold and that it was an effort to ensure that Aramark would not try to block any bidding group with Joe O'Donnell in it out of a fear O'Donnell would install his own concessions company.

Henry and O'Donnell found out about the Aramark contract while they were in what they both assumed would be their make-or-break meeting. Henry was shocked. "At that point, Joe and I are looking to buy the team," says Henry. "In the middle of this, they

---

* Justin Morreale and Daniel Goldberg were of the opinion that O'Donnell and Karp didn't have the money to do the deal. People close to O'Donnell who are familiar with his financial situation insist he simply did not want to put up so much of his personal fortune. Neither O'Donnell nor Karp responded to repeated verbal and written requests for comment for this book, although close associates of both men did speak to me on background. In March 2006, *Boston* magazine listed Steve Karp as tied for the eighth richest Bostonian, with an estimated net worth of $1.6 billion. Joe O'Donnell was listed at number 24, with an estimated net worth of $725 million.

make a deal with Aramark? We're spending a lot of money to buy this team, and we don't have the ability to determine who the concessionaire is going to be? It was outrageous."

Another person involved with the sale is more blunt. "They ran the sale the way they ran the team," says a businessman who had intimate knowledge of the entire sale process but wishes to remain anonymous because he still has dealings with Harrington. "It was like, 'Fuck you.' Harrington was arrogant. They had such arrogance."

At his wit's end, Henry apologized for getting everyone together. Since he and O'Donnell still had not been able to agree on the issue of control, he said he'd simply bow out and let Werner and Lucchino see if they could work out a deal with O'Donnell and Karp on their own. Just as Henry was about to get up to leave, O'Donnell spoke up. "I want to do this deal," he said. "I want you to be the control guy, and I want to be your partner."

Henry was taken aback.

"You're a good fucking guy," O'Donnell said. "Let's make this work." Eventually, they agreed: While Henry, as the group's largest investor, would be the team's control person, O'Donnell would represent the Red Sox at American League meetings. On the night of Monday, December 17, the newly formed partnership set out for Boston's Grille 23 and celebrated their union with steak and champagne.

With just two days left before the bids were due, the groups still had to figure out how their investments would be divided up. Each group, Henry assumed, would be responsible for roughly half of the $695 million bid. It was then, with the hours ticking until the final bids were due, that John Henry and Tom Werner discovered what John Harrington had realized the week before: Joe O'Donnell and Steve Karp weren't keen on putting up a lot of their own money. They were willing to guarantee an investment of only $75 million and, according to Henry, "hope for the rest." "I took the position that that wasn't going to work," Henry says. "I wanted to see the money on the table."

Sometime past eight in the evening on December 19, about 12 hours before the final bids were due, O'Donnell and Karp called

Henry at his lawyer's office in New York. Throughout the day, the two groups had been exchanging faxes and emails, and as the day progressed, Henry had grown more concerned. O'Donnell and Karp kept reducing their financial commitments, and Henry knew he would need to personally come up with whatever money his group's bid needed at the end of the day.

Now O'Donnell and Karp said they were pulling out entirely. "We can't live with giving up control," the two men told Henry before asking him if he and Werner still planned on making a bid the next morning. According to sources within the Boston banking community, O'Donnell and Karp spent much of the evening placing frenzied phone calls to local banks in an effort to find someone who would guarantee the bulk of the money they needed to finance their own bid.

It wasn't until around midnight that Werner arrived, fresh from a dinner he'd attended with Katie Couric at the White House. President Bush, who'd gotten to known Werner when Werner owned the Padres and Bush owned the Rangers and had personally lobbied Bud Selig on behalf of O'Donnell, had been ecstatic that Werner was part of a partnership that would include O'Donnell. Now, Henry and Werner decided they had to call Selig and tell him the partnership had fallen apart. Selig was momentarily shocked into silence by the news.

"I'm stunned," Selig said. "Stunned. I don't know what to say. Figure out what you're going to do and call me back, will you? I'm going to sleep on the couch so I don't wake [my wife]. Call me back."

With less than nine hours left before bids were due, Henry now had to raise hundreds of millions of dollars—the money he'd thought O'Donnell and Karp would be putting up—or lay it out himself. After staying up all night figuring out what to do about their bid, Henry and Werner headed to New Jersey's Teterboro Airport, where they took Henry's plane to Boston. A frenzied three weeks was heading into its final hours.

## CHAPTER 12

# December 20, 2001

ON THURSDAY, DECEMBER 20, *The Boston Globe*'s lead story announced that, despite the fact that final bids weren't due until 9:00 A.M., the Red Sox sale had been all but finalized. "Boston Red Sox chief John Harrington will recommend today that the team's next owner should be a newly combined group led by two former rival bidders, Florida financier John Henry and Boston Concessions head Joseph O'Donnell, according to an executive close to the sales process," Meg Vaillancourt and Steve Bailey's article began. Daniel Goldberg read the piece on his way in to his office. Vaillancourt and Bailey, he thought, seemed to have the story pretty much right. Frank McCourt and Jeremy Jacobs had both dropped out in the days before the final bids were due, and Goldberg assumed that a joint Henry-O'Donnell bid would at least match any of the other offers. When he got to work, Goldberg was going to assemble the final bids before bringing them over to the Red Sox offices at Fenway Park, where the limited partners would vote on who would be the next owner of the team.

Soon after arriving at work, Goldberg heard from Creighton Condon, who called to say that the proposed merger of the Henry-O'Donnell groups wasn't going to happen, and that Henry and Werner were raising their $406 million bid for the Yawkey Trust's share of the team to $410 million, to go along with their $250 million bid for the limiteds' shares. Including the team's $40 million in debt, that meant their total bid would be for $700 million, more than twice the record $320 million Larry Dolan had paid for the Indians almost two years earlier. A little while later, Charles Dolan's lawyer called to increase his bid for the limiteds' shares to $250 million from $230 million. Dolan was also bidding $410 for the Trust's portion of the team, so he was at $700 million as well. Miles Prentice also had a bid in, for $750 million, but Prentice's bid was contingent on his firming up his financing with the New York–based Quadrangle Group and the media giant Comcast. After going over Prentice's offer sheet, Goldberg became concerned that Prentice, despite offering the most money, hadn't followed the rules of the sale. "He could have bid two billion dollars and it wouldn't have been acceptable," he said later that week. Some of Prentice's funding had contingencies and not all of his investors had been preapproved, a requirement in the sale process.* "This was a cash-only sale, and all of the bidders had to prove they had their financing in place," Goldberg says. "Prentice clearly didn't." Goldberg was only waiting for word from the O'Donnell group. Finally, he checked his voicemail. He had a message waiting.

"Dan, this is Kitt," a voice said. Kitt Sawitsky was one of O'Donnell's lawyers. "It's about one on Thursday morning. I want you to know that the discussions with Werner and Henry's group have fallen apart essentially on the controlling interest and we don't think that they're going to be revived, so that's over." Goldberg knew that already; now, he assumed, he'd get O'Donnell and Karp's bid. He was wrong.

"We're also sending you a letter revoking our offer"—O'Donnell and Karp had submitted their own bid for the team on Monday, December 17—"both by hand and fax, and if you have any questions, feel free to call me in the morning."

"There was no explanation," Goldberg says, although he assumed the pair had been unable to come up with enough money to cobble together a bid. He told Justin Morreale what had happened,

---

* Prentice did not respond to written or verbal requests for comment, although I did speak at length with several of his business associates.

and the two men drove over to Fenway Park to go over the final bids with John Harrington. At eleven o'clock, Harrington began his presentation to the team's limited partners by explaining that the Henry-O'Donnell partnership had fallen apart, and that Joe O'Donnell and Steve Karp had withdrawn their bid for the team. He then gave a brief summary of the three remaining bids. At this point, Harrington decided not to make a recommendation himself; instead, he went over the contingencies and conditions of the various deals, then left the room to let the partners discuss the situation alone.

The limiteds began by focusing on the Prentice bid. Initially, there was a desire to try to find a way to make it work; after all, the $50 million more would mean a significant windfall for everyone who owned a stake in the team. (During the day, Prentice called and actually increased his bid.) "The limited partners are sophisticated business people," said Sam Tamposi, a New Hampshire businessman whose family owned about 2.4 percent of the team. "We certainly did not want to leave any money on the table." But they came to agree with what Goldberg and Morreale had already decided: The absence of binding financial commitments attached to Prentice's bid made it too risky. In a letter Tamposi wrote about two weeks after the sale, he said that the partners decided that day that if they "gamble for the long dollar, we subject ourselves to the vagaries of financing that might never come together . . . a lengthy approval process or possibly lack of approval, and a host of other . . . pitfalls and problems that might occur over time."

The limiteds then turned their attention to Dolan's bid and the Henry-Werner bid. One of the partners, former Dexter shoe executive Harold Alfond, initially was leaning toward Dolan because he was just one person, not the motley collection of players who had gone through dizzying permutations since Les Otten filed papers to incorporate Longball LLC more than a year earlier. What's more, Dolan clearly had the money. However, there was lingering concern over everything from Dolan's media holdings—other baseball owners had been wary that large media companies running baseball teams would run up player salaries—to his brother's ownership of the Indians and his dispute with George Steinbrenner.

On the other hand, Bud Selig had already made clear that Henry's group was likely to get a speedy approval. The limiteds also knew that Henry, whose personal wealth was estimated at around a billion dollars, had the money to complete the deal. Finally, they were worried, as Harrington, Morreale, and Goldberg had been, about wrapping up the process in time for the new Red Sox owners to be approved by baseball's other owners at their annual meeting in mid-January. Any delays could put the deal on hold for another year. After going back and forth for about an hour, the partners agreed. While Dolan might ultimately be able to win approval, the uncertain economic outlook for the country meant that any snags in the sale could be disastrous, and since Dolan's bid and Henry's bid were identical, it wasn't worth the risk. The partners chose the Henry-Werner group.

As the limited partners were meeting in Fenway, John Henry, Tom Werner, and Larry Lucchino were ensconced in a suite on the 29th floor of the swanky Sheraton in Boston's Back Bay. All of them were exhausted. As Henry thought through all that had happened in the previous year, he felt a vague sense of vertigo. He'd gone from being convinced he'd be successful in his efforts to build a new ballpark in Miami to being told the Marlins would likely be contracted and he'd take over the Angels to thinking he would simply buy the Angels outright to this last-minute bid to buy the Red Sox. As the hours ticked by, Henry, Werner, and Lucchino restlessly waited for a phone call. Noon passed, then one o'clock. Werner began to grow concerned.

"We're sitting around all day eating lousy hotel food, and feeling more and more disappointed as the day went on," says Werner. "By this time, I was feeling like John and Larry are good friends, and all of a sudden I might never see John again. He'd go back to Florida and I'd go back to California. That was it."

"As it got later in the day and we hadn't heard anything, we assumed it wasn't going to be us," says Henry. "You would have thought they'd call about something—a question, or wanting a little more money, or something. Even just to tell us to prepare for an announcement."

In fact, the limiteds had long since moved on from their decision about which group to award the team to and had commenced squabbling over money. Since the sale of the team had evolved from consisting solely of the Yawkey Trust's controlling portion to including all the other shares as well, the limited partners had begun to question why there was still a need for a buyer to pay a premium for the Yawkey Trust's 53.5 percent of the team. Since the limiteds could veto any deal, they argued, every percent of the Red Sox should now be valued equally. Instead of the Yawkey Trust getting around $7.66 million for each percentage of the team it owned and the limiteds getting around $5.38 million for each percentage they owned, everyone's stake should be proportionately worth the same thing.*

Morreale and Goldberg refused to budge. "We basically said, 'We're not giving away a dime,' " says Goldberg. " 'This is what the bid on our controlling interest was, and this is the value. What's more, we have a fiduciary duty to the charity not to give away any of this money. If you don't want to approve either of these deals, we'll just take the club off the market.' " As afternoon stretched into early evening, Goldberg and Morreale finally proposed a solution the limiteds could accept. "Look," Goldberg said. "The money's going to charity. It's not like it's going to someone's profit. You guys are all wealthy people, and the likelihood is even if you get a little more for your shares, you'll be giving that away. So if you have a favorite charity that you want the Yawkey Foundation to consider, we'll take those views into account and will do our best to direct some funds to those designated charities." After nine hours of meetings and with the local media waiting anxiously for news, the limiteds finally agreed, and plans were made for an announcement.

---

* The limited partners' 23 shares collectively accounted for about 54 percent of the team, with each share worth approximately 2.4 percent of the team. Because the Yawkey Trust owned three of the limited shares (about 7 percent of the team) in addition to the 46.5 percent of the team it controlled outright, the non-Yawkey Trust percentage of the team's ownership was 46.5 percent. (The bids for the Yawkey Trust's portion of the team included the Trust's three limited shares.) Most of the limited partners had bought their shares for $500,000 each in the late 1970s; the $250 million bid for their 20 remaining shares valued each share at $12.5 million.

At the Sheraton, when John Henry heard about the Red Sox's imminent press conference, his heart sank. After all, he reasoned, Harrington would want the winning team on hand, and no one had called to tell them to get ready. Henry thought about David Ginsberg and Lucinda Treat, who'd spent the last year working around the clock on Henry's various plans, first trying to find a way to build a stadium in Florida, then embarking on his bid for the Angels, and finally shifting their attention to this last-ditch effort to buy the Red Sox. Henry had joked recently about sending Ginsberg and Treat to Los Angeles in order to work on a plan to buy the Dodgers; now, he feared that joke might become a reality.

Henry, Werner, and Lucchino began changing out of their suits and into jeans. Someone suggested they call for pizza. "I felt like we had put everything we had into this," says Henry. "It had been an absolutely extraordinary month. We'd all had very little sleep. I mean, just in the past 24 hours we had this partnership where Joe O'Donnell and Steve Karp were supposed to be putting up half of $700 million and they pulled out the night before the bid and we still thought we could do it." Finally, just before eight o'clock, the local stations interrupted their programming and showed a bank of microphones at Fenway. Werner suggested everyone in the room put a dollar in a hat and bet on which group they thought was going to win the team. No one chose their own bid.

"At the time, I just felt like we did the best we could," says Werner. "We had a strategy—we were going to keep the team at Fenway Park. We had ideas about how to staff the operation. We talked to Larry about what we would do with baseball operations. But it didn't look like we'd ever get a chance to tackle it."

"At about two minutes to eight, Creighton [Condon] gets a phone call," says Henry. "We're all watching this big television, waiting to find out who won the team. John Harrington's getting ready to speak. And then Stacey"—Stacey Ballard, Larry Lucchino's then girlfriend and now wife—"said, 'Wait, everybody, look at Creighton!' And Creighton's got this big smile on his face and holding the phone to his ear with one hand and giving a thumbs-up with the other. A couple of people started jumping up and down and I thought, 'My God, does this mean it's us?' And at almost that exact moment John Harrington appeared on TV."

"I am delighted to announce that the Boston Red Sox partners have voted unanimously this evening to sell 100 percent of the team's interests to the group led by John Henry, subject to approval by Major League Baseball," Harrington said. "This has been an intensely competitive process, and the John Henry group has been selected for several reasons." As Henry began to celebrate, Harrington ticked off the reasons: Henry and his partners were committed to Boston, to the Red Sox, and to beating the Yankees and winning the World Series. Finally, Harrington said, "They were the highest qualified bidders."

Henry was overwhelmed. "It was so unexpected," he says. "You can't ever really prepare for owning the Red Sox. It was surreal, and there was so much stress involved in the whole process, and we'd all gotten so little sleep over the past month, when it finally happened I just felt, overwhelmed, I guess. And relieved."

That night, Henry had dinner with Joe O'Donnell at Abe and Louie's, a Boylston Street steakhouse. Later, Henry, Werner, and Lucchino celebrated alone with champagne. Finally, in the early morning hours of Friday, December 21, they went off to get some sleep. When they woke up, they all thought, they'd be entering into a whole new world. "No time to rest now," Henry told Larry Lucchino before they went to sleep. "We have a lot of work to do. Spring training starts in a couple of months."

## CHAPTER 13

# Boston's Second Favorite Sport: Revenge

**IF JOHN HENRY AND TOM WERNER** went to sleep early Friday morning overwhelmed with anticipation about what their ownership of the Red Sox might mean, they woke up later that day and were greeted with the harsh reality of Boston's second-favorite sport: revenge. The *Boston Herald*'s front page ran a mock-up of Fenway's famed manual scoreboard; on it was written, "Visitors 1, Boston 0." In a ranting, raving front-page column, *Herald* business writer Cosmo Macero Jr. complained that because the team had not been sold to Joe O'Donnell and Steve Karp, "the fix was really in."

Dan Shaughnessy did Macero one better. First, he laced into Henry, Werner, and Lucchino for not being sufficiently in touch with Boston history. "Forgive me if I don't trust these guys. Any of them every been to Durgin Park?" he sneered. "Any of them know who hit Tony Conigliaro with that spitball in 1967?" Shaughnessy was just getting warmed up. After calling John Harrington a "cowardly little accountant," he proclaimed that O'Donnell and Karp "should be the new owners of the Boston Red Sox. They were the answer to every question. They have money. . . . But Harrington didn't want the local guys." Without explaining why Harrington—who had, after all, announced the Red Sox were for sale by saying, "God willing, my last act will be to turn this incredible team over to a die-hard Red Sox fan from New England who knows how important the team is to this town and the fabric of this community"—wouldn't have wanted the local guys, Shaughnessy then shifted his attention to baseball commissioner Bud Selig, who, according to Shaughnessy, wanted a Red Sox team with an anemic payroll and little chance of being competitive. "Selig can be forgiven," Shaughnessy wrote sarcastically. "It's OK with him if we become the Kansas City Royals of the East."

Although the sheer vitriol of the press coverage was surprising, Henry thought he and his partners could deal with that; he felt confident that over time, they'd be able to prove to Boston fans that they were worthy caretakers for the team. What neither Henry nor the Red Sox anticipated was the threat of an investigation by Massachusetts attorney general Tom Reilly who, as overseer of the state's charities, argued that he should have oversight of a sale that would benefit the nonprofit Yawkey Trust.

On Friday, December 21, Daniel Goldberg called Reilly's office with the message that he'd prepare documents relating to the sale for the attorney general to go over. That weekend, Goldberg's mother was hospitalized in Philadelphia and he flew out to be with her. Before leaving town, he left another message for Reilly. There might be a slight delay, Goldberg said, because he had to leave town unexpectedly.

During the next week, emissaries of Charles Dolan, Miles Prentice, and Joe O'Donnell and Steve Karp all made their cases to Reilly. The sale, they claimed, had been unfair. Selig had forced the Red Sox to sell the team to his cronies. Higher bids had been rejected. Goldberg, meanwhile, got back to town just after Christmas and began to assemble the relevant documents.

It was too late. On Thursday, December 27, Reilly announced his intention to investigate, and possibly call off, the sale of the Boston Red Sox. Saying he was "troubled" by what he had learned about the sale, he said his office "has a responsibility to make sure the charities get all the money they're entitled to from the sale of the Yawkey Trust's controlling interest in the Red Sox."

Goldberg and Morreale were stunned. They had already set up a meeting for the following week to review the sale with Reilly. But Reilly, who'd been elected in 1998 with the support of O'Donnell and the Boston business community, made it clear he was in a fighting mood, and implied that the fact that Harrington and the limited partners accepted what seemed to be something other than the highest bid meant there had been shenanigans involved.

This was in stark contrast to what Reilly had said about the pending sale a year earlier, in late 2000. As *The Boston Globe*'s Joan Vennochi later reported, shortly after John Harrington had announced the team was up for sale, Reilly attended a private meeting in Boston's Back Bay with local business leaders who wanted to talk about "various scenarios" relating to the sale of the club. The executives, who supported O'Donnell's bid for the team, assumed that O'Donnell would not be the highest bidder and wanted to know whether Reilly felt he'd have a legal obligation to question the sale if O'Donnell was awarded the team anyway. Reilly, Vennochi reported, "gave assurances" that he would not challenge the sale even if the Red Sox were sold to someone besides the highest bidder. In fact, in December 2000, Reilly had said on the record, "The highest bidder is one factor. It's not the only factor. John Harrington will have a lot to say about who the next owner is because the Yawkeys wanted it that way."

Even as Reilly's investigation was gaining steam, Henry and his partners were in a bitter dispute with the Red Sox over which season tickets and luxury suites the team's old limited partners would be able to keep. "They had carved out all the best tickets," says Henry. "And I kept saying I needed tickets to give to my partners, to the people coming in on the deal." On New Year's Eve, Henry was on his yacht in the Caribbean arguing with John Harrington, who was, according to Henry, threatening to call the media the next day to tell them the deal was off. Henry, who had seen other deals fall apart over similarly inconsequential points, decided to end the tiff by building another row of seats along the infield grandstand. (The team actually ended up building two more rows of seats.)

Then, in early January, Henry entered into discussions with Joe O'Donnell and Steve Karp about whether the two Bostonians would join the Henry-Werner ownership group as minority partners.\* Despite the bad blood between the two groups, Henry thought it made sense at least to see if there was any way an alliance could be formed. At seven thirty on Thursday, January 3, Henry met O'Donnell and Karp in Boston for dinner. O'Donnell, according to letters and documents Henry wrote at the time, promised that he could make the attorney general's investigation "go away immediately" and that he could sway the press to Henry's side as well. At around one in the morning, O'Donnell suggested he and Karp drive Henry out to a waterfront location where they wanted to build a new ballpark for the team. Henry was sufficiently concerned about the prospect of an after-midnight trip to Boston's waterfront that he called David Ginsberg to tell him where he was headed, and with whom.

Once the men were at the waterfront, O'Donnell explained how difficult it could be for Henry if O'Donnell and his allies were aligned against him. "Joe played me recordings of voicemails from the house speaker, the mayor, and another who were reacting to Joe's losing out on the Red Sox," Henry wrote in an email he sent his lawyers and several of his partners that morning at 3:05 A.M. "He talked a lot about the sports media and the Herald being in his control or something to that effect." Henry told how O'Donnell had asked that he be made managing partner "if something happened to you." "That," Henry wrote, "was a little scary."

Henry was conflicted, and a bit unnerved as well. Still, he had come to like O'Donnell and Karp despite everything that had gone on, and knew that having the local businessmen as part of his team

---

\* The Henry-Werner group ended up with 15 minority partners: Dexter shoe heirs Theodore and William Alfond; TJ Maxx founder Ben Cammarata; Boston International Group and Junction Investors, Ltd. founder Thomas DiBenedetto; Carruth Management partner Michael Egan; Arnold Worldwide Partners chairman and CEO Ed Eskandarian; Boston-based hedge fund manager Michael Gordon; H.P. Hood and Gulf Oil chairman John Kaneb; medical device pioneer and businessman Phillip Morse; The New York Times Company; San Diego money manager Arthur Nicholas; real estate investor Frank Resnek; real estate developer Sam Tamposi; Mast Industries founder and Staples board member Martin Trust; and money manager Jeffrey Vinik.

would smooth his entry into a city he was quickly discovering could be rough on outsiders. But Henry's partners—particularly The New York Times Company—were put off by O'Donnell, and while the two sides did reach a truce, they never were able to come to terms.

In the coming days, the sale of the Red Sox became even more bizarre. With the baseball owners meeting less than a week away and Reilly's investigation still going full steam ahead, Dolan announced on January 10 that he was increasing his bid to $740 million.

Harrington, Goldberg, and Morreale felt that, with everything else going on, they had to at least discuss Dolan's offer with the team's limited partners. After more than eight hours of conference calls stretched out over two days, the limiteds decided unanimously not to pursue any more "untimely bids" for the team. Undeterred, on January 14, Dolan upped his bid again, finally matching Miles Prentice's bid of $790 million. (Prentice, in response, added another $5 million to his own offer.) This time, the limiteds refused to even discuss the new offers.

Reilly, meanwhile, was engaged in tortuous negotiations with the Red Sox. Convinced that Harrington and the team's lawyers had been disrespectful, he seemed determined to embarrass the team, and particularly John Harrington, publicly. At the same time, he seemed finally to realize that, after a yearlong sale process, there had been only two groups that submitted bids with their financing in place. If he called off the sale (as he was threatening to do), the team could potentially go for much less. At one point, Daniel Goldberg told Reilly that if he were so confident he could get more for the team, the Red Sox would undo the deal and let him sell the team on his own. "But," Goldberg said, "if you don't get as much for charity as we've gotten, then the deal is on your head."

On the morning of the January 16 owners meeting, Reilly, Henry, and the Red Sox finally reached a compromise. Since Prentice's and Dolan's higher bids, if accepted and approved, would have netted state charities another $30 million, Reilly was determined to find some way to raise that much extra money. As a solution, the new owners agreed to create their own charity, The Red

Sox Foundation, which they'd fund with $20 million over the next 10 years. The limited partners, meanwhile, would donate $500,000 per share to the Yawkey Trust, for another $10 million. And the board overseeing the Yawkey Trust would be expanded, a move Reilly argued would give him more oversight, and John Harrington less control, over the charity.

Today, four years later, it's clear there never was a bag job of the type alleged by so many of the city's media provocateurs—a Major League Baseball–coordinated effort that guaranteed Henry and Werner would get the team, regardless of how much they bid or who else was involved in the process. That's not to say that the sale didn't have its peculiarities, or even that Henry and Werner weren't given special consideration in the process. "It is to baseball's advantage for the commissioner to have trust in who he's selling [a club] to," says Charles Steinberg, the Red Sox executive vice president of public affairs. "That's not illicit." Steinberg also points out that Henry, Werner, and Lucchino all had experience with, and sympathy for, the plight of small-market teams. "That was key," he says. "These three knew the plight of the small markets. So now you have a small-market conscience in a big-market club, and that was critical to the future of baseball." These factors obviously contributed to actions Selig took that helped Henry's bid, such as the promise of a put to Henry when he was trying to sell the Marlins, or Selig's advocacy of a change in the rules of the sale to allow Henry and O'Donnell to discuss joining forces. Still, the fact remains that if Charles Dolan's advisors had not panicked and leaked his intention to buy up the entire team; or if Joe O'Donnell and Steve Karp had put together a fully financed bid of their own; or if Miles Prentice had been able to secure approval for his funders before December 20, then one of these bidders would likely be the owner of the Red Sox today.

In the early afternoon of January 16, Major League Baseball's owners voted 29–0\* to approve Henry and Werner's group as the new owners of the Boston Red Sox. As soon as the approval was offi-

---

\* Since John Henry still technically owned the Marlins, he was not allowed to vote for himself.

cial, Lucchino gave notice that things were about to be run a lot differently over on Yawkey Way. The Red Sox, known for taking their fans for granted and for their needlessly ornery approach to public relations, were about to get a major makeover. In a move that recalled Lucchino's arrival in San Diego, the Boston press was told how the new owners were planning a "fan-friendly" marketing effort with a theme of "the New Boston Red Sox."

At the end of the day, Henry once again addressed concerns that he had put together a group of out-of-towners intent on making money. "What I'd really like to do," he said from Phoenix, "is to address the fans of the Boston Red Sox and say today that we're bringing to Boston what I would call a dream team of baseball people. Baseball runs in our veins, like it does yours. We're excited today, and like we said a month ago, we can't wait to get started."

# PART III

# A Fresh Start: 2002

## CHAPTER 14

# "Sweep Out the Duke"

ON JANUARY 10, 2002, six days before baseball's other owners officially approved the sale of the Red Sox to John Henry and Tom
Werner, the Boston chapter of the Baseball Writers Association of
America held its annual fund-raising dinner at the Back Bay Sheraton. The dinner, which every year is advertised as a chance for atten-
dees to mingle for a few hours with a handful of Red Sox officials
and players, began in the 1930s and originally functioned as a fund-
raiser for indigent writers and their families. Today, the Boston
writers donate the money raised from the meal—in 2002, tickets
were $100 each—to various charities. The evening is generally a
ho-hum affair, more of an opportunity for a wintertime check-in
than an occasion to get serious business done. Henry saw the dinner
as a chance to begin forging the kind of relationships he'd had with
many of the Marlins writers when he was in Florida.* That afternoon, from three until six, he met individually with many of the
beat reporters and columnists who covered the team.

In addition to introducing himself, Henry wanted to know what
the reporters thought of Dan Duquette. Since being awarded the

---

*In the coming months, the new owners tried to build bridges to the media
outlets that had been the most critical of their bid for the team. When Larry
Lucchino went to meet with Pat Purcell, the publisher of the *Boston Herald,*
he brought along a hatchet. "Let's bury this," Lucchino told Purcell.

team, Henry had found Duquette increasingly difficult to deal with. When he tried to talk to Duquette about the possibility of his staying on as the Red Sox general manager, Duquette said he thought he deserved to be named the team's president. "My goal was to help the Red Sox win a World Series championship and I wanted to stay and fulfill that goal," Duquette says. "I made it clear I wanted to stay." Henry thought Duquette's approach was bizarre. For one thing, Larry Lucchino had already been named the Red Sox president and CEO.

"I tried to convince him that just being general manager, if we ended up going with him, would be a big enough job," says Henry. Duquette was not assuaged. He began to complain about how little he had been paid while working under Harrington, about how he was unappreciated, about how no one seemed to realize how valuable he was to the club.

Henry was well aware that the Red Sox front office was notorious for being needlessly combative. The previous year's disarray—Duquette's war with former Sox manager Jimy Williams; Carl Everett's meltdown; the Sox's precipitous September swoon—had been well documented. "Before we took over," Henry says, "it seemed as if [the team] was out of control." Prior to making any decisions, Henry felt he needed to determine the extent to which the Red Sox's breakdown was due to circumstances that had nothing to do with Duquette. The team, after all, had been in a much-scrutinized state of flux for almost a year and a half.

The city's assembled newshounds answered that question for him. Many of the reporters told Henry that they'd never had a single significant—or friendly—conversation with Dan Duquette during the eight years he had run the team. The interactions they *did* have were marked by an arrogance and elitism they found insulting and obnoxious. With little prompting, they began telling Henry what covering the Red Sox had been like under the previous regime. One writer described how, in the late 1990s, he'd called the Red Sox training facility in Fort Myers to inquire about injured utility infielder Lou Merloni's physical rehabilitation program. The trainer who answered the phone not only wouldn't discuss Merloni's progress, he refused even to confirm that Merloni was in Florida.

When asked why he couldn't comment, the trainer whispered, "If I talk to you, I'll get fired," before quickly hanging up. Reporter after reporter described an environment in which the writers, the players, and the team's management were needlessly at war with one another. One famously feisty scribe said simply, "Get out your broom and sweep out the Duke."

Henry's one-on-one meetings with Red Sox writers gave Henry a fresh perspective on the team. Just as important, they helped to thaw the decades-long resentment that existed between the media and the Sox front office. In the past, taking shots at ownership had been easy (and fun) to do: When a reporter is treated poorly, he doesn't worry much about being too hard on a subject. Henry, even after emerging from his bruising battle to buy the team, demonstrated immediately his commitment to changing the way business was done in Boston.

"The media was telling me if they tried to interview a minor league pitching coach they were told, 'I can't talk to you because I'll get in trouble,' " Henry says. "I was shocked." To each reporter, Henry promised that things would soon be different. "We were committed to being open and having open lines of communication," says Henry. "That was the opposite of Duquette. And I knew that we had to show we were different as quickly and as aggressively as possible."

That would be easier said than done. Even after the teams' owners approved Henry's group, John Harrington refused to let Henry and his partners make any changes regarding the team until the sale had officially closed, which would likely not occur until late February. They couldn't begin implementing their own plans for ticket sales, or make even the most cosmetic improvements to the Red Sox facilities.* Despite the fact that Henry, Werner, and Lucchino all agreed that Duquette should be replaced, the new owners were forced to begin spring training workouts with a lame-duck GM still convinced he had a shot at retaining his job.

---

* Even so, the Red Sox executive team was being put in place, and during this time, Henry and Werner named David Ginsberg one of the team's vice chairmen and Lucinda Treat the Red Sox chief legal officer.

• • •

On Monday, February 18, John Henry arrived at Boston's spring training home in Fort Myers in a $1 million customized bus he had built when he owned the Marlins. (The bus, which Henry joked that new Marlins owner Jeffrey Loria had lent to him for his trip to Florida's southwest coast from his Boca Raton home, was adorned with an enormous Marlins logo on the side. Loria, whose eventual ownership of the bus became a bargaining point in his negotiations to buy the Marlins, received the vehicle soon after this final trip of Henry's.) Even though the sale of the Red Sox would not officially close for nine more days, Henry was eager to introduce himself to the team.

Henry was, it is safe to say, an owner unlike any the assembled Red Sox fans had ever encountered. He climbed off the bus wearing loafers, pressed trousers, a button-down shirt, a wide-brimmed, pale-cream Stetson Panama hat—Henry is extremely sensitive to the sun—and sporty sunglasses. Before making his way to the Red Sox practice field, he stopped to sign autographs and banter with fans, who seemed almost awed by his presence.

"You play baseball? What position?" he asked a young boy in his soft, almost gentle tenor.

"I usually play first base," the boy answered. "You're too young to play first," Henry said, chuckling. As Henry continued to sign autographs and joke with the fans and reporters, Duquette, still lobbying for a place in the organization, strode into the scrum of people, thrust out his hand, and asked Henry if he'd arrived at the park safely.

The next day, local press reports poked fun of Henry's choice of headwear and his slight build. "Some wondered whether a truly strong gust of wind would send the slightly built owner airborne," one reporter wrote. The habits of a lifetime's worth of antagonism between the media and the Red Sox brass weren't going to disappear in a single afternoon. For the most part, however, the Boston media noted what a welcome contrast Henry made with the old regime.

While Henry was determined to change the face of ownership,

he was soon to learn the character of the team wasn't going to change simply because there was a more thoughtful and considerate group of men running the team. Within an hour of Henry's arriving at the park, one of the team's PR staffers approached Henry. Manny Ramirez, the staffer said, would like to talk to Henry in the Red Sox clubhouse. The new owner assumed the star slugger wanted to say hello and introduce himself.

He was wrong. Henry had barely said hello before Ramirez started venting. "I hate it," Henry says Ramirez blurted out, citing the discord and acrimony that had gripped the team in 2001. "I hate the clubhouse, I hate the pressure. . . . I gotta get out of here." Ramirez explained how he didn't like the team's interim manager, Joe Kerrigan, how he found the atmosphere in the clubhouse poisonous, how the media never left him alone.

Henry was taken aback. "It was not how I wanted to spend my first day of spring training," he says. Henry told Ramirez he'd see what he could do about making the clubhouse more comfortable for the team's players and alleviating some of the pressure from the media. And Kerrigan, Henry thought to himself, would likely be fired soon anyway. Finally, Henry told his disgruntled star he'd ask around and see if there were any trades that made sense for the team. Henry knew that the relationship between the Philadelphia Phillies and Scott Rolen, their superstar third baseman, was problematic, and half-heartedly inquired about a swap.* But, he says, "I just didn't want to do it. Manny was too good."

As he exited the clubhouse, Henry wondered if the rest of the team's superstars were equally unhappy. He ran into Nomar Garciaparra playing catch in the outfield. Two-thousand one had been a difficult year for Garciaparra: After hitting .372 in 2000, he sat out all but 21 games of the following season with a ruptured tendon in his right wrist. Now, Henry was relieved to see, Garciaparra was smiling and seemed at ease. "Mr. Henry," Garciaparra shouted, as he pointed to the Marlins bus, "I hope you're going to get that

---

* Before the 2002 season started, Rolen said he would become a free agent rather than accept a 10-year, $140 million contract extension from the Phillies. On July 29, 2002, Rolen was traded to the St. Louis Cardinals.

painted." Pedro Martinez was equally upbeat, and the two men joked how they had just missed each other when Henry and Werner visited the Dominican Republic, Martinez's native country, over the winter. Modern-day baseball players know better than to get too attached to one city or one team, as it is the rarest of players who spend their entire playing career with one organization. There's also a natural antipathy that exists between players and owners, as both groups fight for a larger share of the game's revenues. Still, Henry's reputation as a caring and thoughtful owner was well known, and even the most disengaged members of the Red Sox were optimistic.

Although the apparent enthusiasm of Garciaparra and Martinez wouldn't last—both superstars would cause more than their fair share of distractions in the months and years ahead—it was Ramirez who demanded the most immediate attention. Two days after Henry made an appearance at camp, Joe Kerrigan scheduled his first full-squad workout. Still unsure if he would have a contract to start the season, Kerrigan wanted to make his mark on the team from the start. He told the players he wanted to give a short talk; the subject would be the importance of always showing up and always giving your all.

Ramirez, whom the Red Sox had signed to the second-largest contract in baseball history before the 2001 season, an eight-year, $160 million deal, didn't show up. By the end of the day, right fielder Trot Nixon, who was named the team's MVP following Boston's disastrous 2001 campaign, took Ramirez to task in the press. "You want to know why the Yankees win so many championships?" Nixon asked the *Hartford Courant*'s Dave Heuschkel that afternoon. "I'll tell you why: Everybody shows up ready to play baseball. . . . They don't come strolling in, pimping around doing this and doing that. Bernie Williams showed up. Derek Jeter made $20 million. He shows up. You can guarantee he shows up on time." Speaking of Ramirez, Nixon said, "He had enough time in the off-season. He should be here. The last thing he needs to do is come in here with any type of grudge of this, that, or the other thing. . . . The biggest thing it does is it shows these younger kids that it's okay, once you start making money, you can come in whatever time you want." Nixon and Ramirez soon made peace, and before long, Ramirez was back in camp, telling reporters, "Everything is all right. Everything is fine. I don't have any complaints." Ramirez then followed these assurances with two patently false lies: that he had met with Joe Kerrigan over the winter and that he had been at Fenway Park on the September 2001 night when the team honored the Baltimore Orioles' Cal Ripken Jr., who had retired at the end of the season.*

With Ramirez, it was, as always, hard to tell exactly what was going on. Was he so dumb as to think that people would believe his obvious untruths? Or was he so smart as to be engaging in a kind of postmodern meta-dialogue with the media, in which he countered some of the many platitudes athletes are required to offer up on a daily basis with a kind of coded message, telling those in the know not to take him seriously? There was no telling. If anyone tried to press Ramirez on anything he didn't want to discuss, he'd pretend his English wasn't good enough for him to understand the question. This was another obvious lie: When he wanted to communicate with people, Ramirez was perfectly fluent in English.

---

* Ripken is best known for his streak of 2,632 consecutive games played, a run that began in May 1982 and went until September 1998. He also holds the record for consecutive innings played, with 8,243—more than 900 games' worth—spanning from May 30, 1982, until September 14, 1987. The irony that Ramirez couldn't be bothered to show up for a game honoring baseball's most diligent player was not lost on local commentators.

## CHAPTER 15

# "Getting Ready to Have a Good Ride"

**ON FEBRUARY 27,** the day before the Red Sox's first spring training game, the sale of the team was, finally, officially completed. Dan Duquette was fired within 24 hours, and Mike Port, who had been a Red Sox assistant general manager since 1993, was named interim replacement.

Duquette may have been gone, but his fingerprints were all over the 2002 team. In the offseason, as the sale of the team to Henry and Werner was being finalized, Duquette finally made a concerted effort to rid the team of its most distracting players, trading Carl Everett, whom *Sports Illustrated* had labeled a "clubhouse cancer," to the Texas Rangers, and ending the team's relationship with a number of unhappy veterans, including outfielders Dante Bichette, Darren Lewis, and Troy O'Leary, infielders Mike Lansing and John Valentin, and pitcher Rod Beck.* He signed Johnny Damon, a free-spirited center fielder who had spent the previous year with the close-knit, rambunctious Oakland A's, to a four-year deal worth more than $30 million. He'd also picked up players known

---

*Beck once told a reporter who'd queried him about the state of the clubhouse's morale, "Other than everybody hating each other? Great."

for being hard-working and conscientious, like first baseman Tony Clark.

Five days after firing Duquette, the Red Sox dismissed Kerrigan. Third base coach Mike Cubbage, former Montreal Expos manager Felipe Alou, and Cleveland Indians bench coach Grady Little all interviewed for the position. Little, who'd been the Red Sox bench coach from 1997 through 1999, was popular with the players, and his laid-back style and nonconfrontational approach were the polar opposite to that of former manager Jimy Williams. In addition to Henry, Werner, and Lucchino, longtime baseball executive Doug Melvin, who'd worked with Lucchino at Baltimore and had been hired as a consultant to the Red Sox, sat in on the interviews. The new owners all agreed that one of their first priorities would be to make Boston the type of club that players wanted to join. "By the end of 2001, no one wanted to be here," says Henry. "We knew we had to change that." The newer members of the team found their acclimization to the Red Sox to be particularly hard. "My first day being in the . . . clubhouse, it was weird," Damon said more than two years later. "No one was playing cards, no one was playing video games." Damon worried that he might be in for a lonely season. "No one was really talking to each other. Everyone was on their own."

Beyond that, there was some disagreement about what, exactly, a manager's job actually was. Lucchino, who began his career in sports convinced that chemistry was basically a bogus notion when it came to team sports—"Don't talk to me about chemistry, talk to me about biology," he used to say—had increasingly come to believe that a baseball manager's main responsibility was keeping his team relaxed and motivated during a grueling seven-month season. At least 75 percent of a manager's job, Lucchino thought, consisted of managing people and personalities; only the remainder concerned making strategic judgments. "These guys get fried," Lucchino says of the players. "It's very draining, and that can create some really difficult mental moments. The psychological dimension of the game is so damn important."

Henry thought more attention should be paid to managers who were more sophisticated with their in-game approach. He was most impressed with Alou, and Lucchino told him if that's whom Henry wanted, the Red Sox should hire him. However, Lucchino said, he and Melvin felt Grady Little would be a better choice. Lucchino emphasized how well liked—almost loved—Little was among the players, and how he'd be able to relax a clearly talented and just as clearly anxious and unhappy team.

Initially, Henry was unconvinced. Outside of stressing that he wanted to use Ramirez more in the outfield—in 2001, Ramirez had played most of his games as the team's designated hitter—Little had not said much that impressed him. Henry also feared that Little's hunch-based approach would be out of tune with the cutting-edge statistical analysis the team planned on incorporating. After all, Henry thought, what good was knowing what matchups or usages were likely to be most effective if the manager didn't take advantage of them? "I couldn't imagine him being our manager based on what I heard in the interview," says Henry. But while forging their partnership, Henry, Werner, and Lucchino had promised each other that despite the fact that Henry was the principal owner and had ultimate authority over the team, the three of them would make decisions by consensus rather than by fiat. Henry agreed to hire Little.

On March 11, Grady Little was introduced as the 43rd manager of the Boston Red Sox. Lucchino's sense that he'd be a good influence seemed to be immediately validated: When Little walked into the team's clubhouse for the first time as manager, the players greeted him with a standing ovation. Meeting with the media that day, Little showed off the folksy style that would become his trademark. "I'll tell you like I'm going to tell the players," he said. "Just buckle up. We're getting ready to have a good ride."

With the team's two most pressing personnel moves completed, Lucchino shifted his focus to remaking the internal workings of a Red Sox organization that had been infected from top to bottom with the paranoia and divisiveness that had marked much of Dan Duquette's and John Harrington's tenures. "I wanted to almost pollinate people here from San Diego, to put people in with a certain work ethic and talent," he says. "I knew the transition would not be so hard if we had people in all areas of the operation who sort of believed in the gospel we preached." Just as he had in San Diego,

Lucchino wanted to import a philosophy he sometimes referred to as WAAF, pronounced waff, for We Are All Fans.

Charles Steinberg was one of Lucchino's first hires, as the team's executive vice president of public affairs. Steinberg would be responsible for reshaping the organization's approach to, and relationship with, the outside world. Janet Marie Smith, the Baltimore-based architect who had helped plan, design, and build Camden Yards, followed soon after. She'd help the team as it made some immediate changes that would make Fenway more accommodating and as the new owners examined whether to stay in the old ballpark for the long-term future. Then Lucchino set his sights on two people he considered the brightest rising stars in San Diego: Padres executive director of corporate partnerships and broadcasting Sam Kennedy and Padres director of baseball operations Theo Epstein.

Kennedy and Epstein had grown up close to Fenway. They'd been teammates on the Brookline High School baseball team, and were members of the school's 1991 graduating class. Epstein's working relationship with Lucchino began soon after; in 1992, while on summer break from Yale, Epstein landed a summer internship with the Orioles, working under Steinberg. A few years later, during a particularly cold and snowy New Haven winter, Epstein read that Lucchino and Steinberg had ended up in Southern California, and he applied for a job with the Padres. In San Diego, Lucchino took Epstein under his wing and encouraged the recent Yale grad to take law school classes at night. Before long, Epstein got his law degree from the University of San Diego, and in 2000, was named the Padres director of baseball operations.

Speaking of Epstein and Kennedy, Lucchino says, "These were two different areas—baseball operations and corporate sponsorship —that were quite important to us. I was pretty determined to press John [Moores] to request permission to talk to them." In baseball, there's an unspoken rule that clubs will allow their employees who are under contract to interview for positions with other teams if the new job would be a promotion. Lucchino's strained relationship with Moores initially squashed the Red Sox's ability even to woo the young executives. "These were not just promotions, but opportunities for them to return home to a sort of dream job they had always

hoped for," Lucchino says. "I couldn't imagine someone standing in the way."

Before long, Lucchino began to joke about "freeing the Brookline Two." By the end of spring training, Moores had relented, and on March 24, Epstein and Kennedy were hired as the Red Sox assistant general manager and vice president of corporate development, respectively, both crucial positions within the organization. Epstein would have more power than traditional assistant GMs, and would report directly to Henry and Lucchino in addition to interim general manager Mike Port. Lucchino intended to groom Epstein as a prime candidate to take over for Port one day. For his part, Kennedy would be instrumental in the organization's efforts to build up its nonbaseball revenue.

"It literally is a dream come true," Epstein said of his job with the Red Sox at the time. "I grew up one mile from Fenway, and bought standing-room tickets and moved down to the box seats because I knew which season-ticket holders wouldn't be there. I got into baseball in 1992 and definitely had a goal in mind to work for the Red Sox. I never thought it would happen so soon." Privately, Epstein was wondering if the new ownership would be able to change how the Red Sox did business. "We were confused by the way things worked in Boston, looking in from afar," he says. "It was an atypical baseball operation structure in terms of how they worked with other clubs. We heard some horror stories about the dysfunction, but I assumed with Larry and the new team in place, it would be different."*

---

* Epstein and Kennedy weren't the only Padres executives to make the trek to Boston. In June, Mike Dee was named the Red Sox vice president of business affairs; he'd oversee the day-to-day business operations of the team. In February 2003, former Padres broadcaster Glenn Geffner was named the Red Sox director of communications.

## CHAPTER 16

# The Love Affair Begins

**SPRING IN BOSTON** is not dissimilar to Thomas Hobbes's famous description of the life of man: nasty, brutish, and short. After the bitter cold of a New England winter, April's temperatures stubbornly stall in the 40s and 50s. By mid-to-late May, there's a glimpse of the idyllic, clear-sky, 70-degree weather that can make the Northeast seem so wondrous. Those days pass quickly, and before these mild days and breezy nights can be properly appreciated, the heat and humidity of Boston's summer take over.

April 1, 2002, Opening Day at Fenway Park, demonstrated once again why baseball's boys of summer much preferred playing when it was actually summertime. As the Red Sox prepared to open their first season under new ownership, the temperatures remained in the 40s, a bad omen for starter Pedro Martinez, who preferred pitching in warmer weather. Despite the cold, it was hard for Red Sox fans not to be optimistic about what lay ahead—maybe *this* season would really be the one that ended without people once again telling themselves to "wait until next year." For the first time since September 2000, the injury-plagued trio of Martinez, Nomar Garciaparra, and catcher Jason Varitek would all be in the lineup on the same day. Those three team stalwarts were, along with Manny Ramirez, Johnny Damon, Derek Lowe, and Trot Nixon, within a year or two of 30, often considered the age at which a baseball player is in his prime. Jimy Williams and Carl Everett seemed like distant nightmares, Dan Duquette and John Harrington safely in the rear-view mirror. If everyone performed up to potential, the team had a good chance of being in the playoff hunt come September.

Even Fenway itself looked better than it had just six months earlier, when the Red Sox ended their mess of a 2001 campaign. Four hundred new seats had been added, most of them in roof boxes along the first and third base lines and on top of the right-field grandstand. In addition, two rows of $200 seats had been built on the field—the dugout seats, they were called.* The paint was touched up, the dugout cleaned out. More concession stands were added throughout the park.

This, John Henry thought to himself, is a good start. He'd been looking forward to this day for months. As the Red Sox finished their batting practice in preparation for an afternoon matchup with the Toronto Blue Jays, Henry made his way down through the park's concourse and walked over to the inside of Gate A, Fenway's first entrance on Yawkey Way. When, at around eleven thirty in the morning, the ancient metal roll-up gates clanked into the ceiling, Henry was there, greeting patrons.

One of the first fans Henry greeted was Tony Pedriali, who announced that he was from the nearby suburb of Quincy. "I'm speechless," Pedriali told a reporter from the *Boston Herald*. "You come into the ballpark and there's the guy who owns the team, thanking you for your support. Could you imagine John Harrington ever doing that?" Pedriali shook his head. "He just said, 'Thanks for coming.' I'm shocked!" Before long, a small mob had formed around the new owner, offering advice (build a new ballpark!), exhortations (bring back Clemens!), and sharing memories (I saw Ted Williams hit one over the Monster!).

The pregame ceremony was the type of nostalgic, celebratory production Charles Steinberg specialized in when he worked in Baltimore and San Diego. An enormous American flag was draped

---

* These were the rows of seats Henry had added after the dispute with Harrington over how many of the team's old partners would be able to hold onto their season tickets.

over the left field wall as Aerosmith's (and Boston's) Steven Tyler sang "The Star-Spangled Banner." When Tyler finished, 22 members of the New England Patriots, fresh off their last-second Super Bowl victory over the St. Louis Rams, emerged from behind the flag. (The Patriots, no one needed to be reminded, were New England's first world champions since the 1986 Celtics of Larry Bird, Robert Parish, and Kevin McHale.) As the Patriots' unofficial anthem, U2's "Beautiful Day," blared from the PA system, quarterback (and Super Bowl MVP) Tom Brady led his teammates onto the field, with defensive back Lawyer Milloy hoisting the National Football League's Vince Lombardi Trophy above his head. "You love this town," Bono sang, as the football stars made their way to the mound. "It's a beautiful day / Don't let it get away." As the sold-out audience cheered, Fenway was as loud as it had been in years.

Even the losing bidders for the team seemed to be reveling in the atmosphere. Before the game, Henry presented Joe O'Donnell with a $150,000 check from The Red Sox Foundation for the Joey Fund, a charitable organization O'Donnell named after his son, who died of cystic fibrosis when he was 12. During the game, Henry and O'Donnell sat in the front row of the new dugout seats; Larry Lucchino and former Senate majority leader and Red Sox limited partner George Mitchell settled in just behind them.

"I think pretty quickly we made some headway," says Werner, speaking of the region's relationship with the team's new owners. "There was some concern that because we were from small-market clubs that we'd have some other agenda instead of winning, so just our continually articulating how important that was helped a lot. And we were creative. We kept coming up with creative ways to thank the fans and to make them feel like an integral part of the experience, and pretty soon, you know, people were saying, 'These guys aren't so bad.' "*

---

* Dan Duquette argues that the new owners' success with fans was a result of the work he and Harrington had done. "They inherited the team at a time when we had a mature farm system, an excellent major league roster, and fans coming to the ballpark every single night," he says. "They had everything, and it came together for them right when they took over the club. Those things don't just happen."

The game itself, alas, did not live up to its hype. Pedro Martinez struggled through one of the worst outings of his bejeweled career, giving up eight runs in three innings. After Boston clawed back, the Sox and the Jays eventually settled into an 11–11 tie before Red Sox closer Ugueth Urtain Urbina let in the winning run in the top of the ninth inning. Urbina, reviled among reporters as one of the nastiest men ever to set foot in a major league clubhouse,* memorably (and theatrically) pumped his fist after recording a strikeout to end the inning, apparently unaware it looked foolish to celebrate after blowing the game.

Unlike in so many years past, though, this Opening Day loss did not feel like a harbinger of things to come. Before the second game of the season, Red Sox players themselves manned Fenway's gates, greeting visibly nonplussed patrons, and soon the team ran up a four-game winning streak. Before long, Pedro Martinez seemed to return to his indomitable form. In mid-April, the Sox took three of four from the Yankees, with Boston's final victory against New York starting a six-game winning streak. By April 22, the team had an 8-0 record away from Fenway, and was off to the best road start in team history. And on April 27, Derek Lowe, who'd been mercilessly booed as the team's star-crossed closer the year before, pitched a no-hitter against the Tampa Bay Devil Rays.

Henry and Werner, meanwhile, found themselves continually marveling at how different owning the Boston Red Sox was from their previous experiences in baseball. For the first time, they could afford to have a payroll with high-priced stars. Instead of begging fans for support, they found a region that was both in love with the Red Sox and almost laughingly appreciative of any efforts the owners made on their behalf. To this day, Werner still remembers how shocked he was after witnessing the devotion of Red Sox fans firsthand. "[Sometime in] that first April, there was a rain delay. It was freezing—like 45 degrees," Werner says. "And it just started to pour.

---

* In November 2005, Urbina was arrested in Venezuela, his native country, and charged with attempted murder for leading an attack on five of his domestic workers. The workers were attacked with machetes and doused with gasoline in an effort to light them on fire. Urbina was reportedly upset that the workers were using his swimming pool without permission.

The rain delay probably lasted 90 minutes, maybe two hours and everyone disappeared—presumably to the comfort of their homes. And when the team took their places again on the field, the whole place miraculously filled up again. I just found that stunning— after having to practically beg fans to come to the ballpark in San Diego, it was amazing. It really said volumes about the passion that Red Sox fans have. And that just makes you want to work all the harder because you want to kill yourself to give something back."

After a May 9, 5–1 win over Oakland, the Sox were 24-7, tops in their division, and riding a nine-game winning streak. Martinez and Lowe were a combined 9-1, and were near the league's best in earned run average. Ramirez was leading the league in batting. The Red Sox looked prepared to make a formidable run.

Charles Steinberg, meanwhile, was showing Boston fans what it felt like to have an organization that didn't take them for granted. With the Red Sox out of town on Father's Day, Steinberg orchestrated an on-field extravaganza. The event sold out in two days, and more than 20,000 people showed up, many of them fathers and sons, equipped with pocket cameras and baseball gloves they used to play catch on Fenway's fabled grass.

That proved to be a warmup for what was to come. The biggest success of the year was the July memorial in honor of Ted Williams, who died July 5 at age 83. Two-and-a-half weeks later, the day before the Red Sox were opening a homestand, Fenway was transformed into a living memorial for one of the greatest hitters who ever lived. On the morning of July 22, the team opened the park to the public, and fans and mourners were allowed to walk out on the field to view Williams memorabilia, including Williams's plaque from the Baseball Hall of Fame in Cooperstown, which had been loaned to the team and placed along the left field wall. A large 9, in honor of Williams's uniform number, had been mowed into the left-field grass and covered in flowers. An American flag was draped across the Green Monster, and the two billboards above the Wall had pictures of Williams. On the infield, the grounds crew had painted .406 (for Williams's 1941 batting average), USMC (for Williams's stint in the Marines), and 521 (his career home run total).

That night, a ticketed event was held to benefit The Jimmy Fund, a Boston-based juvenile cancer charity in which Williams had been active. After a Marine sang the national anthem, the large American flag was lowered, revealing three banners that read, THE GREATEST RED SOX PLAYER OF THEM ALL, AN AMERICAN PATRIOT, and A PIONEER IN THE DEVELOPMENT OF THE JIMMY FUND. John Henry and Tom Werner announced that the exclusive, glassed-in luxury seating area behind home plate, which had been called the 600 Club (for the number of seats located there), was being rechristened the .406 Club in honor of Williams. Finally, a collection of past and present Red Sox players took the field, including Dom DiMaggio, Johnny Pesky, Dwight Evans, Jim Rice, Luis Tiant, Jim Lonborg, Jason Varitek, Tim Wakefield, Johnny Damon, and Nomar Garciaparra. With the players assembled, former Red Sox broadcaster Curt Gowdy re-enacted his call of the Williams's home run in his final at-bat. That night, twice as many people—20,500 fans—heard Gowdy re-enact Williams's last at-bat as had been in Fenway to witness the actual event.

These were thrilling days for the Sox's new management. "When we got [to Boston], people kept telling us what we couldn't do," says Steinberg. "That whole first year, there was a continual sense that we were crazy for proposing ways to bring fans into more intimate contact with Fenway. Father's Day? No way, we were told. The Williams tribute? Won't happen. But I knew that we could make these things happen and that they were important, both for the fans and to establish ourselves in the community."

Steinberg's approach wasn't just evidenced in large-scale efforts, either. His staff hired Fenway ambassadors to answer fan letters and welcome people to the park.* In Steinberg's office, there are thick, three-ring binders full of special requests: from the sick veteran who always wanted to walk on Fenway's lawn, or the eight-year-old girl who broke her arm and wants her cast signed by a player. On almost every one, Steinberg scribbles, "Can we do something about

---

* When Steinberg first arrived at Fenway, he found bags of unopened fan mail in the halls.

this?" or "Let's make this happen" and then hands it off to one of his employees to take care of.

Less than six months into his stewardship of the team, Larry Lucchino had begun recrafting Boston's relationship with the Red Sox. The fact that the Sox of old had taken their fans for granted had almost been part of the identity of the team, and it seemed to add to the Calvinistic faith required to be a true believer. Other stadiums might have clean toilets and friendly ushers, but Red Sox fans were tougher than that. Urinal troughs and surly ticket takers would do just fine.

Now, Lucchino's acolytes were working to show Boston fans that they were an important and valued part of the Red Sox experience. "[In San Diego] we had this anti-arrogance campaign," says Mike Dee. "We'd return every phone call, answer every letter. We needed to do that there because we were trying to fill a 60,000 person stadium in a region without a lot of baseball history. Those experiences really helped us [in Boston]." With Dee and Sam Kennedy drumming up corporate sponsors and Steinberg creating a warm, feel-good aura around the team, the Red Sox made more strides in the first six months of John Henry and Tom Werner's ownership than they'd made in the previous decade. By expanding the pregame and postgame shows on NESN, Werner had even made the experience of watching the team on television more inviting—and profitable.

Unfortunately, as the season progressed, the team's performance on the field did not continue to mirror the new front office's accomplishments. After Ramirez fractured his pinkie finger sliding head-first into home plate in May, he began what would become the annual Manny soap opera in Boston. Instead of recovering with the team, Ramirez chose to rehab in Florida; initially, the team's trainers were worried he wouldn't even get the finger set. When he joined up with the Red Sox's Triple-A affiliate for some tuneup games before coming back to the big-league club, Ramirez made headlines when he dove headfirst into third base, a play in which the slugging left fielder not only risked further injury to his finger but managed to lose a large diamond earring worth $15,000. ("Don't worry about it," Ramirez said when asked later if the earring had ever been found. "I've got money. I can buy another one.")

Still, when Ramirez returned to the team late in June, he picked up where he had left off, proving once again that he was the most dangerous kind of batter: one who could hit for both average and power. (He'd ultimately win the 2002 batting title with a .349 average, and was ninth in the league with 33 home runs despite missing more than a quarter of the season's games.) All the while, Ramirez kept on making news for reasons other than his on-field prowess. On September 9 in Tampa Bay, with the Red Sox's slim playoff hopes slipping away, Ramirez failed to run out a routine grounder. Larry Lucchino got used to answering publicly for his churlish superstar.

Ramirez wasn't the only Red Sox star who made it into the local papers for reasons other than his athletic ability. With two more full years remaining on his contract, Nomar Garciaparra began complaining to, and about, the press. In early September, he hinted that the Sox front office was hiding the truth from the team's fans about contract negotiations. (Garciaparra was signed through the 2004 season.) "Fans are going to miss a lot of good guys," Garciaparra said ominously. "I've said that all along. You like wearing a guy's T-shirt with his name on it—maybe he won't be here next year." On Friday, September 13, in a game in which Garciaparra's soccer-star girlfriend, Mia Hamm, threw out the first pitch at Fenway, the Red Sox lost 8–3 to the Baltimore Orioles. The team's playoff hopes all but ended that day. Garciaparra had been caught leading off of second base during the game, and afterward he blamed third base coach Mike Cubbage for not warning him of the opposing pitcher's pick-off move. When asked why the Red Sox seemed to have so much more success on the road than at home, he snorted sarcastically. "It's a good place to play, right?" he asked. "A lot of positive vibes around here. It's great." The next day, he complained about how "fucking reporters" keep on "mak[ing] shit up."

Pedro Martinez, meanwhile, who was paid $14 million in 2002 and due to make $15.5 million in 2003, said he felt disrespected by the fact that the club hadn't picked up his $17.5 million club option for 2004. If the Red Sox didn't act by the time the 2003 season started, Martinez said, he'd assume his career with the club was over. "It's bye-bye once the year starts," he told reporters. "I'm gone.

I'm just going to pitch. I won't wait until the All-Star break to talk to them."

As Ramirez, Garciaparra, and Martinez moped and griped about their respective lots,* the Red Sox were the very definition of average for the season's final two-thirds. From June 6, a day on which the Red Sox were in first place with a 40-17 record, through the end of the season, Boston only managed a 53-52 record. The Yankees, meanwhile, went 65-36 over that same span, and finished 2002 a full 10.5 games ahead of the Red Sox. For the third year in a row, Boston would not see any baseball in October.

Still, John Henry, Tom Werner, and Larry Lucchino had reason to look back at their first season as stewards of the Red Sox with a fair amount of satisfaction. The club had reached 93 wins for only the second time since the World Series–bound 1986 team won 95 regular season games. There was some only-in-Boston drama, to be sure, but the new owners had gotten high marks virtually across the board, and were lauded for their fan outreach, their respectful dealings with the media, and their charitable involvement with Boston. They had begun to increase revenue, and felt confident there were many more ways they could do so in the future. Despite the testy relationship they had with some of the team's superstars, many of the other players had also grown to appreciate the new owners, who'd instituted regular round-robin meetings in which the players could air their concerns. Henry, Werner, and Lucchino seemed to have done the impossible and transformed the Red Sox into a model organization, with a front office that received adulatory praise from the press and public alike.

They'd even managed to make the Fenway experience a calmer, friendlier one. For years—decades, even—the prevailing wisdom was that there wasn't anything that could be done about the bottlenecks that formed as fans were rushed through the park's turnstiles, or the interminable lines for the bathrooms. The park, after all, was what it was, and there wasn't a way to create more entrances or add

---

* Combined, Garciaparra, Martinez, and Ramirez made $38.5 million in 2002. That year, the entire 25-player Florida Marlins payroll was $42 million; the San Diego Padres payroll was $41.4 million.

more facilities if there wasn't any space. The new ownership solved this conundrum by expanding the perimeter of the park so that it included Yawkey Way, the street that bordered Fenway's main entrances. The street was shut off to non-ticket holders several hours before each game, turning Yawkey Way into a virtual extension of the park's cramped concourses. Food stands and entertainment were set up along the street, which was open throughout the game. Before the start of the next season, more bathrooms were added. Even old hand Luis Tiant got in the act with El Tiante's, which sold Cuban food. Now, with Grady Little having at least partially succeeded in calming down what had been a tension-filled clubhouse, the organization set about reworking its baseball operations crew.

About six months before Michael Lewis's book *Moneyball* would popularize a statistics-reliant, objective method of evaluating players and searching out market inefficiencies as a way to build a competitive team, Henry was already deeply committed to staffing the Red Sox front office with executives who felt comfortable with, and were committed to, combining traditional scouting with sophisticated number-crunching. Henry, with his almost religious belief in the ability of intelligently analyzed historical data to trump hunch-based suppositions, was an early believer in the use of statistics as a way to evaluate baseball players.* Since Henry and Werner had purchased the team, baseball stat geeks had been eagerly waiting for the Red Sox to implement some of the more creative analytical tools available to baseball aficionados. In November 2002, the Boston Red Sox showed just how serious they were about integrating cutting-edge baseball analysis by hiring Bill James, one of the sport's sharpest thinkers.

---

* For almost thirty years, from 1970 until the late 1990s, Henry was a devotee of APBA, a baseball game in which players draft a team that then plays a full season's worth of simulated games. Henry and Kevin Koshi, a trader at Henry's company, so dominated the competition that the two men held a dispersal draft of their players. APBA dates to the 1930s, when it was founded in Pennsylvania. The game combines dice rolls with actual on-field performances of individual players.

## CHAPTER 17

# *Enter Bill James*

**THERE ARE, TO BE SURE,** many reasons why baseball has such an intense hold on the American imagination. The game is unique in the way it seems almost to mirror the randomness and fundamental unfairness of life itself. A beautifully hit ball can happen to land directly in an outfielder's glove, while a lame excuse of a dribbler can snake its way through the infield grass and result in a base hit. Unlike virtually every other popular American sport (golf being the obvious exception), the dimensions of each playing field in baseball are distinct. Like many other work environments, baseball players are dependent on their teammates for overall success but hold their individual fate almost entirely in their own hands. What's more, baseball players, with their swooping potbellies and scrawny chicken legs, physically resemble the rest of the country more than, say, the 7-foot-tall giants of the National Basketball Association or the 350-pound behemoths of the National Football League.

Aside from its on-field poetry and the opportunities it holds for fans to identify with players, another fundamental reason for baseball's vast appeal is its promise of being a riddle whose answer lies, tantalizingly, just out of reach. The game has always provided fans with a vast amount of information. Unlike almost every other team sport, baseball primarily consists of a discreet series of interactions between two individual combatants. The pitcher throws the ball and the batter tries to hit it. The batter hits the ball and the defense tries to field it. The fielder throws the ball and one of his teammates tries to catch it. Unlike basketball, football, and hockey, in which offensive players help to clear a path for the teammate with the ball (or puck), baseball players are usually on their own. There are no defensive blocks or offensive assists in baseball. Because of this, baseball seems as if it should be totally quantifiable, with everything from batting average to the number of pitches a hitter sees per at-bat available to those who are curious enough to go looking. For decades, baseball statistics have been collected and endlessly discussed, from kids swapping baseball cards to adults who go to the game with copies of the previous day's box score in hand.

The very scope of this information seems to present a paradox: If everything in baseball is quantifiable, why isn't it easier to predict what will happen on the field? Part of the answer lies in the vagaries of real life. Players get injured, or they slump, or they are caught cheating on their wives and sink into season-long depressions. But another part of the answer lies in the fact that, for most of the game's existence, the information being analyzed was usually the wrong information, and the way it was used was incorrect as well.

In the 1970s, some fans and observers joined forces to find more aggressive ways of distinguishing between more and less valuable types of data. For instance, at first blush, a pitcher's win-loss record would seem to be a good indication of his skill relative to other pitchers; the point of baseball, after all, is to win games, and surely a pitcher with a good winning percentage is more valuable to his team than one with a poor winning percentage. On further examination, however, this line of logic becomes problematic. A pitcher who loses a string of 1–0 games is probably a much more skilled pitcher than one who wins a bunch of 8–7 games. A pitcher's winning percentage, therefore, is not as good an indicator of his actual abilities as are any number of other statistics. Even a pitcher's earned run average can be misleading, because many pitchers have little control over whether a ball, once hit, will be a base hit or an out. Most of the time, two of the most crucial statistics for pitchers are the number of strikeouts he racks up—those batters can't reach base—and how many total base runners he allows per nine innings.

Similarly, two statistics—batting average and the number of hits a batter gets during the course of a season—were long thought to be reliable indicators of that player's offensive prowess. In fact, batting average is of relatively minor importance compared to on base percentage: When a player is at the plate, his primary purpose is not to get a hit, but rather *not* to make an out—baseball is, after all, essentially nine distinct struggles to score runs before your team makes three outs. On base percentage, a ratio signifying the number of times a player comes to the plate and does not make an out, measures this much more precisely than batting average does. (Batting average does not take into account when players reach base due to walks. For most of baseball's history, walks were thought to be the result of poor pitching rather than discerning hitting; in fact, they usually reflect some of both.) In this same vein, a player's total number of accumulated bases is more important than his total number of hits—the only way to score, after all, is to move one player along four successive bases, from first to home.*

It was partially to discuss and examine these types of statistics that, on August 10, 1971, the Society for American Baseball Research (known colloquially as SABR, an acronym that is pronounced like the word for a sword with a slightly curved blade) was founded. One early SABR devotee was Bill James, a lifelong baseball fanatic who was, at the time, working the overnight shift in the boiler room of a Lawrence, Kansas, pork-and-beans cannery. James coined the word *sabermetrics*, a general term that refers to the use of statistics in the quest for truly objective knowledge about baseball.

James was born in 1949 in Mayetta, Kansas. He didn't become a baseball fan until age 12, but when he did, he began devouring everything he could read about the sport. Unlike many fans, who are basically passive observers, James found he had a hunger to truly understand the game he so loved.

---

* For example, if player A has 100 hits and they're all singles, while player B has 80 hits that were accumulated by hitting 50 singles, 20 doubles, and 10 home runs, player B has accumulated 130 total bases (50*1) + (20*2) + (10*4) while player A has only accumulated 100 (100*1). If all of these bases were collected in a single inning, player B would have scored 32.5 runs, while player A would have only scored 25.

This tendency was apparent by the time James was barely a teenager. Sometime in the early 1960s, he picked up a copy of *Sport* magazine from 1958, which had an article describing how a 25-year-old Chicago Cubs player named Lee Walls had discovered weightlifting in the offseason, which led to what seemed to be a breakout year. In 1957, Walls was a .237 hitter with 6 home runs and 33 RBIs; in 1958, he hit .304 with 24 homers and 72 RBIs. By the time James read the article, Walls had regressed to being the same player he'd been previously: a .250 hitter with not a lot of power.

"That fascinated me," James says. "I puzzled a long time on why this had happened." James, still too young to shave, eventually developed a sort of Gestalt theory of athletic progress. Highly successful players, James thought, had to be supported by "scaffolding" that was, out of necessity, built up gradually over time. It wasn't just skill that accounted for the difference between a platoon player and a superstar: It was also self-confidence, an external support system, and proper development. "The weightlifting winter had projected Walls up to a level that the whole picture of the man would not sustain," James says. A few years later, James's theory was confirmed for him when another Cubs player, a pitcher named Bill Faul, had a midseason hot streak in which he let in just one run over three starts, two of which were complete games. Faul became big news when he began publicly talking about how visits to a hypnotist had helped him relax and throw strikes. James remembers thinking, "This won't last. He's not really that good. It will catch up with him." He was right. Almost immediately, Faul began to struggle; he ended the season with a 6-6 win-loss record and a league average ERA, and only won one game for the rest of his career. This approach to problems became typical of James: Upon hearing of a phenomenon, James looked for evidence that would support or disprove its existence instead of simply assuming it was true.

Throughout high school and college, James continued to spend much of his spare time thinking about and analyzing baseball. He'd start with the question general managers had been pondering since the early 1900s: What are the characteristics of winning teams? Then, unlike many GMs, James set out to examine *why* these things are the characteristics of winning teams. The answers he came up with were often surprising. By the mid-1970s, when James was in his twenties, he'd begun to compile some of his findings.

In 1977, he self-published the first *Bill James Baseball Abstract,* an 80-page, mimeographed compendium of analyses gleaned from his study of box scores. Within a couple of years, James's word-of-mouth operation had become successful, as talk of his work spread from early readers like the author Norman Mailer and journalist and baseball writer Daniel Okrent to a more general audience. James began adding humorous essays and observations to the *Abstracts,* which were published professionally beginning in 1982.

By 2002, baseball could be said to be in the beginning stages of a Jamesian revolution. James had helped come up with new and more effective ways to analyze just about every aspect of the game. Instead of looking at batting average, or even on base percentage or slugging percentage or OPS,* James devised a "runs created" formula, which quantified the number of runs a given player contributed to his team during a season.† Instead of using fielding percentage—the number of fielding plays a player makes without making an error divided by his total number of fielding plays—as a way to measure defensive prowess, James devised "range factor," which took into account the fact that better fielders will be able to reach more balls and should be rewarded accordingly.‡

---

* OPS is an acronym for "on base percentage plus slugging percentage." Since it combines a measure of how effective a hitter is at reaching base with a measure of his power, it is one yardstick by which to judge a hitter's overall offensive ability.

† James's initial formula for runs created was to multiply a batter's total bases by his hits plus his walks and divide that by his total number of plate appearances. (Or RC=[(total bases)*(hits+walks)]/plate appearances.) This formula has since been refined to include everything from grounding into double plays to park factors for different ballparks.

‡ In other words, a defensive player who could cover very little ground and only made it to 10 balls hit in his direction but who properly fielded nine of those balls would have a fielding percentage of .900, while a defensive player with much greater range who made it to 20 balls and correctly fielded 18 would also have a fielding percentage of .900. In fact, the second player made twice as many plays as the first, and range factor helps quantify this.

Not surprisingly, James's work piqued the interest of player agents long before the slow-moving big-league clubs began to take notice. After the 1979 season, the agent duo of brothers Alan and Randy Hendricks wanted to put together statistically based arguments on behalf of their clients as they headed into arbitration hearings. Alan saw one of James's two-inch *Sporting News* ads for that year's *Abstract*—James was selling the books out of his house at the time—and the Hendricks hired James to work with them as a consultant. That year, the Hendricks won a $213,000 arbitration case for Houston Astros reliever Joe Sambito, at the time the largest arbitration award ever.

Over the years, as James's renown grew, he was hired as a consultant by several major league clubs, but for the most part, the baseball establishment ignored him. Despite the clear utility of sabermetric thinking, the front offices of many baseball organizations were still staffed with lifers—longtime scouts or ex-players who were wary of, or simply didn't understand, the intricacies of sabermetrics. There was some lip service paid to James and his allies, but big-league clubs were only hesitantly utilizing their thinking.

By hiring James, the Red Sox gave notice that was about to change. Immediately after making the hire, Henry explained why James's work fit so well with the philosophy Henry used to guide his business decisions. "Usually when making investments, it is implicit that investors believe they have some degree of knowledge about the future," Henry told ESPN's Rob Neyer, a James protégé. "I've had an advantage over the years because I am clear about a couple of things: 1) it is part of the nature of life itself . . . to trend, and 2) I will never have a complete or full understanding of anything. Therefore, all investment decisions should be based on what can be measured rather than what might be predicted or felt. People in both baseball and the financial markets operate with beliefs and biases. To the extent you can eliminate both and replace them with data, you gain a clear advantage. . . . [M]any people think they are smarter than others in baseball, and that the game on the field is simply what they think it is, filtered through their set of images and beliefs. But actual data from the market means more than individual perception/belief. And the same is true in baseball."

At the time of James's hiring, some observers predicted the Red Sox would be transformed into a team that relied on the computations of pasty, number-crunching geeks and completely ignored the tobacco-chewing wisdom of traditional scouts. James found this viewpoint comical. "I believe in a universe that is too complex for any of us to really understand," he says. "Each of us has an organized way of thinking about the world—a paradigm, if you will. . . . But the problem is the real world is vastly more complicated than the image of it that we carry around in our heads." Baseball was roughly divided into the analytical camp and the traditional camp, or the sabermetricians and the scouts. "I created a good part of the analytical paradigm," James says, "but at the same time, the real world is too complicated to be explained by that paradigm." He would never advocate ignoring characteristics like leadership or focus, even if those qualities can't be neatly measured. "It is one thing to build an analytical paradigm that leaves out leadership, hustle, focus, intensity, courage, and self-confidence," he says. "It is a very, very different thing to say that leadership, hustle, courage, and self-confidence do not exist or do not play a role on real-world baseball teams. The people who think that way, not to be rude, but they're children. They may be 40-year-old children, they may be 70-year-old children, but their thinking is immature."

## CHAPTER 18

# Red Sox General Manager Billy Beane

**WHILE JAMES'S HIRING** helped demonstrate the direction in which the Red Sox front office was heading, the team still was faced with finding a permanent general manager to replace Mike Port. Port, who had been given the position on an interim basis before the season started, had done a fine job and was both respected and liked, but it was no secret that the team was looking for a new type of leader. Even while the search process was in its early stages, Henry was forced to answer questions about whether a top-tier candidate would feel comfortable reporting to the strong-willed Lucchino. In San Diego, as reporters kept pointing out, Lucchino had hired the young and untested Kevin Towers as the Padres general manager. Lucchino's admirers argued that this meant that Lucchino was good at recognizing and promoting new talent. His detractors had a less benign interpretation: They said that Lucchino had been unable to hire a more experienced hand because so many people had reservations about working under him.

Henry took pains to make it clear that, in the team's search for a new GM, Lucchino would not be undermined. "Larry is president and CEO of the Red Sox," Henry told reporters at the end of the 2002 season. "Everyone within the Red Sox reports to him directly or indirectly. The GM reports directly to Larry. That won't change." That doesn't mean, Henry said, that whomever was hired wouldn't have a large amount of autonomy. "We all participate in the process one way or another because we are trying to instill a certain philosophy here and we're all on the same page," he said. "We have a wonderful working relationship on the baseball side—all of us. There is a lot of dialogue, but the GM is the GM."

By October, the Sox had asked for permission to speak with Toronto Blue Jays general manager J. P. Ricciardi, a Worcester native and former protégé of Oakland A's GM Billy Beane. The Jays, instead of taking any chances, quickly signed Ricciardi to a five-year contract extension. The Red Sox next turned their full attention to Beane himself, the man Henry had been interested in all along.

Henry had first met Beane several years earlier, when, as the owner of the Marlins, he heard Beane give a speech to baseball executives about competitive balance between large- and small-revenue teams. "He just seemed brilliant to me," says Henry. "Not just his presentation, but how he approached problems. It was very well done, well organized. And after I got to Boston, I began to think that maybe we could work together some day." A brash former top prospect who had failed as a player and excelled in the A's front office, Beane had, by 2002, led the revenue-starved A's to the playoffs three years in a row largely by snapping up players that other teams didn't properly value.

In 2001, the A's won 102 games, but lost three of their best players to free agency: 2000 American League MVP Jason Giambi, who signed with the Yankees; Johnny Damon, who signed with the Red Sox; and closer Jason Isringhausen, who signed with the St. Louis Cardinals. The 2002 season was widely predicted to be the one in which the high-flying A's would return to earth. Instead, Beane's team, with a $41 million payroll, among the lowest in all of baseball, won more games than it had the year before, going 103-59. In the spring, Beane signed a contract extension that would keep him in Oakland for six more years and would eventually pay more than $1 million per year.

Because he was under contract, Beane needed the approval of his boss, A's owner Steve Schott, to interview with the Red Sox. Beane asked for weeks before Schott finally granted him that permission in early November. On Thursday, November 7, Beane flew to Florida and met with Henry and Lucchino at Henry's Boca Raton mansion.

Two days later, Beane had left Florida and arrived back home in Northern California as the new general manager of the Boston Red Sox. After nonstop negotiating, the Red Sox and Beane had come to an agreement on a five-year contract worth around $13 million. His $2.5 million annual salary would make him the best-paid general manager ever. To help assuage Beane's concerns about the toll the job would take on his family, Tom Werner had girlfriend Katie Couric call Beane's wife, Tara, a huge *Today* show fan, to sing "Happy Birthday" on her answering machine.

Beane and the Red Sox owners both had reason to be elated. "We were jumping up and down," says Henry. "We opened champagne. We were celebrating. We were thinking, you know, we just made the deal that's going to win us a World Series." In return for allowing the Red Sox to hire one of their employees while he was still under contract, the A's had a right to compensation, and that night, Beane and Theo Epstein negotiated with A's assistant general manager Paul DePodesta, the man who would almost surely be named Oakland's new GM. DePodesta wanted minor league prospect Kevin Youkilis, a young, balding, not particularly athletic-looking third baseman who had been ignored by most of the baseball world but was highly prized by both the Red Sox and the A's for his unerring batting eye and his amazing ability to get on base,* as well as one of the Red Sox pitchers. "Don't worry, there'll be other Youkilises," Beane told Epstein. "We'll get our Youkilises."

The next morning, still soaring from his recent coup, Henry called Beane to iron out the final details of their deal. Unable to reach him, Henry called Steve Schott to discuss the specifics of the compensation package. He was given an unpleasant surprise.

---

* The A's baseball operations crew had dubbed Youkilis "The Greek God of Walks" despite the fact that Youkilis is a Romanian Jew, not Greek. Youkilis took the nickname in stride, telling a reporter, "It's better than being the Greek God of Illegitimate Children."

"I don't think he's going to go," Schott said. "I just had a 45 minute conversation with Billy and I don't think he's going to go."

"What are you talking about?" Henry asked.

"I told you," Schott said. "He can't make up his mind. This is the kind of guy he is."*

"But we have a deal," Henry said.

"I don't know what your deal is," said Schott. "But I can tell you this: I don't believe there's any chance he's going to go."

Henry got off the phone, stunned. He tried to reach Beane again, to no avail. Finally, that afternoon, Beane called the Red Sox owner. He told Henry that he hadn't slept in days and that he couldn't take the job. If he did, he feared, he would never see his wife and wouldn't be able to be a good husband or father. (Beane's daughter from his first marriage lived in California, and the Sox had agreed to let Beane work from the West Coast for part of the year.) "If I go to Boston, I'll nova," Henry remembers Beane telling him. "I'll burn out. It's not the right thing for either of us. I'm already out of control, and this is the Red Sox. I'll be so much further out of control in my personal life."

Henry pleaded with Beane to sit and think about it for at least a day, but Beane said there was no need to wait. He had made up his mind. That afternoon, Beane announced he was staying in Oakland. At his press conference the next day, he explained how he had called J. P. Ricciardi, the other candidate the Red Sox had unsuccessfully tried to woo and one of Beane's best friends, to discuss the situation. "When I called J. P., I was talking about maybe the premier job in sports. What was going through my mind was that [the Red Sox] were incredibly generous and accommodating [about Beane's familial situation], and the compensation was unbelievable, but I sort of wasn't doing cartwheels. I knew something wasn't right."

At the time, there was speculation in the Boston media that Beane had blanched at working underneath Larry Lucchino.

---

*After high school, Beane initially committed to attending Stanford before coming to terms on a minor league contract with the New York Mets. Before signing, he wanted to change his mind again, but his father wouldn't let him.

Lucchino himself addressed these concerns soon after Beane had publicly turned down the job. "Issues of autonomy were not really troublesome during these discussions," Lucchino told Boston sports-radio station WEEI. He then brought up an example that couldn't have done much to ease the concerns of prospective candidates who wondered how much authority they'd have. "The teamwork element of the baseball side of the operation of the Yankees is a good example," Lucchino said. "[Yankees general manager] Brian Cashman is the quarterback of good evaluators. There's a team there." Cashman, as baseball insiders were all too aware, was constantly being second-guessed and overruled by Yankees owner George Steinbrenner's coterie of advisors. Lucchino was then asked whether he and Beane would have clashed over chain of command issues. "I think," he said, "that's a red herring and a false issue."

## CHAPTER 19

# *Introducing the Boy Wonder*

**WITH BEANE OUT OF THE RUNNING,** the Red Sox brain trust began their search anew. Immediately, both Beane and Ricciardi began advocating for 28-year-old Theo Epstein. In an interview with ESPN's Peter Gammons, who was by now the most visible and popular baseball reporter in the country, Beane said, "Epstein is a pillar, and in all the time we've spent together in this process, I'm convinced he should take the job." Gammons, for his part, quickly concurred. Outside of Sandy Alderson, Beane's one-time mentor with the A's and at the time one of Major League Baseball's executive vice presidents, Gammons surmised that the only person who was likely to fit Henry and Lucchino's particular criteria for the job was Epstein.

The Epstein family was already well known in Boston. Epstein's father, Leslie, was a respected novelist and director of Boston University's creative writing program; his mother, Ilene, was one of three women who ran The Studio, a chic local clothing store. His grandfather, Philip, won an Oscar for the screenplay for *Casablanca,* which he wrote with his twin brother and Howard Koch. Epstein's sister, Anya, was a writer on perhaps the best cop show of all time, NBC's *Homicide: Life on the Street.*

The person to whom Theo would be most often compared was his fraternal twin, Paul. While Theo focused from an early age on a career in sports, his brother went into education, and by 2002, the taller (and balder) Paul was a guidance counselor and social worker at Brookline High, where he also coached the girls' soccer team. Theo referred to his brother as his "moral touchstone."

Both Henry and Lucchino were already convinced Theo Epstein would one day run the Red Sox, but Henry in particular wasn't sure the timing was right. It was hard enough for GMs who had never played professional baseball to gain the respect of star players. Epstein hadn't even played college ball. What's more, he was younger than many of the players on the Red Sox payroll. Instead of getting a chance to learn on the job in a less frenzied city, he'd be working in perhaps the most demanding, all-consuming sports media market in the country. "I thought he was a magical person," says Henry. "And I told him, 'You're going to have a long career as the general manager of the Boston Red Sox one day.' But I was worried. You know, 28-year olds are generally not immature, but this is a serious responsibility. It would completely take over his life." Henry thought that, in a perfect world, Epstein would wait several more years before running the team's baseball operations. By that time, the ownership could establish itself, Epstein's age wouldn't be as much of a factor, and perhaps the Red Sox would have won a World Series.

Epstein, for his part, was also concerned—not about his ability to do the work, because he was always happiest when he was most busy—but about how the job would affect his ability to live a sane and normal life away from baseball. "Being an assistant GM is just one part of your life," Epstein says. "It's great to hear from old friends and hang out with them. I could walk out of the park after the game, and even if the team lost, you can separate the two. I could hang out at bars and no one recognized me. My identity was intact and there was no bullshit. It was one of the better aspects of being unknown." If he was named general manager, he knew all that would change. Besides, Epstein says, he never particularly aspired to land the job. "I always wanted to have an active role [in the team]," he says. "I wanted to have influence, to be in the inner circle where I was in a position where I could help impact what was happening on the field, because that's why I'm in the game. I'm competitive. I wanted to help us win. As long as I had those two things, I didn't really care necessarily what my title was. When I came to the Red Sox, I never thought I would be the GM."

With Beane and Ricciardi out of the running, however, Henry, Werner, and Lucchino had no other obvious candidates in mind. They all agreed that it made no sense to search for a placeholder, a seasoned GM who would man the ship while Epstein was groomed for the job. They knew the kind of organization they wanted to put together and didn't see much point in waiting around a couple of years to do it. With Lucchino assuring Henry and Werner that Epstein had a maturity and perspective beyond his years, the three men decided to offer the young Boston native the job. And so on Sunday, November 24, Larry Lucchino summoned Epstein to Fenway and told him he'd been chosen to lead the team. He was offered a three-year contract that would pay, in total, about a million dollars plus bonuses, or about $2.2 million less per year than what the Sox had offered Billy Beane.

It didn't take long for Epstein to become aware of how his life would be forever altered in ways both large and small. "I knew things would change immediately," says Epstein. "But I didn't know how much." The next morning, as Epstein left his Brookline apartment to make his way to the Fenway Park press conference that would announce his promotion, there was a trio of TV reporters camped outside his front door. The reporters followed Epstein to work. "It was a good symbol for the lack of privacy and amount of attention I was going to get all the time whether I wanted it or not," he says.

The Sox tried to frame Epstein's new posting as another part of the ongoing transition to the "new" Red Sox, another sign that the years of mismanagement and poor communication were things of the past. After announcing Epstein's promotion at a press conference, Lucchino said, "What this means is, I hope, evident to all of you: This is no longer your father's Oldsmobile. The Red Sox are determined to do new and innovative things, work with new approaches and new people, and push the envelope for baseball." Epstein, for his part, charmed the local reporters by demonstrating the extent of his familiarity with Red Sox history, at one point answering a question about Grady Little's job status by saying that Little was "the manager of this nine," an allusion to one of former Sox manager Joe Morgan's famous colloquialisms. Epstein also displayed a sense of humor many of the reporters hadn't seen before. When asked to respond to the skepticism his appointment had provoked, he quickly quipped, "Do people think I'm too old for the job?" On this day it seemed as if Epstein could do little wrong. Even the notoriously contrarian Dan Shaughnessy lauded the move.

Yet there were those who questioned why the Red Sox had not been able to hire any of their top choices. "Think long and hard about the supposed search the Red Sox conducted for the better part of the last two months and ask yourself this: If this is such a desirable place to work, then why couldn't the Sox convince a more experienced man to take the job?" asked the *Herald*'s Tony Massarotti. The entire search process, Massarotti wrote, "either speaks poorly of the current Sox administration or suggests that this is an extremely difficult place to succeed as a major league executive. Or both." Hiring Epstein, Massarotti said, showed definitively that the Red Sox were an institution that "Larry Lucchino . . . clearly knows so extraordinarily little about."

Massarotti's column was only the beginning of the broadsides Lucchino would receive. For the second time in less than a month, he found he was being called on to answer questions about whether his hands-on approach was scaring off some front-office talent. "In no other industry do they call it meddling when a CEO tries to stay active and involved in all facets of his company," Lucchino told the *Herald*'s Gerry Callahan. "I do think there's a role for the CEO of this ball club to be involved in baseball matters. That's not meddling. That's due diligence." Epstein, Callahan noted, "understands and accepts [that] more readily than any of the other 973 GM candidates would have. He has lived and learned under Lucchino for the better part of a decade and has been molded and shaped the way the CEO wants him."

It's true that in 2002, Epstein and Lucchino had a genuinely comfortable relationship. "I worked very closely with Larry [in San

Diego]," Epstein says. "He was a sort of hands-on manager of all the departments. He supervised all the departments beneath him, including baseball operations. He didn't micromanage—he didn't execute trades or stuff like that—but he always wanted to know just what was going on. When we were there, I don't think he overruled anything." Epstein says he likely owes his career in Boston to Lucchino. "He was the one who wanted to hire me," Epstein says. "Had he not joined the Red Sox, I'm not sure I would have had the opportunity."

The day after the press conference announcing Epstein's promotion, Lucchino and Epstein began remaking the Red Sox baseball operations outfit, bringing in some old hands to complement the young general manager. Bill Lajoie was one of the first new hires to come on board. Lajoie, with his almost half-century's worth of experience in professional baseball, had helped construct an impressive number of successful teams, including the Cincinnati Reds of the mid-1970s, the Detroit Tigers of the mid-1980s, and the Atlanta Braves of the 1990s. He had served as GM of the Tigers for seven years. At the Red Sox, he'd be a special assistant in charge of scouting, a kind of yin to Bill James's yang. Soon after Lajoie came to Boston, Epstein hired Colorado Rockies assistant GM Josh Byrnes as his right-hand man. The 32-year-old Byrnes, who cut his teeth in the front office of the hard-hitting Cleveland Indians of the late 1990s, knew all about the pressures of being labeled a boy wonder: When he was named the Indians scouting director at age 27, he was one of the youngest people in the history of the game to occupy that position. Epstein promoted 28-year-old Ben Cherington to director of player development, and 29-year-old Jed Hoyer, who not long before had been working in the Wesleyan College admissions office, was named baseball operations assistant. The Red Sox, led by Epstein, would head into the 2002 season with one of the youngest baseball operations offices in major league history, and the only one in which the ages of many of its employees mirrored the ages of the team's players.

It didn't take long for Epstein and his crew to start putting their mark on the Red Sox roster. Even though Dan Duquette had been fired before the season started, the 2002 Red Sox had been very much the product of his era—outside of a midyear acquisition of outfielder Cliff Floyd, the Sox didn't make many changes to the team during Mike Port's one year as the general manager. The '02 team closely resembled many other teams Duquette had assembled in his years in Boston, with a potent core surrounded by role players who were significantly below average. While Derek Lowe and Pedro Martinez blazed through the league, starters John Burkett and Frank Castillo had earned run averages higher than the league's average. Nomar Garciaparra, Manny Ramirez, Shea Hillenbrand, Jason Varitek, and Trot Nixon had all put up impressive offensive numbers, but first baseman Tony Clark and second basemen Rey Sanchez and Jose Offerman, who accumulated 869 at-bats among them, had a combined on base percentage of .302. (The league average was .331.) The team's bench players were atrocious. As one member of the Red Sox front office says, "The core of that team was plenty good enough to be a playoff team. But basically players 15 through 25 on the roster sucked."

Epstein thought he could successfully remake the offense relatively cheaply by finding players who were likely to take advantage of Fenway Park's peculiar dimensions or had a particular skill set that was important but unappreciated. Back in 2002, the primary importance of on base percentage was not the accepted gospel it is today. "There were at the time still a lot of undervalued players available," Epstein says. "We already had Manny, who you can build a lineup around. We had Varitek, a catcher who's an equally [skilled] offensive [and defensive] player. We had a leadoff hitter [Johnny Damon] in center field. So with those elements up the middle, we thought we could add some value for not too much money." On December 12, Epstein picked up Cincinnati Reds second baseman Todd Walker in exchange for a pair of minor league players. Three days later, he traded pitcher Josh Hancock to the Phillies for Jeremy Giambi, the brother of former American League MVP Jason.

Walker, a subpar defensive second baseman, was due $3.5 million in 2003, and his numbers, at first, didn't look particularly impressive: He'd hit .299 in 2002 with only 11 home runs and 64 runs batted in. But Walker had demonstrated he could get on base at a decent clip, with a .353 on base percentage, almost exactly identical to what Nomar Garciaparra had put up the year before. He was also $4 million cheaper than the Sanchez/Offerman combination that had fared so poorly.

Similarly, to judge by batting average alone, Jeremy Giambi didn't appear to be the kind of offensive force that could anchor first base: He'd hit only .259 in 2002. But he did display a decent amount of power, with 20 home runs. Like his brother Jason, Jeremy Giambi had one of the best eyes in the game, and his .414 on base percentage would have been good for a top-10 finish in 2002 had he spent the year in one league. (He was traded in May 2002 from the American League's Oakland A's to the National League's Philadelphia Phillies.) Since he cost just $2 million, the Red Sox would still be able to look for a platoonmate to split time with Giambi, all for less than the $7.3 million the team had paid to Brian Daubach and Tony Clark the season before.

A new peak in the age-old Red Sox–Yankees rivalry would soon eclipse coverage of these acquisitions. Just before Christmas, the Cuban defector Jose Contreras, a highly regarded pitcher who had never played in the United States, signed a four-year, $32 million deal with the Yankees. Epstein and the Red Sox had also pursued Contreras, and when a reporter from *The New York Times* called Larry Lucchino to get his reaction, Lucchino initially offered up a terse "no comment." Then he changed his mind. "No, I'll make a comment," he said. "The Evil Empire extends its tentacles even into Latin America." Although Lucchino later tried to dismiss the quip as a light-hearted joke, it incensed George Steinbrenner, who'd disliked Lucchino for more than a decade.

"That's BS," Steinbrenner said in response in an interview with New York's *Daily News*. "That's how a sick person thinks. I've learned this about Lucchino: He's baseball's foremost chameleon of all time. He changes colors depending on where he's standing. He's been at Baltimore and he deserted them there, and then went out to San Diego and look at what trouble they're in out there. When he was in San Diego, he was a big man for the small markets. Now he's in Boston and he's for the big markets. He's not the kind of guy you want to have in your foxhole. He's running the team behind John Henry's back. I warned John it would happen, told him, 'Just be careful.' He talks out of both sides of his mouth. He has trouble talking out of the front of it." Steinbrenner's comments were, of course, unfair: Lucchino hadn't deserted Baltimore, but left after an ownership change, and he had increased both the revenues and the on-field performance of the Padres. It didn't matter. Instead of letting the matter drop, Lucchino returned fire. "Is that the best he could do?" Lucchino asked the next day. "I don't think he even gets the reference." The media certainly did. The Red Sox–Yankees rivalry was already the most hyped tug-of-war in sports, and Lucchino and Steinbrenner's sniping only upped the ante. From that day forward, television promotions for Red Sox–Yankees matches were inevitably set to the anthemic music from Star Wars.

**This doesn't look like it'll end well:** With five outs to go in the 2003 American League Championship Series and the Red Sox nursing a two-run lead, Grady Little decides to leave Pedro Martinez in the game to face the Yankees' Hideki Matsui. (Barry Chin/*The Boston Globe*)

**Any bets on who the new manager will be?** From left, Martinez, David Ortiz, Derek Lowe, and John Burkett sit in the visiting dugout at Yankee Stadium after Aaron Boone's 11th-inning, series-ending home run. (Barry Chin/*The Boston Globe*)

**Owner, meet icon:** On his first day at spring training in 2002, John Henry introduces himself to Nomar Garcia-parra. (Jim Davis/*The Boston Globe*)

**In Theo we trust:** One of the new ownership's first hires was Theo Epstein, a young baseball operations executive who'd grown up within walking distance of Fenway Park. (John Huba

**He'll handle that:** Executive vice president of public relations Charles Steinberg (left) calls on a reporter as CEO Larry Lucchino indicates that Theo Epstein will explain why the Red Sox fired Grady Little. (Jim Davis/*The Boston Globe*)

**One last tip of the cap:** Nomar Garciaparra acknowledges fans after his first home run of 2004, a June 22 grand slam against the Twins. He would hit only two more four-baggers at Fenway as a member of the Red Sox. (Jim Davis/*The Boston Globe*)

**The slugger:** David Ortiz prepares to add to his legacy as the greatest clutch hitter in Red Sox history. (John Huba)

**The savior:** As blood seeps out of a sutured ankle tendon, Curt Schilling rests during his dominating Game 6 victory over the Yankees in the 2004 American League Championship Series. (Jim Davis/*The Boston Globe*)

**Champions:** The 2004 Boston Red Sox celebrate their four-game sweep of the St. Louis Cardinals in the World Series. (John Huba)

**United we stand:** After the final out of the World Series, John Henry, Tom Werner, and Larry Lucchino (left to right) embrace in the stands of St. Louis's Busch Stadium. (Julie Cordeiro/The Boston Red Sox)

**The right arm of God:** After seven years with the Red Sox, Pedro Martinez hoists the World Series trophy above his head on what would be his last night in a Red Sox uniform. (John Huba)

**There's a new boss in town:** David Ortiz ain't afraid of no ghosts. (John Huba)

**Another ho-hum day at the office:** Two days after the 2005 trade deadline—and a week after asking to be traded—Manny Ramirez makes nice with Red Sox fans. (Jim Davis/*The Boston Globe*)

**Where do you get your hair done?** A freshly shorn Johnny Damon (right) pals around with Derek Jeter in spring training 2006. Damon's agent never gave the Red Sox a chance to match the Yankees' offer. (AP Photo/Kathy Willens)

**Same as it ever was:** Four months after quitting and a month after rejoining the Red Sox, Theo Epstein (right) watches a spring training workout with John Henry (left) and Tom Werner. (Barry Chin/*The Boston Globe*)

**Remind me of your name again:** Manager Terry Francona congratulates center fielder Coco Crisp during a spring training game. Along with Crisp, the Sox fielded an entirely new starting infield in 2006. (Barry Chin/*The Boston Globe*)

# PART IV

# The Best Hitting Team Ever Assembled: 2003

## CHAPTER 20

# Shopping at Wal-Mart for David Ortiz

**WITH LUCCHINO AND STEINBRENNER** busy sparring in public, Epstein opened 2003 by making another key acquisition: third baseman Bill Mueller, whom Epstein signed to a two-year deal with a team option for a third year. Mueller, Epstein thought, was another player who showed good patience at the plate and who was projected to do well at Fenway. "We thought Bill Mueller was a better player than Shea Hillenbrand," Epstein says. "And we thought if we could sign Mueller, we could trade Hillenbrand for pitching help and that Hillenbrand"—coming off an All-Star season— "would be more attractive as a trade chip than he would be to us." It was the type of levelheaded, coolly rational move that helped build winning ball clubs. Instead of becoming enamored of a player who, for whatever reason, was considered to be more valuable than he actually was, Epstein wanted to use Hillenbrand's inflated reputation as a way to get more value in return.

Then the Sox turned their attention toward finding more offensive power to complement Jeremy Giambi at first base and in the designated hitter spot. One of the team's top choices was Kevin Millar, a scrappy player who'd gone undrafted out of both high school and college and had to fight his way to a major league contract with the Florida Marlins. Millar was not a particularly gifted ballplayer or athlete, but he had better pitch recognition than almost any hitter in the majors. (Unfortunately, he also had an inordinate amount of trouble handling any pitch that wasn't a fastball.) In 2001—John Henry's last year with the Marlins—and 2002, Millar had blossomed, hitting over .300 both years and smacking a combined 36 home runs.

The problem was that the Marlins had already agreed to sell Millar for $1.2 million to Japan's Chunichi Dragons, with whom Millar had agreed to a two-year, $6.2 million deal. In order to complete the transaction, the Marlins first had to place Millar on waivers. Baseball tradition stated that another team would not claim a player a ball club had agreed to sell overseas.

The Red Sox, showing they had little patience for the gentlemen's agreements that had governed baseball for decades, claimed Millar, setting off an almost month-long saga that made news on both sides of the Pacific Ocean, with the will-he-or-won't-he's and back-and-forths surrounding the 31-year-old taking up plenty of ink as the month progressed. The Sox, meanwhile, kept hunting for bargains. At the beginning of the offseason, the team had compiled a list of about 15 first basemen and designated hitters who might be available for a discount. They'd gotten Jeremy Giambi and still hoped to get Millar. As a backup, they had pursued options like free agents Brad Fullmer, Greg Colbrunn, and Travis Lee. Another name on the list belonged to a burly 27-year-old Dominican left-handed hitter: David Ortiz. The Minnesota Twins had released Ortiz in December—Gold Glove winner Doug Mientkiewicz seemed to have a stranglehold on the first base job in Minnesota—and Ortiz's poor defensive skills and injury-riddled history made many teams wary.

Within the Red Sox, Ortiz intrigued virtually everyone involved in the discussions. One of the scouts loved his swing—it was, he said, a thing of beauty. After looking over his hit location charts, Epstein's crew thought he was likely the type of player who would be able to take advantage of the left field wall in Fenway. Bill James liked the fact that, while he only hit .234 in 2001, his secondary average was almost .400.* ("That's my kind of player," James says.) Dave Jauss, a scout who was down in the Dominican Republic for the winter, reported that in the winter-ball leagues on the island, Ortiz was a superstar, as big as Manny Ramirez or the Montreal Expos' Vladimir Guerrero. Finally, Epstein was consciously trying to find players who could help make the Red Sox clubhouse a more positive place to be, and Ortiz, like Millar, had a reputation for being both outgoing and upbeat, which Epstein felt was crucial at that moment in the team's history. "We wanted to get guys who had a certain makeup," Epstein says. "We wanted guys who were supportive of the other 24 guys in the clubhouse, who care more about team winning and losing than they do about their own stats." Epstein thought that Ortiz, like Millar, had the kind of loose personality that could help the team get through the season in a city like Boston.

That's not to say the Red Sox didn't have reservations. Most pressing were their concerns about Ortiz's age—foreign-born players are known to claim to be younger than they really are so it will seem as if their peak years are still ahead of them, and Ortiz had given his age as 17 when he broke into professional baseball in the States a decade earlier. Instead of simply throwing up his hands, Epstein asked James to see if he could find a way to determine anything further about Ortiz's likely age. "I did a study of his career progression up to that point, identifying historical players who had very similar career paths up to that point in time, and concluded that, on average, they were exactly the age that David claimed to

* Secondary average measures a hitter's ability to produce bases independent of batting average. Where batting average is a ratio of hits to at-bats, secondary average is a ratio of bases achieved in other ways to at-bats. It is achieved by taking a player's total number of bases, subtracting his number of hits, adding his walks and his stolen bases, and subtracting the number of times he was caught stealing and then dividing that number by at-bats. (Or: Sec=(TB-H+BB+SB-CS)/AB.) While secondary averages vary more widely than batting averages, the league average is usually similar, somewhere between .250 and .280. A player with a secondary average that is considerably higher than his batting average may be a player who is undervalued or who has a high likelihood of breaking out.

be," says James. "That was a fun little study. I had never done anything like that before." With that settled, Epstein made his move, acquiring the player that would change both Epstein's and the Red Sox's futures. On January 22, 2003, the Red Sox signed David Ortiz to a one-year, $1.25 million deal.

"We knew he had breakout potential," says Epstein. "He was a guy that brought more than just raw power—he used the whole field, he seemed to be closing up some of his holes, just knew how to hit. You put that all together in a ballpark that will reward those tendencies, and yeah, there was always the possibility that he'd become a star." Still, not long before the Sox signed Ortiz they had inked former Yankees pitcher Ramiro Mendoza to a two-year deal worth $6.5 million and, as Bill James notes, "We weren't any more excited about the one than we were about the other."

While Epstein was pleased with his first offseason's acquisitions, Boston's writers were not impressed.* The *Globe* compared the Ortiz signing to the equivalent of "shopping at Wal-Mart" instead of spending the big bucks for luxury goods. The paper noted disapprovingly that Ortiz, Giambi, Walker, and Mueller would make only $8.8 million in combined salary in 2003, "probably less than what the Sox would have had to pay Cliff Floyd" had he accepted arbitration. (Floyd signed a four-year, $26 million contract with the New York Mets in the offseason.) And Ortiz, the *Globe* noted, had "uncannily" similar career numbers to the recently departed and still popular Brian Daubach, who was, the *Globe* made a point of noting, newly engaged and unemployed. The *Herald* highlighted the fact that while Ortiz referenced fellow lefty Mo Vaughn when asked about hitting in Boston, Ortiz's Fenway average was just .212. One rabble-rousing Red Sox fansite ran a headline on the day of Ortiz's signing that read, "Frustration Nation: Many Sox fans dis-

---

* The North Andover *Eagle-Tribune*'s John Tomase did note at the time that while the Yankees "pumped $50 million into the global economy," the Red Sox, "relying on some obscure stat known as 'on base percentage,' signed a bunch of no-names. . . . [H]igh profile signings and high impact signings are two different things. One looks good before the season. The other looks good after it."

gruntled about hot stove* turning to cold shoulder, big names turn to small moves."

Even with Ortiz on board, the Red Sox weren't quite done. By mid-February, the Kevin Millar saga had worked itself out, as the Dragons agreed to release Millar back to the Marlins, who then sold him to the Sox for $1.5 million, $300,000 of which the Marlins donated to charity. Millar soon signed a two-year, $5.3 million deal, with a $3.5 million option for a third year, which vested after a certain number of plate appearances.

As spring training began, the Red Sox brass found they needed to answer for Epstein's financial calculations. For the first time in memory, the team's payroll had significantly decreased, from around $110 million in 2002 to just under $100 million in 2003. That was still the sixth highest payroll in baseball, behind only the Yankees, Mets, Atlanta Braves, Los Angeles Dodgers, and Texas Rangers. Nevertheless, John Henry was forced once again to assure the locals that yes, he did have enough money to keep on running the team, and that the smaller payroll did not signify any less of a dedication to winning. Henry explained that rather than make a big flashy trade that would appease the fans—at one point in spring training, there was a proposed deal that would have sent pitcher Casey Fossum to Montreal for All-Star Bartolo Colon—Epstein and the Sox were committed to making moves that made the most sense for the long term. It's true that Epstein was told to cut payroll; the team hadn't made the playoffs in three years and revenues were stagnant. Just as important, Epstein believed he could assemble a winning team at that payroll level.

For many general managers, simply following this type of careful plan would have been enough of an achievement for their first offseason. Epstein, though, also vowed to transform the way the team used its staff of relief pitchers. Building on Bill James's much-discussed "bullpen ace" model, Epstein announced that, in 2003, the Red Sox would not use a traditional closer (a highly paid, highly

---

* The baseball offseason is commonly known as the "hot stove" season, a reference to fans gathering around a stove during the cold winter months to discuss their favorite team's plans and prospects for the upcoming year.

specialized pitcher brought in to record the final outs of a win when the lead was three runs or less), but would match up the team's bullpen pitchers with the situations they were most equipped to handle.

Under James's model, this means that the "closer"—generally the best pitcher in the bullpen—is called on to pitch in the most crucial situations, whether those come in the seventh inning of a tie game with the opposing team's best hitter at the plate or in the ninth inning of a one-run game with two men on and nobody out. The rest of the bullpen pitchers are used situationally—left-handed pitchers can take advantage of left-handed batters, say, or a curveball pitcher can be used to neutralize a fastball hitter. The logic of this approach is stunningly simple: If one of your less-than-great pitchers has blown the game in the seventh inning, there will be no victory to close out in the ninth. Such logic is rarely used, however, both because baseball players and managers are creatures of habit and because closers have come to love the "save" statistic they receive when they're on the mound at the end of a victory.* There are no glamour statistics for keeping a game tied in the seventh inning, no matter how tough the batters you're facing.

Epstein thought the approach could work with the 2003 Red Sox. He had offered a deal to the team's 40-save closer, Ugueth Urbina, but Urbina had turned it down. For only a little more than

---

* A pitcher earns a save when he satisfies three conditions: 1) He is the last pitcher on the mound in a game won by his team. 2) He is not the winning pitcher (for instance, a starting pitcher who pitches a complete game does not earn a save). 3) He fulfills one of the following: a) he enters the game with his team leading by three runs or fewer and pitches at least one full inning; b) he comes into the game with the tying run either on base, at bat, or on deck; c) he pitches at least three "effective" innings. So, to give some quick examples, a pitcher who pitches the entire ninth inning with his team leading 6–3 would earn a save, because he pitched a full inning with his team leading by three runs or less. A pitcher who came in with his team leading 8–3 with one out and the bases loaded would also get a save, because he came in with the potential tying run on deck. Finally, a pitcher who pitches the seventh, eighth, and ninth innings of a game in which he preserves his team's 10–3 lead would also earn a save, because he pitched three effective innings. The use of the term "save" as a baseball statistic did not begin until 1969.

it would have cost to retain Urbina, Epstein picked up a trio of pitchers, all of whom he thought had the potential to emerge as stars. Along with Ramiro Mendoza, he signed veteran right-hander Mike Timlin, who had worked as a closer with Toronto, Seattle, and Baltimore, to a one-year, $1.85 million contract, and inked Chad Fox, who had been injured for most of 2002, to a $500,000 deal that could be worth as much as $2.3 million with incentives. Epstein and the Red Sox were most optimistic about Mendoza, who, in his seven seasons with the Yankees, had proven himself to be a versatile and dependable pitcher who could start, pitch in long relief, or even close games.

Even before the season began, Epstein's bullpen strategy was drawing scrutiny. In March, he explained his approach to *Sports Illustrated*. "The fact that we don't have a high-profile, proven, late-inning relief pitcher is probably a financial decision," Epstein said. "Using our best relievers to get the most critical outs, that's purely philosophical. We could have had closer X, but we would still be committed to using him in the seventh inning on a given day if it was appropriate." Epstein went on to say he thought the new approach would actually be good for morale. "Whatever you might lose intangibly, you gain from a sense of unity and cohesion in the bullpen," he said. "By forgoing conventional roles and individual stats and replacing them with the common goal of getting the last out and getting a win—not a save or a hold but a win—I think that builds a certain esprit de corps in the bullpen."

The biggest flaw in this plan was the fact that, without a bullpen ace, there was no clear stopper to rely on in those crucial situations. Just as important, the Sox manager, Grady Little, was not capable of dealing with this degree of flexibility and creativity. Little was a genial, soothing man who unquestionably helped the team relax in 2002. But it frequently seemed as if the game moved too quickly for him, and he often appeared frozen when faced with the inning-to-inning challenges of a given game.

CHAPTER 21

# Kim and the Committee

**THE RED SOX BEGAN THE 2003 SEASON** hundreds of miles away from their Fenway home, in Tampa's Tropicana Field, a domed stadium that housed the moribund Tampa Bay Devil Rays. The first inning of Opening Day seemed as though it could serve as a microcosm for the two teams. In the top of the first, the Sox scored three runs on two Tampa Bay errors, a pair of singles by Nomar Garciaparra and Kevin Millar, and a two-run double by Shea Hillenbrand. In the bottom of the inning, Pedro Martinez retired the Devil Rays in order, with a strikeout sandwiched between a pair of groundouts. For most of the game, that was as exciting as it got. The Red Sox scored again in the fifth, and Tampa scratched out an unearned run off Martinez in the seventh. After finishing that inning, Martinez's night was complete, and he seemed to be in prime form. He'd thrown 91 pitches, striking out six while allowing only three hits. Ramiro Mendoza came on in relief to retire the Devil Rays in order in the eighth, and Boston was three outs away from its first victory of the season. With a three-run lead against a team that had finished in last place every year of its existence, this was the perfect opportunity to test the Red Sox's closer-by-committee approach in a low-stress situation.

With three left-handed batters coming up to the plate, lefty Alan Embree was the first pitcher summoned out of the Boston bullpen in the ninth. Embree, a former member of the Padres, had been picked up by the Red Sox on June 26, 2002, four days after he struck out seven of ten Yankees, including the last six in a row, in a game in San Diego. For the remainder of the 2002 season, he had thrown well, pitching in 32 games for Boston with a 2.97 ERA. Epstein was hoping that, in 2003, he'd become one of the linchpins of the Red Sox bullpen.

Embree gave up a single to Travis Lee, the first batter he faced, prompting Tampa manager Lou Pinella to send up the right-handed Terry Shumpert to pinch-hit for the Devil Rays lefty designated hitter, Al Martin. Shumpert, in his 13-year major league career, had only 47 home runs and had batted .235 in 2002. Before the game, the Red Sox advance scouting team had prepared a report on Tampa Bay for Grady Little. With regards to Shumpert, the instructions were clear: Shumpert was all but useless at the plate so long as you don't, under any circumstances, throw him an inside fastball. Embree soon demonstrated that Little had either never read the report or never shared the information with his pitching staff, and Shumpert hit one of Embree's inside fastballs for his 48th home run (and the second to last of his career) to bring the Devil Rays to within a run.* After Embree gave up another single, this one to right fielder Ben Grieve, Little summoned Chad Fox to the mound.

Fox struck out the first batter he faced. With one out and a man on first base, he induced a bouncer up the middle that looked like it would result in a routine, game-ending double play. After stepping on second base for the force out, however, Nomar Garciaparra fumbled the ball as he prepared to throw to first, leaving a man on with two out and the Red Sox clinging to a 4–3 lead. After a seemingly rattled Fox walked pinch-hitter Marlon Anderson, Carl Crawford, the Devil Rays leadoff batter, came to the plate.

Crawford fouled off four straight pitches, putting him in an 0-2 hole. Fox's fifth pitch was high, bringing the count to 1-2. His next pitch was low and inside, exactly where he wanted it, but Crawford

---

* One member of the team's baseball operations staff said of that night, "That's when I had a feeling Grady wasn't going to work out."

got his bat around on the ball, golfing it in to the right-field stands for a game-winning, three-run homer.

It was a tough loss, but it didn't predict anything one way or another about the Sox's bullpen plan. Save for Garciaparra's bobble, Chad Fox would have been out of the inning, and the pitch Crawford hit to end the game was an excellent one. Still, the reaction in Boston was swift and harsh. After a grand total of one game, the *Herald*'s Jeff Horrigan dubbed the Red Sox bullpen experiment "loser[s] by committee." The *Globe* said the opening night loss had given "rise to the darkest fears of the scheme's architects" and reported that a 73-year-old woman had been prompted to call the paper for the first time in her life. She relayed this message: "I'm so disgusted. What's with this closer by committee?" Dan Shaughnessy wanted to "start with a memo to Bill James: Perhaps the seventh inning is not the most important inning to hold a lead." After an offseason "spent reinventing baseball," Shaughnessy wrote, "young Theo saw it all implode in the hideous confines of Tropicana Field."

The bullpen brouhaha was just one of the distractions that would occupy the team during the first half of the season. In April, soon after his $17.5 million contract extension for the 2004 season was exercised, Martinez seemed to falter, sparking a round of hand-wringing and second-guessing. When the team's relievers continued to struggle, the closer-by-committee experiment was more or less discarded, as Grady Little announced that Brandon Lyon and Chad Fox would, until further notice, serve as the Red Sox closers. And in late May, after Martinez landed on the disabled list with a strained muscle in his back, Epstein succeeded in swapping an increasingly bitter Hillenbrand for some pitching help, trading him to the Arizona Diamondbacks for a 24-year-old Korean pitcher, Byung-Hyun Kim.

In 2002, Kim had been an All-Star closer for the Diamondbacks, going 8-3 with 36 saves and a 2.04 ERA. He finished the season particularly strong, with a 1.05 ERA over his final 22 games. In 2003, with Arizona's starting pitching in shambles, the Diamondbacks were transitioning Kim to a starter's role, and while he'd gone only

1-5 in the season's first two months, he'd done so with a respectable 3.56 ERA.

Normally, the acquisition of a young, hard-throwing pitcher who has shown an ability to both start and close games would be cause for celebration. But Kim was best known in baseball for being the man who served up home runs on successive nights in the 2001 World Series when the Diamondbacks blew consecutive late-game leads against the Yankees. The image of the slight, shell-shocked pitcher crouching on the mound in disbelief was burned into many baseball fans' memories. Kim, on the basis of those two games, was labeled a pitcher who choked under pressure.

As is often the case in baseball, the reality looked quite different if one took the time to examine it a little more closely. In Game 4 of the 2001 Series, Kim was brought into the game in the eighth inning with the Diamondbacks leading, 3–1. He struck out all three Yankees batters he faced that inning, then, with one on and two out in the ninth, gave up a game-tying home run to the left-handed Tino Martinez.

It's certainly true that a team's closer is not supposed to give up a game-tying home run in a World Series game. It's also true that, on occasion, these things happen: Baseball, as has often been pointed out, is a game built around failure, and Kim didn't have nearly the success against lefties that he had against righties. At that point, the game was still tied, and as long as the Diamondbacks held the line, they'd have an opportunity to come back.

They almost didn't get the chance. A walk and a single put men on first and second. With the sold-out Yankee Stadium erupting into a frenzy, Kim, facing the most pressure he'd been confronted with in his career, struck out Shane Spencer to end the inning.

By this point, it was obvious to virtually everyone watching the game that the 22-year-old, 5-foot-11-inch, 170-pound Kim was physically spent. Inexplicably, in a move that wouldn't have been out of place in the Red Sox's history, Diamondbacks manager Bob Brenly sent Kim out again in the bottom of the 10th inning. After retiring the first two batters he faced, Kim gave up the game-ending home run to Derek Jeter.

The next night, heading into the bottom of the ninth inning, the Diamondbacks again had a two-run lead. Brenly, once again, summoned Kim to the mound, despite the fact that Kim had thrown more pitches—63—the previous night than ever before in his major league career. This time, Kim's struggles were more predictable, and he gave up a two-run home run to Scott Brosius to tie the game, which the Yankees went on to win.

In the aftermath of the Diamondbacks' back-to-back losses, few thought to consider Kim's exhaustion. While commentators, writers, and fans alike wondered why Brenly had allowed Kim to return to the mound in the 10th inning of Game 4 or to come in at all in Game 5, they laid most of the blame upon Kim instead of Brenly, who had asked an obviously depleted pitcher to keep throwing the ball.

Kim's reputation, combined with his odd workout regimens— he'd obsessively exercise for hours a day, and often stayed up until the early morning hours shadow pitching in front of a mirror to study his mechanics—and the fact that he didn't speak English meant he had a difficult time penetrating baseball's fraternity. Baseball players, for all the many millions of dollars they make, still exhibit the crude tribalism found in high-school locker rooms around the country. Kim already had a hard time fitting in, and few came to his defense when he hit a rough patch.

That made him just the kind of player Epstein was inclined to be interested in: one whose stock was artificially low based on factors that didn't accurately reflect his on-field performance. Kim's 2003 salary was $3.25 million. If the exact same pitcher—a hard-throwing right-hander who could either start games or come on in relief and who almost completely suppressed right-handed batters' power numbers—was on the trading block but was, instead of a sullen Korean, a skinny farm boy from Texas who threw overhand instead of sidearm, he'd have been one of the most sought-after players in baseball. As it was, the Red Sox were able to pick him up for what was essentially a redundant player on their roster.

Kim fit almost perfectly with the Sox's plans. He began as a replacement starter for the injured Martinez. In July, he was moved into the bullpen, taking over as the team's closer and anchoring the team's relievers for the rest of the season. "I didn't do a good job of choosing the pitchers before the season started," Epstein says. "But the whole bullpen thing in 2003—it's not that we didn't want a closer. We wanted to use our closer more aggressively, and we also didn't want to overpay for that closer. We offered [Ugueth] Urbina what we thought was fair, and he didn't take it. We tried that winter to find a closer, but it was a really bad market. So at that point we figured, maybe one will emerge out of this group. Chad Fox had closed very recently. Timlin might have worked. And if not, well, we'll have to trade for one." And that, says Epstein, is exactly what happened. "It worked out, but not without a lot of controversy," he says. "We got our closer. We got our relief ace. But it took until May, and it took Hillenbrand, who was only available because we signed Bill Mueller to a two-year deal when other teams didn't seem to want him. We ended up with relatively cheap contracts for Bill Mueller, David Ortiz, [Kevin] Millar, and Kim, which helped us that season and also gave us the flexibility we thought we'd want in that offseason."

CHAPTER 22

# "You Want Me to Hit Like a Little Bitch?"

WITH KIM ON BOARD AND HILLENBRAND GONE, the 2003 Red Sox truly began to take shape. Millar quickly became the clubhouse leader and offensive catalyst Epstein was hoping he'd be, hitting timely home runs and helping keep the team's clubhouse relaxed. "We play a game for a living," he said that spring, as Martinez's contract negotiations and health and Garciaparra's brooding threatened to take center stage. "I think sometimes people lose perspective of that. If I didn't make a dollar out there on that field, I'd still be out there playing. I love it." Millar's attitude was infectious, and in time, the divisive, bitter team that imploded in 2001 seemed a distant memory.

Certainly, it was easier to relax and have fun while hitting the ball the way the Sox were doing. By midseason, it was clear the 2003 team was an offensive powerhouse on par with baseball's all-time best. For the month of June, the Red Sox had four of the top 10 batting averages in the league: Garciaparra (.398), Millar (.373), Trot Nixon (.356), and Manny Ramirez (.351). The Sox led all of baseball that month with a teamwide .315 average. Combined with the teamwide .308 average in May, the entire roster had compiled one common benchmark for batting excellence over the course of two full months. In June, the team hit more home runs—42—than in any month since 1998 and scored more runs than in any month since 1961.

Perhaps most incredibly, they were doing this largely without the offensive firepower of David Ortiz. Ortiz began the year platooning at first base and designated hitter and hit only one home run in April, one more in May, and two in June. Halfway through the season, Ortiz had a total of only four home runs, half as many as Todd Walker, the team's second baseman.

Still, the 6-foot-4-inch slugger had already become one of the most popular people in the Red Sox clubhouse. He was, along with Millar, one of the team's unrepentant cutups. His pendulous swagger and his ribald, needling sense of humor helped shift attention away from the increasingly sulky Garciaparra. When he arrived at the ballpark the afternoon of a game, Ortiz would stride into the Sox clubhouse wearing fluorescent polo shirts and wrap-around sunglasses and shout, to no one in particular, "What up, bitches!"*

Even before he started playing every day and hitting for power, Ortiz was happier in Boston than he'd been in Minnesota. His six seasons with the Twins had been difficult ones. There had been the injuries, sure—the Minneapolis Metrodome's artificial turf is punishing on players' knees—but just as frustrating to Ortiz was the way in which the Twins coaching staff had tried to turn a proud home run hitter into a singles batter who slapped balls over infielders' heads.

"When I first came to Minnesota, that's when I was told, 'Stay inside the ball . . . hit the ball the other way,' " Ortiz said after coming to Boston. "I was always a power hitter in the minor leagues. Everything changed when I went to Minnesota. Whenever I took a big swing, [the coaching staff would] say to me, 'Hey, hey, what are you doing?' " Ortiz tried to go along with the Twins plan, but he wasn't happy about it. "I said, 'You want me to hit like a little bitch, then I

---

* Other often-used Ortizisms include, "Shiiiiit," "Let me tell you something, bro," and "That's some fucking bulllllllshit." There's also his trademark exhortation to reporters at the conclusion of his postgame press conferences: "Now go home and get some ass."

will.' But I knew I could hit for power. It was just a matter of getting the green light."

Watching Ortiz, it seems hard to believe any coaching staff had ever asked him to cut down on his monstrous swings. As big and strong as Ortiz's upper body is, it's his lower body that is most impressive. As the ball approaches the plate, his back hip remains stationary, while his front hip closes slightly as he cocks his leg to time his swing. Then, using his flattened front foot as an anchor, he whips his bat through the strike zone in a motion one writer describes as "torquing like a motherfucker." When Ortiz connects squarely, it is an inspiring sight, perhaps to no one more than the slugger himself: Ortiz admires his clouts in a style Todd Walker once compared to "pimpin'." Ortiz makes no apologies. "If they don't like it," he said of opposing pitchers, "don't let me hit it out."

The Red Sox didn't want to see this power go to waste. During Ortiz's first at-bat during spring training, he came to the plate with a man on first base. He tried to do what he had been taught in Minnesota: move the runner along to second. When he returned to the Red Sox dugout after his at-bat, Grady Little told him, "Hey, you've got to bring that guy in."

"OK," Ortiz replied, a smile breaking out on his expansive face. "I guess I've got the green light to swing."

With Jeremy Giambi ahead of Ortiz on the Sox's depth chart and the emergence of Kevin Millar as Boston's clutch-hitting mascot, Ortiz didn't get a chance to build up momentum during the season's first half. In April and May, he rarely played two full games in a row. Even in June, he only played sporadically.

That pattern was about to change. When Giambi—who, much to everyone's disappointment, was batting only .173—landed on the disabled list, Ortiz got his chance. He'd soon emerge as one of the game's premier power hitters, and one of the best clutch performers in all of sports. Even before becoming a starter, he'd shown a penchant for coming up big when the game was on the line: His first home run of the season was a game-winning blast in the 14th inning of an April 27 game against the Anaheim Angels in which Ortiz had been sent in as a pinch-hitter for Giambi.

By July, Ortiz began to truly show Boston fans what he was capable of. In a July 3 game against the Devil Rays, he hit his fifth home run of the year. The next day, the Sox began a three-game trip to Yankee Stadium. On Friday, July 4, Ortiz, hitting in the sixth spot behind Kevin Millar, smacked a pair of solo home runs in a lopsided, 10–3 Boston win. The next day, he hit two more homers in another easy Boston victory. In three days, he had more than doubled his home run total from the season's first three months. More—much more—was yet to come.

## CHAPTER 23

# The Manny Sagas, Part 1

**MICHAEL LEWIS'S** *Moneyball* was published in May 2003. The book, which chronicled the 2002 Oakland A's season by shadowing Billy Beane, was an instant success—*The New York Times* called Lewis a "terrifically entertaining explicator" and said Lewis had hit *Moneyball* "out of the park."

Most of the press attention, and most of the attention the book received inside the baseball community, focused on Lewis's description and analysis of Beane's approach to building a small-budget team that could rack up wins. Three decades after the founding of the Society for American Baseball Research, Beane's interest in and use of statistics was seen as revolutionary. Journalists often summed up the sabermetric principles described in the book thusly: batting average should be ignored in favor of on base percentage. Occasionally, some other notions—the benefit that comes from stealing a base is rarely worth the risk of getting caught; a team will score more runs by swinging away than by trying to sacrifice runners along the base paths—were thrown in for good measure.

It's true that Beane, and sabermetric thinkers generally, believed in the importance of on base percentage, but simplifying Beane's philosophy (or Lewis's description of Beane's philosophy) down to this level was akin to saying that the strategy of good investors is to buy stocks whose price will go up in the future. What was much less discussed, at least within baseball itself, was Beane's reliance on the notion of inefficient markets. Baseball, as Beane so memorably illustrated in Lewis's narrative, has for most of its history been inefficient: The prices players were paid didn't accurately reflect their true talent levels because of a lack of understanding about what combination of skills most helped a team win ball games. (Put another way, too few people had figured out that the important question to ask is not, "What are the characteristics of winning teams?" but Bill James's "*Why* are these the characteristics of winning teams?") Thus, there were many factors that a general manager who was determined to run his team more rationally could take advantage of. During the year Lewis spent trailing Beane, the easiest inefficiency to take advantage of was the lack of attention paid to the importance of on base percentage. That would soon change, as Lewis's book prompted executives and analysts around the baseball world to treat on base percentage in the same simpleminded, crude way in which they had previously treated batting average. Baseball broadcasts began showing on base percentage on screen, along with batting average, home runs, and RBIs. Instead of applying the underlying philosophy Lewis illustrated, baseball executives and journalists alike simply began replacing one statistic they didn't understand terribly well with another, while ignoring the thinking that led GMs like Beane—and Theo Epstein—to realize that hidden value could be found in on base percentage in the first place.

Within the Red Sox, there was considerable anxiety about *Moneyball*'s publication even before it was released. Just as Beane, whose 2003 payroll was around $50 million, was trying to compete with richer clubs in his division like the Anaheim Angels and the Seattle Mariners, so too were the Red Sox trying to compete with the significantly wealthier New York Yankees, their rivals in the American League East.* If Lewis disclosed the extent to which

---

* Because of baseball's unbalanced schedule, teams not only compete within their own division for playoff spots, they play their division rivals far more each year than they play other clubs in their league: Teams in the same division play each other 18 or 19 times each year while playing other league rivals not in their division as few as six times a season.

baseball players were improperly valued, one of the most potent tools the Red Sox had in their arsenal would, they feared, be neutralized.

In the meantime, the team's baseball operations crew searched for even more sophisticated ways to analyze players. With more accurate and nuanced information at their fingertips, they figured, they'd be able to find new inefficiencies to exploit—perhaps middle relievers were undervalued, or maybe players who could hit well but played poor defense were overvalued. In 2003, Bill James undertook two studies that attempted to build whole new sets of data to use as a means of analyzing baseball players. Both required tracking every single play of every single game for an entire season.

The first of James's 2003 studies calculated the incidents in which a player's failure to hustle negatively affected his team. For as long as baseball has been played, some players have been considered showboats who never put in enough effort while others were lauded for their grit and all-out determination, but no one had ever endeavored to analyze the extent to which a lazier player negatively affected the outcome of a game. For James's study, a player was noted as exhibiting a "failure to hustle" only if the final result of that play could have been affected by an increase in effort. For example, a player who fails to run down the first base line on a hard-hit ball to the second baseman would not be marked down—he would have been out even if he'd been running at full speed.

Similarly, if, on that same play, the second baseman threw the ball into the dugout and the runner was safe because of an error, the batter would not be marked down; he didn't need to run full speed in order to make it to first safely. If, however, the second baseman bobbled the ball, recovered, and threw to first in time to nail the lollygagging runner by a half step, he'd be marked down for a failure to hustle. The reason for this, like the reasoning behind much of James's work, is wonderfully straightforward: James was only interested in the actual, real-life impact of a player's actions. If a player didn't run hard out of the batter's box 100 times during the course of a season, but his slowness only resulted in three unnecessary outs, it would be safe to conclude that, as frustrating as that player's attitude was, it didn't really affect the outcome of a season's worth of games. If, on the other hand, he didn't run hard 30 times and that resulted in 15 extra outs, that was a whole other story.

James also set about tallying and examining the team's defensive miscues as distinct from a compendium of errors, because a player generally received an error only if he came into contact with a ball while it was in play. James also wanted to tally balls an outfielder should have gotten to but didn't because of a poor approach to the ball, or times a catcher should have been able to apply a tag to a runner trying to score but failed to do so. Both of these studies were efforts to develop a more complete framework through which to view baseball players.

The results of James's studies highlighted the impact of one player: Manny Ramirez. In 2003, second baseman Todd Walker led the team in defensive miscues—he had so little range as to appear immobile at times, and infielders get far more fielding opportunities over the course of a season than outfielders—but Ramirez was not far behind. Ramirez also had about half of the team's nearly 60 "failure to hustle" plays that James recorded during the course of the season. To the rest of the baseball world, Manny Ramirez looked like a hitting savant who was anchoring a prodigiously potent lineup. To the Red Sox, he was, with his $20 million per year price tag, looking more and more like a player making too much money for his aggregate contribution to the team.

It would have been hard to make that argument to many Boston fans—or many baseball observers—in 2003, a year in which Ramirez led the American League in on base percentage and was in the top 10 in runs, hits, home runs, and walks. With Ramirez stroking the ball and David Ortiz blossoming at the plate, the Red Sox began to hit like the 1927 Murderers' Row New York Yankees of Babe Ruth and Lou Gehrig. Halfway through the season, the Sox were collectively hitting .299. Bill Mueller, the gimpy-kneed third baseman to whom no one wanted to risk offering a two-year contract, led all of baseball with 30 doubles and had a .328 batting average. By the end of July, the Red Sox, as a *team,* had a slugging percentage of over .500, which meant that for every two trips to the plate, the Sox would gain one base. No team in history had ever amassed a .500 slugging percentage over the course of a season.

Perhaps as remarkable was that the Red Sox were, for the first time in years, clearly having fun. Millar, the free-spirited Texan, bestowed an unofficial motto upon the team: "Cowboy Up." The Red Sox became affectionately known as the Dirt Dogs, with right fielder Trot Nixon, whose batting helmet was so coated with pine tar it was hard to make out its red B, personifying the team's gritty identity. Someone unearthed an old home video of a college-aged Millar lip-syncing Bruce Springsteen's "Born in the U.S.A.," and soon the clip was being shown on Fenway's JumboTron during games under the heading RALLY KARAOKE GUY. David Ortiz was not only knocking the ball all over the park, he was taking his place as one of the most popular and charismatic members of the team. He strode around like a hip-hop star, but one who loved doling out hugs, and looked vaguely like an overgrown child. He constantly peppered his speech with the word "bitch," but he did it so good-naturedly that no one ever minded. Take the time when, during one of Grady Little's pregame meetings with reporters, Ortiz stuck his head into the manager's office to give his take on how that after-noon's contest would unfold. "We're going to kick their ass, drink their beer, and rape their bitches," Ortiz announced. From another player, such a pronouncement would have come off as an uncom-fortable attempt to appear either thuggish or cool. Ortiz, with his youthful glee and broad smile, seemed more like a wanna-be pirate. The room full of reporters burst into laughter.

During the season—and against the backdrop of Larry Luc-chino's "Evil Empire" quip—this ragtag group of ballplayers was transformed by the national press into a group of rebels trying to topple the imperious, arrogant, overbearing Yankees dynasty. The contrast could not have been starker. The Yankees had won four World Series between 1996 and 2000 and had taken the Diamond-backs to seven games in 2001; the Red Sox hadn't won a title in 85 years and hadn't played in the World Series since 1986. The loud-mouthed George Steinbrenner treated every baseball game as a win-at-all-costs contest and threw money at superstars past their prime; the soft-spoken, gentle-seeming John Henry believed in the cool, ra-tional analysis of players. The Yankees, with their prep-school regu-lations about hair length and facial grooming, seemed like a bunch of corporate stiffs; the Red Sox, with their cornrows, muttonchops, and motley beards and goatees, looked like frat-house refugees.

With that rambunctiousness came a fair amount of turmoil, to be sure. Ramirez, in particular, seemed to be doing his all to alienate himself from his teammates and his fans. On Friday, August 29, while saying he was too sick to play, Ramirez told ESPN he'd like to play one day for the Yankees. The next day, he said once again he was too ill to take the field—he was, he explained, suffering from a throat inflammation, although that night he was seen socializing with New York's Enrique Wilson in the lobby of Boston's Ritz-Carlton. On Sunday, he didn't show up for a Fenway Park doctor's appointment.

And on Monday, September 1, Ramirez capped what might have been the sorriest four-day stretch of his Red Sox career when he refused to pinch-hit in a game against the Philadelphia Phillies. Heading into the ninth inning, Boston was down, 9–7. Boston mounted a comeback, with little-used role players like Damian Jackson and Lou Merloni delivering crucial hits while Ramirez stayed on the bench. The Sox clawed back that day, and Trot Nixon won the game with a grand slam. Afterward, Nixon said, "I'm sure a lot of guys would like to have seen Manny up there. Well, I'm just as confident with the people who went to the plate."

Ramirez's insubordination posed perhaps the starkest challenge of Grady Little's managerial career. In 2002, Little had made no secret about the fact that he felt players such as Ramirez and Pedro Martinez were essentially uncontrollable. At one point, he explained his attitude about the team's spoiled superstars to the *Herald*'s Tony Massarotti. "Let me ask you something," Little said. "If someone gives you a dog and that dog has a habit of peeing on the floor, can you change them?" Now, Little apparently felt it was time for Ramirez to be house trained, and the next day he refused to put him in the lineup.* After the season ended, Tim Wakefield pointed

---

* Little did not bench Ramirez in 2002 when he failed to leave the batter's box after hitting a ground ball. He later said he regretted that decision. "I should have taken him out of the game right there," Little said the day after the 2002 incident, which had occurred in Tampa Bay. "It was a mistake I won't make again."

to the day Little had benched Ramirez as the turning point in the Red Sox's season. "I think that brought us even closer together and then [Ramirez] realized, I think, that he wants to be part of this team. If you noticed, his numbers got a little better," Wakefield said. "He started playing harder."

Ramirez's meltdown was, people assumed, just another case of "Manny being Manny." Everyone, from his manager to his teammates to the reporters covering the team, thought that was the end of it. But, in fact, Ramirez had gone to John Henry in August and asked, for the second time in two years, to be traded.

"I thought he was happy," Henry says. "We all thought he was happy. And since that first day [when Ramirez had asked at spring training in 2002 to be traded], we'd had a great relationship. But he said, 'I can't do this for five more years.' And I said, 'I give you my word: I'll do everything I can to get you out of here. But it's obviously not going to happen until the end of the season.'"

A couple of weeks later, Ramirez passed Larry Lucchino on the field before a game. "We've got a deal, right? We've got a deal?" Ramirez asked. "Not until the end of the season, Manny," Lucchino answered. "Let's wait until the end of the season."

Even with Ramirez taking himself out of the lineup for days at a time, the Red Sox kept hitting, and the team kept winning. By the end of the year, the scope of the team's offensive accomplishments was astounding. The team had set a major league record for most extra-base hits in a season, 649, and one for the most total bases in a season, 2,832. They'd broken the 1927 Yankees record for the highest slugging percentage in a season, at .491. They had eight players on their roster with 30 or more doubles, another record. The Sox's eight players with 80 or more runs batted in and nine players with more than 100 hits both tied previous baseball records. Instead of collapsing under the weight of a fractious clubhouse, the 2003 Red Sox succeeded despite some of their superstars' petulance. "Theo deserves a lot of credit," says Kevin Millar. "He brought baseball players [to Boston]. Myself and David Ortiz and Billy Mueller— these guys no one wanted. David Ortiz was nontendered by the Minnesota Twins. I mean, I was going to Japan. Billy Mueller, coming off knee surgery with the Chicago Cubs, no one wanted. This guy wins [the American League] batting title [in 2003]."

As potent as the Red Sox were, they weren't quite good enough to overcome the Yankees in the regular season, and the Sox finished Epstein's first year as general manager with a 95-67 record, six games behind New York in the American League East. Still, it was good enough for the third best record in the league, which meant the Sox were crowned one of baseball's wild-card teams.* For the first time since 1999, the Red Sox were headed to the playoffs.

---

* The American and National Leagues are each divided into three divisions: East, West, and Central. The top team in each division makes the playoffs, as does the nondivision winner with the best record of the league's remaining teams.

## CHAPTER 24

# Gumped: A Cautionary Tale

**HEADING INTO THE PLAYOFFS,** life in what had increasingly come to be known as "Red Sox Nation" seemed to be going fairly smoothly. The team was gelling and the offense was ferocious. Even the bullpen had been transformed into one of the team's strengths, with Byung-Hyun Kim serving as the team's closer and the newly acquired Scott Williamson joining Mike Timlin and Alan Embree to create a strong staff of hard throwers.

But this might have been the rare instance in which the team's front office was more pessimistic than most of its fans. The team, now under Grady Little's tutelage for a second year, had not been managed the way the Sox's top brass had envisioned. Little's usage of Kim was a prime example. By July, Kim was shifted to the Sox bullpen after almost half a season in which he'd worked as a starter, training his body to be prepared to pitch once every five days.* Lit-

---

* The mechanics involved in pitching a baseball produce some of the most violent motions in all of sports. Tests done by a biomechanical engineer at the American Sports Medicine Institute in Birmingham, Alabama, showed that an average human ulnar collateral ligament, which connects the large bone that runs from the shoulder to the elbow to one of the two bones that make up the forearm, would snap when placed under the amount of pressure a major

tle (who'd acquired the nickname "Gump" after the Tom Hanks character in *Forrest Gump*) almost immediately started using Kim for three, four, and even five games in a row. Little had been terrified by the Red Sox's early-season bullpen collapses; the first-time manager's contract ran out at the end of the year, and expectations for the team were high. He decided that as soon as he found a formula that worked, he was going to ride it into the ground.

In the final half of the season, Little used Kim a total of 42 times; extrapolated out over an entire season, that would be 84 appearances. In 14 out of the last 18 years, no American League reliever has appeared in 84 or more games. Nine of Kim's 42 appearances were for more than one inning, and five were for two or more. In 2005, when the Red Sox's Mike Timlin led the league with 81 appearances, only 14 of his stints were for more than an inning, and only four were for two. From July 6 through the end of the season, Kim pitched in six out of seven games three times. From August 26 to September 3, he pitched in seven out of eight games, including one appearance of two innings.

His use of Kim was a perfect illustration of how Grady Little's shortsightedness and lack of creativity hamstrung the Red Sox. When, in July and August, Kim seemed to be the answer to the bullpen's problems—in 13 out of his first 15 relief appearances after joining Boston's bullpen, Kim didn't allow an earned run—Little decided to hold onto him for dear life. When, at the end of August, Kim gave up seven earned runs in eight games, the shortsighted Boston fans and media blamed Kim instead of Little. Still, in Sep-

---

sure a major league pitcher uses to throw a fastball. When pitchers talk of building up "arm strength," they're talking of building up their muscles so as to decrease the possibility of muscle tears. Obviously, the physical strains of throwing approximately 100 pitches every five days—a normal workload for a starting pitcher—are different from throwing 15 pitches every other day, a more average load for a closer, and one of the most important aspects of maintaining pitching health is allowing the body to properly heal between appearances. A starting pitcher throws more each time out, but he has more time between starts for his body to repair itself. This is why a healthy starting pitcher can average more than 200 innings pitched per season, while it is incredibly rare for a reliever to amass more than 100.

tember, Kim came back to throw 13 innings without giving up an earned run, going 3-1 with 5 saves for the month.

If few members of the media had noticed how Little's managerial approach was affecting the team, it certainly wasn't lost on the Red Sox high brass. Epstein's baseball operations crew was providing the team's coaching staff with voluminous reports—on upcoming opponents, on how best to use the players on the team—which Little largely seemed to ignore. "Grady Little was a hunch manager," says Tom Werner. "That's not our style." John Henry is even more blunt. "My feeling was that we were here to win a championship, and I thought that, sooner or later, when it came down to crunch time, he was really going to hurt us." By the middle of the season, Henry had conversations about firing Little. "There was a total lack of preparation," says Henry, which went all the way back to the Opening Day debacle in Tampa. By season's end, Henry had taken to joking that if the Red Sox did win the World Series and he was tapped to star in one of the iconic "I'm going to Disney World" commercials, he would instead announce to the world, "I'm going to fire Grady Little!"

In the 2003 American League Division Series, the Red Sox would face Billy Beane's Oakland A's, the team assembled by the man they'd thought they'd hired not even a year earlier. Both teams were entering the postseason with something to prove. It was Epstein's first playoff series as a general manager, Henry and Werner's first playoff series as the team's owners, and the Red Sox's first playoff appearance in four years. Beane's A's, for their part, were trying to shake off a reputation for being postseason chokers. Two-thousand three was the fourth year in a row Oakland had made the playoffs— since 2000 Oakland had won more games than any team in baseball except Seattle—but in each of the previous three years, the A's had lost the clinching fifth game of their first round series.* As if that

* Baseball has three rounds of playoffs: the League Division Series, in which the wild-card team plays the division-winning team with the best record that's not in its same division and the other two division winners play each other; the League Championship Series, in which the winners of the Division

weren't enough to whet fans' appetites, the matchup looked as if it had the makings of a classic duel, with the Red Sox's record-setting offense squaring off against the A's spectacular pitching.

In Game 1, played in Oakland, Pedro Martinez pitched a workmanlike seven innings before heading to the showers with the Red Sox leading, 4–3. After Mike Timlin retired the side in the eighth inning, Grady Little summoned Byung-Hyun Kim for the game's final three outs. With one out, Kim walked Billy McMillon and hit Chris Singleton with a pitch, putting runners on first and second. He then struck out Mark Ellis, leaving the Sox one out away from a win. The next batter was the A's left-handed designated hitter, Erubiel Durazo.

Before Durazo could dig in to the batter's box, Grady Little bounded out of the Sox dugout and headed for the mound. He held out his left arm and pointed toward the bullpen: He wanted lefty Alan Embree to come face Durazo. It was, casual fans everywhere knew, a high percentage move. Left-handed batters generally have a much more difficult time facing left-handed pitchers, and Kim fared much better against right-handers.

Except Erubiel Durazo was not your typical left-handed batter. He actually had what's referred to as a reverse split. He hit better—much better, in fact—against lefties than he did against righties. In 2003, Durazo's batting average was 36 points higher when facing lefties, and his slugging percentage was 39 points higher. What's more, in 2003, Embree exhibited a reverse split, too, with lefties hitting 42 points better than righties against him. Finally, Little had just shown up his closer by telling Kim he didn't have confidence in him to record the game's final out. "I thought I was going to have an actual fit when I saw Grady coming out of the dugout," says one member of the team's baseball operations crew. "In that instant, [Little] not only lost the game, he lost his closer for the rest of the

Series play each other, and the World Series, in which the American League champion plays the National League champion. In 2003, the wildcard–winning Red Sox played the A's, the American League West winners, while the American League East's Yankees played the American League Central's Twins.

postseason." With the Coliseum crowd going wild, Durazo slapped an Embree fastball into left field, scoring the game's tying run.

The inning hadn't even ended before Kim was, once again, labeled the goat. (Since he was responsible for the runner who scored the tying run, it was Kim, not Embree, who was charged with a blown save.) It was, as no one hesitated to point out, the third time Kim had blown a postseason game in which his team had had the lead heading into the ninth inning. But it was Little's pitching substitution that helped set up Durazo's game-tying hit. Three innings later, with planned Game 3 starter Derek Lowe called in for an emergency relief appearance, the Sox lost on, of all things, a bases-loaded bunt single.

The Sox lost the next day, too, as Barry Zito shut down Boston's vaunted offense and the A's scored five runs in the second inning off Tim Wakefield. Heading back to Fenway, the Sox found themselves facing three elimination games in a row.

If you looked back at the box scores from those first two games in an effort to determine what had gone wrong, a few things would likely pop out. The two pillars of the Red Sox offense, Manny Ramirez and David Ortiz, had gone a combined 1-for-17 with no runs batted in. (Second baseman Todd Walker, meanwhile, was 4-for-9 with two home runs and three RBIs.) And, of course, there was that five-run second inning in Game 2, an inning that was prolonged by a Red Sox error.

What you wouldn't see was any indication that, in both games, the Red Sox's best chance at victory may have hinged on something Manny Ramirez did while not in the batter's box. In the 12th inning of Game 1, with two outs, Ramirez on second, and Bill Mueller on first, Boston's Gabe Kapler hit a shot down the third base line. Coming off the bat, it looked to be a sure single, and Ramirez began trotting toward third. But Oakland's third baseman, Eric Chavez, made a terrific play to stop the ball. Seeing that Ramirez hadn't been going all out, Chavez raced back to the bag, barely beating a sliding Ramirez for the out. Instead of loading the bases, the Red Sox's inning was over, and the A's won the game in their turn at bat.

The next afternoon, a Ramirez defensive miscue led to four of the five runs the A's scored. With one out and runners on first and second in the second inning, Oakland's Eric Byrnes hit a high fly ball to left field. Ramirez tried to track the ball and got turned around before Byrnes's pop-up fell behind him for a two-run double. Had Ramirez caught the ball, Wakefield would have likely escaped from the inning after allowing only one run. Ramirez seemed to be doing his best to provide the Red Sox with yet more proof of his lack of hustle and subpar defensive performances.*

It was the A's whose mistakes cost them Game 3, as the Red Sox took advantage of a pair of Oakland base-running blunders to win, 3–1. The next afternoon, David Ortiz won Game 4 with a two-run double off Oakland closer Keith Foulke in the eighth, tying the series at two games apiece. On Sunday night both teams flew back to California for the next evening's deciding game, in which Martinez would face Zito, the laid-back left-hander who'd edged Martinez to win the 2002 Cy Young Award.

Both pitchers started well, and Oakland was nursing a 1–0 lead as Boston came to bat in the top of the sixth inning. Finally, the big Boston bats woke up. Jason Varitek led off with a home run, and three batters and one out later, Ramirez hit a three-run blast to give Boston a 4–1 lead. There were only 12 outs to go, and even after the A's got back a run in the sixth, Boston's lead appeared safe. Martinez retired the first two batters in order in the seventh, and then Jermaine Dye lofted a pitch into the no-man's-land between second base and center field.

Grady Little had lifted the defensively challenged Todd Walker when the Red Sox got the lead in the sixth inning, and the athletic Damian Jackson was sent in to replace him at second base. As soon as the ball left Dye's bat, Jackson went into a full sprint out toward center, tracking the ball over his shoulder. Johnny Damon, meanwhile, had started dashing in at the exact same time. As they con-

---

* In contrast to David Ortiz, who patiently answered reporters' questions about his offensive slump, Ramirez refused to speak to the press at all following the first two games in Oakland. At one point, when surrounded by a group of writers, Ramirez ignored question after question. Finally, in an effort to shoo away the last remaining scribes, he sprayed an overwhelming amount of cologne into the air. "Media repellent," one Red Sox official quipped after watching this scene unfold.

verged in shallow center field, Jackson dove and the ball landed in his outstretched glove at almost the exact moment that Jackson's and Damon's heads struck in a gruesome collision. As the ball trickled away and Dye tried to sprint to second, both Jackson and Damon lay prone on the field. Only a head's-up play by Nomar Garciaparra, who ran out, plucked the ball off the ground, and fired it to second, kept Dye from reaching base safely.

With the inning over, every Red Sox player on the field gathered around the two players as the team's trainers and doctor sprinted from the dugout. Jackson was groggy but alert. Damon was out cold. "When I got there," said right fielder Trot Nixon after the game, "he was breathing kind of heavy. . . . I said a prayer for Johnny and said the Lord was with him. In those kinds of situations, it makes this game real small." It only took a minute for Jackson to struggle to his feet. Damon, however, remained motionless. Two minutes passed. Then three. Finally, four minutes after losing consciousness, Damon began to stir. He was lifted into a stretcher and, after raising his right arm to acknowledge the crowd, was taken off the field in an ambulance. Only ten minutes had passed, and the Red Sox had just six outs to go to win the series, but the game felt very different.

Pedro Martinez was sent back to the mound in the eighth, and he allowed another Oakland run, bringing the game to 4–3. With that, his night was over. Alan Embree and Mike Timlin were called in to finish the inning off, leaving the Sox with just three outs to go, Grady Little had lefty Scott Sauerbeck,* who hadn't yet pitched in the playoffs, and Scott Williamson still remaining in the bullpen. (Byung-Hyun Kim had further alienated both his teammates and Boston fans when he gave the middle finger to the Fenway crowd after being booed during the introductions to Game 3. Before that game began, Kim told Little he was unavailable because of a sore shoulder.) Thus far in the playoffs, Williamson had been stellar, striking out eight while giving up only two hits and one walk in five playoff innings.

On this night, however, Williamson's always shaky command

---

* Sauerbeck required offseason surgery for a torn labrum and punctured rotator cuff, and missed all of the 2004 season.

seemed to have deserted him, and he walked the first two batters he faced. Little next called on Derek Lowe, who had thrown seven innings as Game 3's starter two nights earlier.

Lowe was one of the most intriguing personalities on the Red Sox. A lanky, 6-foot-6-inch right-hander, Lowe had arrived in Boston via one of the best trades in Red Sox history: In 1997, Dan Duquette sent closer Heathcliff Slocumb to the Seattle Mariners for Lowe and Jason Varitek. Lowe had achieved considerable success in a Red Sox uniform. In 2000, he was named an All-Star and led the American League with 42 saves. He'd also reached considerable depths. In 2001, Lowe seemed to unravel, as he coughed up leads and appeared to be close to tears on occasion. (His tendency to wear his heart on his sleeve caused Red Sox fanatic Bill Simmons, made famous as ESPN's "Sports Guy," to dub any particularly mopey expression, "The Derek Lowe Face.") By mid-April, fans and the media alike were questioning whether Lowe had the mental toughness to be a big-league closer.

In 2002, after being converted to a starter, Lowe did better than anyone could have reasonably expected, going 21-8, throwing a no-hitter, starting the All-Star Game, and placing third to Zito and Martinez in the Cy Young Award voting. In 2003, he continued his forward-backward routine, compiling a 17-7 record mainly on the strength of the Red Sox's offensive might, as his 4.47 earned run average was barely better than the league average. Even the playoffs seemed a microcosm for his career: In Game 1, he'd been the losing pitcher, and in Game 3, his seven innings of one-run ball likely saved Boston's season. Now, with two men on and one well-placed hit the difference between a heartbreaking loss and a series victory, which Derek Lowe would show up?

The first batter Lowe faced, catcher Ramon Hernandez, tapped a sacrifice bunt down the third base line, putting men on second and third with one out. The next man to the plate was veteran Jermaine Dye. Grady Little signaled from the dugout to intentionally walk Dye, which would load the bases and create a force out at any base. Just as Dye was about to stand in, Varitek and the home plate umpire told him he was being signaled for from the A's dugout. Oakland manager Ken Macha was inexplicably sending the little used switch-hitter Adam Melhuse up to pinch-hit for Dye *after* an intentional walk had been called for. Little decided to call off the intentional pass and let Lowe pitch to Melhuse.

Lowe's best pitch is his sinker, a sharply diving fastball. When thrown well, it's almost impossible to hit solidly. When thrown to a right-hander, the ball starts off the plate, then dives back in over the outside corner. This is known as a "backdoor" strike. If thrown too far outside, it's a ball.

With a left-handed batter the risk is far greater, since the ball appears, at first, to head directly for the batter's waist before diving over the inside part of the plate at the last moment. If the pitcher misses too far inside against a lefty, the result is a hit batsman. If he doesn't throw inside enough, the ball will fall over the heart of the plate, every hitter's favorite zone. As Lowe pitched to the left-handed hitting Melhuse, he noticed the batter kept looking out over the plate, seemingly waiting for a pitch away. "You can't look for a pitch on both sides of the plate," Lowe thought to himself. That meant Melhuse would be vulnerable to his sinker, but in order to throw it he had to have complete confidence in his ability to execute the pitch perfectly. It took Lowe a long time—almost a year and a half—to get to the point where he was comfortable throwing it against left-handers in game situations. Now, he had to have faith he could do it again. With two strikes on Melhuse, he settled into his windup, aiming the ball directly at him. It worked perfectly. Lowe froze the A's hitter. The ball tailed back over the inside corner. Strike three.

Lowe pitched around center fielder Chris Singleton, walking him rather than risk throwing a hittable strike. With two outs and the bases loaded, Terrence Long pinch-hit for Frank Menechino. With the entire Coliseum crowd on its feet, Lowe worked Long to two strikes. Once again, he turned to his sinker. For the half-second it took the ball to travel the 60 feet, six inches from the mound to the plate, hundreds of thousands of Red Sox fans across the country had the same thought: "Perfect. Boston will take a lead into the ninth inning of a deciding playoff game and blow it on three walks and a hit batsman." As Long tensed in advance of the inevitable impact, the ball cut down and in, landing in Jason Varitek's glove on the inside corner of the plate.

For a moment, no one moved. Varitek's glove stayed perfectly still. Long looked down at home plate. Lowe peered in from the mound. And then home plate umpire Tim Welke turned to his left and rung up the batter. Strike three. Game over. For the second time in five years, the Red Sox had come back to win a five-game series after losing the first two games.

Though it wouldn't be long before Lowe's agent would hire a sports psychologist in an effort to determine why Lowe alternated between being one of baseball's best and one of its worst pitchers, on this night, at least, Lowe seemed impervious to the pressure. "The biggest thing you have to do is trust it," Lowe said later. "I found myself in situations [during the game] where I've thrown this pitch a hundred times. Throw it through the target, and it worked out well. I've thrown it that well before, but it goes unnoticed because it might be strike one in the second inning to the number seven hitter."

Tom Werner was watching the game from one of the Coliseum's luxury boxes, and when Lowe struck out Terrence Long, he had to fight back tears. The game had been incredibly unpleasant for Werner—sheets of clear glass divide Oakland's luxury boxes from one another, and a drunken fan in the next box had spent the game cursing at Werner and writing obscene notes he'd press against the glass. (The fan was eventually arrested.) As he watched Lowe's pitch settle perfectly into Varitek's glove, Werner "felt blessed. . . . With the Padres, we had never gotten to the postseason, and here we had just won our first series [as owners of the Red Sox]."

Boston's celebration that night was tinged with anxiety—Johnny Damon was still in the hospital, where he'd remain overnight. But both the Red Sox and Derek Lowe felt as if they'd lifted a monkey off their backs. "I don't know anyone else in baseball with as much heart as Derek to throw those two pitches," Theo Epstein said in the Red Sox clubhouse after the game. "I think we put a few things behind us historywise, winning this kind of game and this kind of series."

Come morning, no one would think a first round series against the Oakland A's gave Boston the right to put anything behind it, historywise. Up next, for the right to play in the World Series, were the New York Yankees.

## CHAPTER 25

# *Not Again*

**LESS THAN 48 HOURS** after clinching their first round series in Oakland, the Red Sox were loosening up at Yankee Stadium. The team was in rough shape. After Monday night's game, Johnny Damon had been diagnosed with a serious concussion, and while he remained on the Red Sox roster, he wasn't sure whether he'd be able to contribute meaningfully. Byung-Hyun Kim was left off the team entirely. Since Pedro Martinez had pitched the final game of the Oakland series, he'd likely be unavailable until Game 3, and Lowe, the team's second-best starter, wouldn't be able to pitch until Game 2.

The Yankees, in contrast, were rested and healthy. They had dispatched their first round opponent, the Minnesota Twins, in four games, which meant none of their four starters—Mike Mussina, Andy Pettitte, Roger Clemens, and David Wells—had had to pitch more than once. While the Sox bullpen had been performing better recently, the Yankees had Mariano Rivera, the most dominant postseason closer in the history of the game. And, of course, the Yankees had history on their side, with their 26 championships, too many of which had come at the expense of Boston.

The Red Sox–Yankees series felt like the culmination of everything that had happened since Henry and Werner had bought the Red Sox less than two years earlier. From the day they were awarded the team, the group had spoken of their determination to beat the

Yankees and bring a World Series victory to Boston; it was as if a Series victory would count for less if the Sox didn't go through the Yankees first. The tension between the teams' front offices had been steadily building. George Steinbrenner was almost comically obsessed with the Red Sox. Some of his lieutenants joked that, judging from Steinbrenner's preoccupation with Boston, you'd have guessed it was the Red Sox who always seemed to have the upper hand. There was no love lost between the teams' players, either. Pedro Martinez was likely the most hated ballplayer in the Yankees clubhouse, while Boston fans still smarted from the sight of Roger Clemens in Yankee pinstripes.

Since the beginning of the 2002 season, Boston and New York had played each other 38 times, and the two teams were almost evenly matched—almost, but not quite. Both years, the Red Sox compiled a 9-10 record against the Yankees, even though in 2003 they outscored their rivals, 109–94. Before the series began, the Yankees were the favorites, but only by the slimmest of margins. In fact, for what felt like the first time in the team's long history, the Red Sox entered the 2003 American League Championship Series on more or less equal footing, and Boston and New York both knew it. Here, finally, was a Red Sox team that didn't fear the Yankees.

For the first game of the series, on Wednesday, October 8, the Yankees sent righty Mike Mussina to the mound. Back in 2000, Mussina had, along with Manny Ramirez, been one of baseball's prize free agents, and both the Red Sox and Yankees had pursued him. A five-time All-Star during his decade with the Baltimore Orioles, Mussina was one of baseball's most dependable pitchers.

He also was known as someone who was consistently good, but not quite good enough. He'd won 18 games in a season three times and 19 games twice, but the common benchmark for excellence, 20 wins, had always eluded him. Twice he'd carried a perfect game into the ninth inning only to have it slip away: On May 30, 1997, in an Orioles game versus the Cleveland Indians, Mussina gave up a hit with one out in the ninth, and on September 2, 2001, he lost a perfect game against the Red Sox with two outs in the ninth when, batting with two strikes, pinch hitter Carl Everett hit a single into left field. (Mussina also lost a bid for a perfect game with two outs in the eighth inning of a 1998 game against the Detroit Tigers.) A Stanford graduate, Mussina had a reputation for both being aloof and somewhat soft, and some of his former teammates had been known to refer to him as "Pussina."

Red Sox Game 1 starter Tim Wakefield could not have been more different. Whereas Mussina, a taut 6-feet-2-inches and 185 pounds, relied on pinpoint location of his fastball and an array of breaking pitches, Wakefield, a considerably dumpier 6-feet-2-inches and 200-plus pounds, was a knuckleball pitcher. Knuckleballs have been around almost as long as baseball has been played, and for most of that time, they've been held in only slightly higher esteem than a goof pitch. Watching Wakefield, it wasn't hard to see why. His pitching motion looked ridiculous next to the simultaneously violent and balletic windups of his teammates and rivals. Instead of using his fingers to grip the ball, he perched the ball between his thumb and his three middle fingers, his pinkie extended as if he were a cartoon aristocrat daintily holding a flute of champagne. Wakefield heaves the ball toward the plate more than throws it, coming down on his legs in quick succession as if he were hopping inelegantly over a puddle. Whereas many pitchers—like all four of the Yankees starters—had fastballs that clocked at over 90 miles per hour, a typical Wakefield pitch came in at somewhere between 60 and 70 mph.

What the knuckleball lacked in speed it made up for in unpredictability. It seemed to flutter toward the plate—like a butterfly, batters often said—dancing up and down, side to side.* Corralling the knuckler was so exhausting that Wakefield had what amounted to his own private catcher, Doug Mirabelli, and even Mirabelli had to use an almost comically oversized mitt while working behind the plate.

Historically, knuckleballers were known as being as flighty as

---

* Befitting the knuckleball's reputation as a rogue pitch, it's difficult to describe why the knuckler dances without an advanced knowledge of physics. Here's the simple version: The knuckleballer's grip allows him to release the ball with virtually no spin. As the stitches on the ball interrupt the flow of the air around the ball, pockets of lower pressure are created, and they send the ball dropping downward.

their signature pitches, but Wakefield, the longest tenured member of the Red Sox, was as stand-up a guy as could be found on a major league roster. After Wakefield was drafted as an infielder by Pittsburgh in the eighth round in 1988, a Pirates minor league coach saw him fooling around with a knuckleball one day and converted him to a pitcher. In 1992, his rookie year, Wakefield went 8-1 and won two playoff games for Pittsburgh. Two years later, he'd been demoted to the minors, and when Pittsburgh cut Wakefield early in the 1995 season, the Red Sox quickly signed him. He was an excellent acquisition for Boston that year, going 16-8 with a 2.95 earned run average and finishing third in the Cy Young Award voting. Over the next eight seasons, Wakefield filled almost every role on the Sox pitching staff, working as a starter, a closer, and a middle reliever. In an often-unpredictable Boston clubhouse, Wakefield became the very measure of constancy, quietly going about his business, concentrating on his knuckleball, his family, and his charitable endeavors. Still, as beloved and respected as Wakefield was, Boston fans weren't eager to see him on the mound in Game 1—Wakefield, after all, had been left off the Red Sox roster the last time the team made the American League Championship Series, in 1999.

On this cold night in the Bronx, Wakefield's knuckler was dipping and floating like a drunken honeybee. At one point, from the second to the seventh innings, he retired 14 straight New York batters. Boston's hitters weren't having any such problems with Mussina, as both David Ortiz and Manny Ramirez bounced back from their power outages against Oakland. In the fourth, Ortiz drove a ball into the third deck of Yankee Stadium, and Ramirez and Todd Walker followed up with homers of their own in the fifth. By the end of the night, Tim Wakefield had earned his first playoff victory since his 1992 rookie year with the Pirates, and the Red Sox had won Game 1, 5–2. The next night, the Yankees' Andy Pettitte bested Derek Lowe, 6–2, leaving the series tied at a game apiece as the teams headed to Fenway Park.

Game 3, on the afternoon of Saturday, October 11, was already being billed as the matchup of the century. For the second time in five years, Pedro Martinez, the best Red Sox pitcher of the 1990s, would take the mound to face New York's Roger Clemens, the best

Red Sox pitcher of the 1980s. The first time the two fireballers met in the postseason—on October 16, 1999—it was a Boston rout, with Clemens not making it out of the third inning and Martinez striking out 12 en route to a 13–1 Boston victory.

It was clear early on this would be no repeat. Martinez didn't have his best stuff, and in the fourth inning, the game was tied, 2–2. After Martinez gave up a run on a walk, a single, and a double to lead off the inning, New York began doing the unthinkable: taunting one of the best pitchers ever to play the game. "You've got nothing," they shouted from the bench. Martinez, one of the proudest men in baseball, didn't acknowledge the Yankees, but it was clear he'd heard the jeers. With men on second and third, Martinez went into his windup, reared back, and sent one of his fastballs sailing toward the head of Karim Garcia, a little-used Yankees outfielder. The pitch hit a shocked Garcia in the back. Sox catcher Jason Varitek hadn't even retrieved the ball when Martinez had snapped his glove up, indicating he wanted it back. Martinez, as he'd done so many times in his career, had delivered a message: Whatever you do, don't disrespect me.*

As Garcia and Martinez began jawing at each other, the Yankees bench joined in the fray, with Clemens, catcher Jorge Posada, and 72-year-old Yankees bench coach Don Zimmer the most verbal. Martinez later said that Posada had been screaming at him in Spanish and had at one point insulted Martinez's mother. "Posada is Latin," Martinez said. "He should know, if you don't want to fuck with someone, you don't say anything about their mother." Before play resumed, Martinez pointed first at his head, then at Posada. He was, he said later, only telling Posada he'd remember what he said. Others had a less generous interpretation, and lip readers swore Martinez was mouthing "I'll hit you in the head" to the Yankees catcher. Whatever the message, the Yankees scored another run before the end of the inning, giving New York a 4–2 lead.

Manny Ramirez led off the bottom of the fourth inning, and

---

* It's worth noting that in the three-plus innings he pitched before hitting Garcia, Martinez gave up six hits and a walk. In the four remaining innings he pitched that day, not a single Yankees batter reached base.

Clemens, in the fourth pitch of the at-bat, threw a ball that was high and inside—a purpose pitch, one designed to back Ramirez off the plate, but not one close enough to the hitter to be of much concern. Ramirez saw it differently, and began yelling at Clemens before starting toward the mound, bat in hand. The melee that followed added another ugly chapter to the Red Sox–Yankees history. Many baseball fights are little more than show, with both teams assembling around home plate and puffing out their chests before everyone goes back to their respective benches. This one was for real, and it culminated with the elderly Zimmer charging directly at Martinez. "He reached for my right arm," the right-handed throwing Martinez said later. "I thought, 'Is he going to pull it? Is he trying to hurt me?' " Martinez stepped to the side and pushed Zimmer down in a movement that resembled a matador dodging a bull. It had been Zimmer who ran at Martinez, but the image of the voluble pitcher flinging an elderly man to the ground further cemented Martinez's status as New York's favorite villain. The fact that the Yankees held on to beat Martinez and the Red Sox, 4–3, did not dull their anger any.

On Monday, Wakefield beat Mussina for the second time in a week, and the 3–2 Boston victory tied the series at two games apiece. After David Wells beat Derek Lowe in Game 5, the two teams headed back to the Bronx. Boston needed two consecutive wins to advance. An improbable Boston victory in Game 6—the Red Sox rallied from a 6–4 deficit in the seventh inning against Jose Contreras, the Cuban pitcher whose acquisition by the Yankees had prompted Lucchino's "Evil Empire" comment—created a Martinez-Clemens rematch on October 16, 2003. Game 7, winner take all. Fittingly, the game would mark the first time in baseball history two teams had faced each other more than 25 times in a single season. Dan Shaughnessy called the matchup "hardball heaven in the Hub, potentially the greatest sports event in the long history of our city."

While John Henry and Larry Lucchino made the trip to New York for the final game of the series, Tom Werner remained at home in California. He was still rattled by his experience in Oakland during the final game of the previous playoff series, and he'd had a particularly unpleasant encounter in Yankee Stadium back when he was the owner of the Padres. While Werner walked through the stands wearing a Padres cap, a fan pushed him and told him to take off his cap. Werner glanced up at a nearby policeman, and after he was pushed again, Werner asked the cop if he would do anything about the situation. "He said to me, 'You're lucky he didn't slug you,' " says Werner. On this night, he'd watch the game from home. John Henry was sitting in seats near the visitors' dugout, while Epstein was in a seat directly behind home plate.

Now, finally, momentum seemed to be on the Red Sox's side. Johnny Damon had gutted his way back into the lineup, and had worked three walks the night before. Nomar Garciaparra had emerged from his postseason slump, and Ortiz and Todd Walker continued pounding the ball. Down three games to two, the Red Sox had been expected to fold, but hadn't. Now the pressure was on New York. And early in the game, the pressure seemed to be getting to them. Clemens didn't make it out of the fourth inning, while Martinez was cruising. After six innings, it was Boston 4, New York 1. As Martinez sat down in the Boston dugout between innings, he turned to assistant trainer Chris Correnti. "Chris," he said, "I'm a little fatigued."

In the seventh, Martinez did appear to tire. With one out, Jorge Posada hit a sharp drive to center field, which Damon caught. Jason Giambi followed with his second home run of the game, and the next two Yankees batters reached on hard-hit singles. With two out and the go-ahead run at the plate, Martinez struck out Alfonso Soriano in a six-pitch at-bat, bringing his pitch count for the game to 100. As he walked off the mound, he looked at the sky and pointed in the air, his way of acknowledging God after a night's work. Boston pitching coach Dave Wallace pulled out a notebook from his pocket, crossed out Martinez's name, and wrote in Alan Embree's, whom he assumed would start off the eighth to face the left-handed Nick Johnson. Both Correnti and Wallace indicated to Martinez his night was over, and Martinez began heading toward the steps that led from the dugout to the showers.

In the stands, both Theo Epstein and John Henry also assumed Martinez was finished, and, with six outs to go, they felt confident the team's bullpen could finish the game. The relievers' spring troubles were well in the past. Even without Kim, the combination of Embree, Mike Timlin, and Scott Williamson had been dominant in the playoffs, combining for 22⅔ innings in which they gave up only 12 hits, 4 walks, and a single earned run, while striking out 25. It was one of the most overpowering bullpen performances in recent memory, and all three pitchers were ready to go. What's more, as Epstein had told Little time and time again, the Pedro Martinez you get with pitches one through 105 was vastly different from the Pedro Martinez you got from pitch 106 on. The former was an all-time great; the latter very mortal, particularly that season, when hitters' batting average against him leaped from .231 on pitches 91 through 105 to .370 on pitches 106 through 120.

Little, however, suddenly decided he couldn't depend on his bullpen. Perhaps he was thinking back to the first game of the Oakland series, or to the team's early season struggles, or maybe even to 1986, when Roger Clemens left Game 6 of the World Series with the Red Sox leading 3–2 only to watch from the bench as his team lost the game. Little stopped Martinez just as he was exiting the dugout. As Martinez later told *Sports Illustrated*'s Tom Verducci, Little asked him, "I need you to go one more [inning]. Can you give me one more?"

"I didn't know what to say," Martinez told Verducci. "If anything happens, everyone will say, 'Pedro wanted to come out.' I wasn't hurt. I was tired, yes. I never expressed anything about coming out. The only way I would say that is if I was physically hurt. The only way." As David Ortiz hit a home run off David Wells to give the Sox a 5–2 lead, Martinez told Little he could give him one more inning. "I'll tell you what, Petey," Martinez said Little told him. "Why don't you try to start the eighth. I might even send you out there just to warm up. Help is on the way." At that point, Martinez said later, he assumed that if even a single runner reached base, Little would summon Embree from the bullpen.

When Pedro Martinez returned to the mound in the eighth inning of Game 7, John Henry felt as if he were watching a horror movie. He knew Martinez was spent; hell, Henry thought, any sentient being watching the game knew the pitcher was cooked. He looked over at Epstein, sitting a couple of sections away, and the two men caught each other's eye. Epstein gave a little shrug, as if to say, "I have no idea what he's doing out there, either." Martinez got the first batter to pop-up to shortstop, putting Boston five outs away from victory, and a trip to the World Series. Then, in an instant, the Yankees bats began lashing at Martinez's pitches. Derek Jeter sized up a shoulder-high 0-2 fastball and smacked it into right field, where Trot Nixon misplayed a catchable ball into a double. With Bernie Williams at the plate, even the TV announcers were saying that, regardless of what happened here, Embree would likely come in to face the left-handed Hideki Matsui, who was on deck. Williams hit a sharp single to center, scoring Jeter, 5–3.

Now, finally, Little shuffled out of the dugout and over to the mound, where he conferred with Martinez. In his seat, Henry was beside himself. At least, he reassured himself, there's still a two-run lead and Martinez was finally coming out of the game. Then, inexplicably, Little walked back to the dugout alone, leaving Martinez on the mound to face the dangerous Matsui. Henry turned to Lucchino. "Can we fire [Little] right now?" Henry asked. "I felt pure rage," he says. Matsui proceeded to hit the Yankees' second double of the inning, sending Williams to third. By this point, Martinez had thrown 118 pitches. His average during the season was less than 100, and he very rarely went over 110. What's more, only a couple of weeks earlier Martinez had thrown 130 pitches in the first game of the Oakland series, the most pitches he'd thrown all year. Now, even Martinez was convinced his night was over.

Still, Little stayed in the dugout. With his nemesis Jorge Posada at the plate, Martinez reared back and threw a cut fastball for ball one. He got a called strike with his next pitch, a curve, before missing again with the third pitch of the at-bat. Another curve fooled Posada into swinging, evening the count at 2-2. Now, with his 123rd pitch of the night, Martinez threw a 95 mile-per-hour fastball in on Posada's hands, which Posada fisted into shallow center field, where it dropped. As Posada scrambled to second base, he saw that both Yankees runners had scored, tying the game. He began to clap his hands furiously. Here, finally, was retribution for all the times Martinez had mockingly referred to Posada as "Dumbo" because of his large ears, retribution for Saturday's Game 3, when Martinez had looked at Posada and pointed at his head. Only then, with the game tied, did Little hurry out to the mound and take Martinez out of the game. There was no pointing at the sky this time around. As Yankee Stadium howled—Posada later said it was louder than he'd ever heard it—Martinez walked back to the Red Sox bench, his head hanging.

For the remainder of the eighth and the ninth innings, Alan Embree and Mike Timlin did what they had been doing all series—they shut down the Yankees. In the 10th, with the game in extra innings, Little summoned Tim Wakefield, who had two wins in the previous six games and would undoubtedly have been the series MVP had the Red Sox found a way to win. Wakefield retired Matsui, Posada, and Giambi on 14 pitches in the 10th. In the top of the 11th inning, Mariano Rivera, the Yankees closer, retired the Red Sox in order. It was Rivera's third inning of work, and he'd thrown 48 pitches—both highs for the season. As Wakefield prepared to pitch to light-hitting Yankees third baseman Aaron Boone in the bottom of the 11th, TV analyst Tim McCarver was telling viewers that the longer the game went on, the more it tilted in Boston's favor. After all, McCarver said, Wakefield could throw forever, and Boston still had Scott Williamson in the bullpen. Rivera, on the other hand, was likely done for the night.

Wakefield's first pitch to Boone didn't have the knuckleball's usual movement, and Boone took a mighty swing. As soon as it left the bat, it was clear the ball would not be landing in the park. As it soared toward the left-field bleachers, Boone threw his bat down and held both his arms in the air. He'd done it. Just like Bucky Dent 25 years earlier, Boone had hit a season-ending home run against the Boston Red Sox. As Boone ran the bases and the Yankees poured out of their dugout to embrace him at home plate, Tim Wakefield walked stoically off the mound, head down, convinced he'd just become the young century's Bill Buckner, that his name would forever be associated with yet another heartbreaking Red Sox failure. In the glum Red Sox clubhouse, Derek Lowe said, "If we played 100 times, I think we'd win 50 and they'd win 50." He was wrong. That year, it seemed that if the Red Sox and Yankees played 100 times, New York would win 51 games to Boston's 49.

In California, Tom Werner felt as if he'd been punched in the gut. "I was very devastated by that loss," Werner says. "I was experienced enough to know that it would be very difficult to get back to that position. It's so hard to even get to the postseason, and then it's hard to win a Division Series. We were very fortunate to have beaten Oakland. I just thought it would be very difficult." Werner was, he says, "comatose" for a couple of months.

Instead of feeling shock or sadness, the first emotion John Henry felt that night in Yankee Stadium was an anger bordering on rage. "I knew at some point he was going to blow the season for us," Henry says of Little. "And he did." When he got to the Sox clubhouse and heard Little telling everyone that there was no reason to be upset, that they'd had a great year and had entertained a lot of people, Henry had to hold himself back from erupting right there.

Adding even more poignancy to the loss was the fact that in the World Series the Yankees would face the Florida Marlins, the team Henry had sold just two years earlier. "As much as I love some of the Marlins players and root for them, I have no interest in watching this series," Henry wrote in an email in late October. "The only interest I currently have in baseball is to prepare for next season." He explained that the Sox's loss had taught him of the true devotion of the team's fans. "I thought initially New Englanders would just finally throw up their hands," he wrote. "But their level of commitment and resolve is astonishing and deserves our full attention." Theo Epstein and Larry Lucchino, Henry said, had not taken even a day's break following the team's defeat as they began preparing for the 2004 season: "The franchise is in very good shape with these two leading it," he wrote.

Henry was right: Neither Epstein nor Lucchino had taken any time off. By Friday, October 17, less than 24 hours after their season had ended, the two men were busy preparing for the next campaign. With Martinez, Lowe, Garciaparra, Varitek, and Trot Nixon all heading into the last year of their contracts, the powerful core of the team was beginning what was likely their final year together. The Red Sox would have one more chance with this crew, and they intended to make it count.

## CHAPTER 26

# Nomar Wants to Know Where He Fits in

**EVER SINCE HE WAS A CHILD,** Anthony Garciaparra was known by his middle name: Nomar, for his father's name, Ramon, spelled backward. He was born in Whittier, California, about 20 miles southeast of Los Angeles. Lithe and graceful, Garciaparra was a natural athlete, and by high school, he was being touted as one of the top baseball prospects in the country. Unlike many schoolboy phenoms, Nomar didn't much look the part: His prominent nose, delicate cheekbones, and skinny frame gave him the appearance of a Baroque painting, and his high-school classmates gave him the nickname "Glass," because he appeared as if he might break. When he was just 17, Garciaparra was drafted by the Milwaukee Brewers; instead of signing with the team, he opted to go to Georgia Tech, whose varsity baseball team at the time also featured future Red Sox catcher Jason Varitek. In 1994, the Sox made Garciaparra the 12th pick of the draft. Two years later, on the last day of August 1996, Garciaparra made his Red Sox debut, and played in most of the team's games during the last month of the season.

The mid-1990s were barren years for the Red Sox. Outside of a division title in the strike-shortened 1995 season, Boston fans found little to cheer about between 1992 and 1996. In 1997, Garciaparra changed that. Twenty-four years old, skinny, and a bit guarded, the young shortstop was filled with odd superstitions and perversely fascinating routines. When heading out for his turn at bat, he'd climb on each step of the dugout with both feet, almost like a child gingerly making his way up a flight of stairs. In the batter's box, he repeated the same obsessive routine—tapping his toes into the dirt, adjusting and readjusting his batting gloves, genuflecting at the plate—before every single pitch of every single at-bat. ("It's important how my feet feel and the way my hands feel," Garciaparra once explained.) All of this would have been seen as distracting, or perhaps even annoying, except for one fact: The preternaturally talented Garciaparra was hitting the ball like no Red Sox rookie since Fred Lynn two decades earlier. By the end of the year, Garciaparra had put up truly awesome numbers, hitting .306 with 30 home runs, 98 runs batted in, 209 hits, and 22 steals. He set a major league record for RBIs by a leadoff batter, and his 30-game hitting streak broke the American League rookie record by four games. A unanimous selection for the American League Rookie of the Year, Garciaparra, by the end of his first full year in baseball, had become the public face of the Boston Red Sox.

Boston fans wholeheartedly embraced the quirky, oftentimes shy Mexican-American kid from Southern California. Three months into the 1997 season, the *Globe*'s Gordon Edes compared Garciaparra's arrival in Boston to the first 100 days of the Kennedy administration. Edes would later write how Boston fans and sportswriters alike realized they were witnessing "one of the greatest players to put on the uniform of the Olde Towne Team, a toe-tapping, glove-tugging manifestation of all the qualities we hold so dearly in ballplayers who steal our hearts: an obvious love for the game, a run-out-every-pop-up effort, a priority list that placed winning as a team over individual achievement."

During spring training of 1999, Garciaparra's prodigious skills were acknowledged by Ted Williams, the greatest Boston baseball legend of them all. "Boy, I'm looking at someone who is going to be as good as anyone who ever played the game," the wheelchair-bound Williams said, gazing at Garciaparra sitting next to him. "I say that, and boy, I believe it, too. And the best thing about it, he's a terrific kid. Boy, he's got so much going for himself. You'll be here, 10 to 15 years from now, singing the praises of Nomar Garciaparra. I can't say enough about him."

But the role of savior in baseball-obsessed Boston was not one to which Garciaparra was well suited. Despite the almost universal acclaim he received, he soon discovered that the constant attention and scrutiny made him uneasy, even upset. Over time, his natural sensitivity morphed into a paranoid thin-skinnedness, a dangerous characteristic for a star in a town where some of the city's columnists view knocking local sports icons as a kind of civic duty. Within a couple of years of arriving in Boston, even as he was being fulsomely praised as one of the greatest players ever to wear a B on his cap—and even though he seemed to be the only athlete in town immune from criticism—Garciaparra began to keep track of every slight, real or imagined, and would spend hours a day thinking about how he was being, or might be, portrayed by the press.

"[Playing in Boston is] like playing three games a day," Garciaparra says. "You play the mental game of preparing for the press before the game, and the questions you have to answer then. There's the mental anguish of the game itself, and the mental anguish of what you have to talk about at the end of the game." Whereas some players barely speak with the press and others don't worry much about what they say, Garciaparra devoted the same obsessiveness to his interactions with the fourth estate as he did to his batting routine. During games, Garciaparra says he'd often think about what he had said in the clubhouse before the game. "How are they going to take it? What's it going to come out like? You focus on the game but you are thinking about that," he says. As soon as a game ended, Garciaparra would begin worrying again: "OK, what are they going to ask me [now]? How am I going to answer?"

Since baseball's inception, the shortstop has been acknowledged as the most important defensive player on the field. Unlike the other infielders, who are to a greater or lesser extent tied to their bags, the shortstop is free to roam. Since most hitters are right-handed, their natural swing carries the ball toward left field,* meaning the shortstop will see far more balls than any other player in the field. What's more, for balls hit to the third base side of the shortstop, the player has to run in one direction, field the ball, stop, set himself, and throw all the way across the diamond to first.

Because they were so important on the field, even elite shortstops tended to be only average offensive players. Take the Brooklyn Dodgers' Pee Wee Reese, who averaged fewer than 10 home runs a year, or the Yankees' Phil Rizzuto, who hit only 38 homers in his entire career. Perhaps no one personifies this model better than the St. Louis Cardinals' Ozzie Smith, nicknamed the Wizard. The 150-pound Smith hit under .260 in nine out of his 19 seasons in the majors and averaged just one-and-a-half home runs a year. He was elected into the Hall of Fame in his first year of eligibility.

The Baltimore Orioles' Cal Ripken changed the conventional wisdom concerning what a shortstop could do. At 6 feet, 4 inches and well over 200 pounds, he looked more like a prototypical slugging first baseman. In 1982, at age 21, Ripken hit 28 home runs, the first of six straight years in which he hit more than 25 homers. Ripken was just as good with his glove, and over his 19-year career, he won two Gold Glove awards at short. Aspiring ballplayers suddenly realized that playing shortstop didn't mean neglecting their offensive skills.

By the late 1990s, the impact of Ripken's ascendance was clear. Those years were a golden age for shortstops. Garciaparra, Derek Jeter, and Alex Rodriguez were three of the best players in the game, and their friendly rivalry only stirred interest in these hard-hitting field marshals. The game hadn't seen three similarly dominant and popular players at one position in a half-century, since future Hall of Famers Mickey Mantle, Willie Mays, and Duke Snider patrolled center field for the Yankees, the New York Giants, and the Brooklyn

---

* Since a right-handed batter stands on the left side of the plate, a hit to right field would be to the "opposite" field. The follow through of a batter's natural swing means the ball will usually go to the same side of the field on which he's standing; to hit a ball to the opposite field, a hitter needs to punch the ball rather than drive it. Hitters who can consistently hit opposite-field home runs are relatively rare for this reason.

Dodgers in the 1950s. From 1998 through 2000, Garciaparra could make a valid claim to being the best of the bunch. While playing defense, he exhibited what seemed to be a philosophical refusal to set his body before he threw, and his acrobatic contortions as he whipped the ball to first base while on a full run became as iconic as his prepitch batter's box routines. On offense, he was nothing less than a monster. He hit .357 in 1999, and followed that up with a .372 average in 2000.

At that point, Garciaparra was in the third year of a five-year deal he'd signed in the spring of 1998, when he'd had only one full season under his belt. The contract was worth $23.25 million, for an average of $4.65 million a year, and the Red Sox held options worth around $11 million a year for 2003 and 2004. Neither Jeter nor Rodriguez had signed this kind of lucrative contract early in his career. Instead, after the 2000 season, both players signed gaudy long-term deals.

By that point, Rodriguez, only 25 and already eligible for free agency, was seen as the person most likely to be considered the next decade's best all-around player. He had excellent power, intense ambition, good range, and was a threat on the base paths. Garciaparra was good, to be sure, but he wasn't quite as fast, wasn't quite as savvy a base runner, hit for a little less power, wasn't as good a defender, and perhaps most important, was two years older. In December 2000, Texas Rangers owner Tom Hicks offered Rodriguez an incredible $252 million, 10-year deal. It was, many said at the time, a foolish move: Rodriguez's next-highest suitor offered around $100 million less. But Hicks thought Rodriguez would bring him, and the Rangers, instant credibility. That same winter Jeter, who out of the three marquee shortstops had perhaps the highest baseball IQ but the lowest level of natural ability, was signed to a 10-year deal for $189 million. That was also a hugely inflated price, but it was what Yankees owner George Steinbrenner was willing to pay to ensure that Jeter, who'd joined the team as a full-time starter as a 21-year-old in 1996, spent most of his career in New York. Those deals came to gnaw at Garciaparra. "He felt like he was in the same category as an A-Rod or a Jeter," says Johnny Damon, "and that he should be paid like that. . . . At the time when

Jeter signed that contract, Nomar was actually considered the better player."

As the years went by, Garciaparra, often known simply by the Bostonism "Nomah" or the affectionate diminutive "Nomie," became more and more beloved throughout New England. By the time he retired, he would, everyone agreed, take his place in a pantheon that included Boston sports heroes like the Bruins' Bobby Orr, the Celtics' Larry Bird, and Ted Williams. In the spring of 2001, he was honored with the cover of *Sports Illustrated*'s baseball preview issue. "A Cut Above," read the headline. "How Nomar Garciaparra made himself the toughest out in baseball."* Garciaparra was photographed shirtless, holding a baseball bat parallel to the ground, a Red Sox cap perched on his head. His face, with its high cheekbones and aquiline nose, was immediately recognizable to any baseball fan in the country. But the body bore little resemblance to that of the skinny rookie who had impressed the world four years earlier. His waxed chest was bulging, his latissimus dorsi—the middle back muscles that run from just below the shoulders to the waist—so large they were clearly visible from a straight-on frontal shot.

Days later, Red Sox officials announced that Garciaparra would be sidelined for a couple of weeks with a split tendon in his right wrist. Garciaparra said he wasn't sure what, exactly, had caused the injury. He'd first hurt his wrist a year-and-a-half earlier, when, on September 25, 1999, Baltimore's Al Reyes hit him flush with a pitch, but he had been able to play most of the 2000 season with only minor pain.

The uncertain cause of Garciaparra's injury, coupled with his muscle-bound *Sports Illustrated* cover appearance, put the first chinks in Garciaparra's armor. The late 1990s featured an unprecedented display of power across baseball, as hitters like Mark McGwire, Sammy Sosa, and Barry Bonds smashed balls out of ball-

---

* Even in 2000, the year he hit .372, Garciaparra was far from the toughest out in baseball: That year, he was eighth in on base percentage, behind, among others, Jason Giambi, Frank Thomas, Gary Sheffield, and Barry Bonds, all of whom hit below .335. As on base percentage became more valued, Garciaparra's free-swinging ways were increasingly frowned upon.

parks in unprecedented numbers. Before 1997, there had been only six single season performances in the history of the game in which a player had hit more than 55 home runs. From 1997 through 2001, the feat occurred 11 more times. Rumblings about a steroid problem in Major League Baseball were just beginning, and Garciaparra's injury added him to the list of suspect players: Tendon tears are one common side effect of steroid abuse, as bursts of training and sudden muscle growth overload static tendons and ligaments. During his year on the sidelines, Garciaparra, who had always been obsessive about his image and his routines, found the occasional whispered questions increasingly difficult to bear.* He became even more distrustful of the local press and felt boxed in by the constant attention he received.

Garciaparra made a near-full recovery in 2002, batting .310 with 24 home runs. By the end of the season, he was back among Boston's beloved. At the same time, he was growing more bitter about what he saw as his below-market contract. Even in his rookie year, Garciaparra thought, he'd hit for a higher average, hit more home runs, had more runs batted in, and had more hits than Jeter and Rodriguez. On the Red Sox, both Manny Ramirez and Pedro Martinez, neither of whom would ever be accused of being team players, were making more. "You look at your teammates, what they are making," Garciaparra says, speaking in detail for the first time about his con-

---

* In 2004, when the debate over steroid testing was at its peak, Garciaparra became one of the most outspoken opponents of Major League Baseball–implemented testing. "I don't trust testing," he said. "Testing is just not the answer." In April 2005, Garciaparra crumpled to the ground when running out of the batter's box; he had torn his groin when muscle ripped away from bone. That injury resulted in printed speculation about possible steroid use. "Look, I'm hardly the first person to raise the question," Bob Ryan wrote in the *Globe*. "[H]e did go from, like, standard athlete issue normal to ultra-buffed in one winter, and he has been . . . systematically breaking down for the past six years." Garciaparra angrily laughed off the accusations. "If I was taking steroids, can I send them back and get the good ones?" he said that year. "Cause these don't work. . . . I just laugh. I mean, come on. It's ridiculous." Garciaparra began the 2006 season with a strained rib-cage muscle. That injury occurred during Garciaparra's first at-bat of the spring's final exhibition game.

tract negotiations with the Red Sox. "Manny's making 20 [million dollars a year]. Pedro's making 17 [million]. You see where you fit in, you see what you do. Alex is making 25 [million], Jeter's making 19 [million]. I mean, where do I fit it in? Let's figure it all out."

As this was occupying the obsessive Garciaparra, Henry, Werner, and Lucchino approached Garciaparra and his agent, Arn Tellem, to begin discussions about a contract extension. Garciaparra had two years left on his deal, but the three partners all agreed they wanted to find a way to keep the shortstop on the team for the long term. "We saw him as a potentially iconic figure for the franchise," says Lucchino. The three Red Sox executives met with Garciaparra and Tellem on John Henry's yacht during spring training in 2003.

That day, the Red Sox proposed a four-year contract extension worth $60 million, which would keep Garciaparra with the Red Sox at least until he was 35. Lucchino says the Red Sox were obviously aware that this was a lower annual salary than Jeter and Rodriguez had gotten a few years before, but they felt it was a fair offer, even a generous one. "We tried to explain that there seemed to be a changing landscape, a changing market," Lucchino says. Indeed, since Rodriguez, Jeter, and Ramirez had signed their deals before the 2001 season, no one else had gotten a deal worth $20 million a year.

"I said, 'Great,' " Garciaparra says. "Four years, $15 million, fine: We agree on that. That is great. What I would like, though, I asked for a signing bonus for $8 million." That would bring the average annual value of his contract to $17 million—"less than everybody [else]," Garciaparra points out, referring to Boston's two highest paid players, along with Jeter and Rodriguez—but still enough so that he wouldn't feel resentful. In Garciaparra's mind, the signing bonus would actually be divided up between the next two years of his previously signed deal, when he was slated to make about $11 million a year. That way, he says, the four-year extension would feel more like a six-year deal at $15 million a year. In either case, Garciaparra says, he thought that they'd agreed on a baseline from which they'd work as they moved forward. "Shoot," he says, "I'm already accepting the $15 [million]."

The Red Sox, however, saw things differently. "We just weren't doing a contract for that kind of money," says Lucchino of Tellem and Garciaparra's $68 million counteroffer, "so it was kind of back to the drawing board." The two sides agreed to keep talking, but when no deal had been reached by the beginning of the season, they decided to revisit the issue at the end of the year. "I thought, great, we're almost there," says Garciaparra. "Let's go into the season and we'll work out the specifics afterwards." In Garciaparra's mind, this would already cost him the $4 million of his requested "signing bonus" that he'd wanted to tack onto his 2003 salary. "My thought throughout the season was, 'One season's over, I probably won't get that $4 million.' . . . I don't know if they really grasped it."

Certainly nothing happened during the 2003 season to make Garciaparra feel that his value had dropped. That year, he made his fifth All-Star team and, even after a horrendous end-of-season slump—he hit only .170 in September—he ended the year at .301 with 28 home runs and 105 runs batted in. "It was an exciting year," he says. "Everything was great, and going into the offseason, now it was just a matter of hearing from them."

## CHAPTER 27

# *The Epic Offseason Begins*

ON SATURDAY, OCTOBER 25, 2003, 23-year-old Josh Beckett pitched a complete game shutout on short rest to lead the Florida Marlins to a World Series victory over the Yankees, four games to two. Two days later, on the morning of Monday, October 27, the Sox told Grady Little he wouldn't be invited back for the 2004 season. Little's dismissal surprised no one. The local media predicted the Sox's search for a new manager would take center stage alongside the questions of whether to pursue pitchers such as Bartolo Colon and Kevin Millwood, and how to fix the bullpen. "Boston's baseball brain trust is gearing up for one of the hottest offseasons in recent memory," the *Globe* wrote on October 29.

They had no idea. A series of deals made in the Dan Duquette era were all coming due at the same time, and four of the team's nine regular starting players (Garciaparra, Trot Nixon, Jason Varitek, and the Epstein-signed David Ortiz), as well as two of its five starting pitchers (Pedro Martinez and Derek Lowe), had contracts that expired at the end of the 2004 season. Epstein had never agreed with Duquette's approach, with its emphasis on a handful of big-name superstars who invariably demanded enormous contracts. He also thought that one of the team's historic problems was its fixation on immediate gratification. Instead of building a strong farm system that would produce high-quality players whose inexpensive early years would be under the team's control, the Sox scrambled year after year, trading away their future for the fantasy of succeeding in the present. Ironically, it was Epstein's very belief in long-term planning that emboldened him to shoot for the moon in 2004. The Red Sox wouldn't sign all of their impending free agents precisely because it wasn't worth paying exorbitant sums for stars on the downside of their careers. But there was no reason to waste the team they had. It was time for the Red Sox to go for it, and Epstein, by not gorging on high-priced contracts in his first year as general manager, had the flexibility to search for high-impact players who could be signed to reasonable deals.

Already, Boston was deep in talks with the Texas Rangers in an effort to trade for Alex Rodriguez, who, at 28, projected to have plenty more great years ahead of him. Since arriving in Texas, Rodriguez had performed pretty much as advertised. However, the Rangers had still gotten worse every year and finished in last place in the American League West three years running. Owner Tom Hicks decided he wanted to free up payroll, creating what seemed like a perfect opportunity for Boston. "[Hicks] called me and told me he was interested in moving A-Rod, and Boston was one of the places he was willing to go," says Lucchino. Hicks told Lucchino the Rangers wanted Garciaparra and some of the Red Sox's young pitchers in return.

The day after the 2003 World Series ended, Lucchino and Hicks met at the St. Regis Hotel in Manhattan. The market for Rodriguez, small to begin with, was shrinking: The Yankees had already told Hicks they weren't interested in trading for A-Rod. That day, Lucchino said Boston wasn't willing to part with Garciaparra, but they would consider a deal in which Texas would take Manny Ramirez. The Sox, according to John Henry, were hoping that should the deal work out, either Garciaparra or Rodriguez would move to second or third base.

Within days of this discussion, Henry, Werner, and Lucchino

had a meeting with Ramirez and his agent, Jeff Moorad, to discuss Ramirez's latest trade demands. Ramirez, who still had five years and almost $100 million in salary left on his contract, gave a list of teams he'd be willing to play for—both the Mets and the Yankees were acceptable, along with the Seattle Mariners, the Minnesota Twins, and the Toronto Blue Jays. If he weren't going to New York, Henry says, Ramirez indicated he "wanted to play in a city where he wasn't such a big deal to people, where there wouldn't be so much of a spotlight on him." Since a trade with one of those teams on Ramirez's list seemed unlikely, the two sides discussed putting Ramirez on irrevocable waivers, which meant that any team in baseball could claim him as long as they were willing to pay his salary. The Red Sox didn't expect anyone to claim Ramirez, but they hoped the process would prove to him that he had to be more realistic about his options.

When the news about Ramirez being placed on waivers was leaked, the response was swift and furious. The move, the *Herald* wrote, "tests the boundaries of weird" and "strongly suggests the Boston franchise has cast planning to the wind and blindly is flailing about in the aftermath of [its] difficult defeat [in the 2003 American League Championship Series]." As Jeff Moorad began telling anyone who'd listen that his client would love to play for the Yankees, Ramirez's teammates showed the extent to which they'd been upset by his behavior in 2003. "If he doesn't want to pull on the same rope as the rest of his teammates, then you know what, he can go somewhere where he can be happy," Kevin Millar said, while David Ortiz, who had made $1.25 million in 2003, said, "If I'm making that kind of money, I'd be happy even if I'm playing for the Tigers." (The Tigers finished the 2003 season with a record of 43-119, baseball's worst single-season record since the 40-120 record the New York Mets compiled in their inaugural 1962 season.) "That's some money, $160 million."

At the same time, Theo Epstein and Arn Tellem were renewing their discussions about Garciaparra's contract. Tellem was still pushing for a four-year deal whose average annual value was around $17 million. But the Red Sox felt that during the course of the season the market had shifted even more.* Two-thousand three's top free agent, the Montreal Expos' Vladimir Guerrero, wasn't expected to command a deal for even $15 million annually, and Oakland A's shortstop Miguel Tejada, the 2002 American League Most Valuable Player, was expected to sign for somewhere around $8 million.† The Red Sox were now thinking more along the lines of $12 million a year, still a sizable amount more than the initial offers Tejada was getting. But Tellem wouldn't budge. If that was the best the Sox could do, he said, then they should simply try to trade Garciaparra before the season began.

In the meantime, no one claimed Ramirez off of waivers, which meant that by the middle of November, the Red Sox had a $20 million per year left fielder who wanted out, an $11 million per year shortstop who was so insulted by the team's offer for an extension that his agent had told the Red Sox to trade him, and in Pedro Martinez, a $17.5 million per year starting pitcher who was already warning the team that if they didn't sign him to an extension before the season began, he wouldn't even speak with them once it was over. In the midst of all this, the Red Sox decided to pursue one of the most outspoken, controversial pitchers in baseball.

---

* Although Garciaparra's 2003 numbers were good, they were by no means outstanding. On his own team, he was tied for third in home runs, placed fourth in batting average, was fifth in slugging percentage, and tied for seventh in on base percentage.

† In January 2004, Guerrero signed a five-year deal with the Anaheim Angels worth approximately $70 million, or $14 million per year. Guerrero, in addition to being three years younger than Garciaparra, was by 2004 clearly a superior offensive player. Tejada, who is also three years younger than Garciaparra, ended up signing a six-year, $72 million contract with the Baltimore Orioles worth $12 million a year. Guerrero went on to win the American League MVP award in 2004.

## CHAPTER 28

# "This Is About Winning the World Series"

**THE BOSTON RED SOX** drafted Curt Schilling in 1986, the same year Roger Clemens was steamrolling his way to his MVP season. The two hurlers appeared similar: Both were hulking, 6-foot-4-inch right-handed power pitchers. There was, however, a major difference between them. Clemens had a tireless work ethic to go with his superior natural talent, while Schilling was a flake who talked too loud, drank too much, and jawed off in public. When, in 1988, the Sox traded Schilling (who was still in the minors) and Brady Anderson to the Baltimore Orioles for pitcher Mike Boddicker, there was no outcry, no concern that the Sox might have just gotten rid of a man who would become one of the most dominant pitchers of his generation. Indeed, in his first four years playing major league ball—three of which were spent with the Orioles and one with the Houston Astros—Schilling threw only 145 innings, had a record of 4-11, and looked like he was on the fast track toward becoming another hot prospect with plenty of natural talent and not enough determination or fortitude. In the 1991 offseason, the 25-year-old Schilling was working out in the Astrodome while Roger Clemens, then still the Red Sox ace, was using the facility's weight room. "I was kinda going through the motions of getting my time in, whatever I had to do," Schilling said later, describing that day. "Roger wanted to talk to me." Great, thought Schilling. He loved talking about pitching. But Clemens didn't want to discuss the vagaries of the split-fingered fastball. "I went over there and he proceeded to chew my ass off for about an hour and a half," Schilling said. "I had lost my father three years before that, and I had not really had that guy in my life that said, 'Listen, you know what? You need to sit down and shut up and listen. This is how it's going to work.'" Clemens told Schilling he was wasting his career and cheating the game. "I didn't turn it around that day . . . but I think it started that day," Schilling said. "That was the biggest step."

As far as the Astros were concerned, it was too late. Houston had given up on Schilling after just one year, and before the 1992 season, he was traded to the Philadelphia Phillies for reliever Jason Grimsley. It was in Philadelphia, with Clemens's admonishments still ringing in his ears, that Curt Schilling changed his approach to the game and began the hard work that would transform his career. His first year with the Phillies, Schilling won 14 games. He led the team in wins and strikeouts, and his 2.35 earned run average placed him fourth in the league. The next year, he led the Phillies' run to the World Series and began to establish his reputation as one of the best postseason hurlers in the history of the game, winning the National League Championship Series MVP award.

Schilling stayed in Philadelphia for eight and a half years until, midway through the 2000 season, he was traded to Arizona. His pitching seemed to improve as he got older. In 1997, at 30, Schilling struck out 319 batters. For many of his years with the team, the Phillies were awful: Following the team's 1993 trip to the playoffs, Schilling's Phillies teams finished last twice, and never placed higher than third. It was during these lean years that Schilling first met and became close to Terry Francona, who managed in Philadelphia from 1997 through 2000.

At the same time that he was building his reputation as a big-game pitcher, Schilling was also becoming known as a blowhard and an attention hog. More eloquent and outspoken than many baseball players, Schilling took it upon himself to let everyone— players, reporters, talk-radio hosts—know what he thought about everything ranging from politics to the management of the team. It was true that he'd become one of the best-prepared pitchers in baseball. It was also true that he took pains to let everyone know this. One of his former managers nicknamed Schilling "Red-Light Curt" because of how he gravitated toward television cameras, and Phillies general manager Ed Wade, referring to a starting pitcher's workload of one game out of every five, once said Schilling was "a horse every fifth day and a horse's ass the other four."

In Arizona, Schilling was teamed with Randy Johnson, and the two became the twin terrors of the National League. In 2001, Schilling's first full season with the Diamondbacks, he led the league in wins with a 22-6 record and posted a 2.98 ERA to go along with his 293 strikeouts, while Johnson went 21-6 with a 2.49 ERA and 372 strikeouts. The two pitchers were first and second in the National League in strikeouts, innings, and earned run average. It would be the first of two consecutive years in which Johnson won the Cy Young Award as the outstanding pitcher in the league and Schilling came in second. In the postseason, Johnson and Schilling almost single-handedly carried the Diamondbacks to their World Series victory over the Yankees.

Two years later, the Diamondbacks were in rebuilding mode. Diamondbacks owner Jerry Colangelo decided that Schilling, who was signed through 2004, would likely be on the block. Schilling had a no-trade clause in his contract, and he let it be known that there weren't a lot of teams he'd consider playing for and that he would need a contract extension before agreeing to a trade. He wanted at least two more years added on, which would take him through 2006, when he'd turn 40.

"[My wife, Shonda, and I] wanted to go somewhere that we were familiar and comfortable with, and we wanted to be on a contending ball club for the remaining years of my career," Schilling says. "I knew this was going to be the last contract for me. And the two teams that kind of jumped out at us were the Phillies and the Yankees."

It became apparent early on that the Phillies would not be suitors. "I made it very clear to them, through back channels, that I'd go there for a lot less than I ended up signing for, for a lot shorter period of time, because we wanted to go back to what we considered home," says Schilling. But it wasn't just about what Schilling wanted. He learned that he had burned some bridges in his first stint in Philadelphia, and returning to the team where he had made his name wouldn't be a possibility. That left New York. Schilling relished the idea of playing on baseball's biggest stage, and the Yankees, of course, were perennial postseason contenders. The Red Sox didn't really even cross his mind. "Boston wasn't a team I was even contemplating, because I didn't know anything about them," Schilling says. "I didn't know anything about the organization or the people."

Still, the Red Sox approached the Diamondbacks and asked what it would take to get Schilling. The Yankees, intent on pursuing Montreal's Javier Vazquez, had had only tepid discussions with Arizona, and it took only a couple of days for the Diamondbacks and the Red Sox to agree on a tentative package of players. When word leaked out that the Red Sox were interviewing Terry Francona as Grady Little's possible replacement, Schilling decided he might be willing to go to Boston after all. Within 12 hours of Schilling's informing Diamondbacks management that he'd consider going to the Red Sox, Boston and Arizona had finalized their deal: Schilling would go to Boston in return for pitchers Casey Fossum and Brandon Lyon and minor leaguers Jorge de la Rosa and Michael Goss.

Now came the hard part: The Red Sox had to work out the details of a contract extension with Schilling. Under Major League Baseball rules, once a trade has been agreed upon for a player who has a no-trade clause, the player and his prospective new team have 72 hours in which to negotiate. As it happened, this time fell on the Wednesday before Thanksgiving, Thanksgiving Day, and the Friday after Thanksgiving. Schilling, who prided himself on not using an agent, would represent himself.

"We'd been nonstop preparing for a couple of days" in anticipation of making a deal, says Jed Hoyer, then an assistant to general manager Theo Epstein. The team knew Schilling was concerned about Fenway's reputation for being a home run ballpark—Schilling, as a fly-ball pitcher, was susceptible to the long ball—so Epstein asked Bill James to work up a presentation on how

Schilling could be expected to perform in Boston. The team's baseball operations crew had put together DVDs illustrating how Clemens, who, besides being Schilling's idol, had a very similar pitching style, had performed in Fenway. Epstein and Hoyer investigated Schilling's personality, the best way to approach negotiations with him, what he'd expect from the organization, and what they could do to make him and his family feel comfortable in Boston. Schilling's wife was very active in philanthropies in Arizona, and both Schillings prided themselves on their involvement in their community. Epstein and Hoyer integrated all of this into their planned sales pitch.

On Tuesday, November 25, Hoyer and Epstein flew from Boston to Arizona. They brought with them a letter of introduction. "We thought it was a good way to start the negotiations," says Hoyer. It was, they agreed, a way to give Schilling a chance to think about some of the issues they hoped to address before the two sides actually sat down to meet Wednesday. But the two young baseball executives didn't know how to get the letter into Schilling's hands. They ended up taking a limo to Schilling's house and delivering it in person. Hoyer, who was 29 at the time, is less than six feet tall and looks as if he's barely out of college. When he rang the Schillings' bell, the 36-year-old Schilling answered the door in flip-flops and a T-shirt. Hoyer handed him the letter—awkwardly, he admits—and said they'd be back the next day at one in the afternoon.

On Wednesday, Epstein and Hoyer met up with Larry Lucchino, who'd flown in from San Diego, and the three men went to the Schilling house. For the remainder of the day, the two sides talked about Boston, about the front office's dedication to pitching, about ownership's goals for the team. The Red Sox executives knew how fanatical Schilling was about preparation, and they assured him they were equally committed to planning for every pitch of every game. They also appealed to his ego. What's one more championship for the people of New York, they asked. Win one in Boston, they told Schilling, and you'll be a god throughout New England for the rest of your life.

Schilling's initial wariness was noticeably softening. "The preparation they did in getting ready was big for me," he says. "It was impressive. It was clear, they're a very forward-thinking group of guys, and I knew that was going to mesh with what I was trying to do. There was just a lot of common ground." That night, the Sox made their initial proposal—three years with a club option for a fourth year or four guaranteed years at less money.

Schilling contemplated the offer, pointedly playing with his gaudy World Series ring. "Look," he said. "You guys are bringing me here for one reason. It's not to make the playoffs. It's to get beyond where you were last year and win the World Series. Let's make that very clear." Since that was the case, Schilling said, why not build in a World Series clause into his contract: If the team won the championship while he was in Boston, he'd get a raise for every year remaining on the deal. "I don't want a clause that says, 'If we make the World Series,' " Schilling said. "This is about winning the World Series. That's all I care about. That's what I'd be there for."

As Hoyer says, "We were like, 'Yeah. That's pretty cool.' " Lucchino had to return to San Diego for Thanksgiving, and as Hoyer and Epstein were preparing to leave, Schilling asked them what they were doing the next day. "This is your time," Epstein said. "We're just going to play some golf." Schilling insisted the two join his family for Thanksgiving. "I'll be insulted if you're not here," he said.

Epstein and Hoyer spent Thanksgiving at the Schillings' house, and after a couple of hours in which they ate turkey and watched football, they retired to Schilling's study and began talking numbers. The Red Sox initially offered around $11.5 million a year, along with a $2 million World Series clause. Schilling wanted at least $13 million a year as a base salary. When Epstein and Hoyer finally left for the night, with one day left before their 72-hour negotiating window closed, they felt a compromise was still a long way away. So, too, did Schilling. "Shonda and I, after Thanksgiving Day, were excited about the possibility [of playing in Boston], but disappointed because we didn't feel like it was going to work out," Schilling says.

Epstein and Hoyer returned to their hotel that evening, confident that Schilling would agree to sign if the Sox came up to $12.5 million a year. As Epstein called Henry and Lucchino to discuss the team's offer, Hoyer, who felt under the weather, returned to his room. Epstein discussed the team's other options with the team's owner and the CEO. Montreal's Vazquez still hadn't been traded and free agent Bartolo Colon was also available. Both of those pitchers were younger and would likely require less money. But Schilling, they felt, was worth going up to $12.5 million.

Hoyer, meanwhile, found himself in the throes of a vicious stomach virus that left him vomiting for much of the night. The next morning he tried to drink some Gatorade before going up to Epstein's suite to type out the team's final offer. While standing on Epstein's balcony he became nauseated once again. "I was looking out at everybody sunning themselves and I felt it coming," Hoyer says. "I tried to run back and ended up projectile vomiting in about three different places in Theo's room." After a hasty cleanup, Epstein and Hoyer set out to pick up Lucchino from the airport; from there, the three of them would drive back to the Schilling house to make the team's final offer. (Lucchino had to give Hoyer a pair of socks from his bag, since the only remaining pair of dark socks Hoyer had were speckled with puke.) "I spent the rest of the day just trying to move as little as possible," Hoyer says. "But since the three of us had been there on Wednesday, we thought we should all be there on Friday as well."

As the Red Sox executives were heading back to Schilling's house on Friday afternoon, they were hopeful they could seal the deal, but they knew that if Schilling didn't agree to their new offer, they'd have almost no time to renegotiate. When they arrived at Schilling's house, they presented him with their latest offer. Schilling took the piece of paper on which they had written out all of the specifics—the World Series clause, the award bonuses, the club option—and was silent for several minutes. Finally, he looked up. "I think we're really close," he said. The final deal was for three years and $37.5 million—an average annual value of $12.5 million a year—with a $13 million club option for 2007. The option, along with Schilling's $2 million raise, would vest automatically if Boston won the World Series. (For his part, Hoyer managed to avoid throwing up in the Schilling residence.)

Over the next several weeks, the Red Sox would make plenty of news. The team did, indeed, sign Terry Francona as its new skip-per—the interview with the former Philadelphia manager was, John Henry said, the single best interview he'd ever had in baseball. Francona seemed to intuit the need to combine a deft interpersonal approach with the utilization of as much information as he could possibly get his hands on. It was clear that Francona would never es-chew the detailed reports the team put together, as Grady Little did when, before the 2003 playoff series with the A's, he failed to even hold a hitters meeting for the Red Sox. The team also signed free agent closer Keith Foulke to a guaranteed three-year deal worth $20.75 million, with a $5.75 million option for 2007. The 31-year-old Foulke had gone 9-1 with 43 saves and a 2.08 ERA for Oakland in 2003, and was considered one of the game's elite relievers. It had already been a busy offseason. The rest of January and December would make the previous six weeks seem like a vacation.

CHAPTER 29

# The A-Rod Chronicles

**AFTER THEIR INITIAL DISCUSSIONS,** both the Red Sox and the Rangers tried to keep word of a potential A-Rod trade quiet. In early November, commissioner Bud Selig gave Henry and Rodriguez permission to meet in order to discuss a possible deal. It was an unusual move—teams are generally prohibited from negotiating with players before a trade has been made—but the desire of the Rangers, the Red Sox, and Rodriguez to get the deal done convinced Selig to make an exception. The meeting at Henry's house in Boca Raton was also unusual because Henry and Rodriguez met without Scott Boras, Rodriguez's agent and the man generally considered one of the shrewdest negotiators in the business. "We were concerned that we'd be less likely to have a deal with A-Rod if he didn't take a lead role in the negotiations," says Lucchino, a long-time Boras adversary. "If we just left it to Scott, we didn't think we'd be able to get from here to there. Scott's a very tough and difficult and time-consuming negotiator." Since Rodriguez had said emphatically that he wanted to come to Boston, the Red Sox were hoping they'd be able to restructure his contract, which still had around $180 million remaining on it, to be more palatable to the club. "We knew he'd be involved—we weren't trying to sidestep him entirely," says Lucchino of Boras. "We were just trying to get a little momentum going with respect to this deal because of the player's initiative."

Rumors about a possible swap began to circulate by the middle of November. When, on November 17, Rodriguez won the American League's Most Valuable Player award (David Ortiz placed fifth, Manny Ramirez sixth, and Garciaparra seventh), he spent most of that day's obligatory conference calls with reporters answering questions about where he'd be playing in 2004.

Then, on Saturday, December 6, the *Herald*'s Tony Massarotti broke the news about the face-to-face meeting between Rodriguez and Henry. Massarotti's scoop led to a frenzy of media coverage around the country. Garciaparra, who was in Hawaii honeymooning with Mia Hamm, whom he'd married just two weeks earlier, says hearing that the Red Sox owner had been personally wooing another shortstop was hurtful and insulting. Within days, Garciaparra and his agent joined the fray, with Garciaparra calling Boston's sports-radio station, WEEI, from Hawaii to say publicly that he wanted to remain in Boston. That same day, Arn Tellem called John Henry's discussions with Rodriguez "a slap in the face to Nomar." Garciaparra's goal, Tellem said, "which we've communicated to the Red Sox, has always been to return to the Red Sox and play out his entire career in Boston." No mention was made of Tellem telling Theo Epstein that the Red Sox would be better off trading Garciaparra than offering him $12 million a year. Henry, furious, responded by calling Tellem's comments "the height of hypocrisy."

Garciaparra says that he hadn't yet learned of the Red Sox's four-year offer for $12 million a year at this point, and therefore couldn't have told Tellem that he was so offended by the offer that he wanted to be traded. (Tellem, who wouldn't comment for this book, did arrange for Garciaparra to speak in an on-the-record interview.) Multiple sources on the Red Sox have independently confirmed the fact of Tellem's requests to the team, making it seem likely that Garciaparra's agent was fudging his client's position a bit in order to increase leverage with the team. This isn't unusual in baseball, where players rarely insist they be kept informed of every stage of the negotiating process. From the first days of their careers, ballplayers are told that team owners should in no way be trusted; after all, owners want to sign players for as little money as possible, and they don't think twice about trading or getting rid of a player who is no longer useful. Agents often become a kind of all-purpose confidant and advisor, and their advice is rarely questioned.

But the agent's actions and the player's best interests don't always coincide. It seems likely that when Epstein made the Red Sox's four-year, $12 million a year offer to Tellem immediately after the 2003 season, Tellem thought he'd be able to get the team back up to $15 million a year by telling them Garciaparra would rather be traded than sign such a deal. After all, there was no reason for Tellem to think at the time that the Red Sox were seriously considering a future without Garciaparra on the team. Instead, the Red Sox took Tellem's request that the team trade Garciaparra at face value. Tellem, says Henry, "made it pretty clear that we wouldn't be able to sign Nomar." The Red Sox might have kept on pursuing Rodriguez regardless, but this made the decision a whole lot easier.

Whatever the situation, Garciaparra insists that he thought the $15 million a year, four-year deal was still on the table. When, immediately after the spat between Henry and Tellem erupted in public, the Red Sox leaked to the *Globe* that Garciaparra had turned down the $60 million offer the team had made in spring training, Garciaparra was shocked.

"I was like, 'Whoa, what is going on here?' " Garciaparra says. "Since when did I turn it down? At what point did I reject this? I'm scratching my head." If Garciaparra wasn't upset before, he definitely was now, and the many months of negotiations were only fueling his paranoia. (At one point during the 2003 season, Garciaparra had confided to friends that he thought management was instructing the team's grounds crew to rough up the dirt in front of his shortstop position so he would have a harder time fielding balls. Garciaparra believed this was done so he would make more errors, lessening his value before he signed a new deal. He also told at least one person he thought the team was bugging his phone.) Just as upsetting as the front office's stance was the press coverage of the potential trade. Everyone, it seemed, preferred Alex

Rodriguez. Garciaparra, once seen as the heir to Ted Williams and Carl Yastrzemski, was the golden boy no longer.

By mid-December, newspapers around the country were reporting that a Rangers–Red Sox deal was all but completed. Boston would send Manny Ramirez (as well as some cash to help pay the $98 million still owed him) and minor league pitcher Jon Lester to the Rangers. The Rangers would send Rodriguez to the Sox, and Rodriguez, in return for getting the chance to play for a contender, would reduce the annual value of the years left on his deal. A corollary deal would send Garciaparra to the Chicago White Sox for outfielder Magglio Ordonez.

And that was supposed to be that. Garciaparra's teammates readied themselves for a new shortstop, a prospect that they were frankly looking forward to. "When you're talking about a guy who's going to be a leader and be the face of the organization, that's Alex Rodriguez," Kevin Millar said on December 16 on ESPN. "Manny leads in the batter's box and Nomar prepares himself to play hard every day but you're talking about a leader in Alex Rodriguez. . . . I mean, A-Rod's the best in the game."

Because of the high profiles of the players and the enormous sums of money involved, officials at Major League Baseball and the players association, the union for professional baseball players, had joined in the discussions even before a deal had been finalized. Gene Orza, a top union official, had given Rodriguez the requisite permission to discuss a restructuring of his contract with the Red Sox. According to an article by *The Boston Globe*'s Gordon Edes, Orza also called a top official in Major League Baseball's central office and said, "I want you to get word to Larry [Lucchino] that we'll do everything within our power to get this thing done—it's great for baseball and we love Alex—but I hope Larry doesn't abuse the process, as he is wont to do." Soon after, Lucchino and Orza had a conversation in which Orza reminded Lucchino that any reduction in the average annual value of a player's contract needed to be offset by some other "added benefit" that the player received.

The Red Sox and Rodriguez ended up working out a deal in which Rodriguez would cut approximately $4 million a year off the last seven years of his deal in return for some licensing rights and the ability to declare free agency at different points during the remaining years of his contract. When the two sides presented the deal to Orza, he was dumbfounded. No one had signed a contract for as much as $20 million in years, Orza said. That made the offer of free agency essentially worthless; there was no way Rodriguez would be offered a *more* lucrative contract in the future. Orza made a counterproposal he said the union would be able to accept, in which the Red Sox would save a total of about $12 million as opposed to $28 million. The Red Sox initially rejected Orza's figure, but both sides assumed they'd keep working toward a compromise.

Then, on the same night in which Orza had presented his proposal, Larry Lucchino issued a statement. "It is a sad day when the players association thwarts the will of its members," Lucchino said. "The players association asserts that it supports individual negotiations, freedom of choice, and player mobility. However, in this high-profile instance, their action contradicts this and is contrary to the desires of the player. We appreciate the flexibility and determination Alex and Cynthia Rodriguez have shown in their effort to move to Boston and the Red Sox."

The move was typical of Lucchino. Despite his unprecedented record as a CEO and despite the high esteem in which his many admirers held him, Lucchino had a hair-trigger sense of being slighted and often seemed to be spoiling for a fight. Now, not only was Orza angry, but Rodriguez, according to people close to him, was upset, both that Lucchino would give the impression he was speaking for Rodriguez and that Lucchino would draw Rodriguez's wife, Cynthia, into the picture. By trying to create the impression of a rift between the union and Rodriguez, baseball's highest paid player, Lucchino actually made it less likely Rodriguez would make a stand about the issue. Rangers owner Tom Hicks was annoyed as well, and within days, the Boston newspapers were reporting that Lucchino had been pulled off of the A-Rod negotiations and that Tom Werner had taken over.

Lucchino characterizes what happened differently. "I was frustrated," he says, talking both about the union negotiations and his efforts to get Hicks to reduce the amount of money he was asking for to augment Manny Ramirez's salary. "At one point, I was talking to Tom and John and I said, 'One of you guys should try to talk to [Hicks], maybe you'll have better luck.' And Tom said, 'I'll call him.'" John Henry agrees with Lucchino's recollection. "Larry went for Christmas to see his mother in Pittsburgh," Henry says. "We didn't send him out of town. Tom still tried to get the deal going, but it wasn't like we'd lost faith in Larry." In the coming weeks, there would be various attempts to resurrect a deal—all to no avail. By January, the Rangers and the Red Sox had ceased discussions.

Before long, the media began lacing into the Red Sox CEO, which tapped into Lucchino's sensitivity about always being the one to get blamed when things went wrong. Peter Gammons was one of the first to finger Lucchino, repeating his charges on ESPN and on his frequent radio appearances in Boston. On WEEI, Gammons said that Rodriguez was not a member of the Red Sox because of "Lucchino's infamous blast, [his] personal attack on Gene Orza." The local papers weren't being much kinder: the *Globe* wrote that "Lucchino's temperament and hubris had something to do with the . . . failed negotiations."

Theo Epstein, in contrast, was only growing in stature. In late 2003, *Esquire* profiled the young GM in its Genius issue. "All of the uncertainty about Epstein's age lasted about as long as it took for him to put together a delightfully entertaining ball club that made the playoffs and won more regular-season games than any Red Sox team since 1986," the article read, adding that Epstein had brought the Sox "into the modern baseball economy." Somehow, even the Red Sox's tumultuous offseason was being portrayed as a sign of Epstein's acumen. "Epstein's confidence is one of the most encouraging things the Red Sox have going for them these days," wrote Gerry Callahan in the *Herald*. "He can waive his highest-paid player or trade his two-time batting champ/folk hero, and not turn away in shame when he comes face-to-face with the disgruntled player." The press wasn't telling Bostonians anything they didn't already think; Epstein had been transformed into a folk hero in his hometown, and "In Theo we trust" became a kind of mantra for Red Sox Nation.

If the aborted A-Rod deal highlighted a distancing in the public perception between Lucchino and Epstein, it also amplified a growing rift between the two men. Although he never said so publicly, Epstein was inclined to agree with some of what was being said about his boss—Lucchino's comments *had* hindered the trade discussions. The fact that Epstein even felt this was itself a violation of Lucchino's code of honor, which dictated that subordinates must always be loyal to their bosses, in thought as well as in word and action.

"[Larry] believes that the loyalty in which he takes a bullet for his bosses is the same loyalty that his subordinates, he would hope, would have for him," explains Charles Steinberg, one of Lucchino's staunchest supporters on the team. "You are loyal up. . . . It's not that you say to your boss, 'You're right, bud, anything you say, bud, anything you want, bud.'. . . [You] argue, challenge, debate. And when it's over, you loyally carry out what your boss wants you to do." This time, Epstein wasn't taking the bullet, which meant Lucchino was feeling the full brunt of the media's fire.

Soon, the Red Sox CEO became convinced that Epstein had been one of the people who'd been telling the media that Lucchino was to blame for the offseason's follies. "Someone told Larry that Theo was at the bottom of that," says a high-ranking Red Sox executive. "At that point, Larry thought that Theo had committed a sin, and he never moved off of that. From December 2003, [Lucchino] operated on the assumption that [Epstein was] throwing [him] under the bus." Lucchino didn't confront Epstein about the perceived backstabbing. The relationship between the two men would never be the same.

PART V

# The World Champion Boston Red Sox: 2004

CHAPTER 30

# *Welcome to the Jungle*

**THE RED SOX** would begin spring training in 2004 with both Manny Ramirez and Nomar Garciaparra, two players they'd openly tried to get rid of, on their roster. The Yankees, meanwhile, had pulled off one of baseball's most stunning coups, snatching up Alex Rodriguez in a trade for second baseman Alfonso Soriano after the Red Sox and the Rangers had ended their discussions. New York would open the season with Rodriguez at third, Derek Jeter at shortstop, and the always dangerous Gary Sheffield in right field. Not only had the Sox lost out on A-Rod, they'd been embarrassed by the Yankees, who seemed to be operating more effectively and efficiently.

Even without all the offseason drama, the Red Sox looked to be in for a tumultuous year. There was, to start with, the issue of the players who had contracts expiring at the end of the year. While right fielder Trot Nixon quickly agreed to a three-year contract extension that would run through 2007, and Jason Varitek and David Ortiz seemed content to do their jobs and worry about their deals later, Nomar Garciaparra, Derek Lowe, and Pedro Martinez would all require lots of attention.

With all of this going on, the Sox came into camp loose and determined to avenge their painful playoff loss in 2003. Players like Ortiz and Kevin Millar hadn't been in Boston long enough to become fixated by the Curse or to worry they'd always lose to New York. Johnny Damon, who spent much of the offseason with lingering wooziness as a result of his concussion, arrived at spring training with a flowing beard and mangy hair and said he'd spent the winter chasing cars to stay in shape. He was soon dubbed "Jesus," and he greeted fans by flicking water at them from his water bottle and intoning, "Bless you, bless you all." Soon, T-shirts featuring a beatific Damon ringed with the inscription "W.W.J.D.D.: What Would Johnny Damon Do?" became a hot-selling item. When asked whether the previous year's loss convinced him of Boston's cursed fate, pitcher Bronson Arroyo quipped, "What curse? We have Jesus on our side."

Garciaparra, the most popular Red Sox player of the previous decade, now found himself on the outside looking in. Not only had management tried to dump him in the offseason, but the clubhouse's personality had clearly changed. "He was really worried about what was being said about him," says Damon. "Nomar was Mr. Boston, and then the media started coming down on him a little bit." The issue, says Damon, wasn't money—it was respect. "There's always all kinds of disparities in this game," he says. "Guys are always jealous if someone's making more than them."

By early March, it seemed as if even the team's contract negotiations would take a backseat to other concerns. Nixon injured his back driving to the Sox's spring home in Florida, and Garciaparra was sidelined with what was described as tendonitis in his right Achilles tendon, an injury that predictably became another flashpoint. Garciaparra insisted he suffered the injury in a March 5 exhibition game against Northeastern University, although he never was able to identify who hit the ball that struck him, and no one on the Red Sox seemed to have seen the incident. There were suggestions that Garciaparra had hurt himself playing soccer with his wife, Mia Hamm. And, while speculation didn't reach print, more than one reporter noted that for the second time in three years, Garciaparra was suffering from a suspicious tendon injury—a warning sign of steroid use.

Finally, the Red Sox were rocked by the arrival of Curt Schilling. Even before he signed his deal with Boston, Schilling had logged numerous hours on a popular Red Sox Internet fansite called Sons of Sam Horn. (Horn was a below-average slugger for the Red Sox in the late 1980s.) As soon as the deal was completed, Schilling became an active participant on the site, and quickly demonstrated why he had a reputation for being someone who liked to hear himself speak. In December, at the end of the A-Rod trade discussions, Schilling responded to press reports that Garciaparra had become estranged from some of his teammates by writing, "The media has no idea what the state of our clubhouse is, or isn't," despite the fact that the closest Schilling himself had been to the Red Sox clubhouse occurred in June 2002, when the Diamondbacks had played the Red Sox at Fenway Park. "Until you hear otherwise assume Nomar is doing just fine," Schilling wrote. "He's a grown man, and he doesn't need people reading tea leaves to tell you how he feels." Garciaparra, who says he had not spoken with Schilling about his feelings during this period, was, in fact, estranged from some of his teammates and upset by the Red Sox's overtures to Rodriguez.

A couple of weeks later, Schilling also belittled players who used agents to negotiate their contracts, a list that included almost every major league ballplayer except for himself. "At some point there becomes zero need to have an agent represent you," he wrote. With so many of the team's players entering their contract years, he went on to say, "If you have an ounce of integrity, pride, you know your place in that market, you know your worth within the sport." He followed this up by taking a swipe at Scott Boras, who represented both Derek Lowe and Jason Varitek, among others. "With someone like Boras," Schilling wrote, "the groundrules are laid out. . . . IF that's what a player is after, top dollar, then that's your guy I guess. I have never liked Scott Boras, nor anything he's done." Despite the fact that almost none of the other players on the team were known to frequent the website, word of Schilling's late-night missives got around. Before spring training even began, some players were saying it seemed as if Schilling thought he was better than they were. For a player who made a point of how perceptive he was, Schilling failed to take an accurate pulse of his new teammates, and his constant appearances, newly ubiquitous ad campaigns, and self-anointment as the new face of the team rankled many of Boston's players.

No one was more upset by Schilling's arrival than Pedro Martinez. Thirty-two years old, Martinez had been the best pitcher in baseball for most of the six years he'd been with the Red Sox, and in 2004, he would be the highest paid pitcher in history. Martinez had begun his career with the Los Angeles Dodgers, where manager Tommy Lasorda had questioned whether the slight Martinez, listed at 5 feet, 11 inches but actually about an inch shorter, had the size or stamina to be a successful starting pitcher. He was traded to the Montreal Expos before the 1994 season, where the fiercely proud Martinez blossomed into one of the most dominant hurlers in the history of the game. "I just didn't like the comments they made about being too small, and not being able to last 200 innings," he said. "It was good being able to prove them wrong." In the late 1990s, Martinez featured a ferocious fastball that he could throw at more than 95 miles per hour, but his dominance stemmed from the fact that his changeup and his curveball were also so devastating. This combination of three "plus" pitches, Bill James once wrote, was the difference between Martinez being good and being one of the all-time greats.

Impish and playful, Martinez lived by his own set of rules. Since coming to Boston in 1998, Martinez habitually arrived at spring training late, clowned around in the dugout, and skipped the team's annual photo. But once he was on the mound, no one questioned his fierce competitiveness. For all his light-heartedness, Martinez was also driven by an irrational (and slightly contrived) fear of being disrespected, and the Red Sox's pursuit and acquisition of Schilling gnawed at him. Boston, after all, was supposed to be his town. "I can't help that they wanted to sign Schilling," Martinez said in February. "If it doesn't belong to me, it doesn't belong to me. If I don't belong in Boston, it's up to Boston. They run the team. They know what they're doing." Instead of viewing his new teammate as one more weapon in the Red Sox's arsenal, he saw Schilling's arrival as a potential challenge to his supremacy. Days before the season started, he asked a reporter, "If they want him [more than me], why don't they just say that?"

Martinez's wounded pride could, potentially, have been a good thing for the Red Sox. Martinez was often most effective when he felt as if he had something to prove—witness his transformation after Tommy Lasorda questioned his potential. But in 2004, Martinez was in a much different place than he had been a decade earlier, when the Dodgers shipped him to Montreal. No one questioned his abilities anymore; by this time, the debate was whether his 1999 and 2000 seasons had been the best two-year run ever by a pitcher. Now, Martinez was more worried about his health than his legacy. He'd missed much of the 2001 season with a frayed rotator cuff, and ever since then, there'd been speculation in the press that his shoulder hadn't fully healed. More recently, there'd been concern about Martinez's labrum.*

Rotator cuff tears and labrum tears both occur for the same reason—the force used to throw a baseball rips apart the very supports that are supposed to hold the human shoulder together—but players can generally rebound from rotator cuff injuries, while ripped labrums often mean the end of one's career.† What's more, labrum tears are almost impossible to detect with any degree of accuracy; the only real way to tell the extent to which a labrum is damaged is to do exploratory surgery. Most shoulder trouble manifests itself as pain that comes when throwing hard, and that discomfort often brings with it an attendant loss of speed. Labrum tears may also cause a pitcher to feel a catch in his overhand pitching motion. Since 2002, Martinez, as the Red Sox baseball operations staff was well aware, had taken to throwing from a three-quarter-arm angle

---

* The rotator cuff is a group of four muscles that secure the humerus, or upper arm bone, to the shoulder socket. The labrum, a thin sheath of collagen, rests between the head of the humerus and the scapula, or shoulder blade, functioning as both connective tissue and as a shock absorber.

† Curt Schilling, who had surgery in 1995 to fix his labrum, is perhaps the only pitcher of note to come back from a labrum tear to anything like his previous form.

more often, eschewing the full overhand delivery that is more powerful but carries more risk.

Martinez knew all too well that an injured shoulder could mean the end of a once-great pitcher's career. By the time Martinez arrived in Los Angeles in the early 1990s, his older brother, Ramon, had already established himself as one of the Dodgers aces. Ramon Martinez was one of his younger brother's biggest influences; Pedro had once said, "What I know about baseball and life off the field, I owe to my brother, Ramon." Ramon Martinez instructed his younger brother to become as fluent as possible in English because it would ease his transition into professional baseball. Ramon never was fully comfortable with English, while Pedro became the best-spoken non-native English speaking player in the game.

In 1990, at age 22, Ramon went 20-6 with a 2.92 earned run average and struck out 18 batters in one game. In 1995, Ramon went 17-7 and threw a no-hitter against the Florida Marlins.* After that season, he signed a three-year deal with the Los Angeles Dodgers, with a club option for 1999, and from the beginning of the 1996 season through the middle of June in 1998, Ramon compiled a 32-14 record with an ERA of 3.34. The Dodgers, it was all but assured, would exercise his option for 1999. Pitchers with his track record were valuable commodities.

But, on June 14, 1998, the 30-year-old Ramon Martinez injured his shoulder. An MRI revealed he had tears in both his rotator cuff and his labrum, and the Dodgers cut him loose. Ramon pitched only 164 more major league innings in his entire career—70.1 innings fewer than he'd pitched in his first full season in Los Angeles. In 2000, while playing with the Red Sox, he amassed a 6.13 ERA. He

---

*Pedro Martinez has never thrown a no-hitter; however, 41 days before Ramon's no hitter, Pedro threw nine perfect innings while pitching for the Montreal Expos against the San Diego Padres. The Expos failed to score until the top of the 10th. In the bottom of the 10th, Padres left fielder Bip Roberts led off with a double. Martinez got credit for the win, but under baseball rules Martinez's 27 consecutive outs to begin the game did not count as either a perfect game or a no-hitter.

started four games in 2001 for the Pittsburgh Pirates, giving up 15 earned runs in 15⅔ innings. And after that, his baseball career was over. The lesson for his younger brother was clear: Career-ending injuries can occur at any moment.

With Schilling on board, Martinez wondered if the Red Sox were planning on keeping him around beyond the 2004 season, and without a contract, he was both hesitant to risk further injury and worried about giving the impression he was less than totally healthy. Martinez's anxiety about pitching during one season before he knew if he'd get paid for the next had been apparent since 2003, when, during spring training, he began agitating for the Red Sox to pick up his 2004 option. Now, when he spoke of Grady Little's decision to leave him in during Game 7 of the previous fall's American League Championship Series against the Yankees, he talked not of the fact that the game was on the line but of the risk to his arm. "I was actually shocked I stayed out there that long," he told *Sports Illustrated*. "But I'm paid to do that. I belong to Boston. If they want me to blow my arm out, it's their responsibility."

The same fragility that made Martinez anxious about securing a long-term deal made the Red Sox concerned about giving him one. "The arm angle Pedro had in spring training was very worrisome," says John Henry. When Henry asked one of the team's top baseball operations executives what kind of season Martinez would likely produce, the answer stunned him: "I was told, 'He'll win 12 or 15 games, have a 4.00 ERA or a 3.50 ERA.' And I was like, 'Fuck.' " Despite this prediction, the team wanted to re-sign its star. "I thought he should finish his career in Boston," says Henry. In an effort to hedge their bets, the Red Sox tried to find a local insurance company to insure Martinez's contract. Henry thought the move could be a public relations coup for the insurer, especially since Martinez had agreed in advance to do advertisements for whichever company signed on.

"We essentially struck a long-term deal," says Henry of the preseason negotiations with Martinez. "We didn't come to complete terms on dollars, but we pretty much had a deal—it was just about getting insurance. And we couldn't. . . . [The insurance companies] took the position that the worst thing that could happen is for people to know publicly that they've insured him, because if he breaks down, they'll look like idiots." As spring training wound down, Martinez and the Red Sox remained at a stalemate, but continued talking.

## CHAPTER 31

# *Treading Water*

**CURT SCHILLING AND KEITH FOULKE** were obviously the offseason's biggest pickups, but, just as he'd done the year before, the Red Sox looked for undervalued players they could snap up. They'd signed Calvin "Pokey" Reese, a two-time Gold Glove winner, to a one-year, $1 million contract to play second base, and nabbed Mark Bellhorn from the Colorado Rockies in exchange for a minor leaguer. Bellhorn, who made less than a half-million dollars in 2004, was just the type of player Boston was inclined to take a flier on. Most years, he had a low batting average, a high on base percentage, and had some stretches during which he'd hit for considerable power. The Sox had also re-upped Byung-Hyun Kim to a two-year deal worth $10 million, with the intention of having Kim pitch as one of the team's starters.

On April 4, the Red Sox began their season in Baltimore. Nomar Garciaparra and Trot Nixon were both on the disabled list. Pedro Martinez got the start, and Gabe Kapler took over in right field with Bellhorn manning second base and Reese playing shortstop. The Sox lost, 7–2, and while Martinez pitched well, he wasn't dominant. Two days later, Curt Schilling made his Red Sox debut, going six innings and allowing only one run while striking out seven. It was Schilling, the team's new star, and not Martinez who set the tone for the rest of the month, in which the Sox went 15-6. More than a third of Boston's victories came at the expense of its rivals from New York, with the Red Sox winning six out of seven contests against the Yankees. (Almost as satisfying as the wins was the fact that Alex Rodriguez, the latest pinstriped villain, went 2-for-17 in his first four-game series at Fenway as a member of the Yankees.) The Red Sox pitching staff looked as if it might be poised for a historic season, and at one point late in the month, the team's pitchers threw 32 consecutive scoreless innings—more than three full games' worth.

Then, on April 30, as the Red Sox sat in the visiting clubhouse in Arlington, Texas, waiting for a thunderstorm to pass, Martinez decided to chat with the *Herald*'s Michael Silverman, his favorite reporter on the beat. Martinez told Silverman he was cutting off all negotiations with the Red Sox until season's end. "I'm just really sad for the fans in New England who had high hopes that . . . I was going to stay in Boston," Martinez said. "[The fans] don't understand what's going on, but I really mean it from my heart—I gave them every opportunity, every discount I could give them to actually stay in Boston and they never took advantage of it. Didn't even give me an offer." His contract status, he said, wouldn't be a distraction for him or the team "because I'm not going to allow it."

The Red Sox proceeded to lose the next five games, including one the next day in which Martinez gave up six runs in only four innings. Boston stumbled through May, a month in which the team went 16-14 and lost its lead over the Yankees in the American League East. Derek Lowe, after talking in spring training about how a dominant year would only make him more expensive for the Red Sox to re-sign, was particularly bad, and became convinced the team was trying to limit his effectiveness in order to drive down his price on the free agent market.* He went 1-4 with an 8.19 earned run average in May. The Derek Lowe Face was back with a vengeance.

---

* After consecutive April rainouts, Terry Francona decided to simply skip one of Lowe's starts instead of moving everyone in the rotation down a couple of days; as a result, Lowe didn't pitch from April 7 to April 18. He spent the rest of the season thinking the Red Sox had conspired to deny him a chance at another win and were trying to throw off his rhythm. As the season progressed, he became more and more upset.

But there was good news for Boston, too, in the forms of Manny Ramirez and David Ortiz, the team's Dominican sluggers. Ramirez, after repeatedly asking for a trade and moping his way through 2003, began 2004 on an inauspicious note. Despite his and his agent's constant conversations with Red Sox management during the offseason, Ramirez had unleashed a bizarre rant on Red Sox executives during spring training, calling them "motherfucking white devils" for trying to trade him to the Rangers. His introduction to Terry Francona, his new manager, wasn't much better. When Francona first saw the star at spring training, the manager stuck out his hand to introduce himself. Ramirez responded by swearing at him as well, and proceeded to skip the start of the first team meeting of the spring.

None of that frustration or unhappiness followed Ramirez into the season. Red Sox staffers joked that he seemed to have gotten either a personality transplant or access to some strong medication. In 2004, he was not only hitting as well as ever, he also seemed to be having fun for the first time since arriving in Boston in 2001. On May 10, Ramirez missed his first game of the season—but only, he said, so he could travel to Miami for a ceremony granting him U.S. citizenship. Upon returning to the team, he joked with reporters, "It was 15 questions. They give you the book. It's not hard." The next day, he ran jubilantly onto the field, waving a small American flag. About a month later, Ramirez flubbed a routine fly ball in the top of the ninth that would have sealed a 1–0 victory against the Los Angeles Dodgers. Upon returning to the dugout, he sat down and deadpanned, "Well, there goes my Gold Glove," as his teammates burst into guffaws. (The Sox won the game, 2–1, in the bottom of the ninth.) Ramirez later explained, not very convincingly, that he'd always wanted to be more outgoing but was insecure. "I decided to open up more to the press because before I was kind of shy," he said. "But I try to give [reporters] five, 10 minutes, at least guys are going to say, 'I know he's not that good [speaking English], but at least he's trying to talk to us to get to know him.'" Ortiz and Ramirez combined for 41 home runs in the first half of the season, and Ortiz, with little fanfare, signed a two-year extension with the Red Sox that would keep him in Boston through 2007.

For all their offensive prowess, the Red Sox were having trouble getting into a groove. Even when Schilling and Martinez performed like the dominant duo the Sox had envisioned, the rest of the club seemed to falter. In June, for example, the two aces at the top of the Red Sox rotation went 7-1, while the rest of the staff went 4-13. Some of the problem was erratic starting pitching—Derek Lowe in particular continued to struggle—and some of it was an increasingly porous infield defense. For that, Nomar Garciaparra, still generally considered the most popular Red Sox player of the last decade, got most of the blame.

Garciaparra rejoined the Red Sox on June 9, after missing the first 57 games of the season. He received a rousing welcome from the Fenway faithful in his first trip to the plate, and responded by smacking a single to left, prompting another standing ovation. But already it was clear that the relationship the city of Boston and the Red Sox had with Garciaparra had been altered. At the press conference announcing his return to the team, Garciaparra was asked whether his mysterious injury had been a case of the shortstop "sticking it" to the only team he'd ever played for. Even Garciaparra's approach to the game was being criticized. His penchant for swinging at the first pitch of an at-bat, regardless of where it was in the strike zone, was at odds with the Red Sox's new organizational philosophy, which tried to teach batters to force opposing pitchers to throw lots of pitches. Balls he'd once been able to drive were now coming off of his bat as weak flares, and soon, "Nomie" was increasingly being referred to with a new nickname: "Garciapopup." Unlike Pedro Martinez, whose intelligence allowed him to remain a dominant pitcher even after his years as a physically blessed flamethrower had passed, Garciaparra seemed simultaneously confused by his inability to perform as he once had and unwilling to alter his approach to the game. Just as glaring as his diminished offense was his woefully erratic defense, which drew a sharp contrast to his April and May replacement, fan favorite Pokey Reese.

The quiet, businesslike Reese was, in many ways, a throwback to an earlier era when shortstops were expected to play spectacular defense and not much else. Reese fit that description perfectly, and during his first several months on the team, he made spectacular plays seem like the norm, as he vacuumed up balls hit anywhere near him. During the times he did have success at the plate, Boston fans responded by showering him with adoration.

Take his performance in a May 8 game against the Kansas City Royals. In the fifth inning, Reese hit a ball deep into Fenway's right-field corner, and as it rolled around, Reese scrambled around the bases for an inside-the-park home run. The next inning, Reese hit a ball over the Green Monster. He'd hit only two home runs all year, and they came in successive innings. The crowd called him out for a curtain call and chanted his name in the traditional Fenway singsong for the rest of the game.

Garciaparra's return, coupled with the surprising offensive prowess demonstrated by shaggy-haired Mark Bellhorn, exiled Reese to the bench. Garciaparra, who'd always been less effective going to his left, was further limited by his heel injury. The contrast with Reese grew starker as Garciaparra began making errors on routine plays, missing balls, and throwing wildly. On rare occasions he was even booed, and every now and then, in a quiet moment at Fenway, a fan would shout "Pokey's better!" into the night.

A June 13 home game against the Los Angeles Dodgers encapsulated the relative fortunes of Garciaparra and Reese. It was Garciaparra's fourth game back, and he'd picked up only one more hit since the single in his first trip to the plate. Martinez was on the mound, and in the seventh inning the Red Sox were leading 4–1. Martinez's pitch count was mounting, and the seventh would likely be his last inning of work.

Adrian Beltre began the inning by grounding out to third. Juan Encarnacion was up next, and he hit a grounder up the middle, just off of the second base bag. Garciaparra ran to his left but couldn't quite reach the ball in time. With Encarnacion on first, Martinez struck out Olmedo Saenz, bringing Alex Cora to the plate. Cora roped a grounder in between shortstop and third base, and while Garciaparra was able to get a glove on the ball, he couldn't make a play.

Both of the runners that reached base had hit the ball in Garciaparra's direction, and while the shortstop wasn't given an error on either play, there was a palpable sense at Fenway that had Reese—

playing second base for the night—been at short, the inning would have been over. Now there were men on first and second with two outs and Dodgers center fielder Dave Roberts at the plate. A base hit would likely score a run, and it would almost certainly be the end of Martinez's night. What had felt, only moments earlier, like a sure victory began to appear less secure. Roberts, known more for his speed than his bat, hit a flare that looked to be headed directly into center field, and the fans at Fenway let out a collective groan. Then Reese, playing about 10 feet to the right of the second base bag, hurled his body upward, his arm stretched out at full extension. "I thought the ball was in the outfield already," said Martinez after the game. Reese was able to snare the ball in the top of his glove, and as he tumbled back down to the field, the crowd erupted. "It wasn't real!" said Martinez, as he ran over to Reese. Fenway began a thunderous chant of "PO-KEY, PO-KEY." It was still going strong in the bottom of the seventh, when Garciaparra popped out to third base to end the inning.

By the end of June, the Red Sox were badly slumping and Garciaparra had become as dispirited as he'd been at any point in his professional baseball career. His teammates were telling reporters—on background, of course—that he'd become a distraction, always moping around his locker just to the left of the clubhouse door. When the Red Sox baseball operations office took an informal poll among players about whether they'd be upset if Garciaparra was traded, virtually everyone agreed it would be better for Garciaparra and the team if he were playing somewhere else. Kevin Millar, Johnny Damon, David Ortiz, and even Manny Ramirez personified the free-spirited, fun-loving Boston Red Sox. Garciaparra didn't seem to fit in with the team's new mood.

When the Red Sox headed into Yankee Stadium for a three-game series on June 29 and 30 and July 1, Boston had lost five of its last eight games and was trailing the Yankees by five-and-a-half games. In the three weeks since he'd been back, Garciaparra hit just .233 with a single home run. The Yankees series did not begin auspiciously: Garciaparra made an error during the Yankees' first at-bat. Three innings later, another Garciaparra error led to three un-earned runs for the Yankees, who cruised to an 11–3 win. The next night, an eighth inning error by Garciaparra preceded two more Yankees runs, and the Sox lost, 4–2.

The last game of the series felt like a must-win contest for Boston. Martinez was on the mound, matched up against Brad Halsey, essentially a spare part called on to make a handful of replacement starts for New York. Garciaparra, who'd played the last nine games in a row, was not in Boston's starting lineup; both Garciaparra and manager Terry Francona said only that the shortstop needed to rest his heel.

From the outset, the game had the makings of an exciting contest. In the first inning, the Yankees' Gary Sheffield stepped out of the batter's box after Martinez had already begun his windup. Moves like this are part of the normal gamesmanship that occurs in baseball, but for Martinez, it signaled an unacceptable lack of respect, and he nailed Sheffield in the back with his next pitch. The Yankees scored first, on a two-run Tony Clark home run in the second, and Jorge Posada followed that up with a solo shot in the fifth. Pokey Reese made a breathtaking catch to end that inning, as he raced from shortstop into foul territory outside of third base to catch a Kenny Lofton pop-up. Reese slammed into the wall separating the field from the seats and jackknifed into the stands, but still managed to hold onto the ball. In the sixth, Manny Ramirez put the Sox on the board with a two-run shot, and Boston tied the game the next inning. The score stayed knotted at 3–3 for the rest of the seventh, the eighth, and finally through the ninth and 10th innings.

In the top of the 11th, Boston loaded the bases with nobody out. Kevin Millar hit into a double play that didn't score a run, leaving men at first and second with two out. Everyone, it seemed, knew what would come next: With weak-hitting Dave McCarty due up, Terry Francona would send Nomar Garciaparra to the plate to pinch-hit.

But Garciaparra didn't stir from his seat on a corner of the Red Sox bench, far removed from the rest of his teammates, who were huddled together on the top step of the dugout, nervously watching the action out on the field. McCarty stepped up to the plate—and flied out to end the inning.

Garciaparra's absence was made all the more glaring by what

happened an inning later. With two outs and runners on second and third in the top of the 12th, Trot Nixon lofted a ball that looked as if it would land just inside the third base line for a fair ball; if it dropped, both runners would probably score, giving Boston its first lead of the night. As soon as the ball left Nixon's bat, Derek Jeter took off on a dead sprint from his position at shortstop. He somehow managed to snag Nixon's flare, but his momentum propelled him forward, and he tumbled into the stands. When he emerged, his face bruised and his uniform bloodied, he still had the ball in his glove. Inning over.

The Red Sox finally scored in the 13th inning on Manny Ramirez's second home run of the game. They looked poised to add more when Boston put two men on with one out, but Cesar Crespo, a lifetime .192 hitter, was sent to the plate as Garciaparra again remained on the bench. Crespo hit into a double play, and in the bottom of the 13th, the Yankees rallied to win the game, 5–4.

Now, for the first time, Garciaparra is willing to talk in detail about what happened that night. "I couldn't play that day," says Garciaparra. When Garciaparra talks, he often gets a slightly bemused look on his face, as if he almost feels sorry for the people who can't see the truths so readily apparent to him. "It was funny, because everyone knew that I wasn't going to play every fifth day because of my [Achilles] tendonitis . . . but prior to the Yankees game I played sixteen games straight." (Garciaparra had played in nine straight games previous to July 1.) That night, Garciaparra says, the trainers told the coaching staff that he should rest his ankle. "The trainers are going, 'You haven't had a day off,' " he says. "I didn't ask for one." When the game went into extra innings, Garciaparra says he told Francona he was available to pinch-hit, and even tried at one point to get loose. He was, he says, sitting alone on the bench only because it was his good luck spot. When he tried to move, he says, "My teammates go, 'Get back in your spot because we need to score some runs.' "

Francona has a different recollection of the game. At the winter meetings following the 2004 season, Francona told Red Sox beat reporters that Garciaparra had asked to sit out the game because he was upset about the three errors he'd committed in the first two games of the series. After Reese's and Jeter's spectacular catches, Francona said, Garciaparra asked into the game. Francona refused to play a player who had already made clear he would put himself and his own sensitivities above the team.

No sooner had the four-hour-and-23-minute game ended than commentators began referring to it as the best regular-season contest ever played. Even the Boston players agreed. "It was one of the best games I've ever seen," said Martinez in the clubhouse, adding, "You saw Jeter over there leaving his skin and everything, his body, out for the team." His rebuke to Garciaparra couldn't have been much clearer. The Red Sox, with their $127 million lineup, had lost eight of their last 11 games and were now eight-and-a-half games behind New York. Since May 1, the team had gone a miserable 27-29. The 2004 Boston Red Sox, the team that had been assembled specifically for the purpose of making a last-chance run at a title before the team's powerful core hit the free agent market, seemed to be a bust.

If the July 1 game against the Yankees was one of the low points of Boston's 2004 season, another contest against New York three weeks later may very well have turned the season around. On Friday, July 23, the Sox opened up a three-game series against the Yankees at Fenway. The Yankees were leading 7–4 in the sixth, before the Sox picked up a run in three straight innings, two of them on Kevin Millar home runs. (Millar had three four-baggers on the night.) But, in the ninth, Alex Rodriguez drove in the game-winning run off Keith Foulke who, after a bout of early season dominance, had blown four of his last six save opportunities.* At the end of the day, Boston was

---

* Foulke was rightly credited as being one of the most valuable members of the 2004 team. It's worth comparing his numbers with those of Byung-Hyun Kim's from a year earlier. From July 1, 2003, through the end of the season, the period during which Kim served as the Red Sox closer, he converted 16 of 19 saves, for a success rate of 84 percent, and put up a 2.28 ERA. In 2004, Foulke converted 32 of 39 saves, for an 82 percent success rate, with an ERA of 2.17.

nine-and-a-half games behind New York, and the season seemed to be slipping away.

Saturday's game was scheduled to begin at 3:15 P.M. Morning rain showers had soaked Fenway's grass, whose field was, at the time, one of the slowest to drain in all of baseball, and early that afternoon, the Fenway grounds crew recommended calling off the game. But Johnny Damon, Kevin Millar, and Jason Varitek went into Terry Francona's office and told him the players were passionate about getting the game in. Their pride was on the line. After a 54-minute delay, Boston's Bronson Arroyo threw out the first pitch of the afternoon.

The game did not begin well for the Sox: By the top of the third inning, the Yankees had a three-run lead. Then Arroyo, who led the league in hit batsmen in 2004, plunked Alex Rodriguez on the elbow. Instead of taking his base, Rodriguez stood at the plate, staring out at Arroyo.* Varitek jumped up and stood between Rodriguez and his pitcher. "I basically told him to get the fuck down to first base," Varitek said later, and soon the two players were pushing and shoving each other's faces.† Both benches cleared, and in a scene reminiscent of their brawl in the 2003 playoffs, the Red Sox and Yankees went at each other with a viciousness rare in baseball. Boston took a 4–3 lead in the fourth, fell behind 9–4 by the sixth, and was trailing 10–8 by the bottom of the ninth. With Mariano Rivera on the mound, the Red Sox looked finished: The Yankees reliever had converted 23 straight save opportunities and had allowed only one home run all year.

Garciaparra, who already had two hits and two runs batted in for

* Arroyo already had a reputation for hitting Yankees batters. In Game 2 of the 2003 American League Championship Series, Arroyo—in his first-ever playoff appearance—hit Alfonso Soriano in retaliation for Yankees pitcher Jose Contreras throwing a pitch near David Ortiz's head. "That's the way the game goes," Arroyo said at the time. "Anytime you go out there and show people you've got a little bit of balls, people respect that."

† The image of Varitek seemingly trying to stuff his catcher's mitt into Rodriguez's mouth has become one of the most iconic images of the 2004 season, and was featured on the cover of Stephen King and Stuart O'Nan's *Faithful*. Varitek made it the screensaver for the laptop he used to prepare for games for the remainder of the year.

the game, led off the ninth with a double, and a deep fly ball by Trot Nixon moved him to third. Kevin Millar followed with a single that scored Garciaparra and brought the Red Sox to within a run. Bill Mueller, Boston's often-overlooked third baseman, was up next. Unlike Millar or Damon, Mueller didn't seek out the spotlight, and when he spoke to the press, he was usually so bland that his quotes were all but worthless. He wasn't a multimillionaire All-Star like Garciaparra or Ramirez, wasn't a prodigious slugger like Ortiz. But he was one of the key players on the team, and he turned in consistently above-average defense and clutch hitting. He dug into the batter's box, left leg twitching, bat waving gently in the air, a sneer settling onto his face. After working the count to 3-1, Mueller found a pitch he thought he could handle and he uncorked his swing, his top hand flying off the bat. The ball soared into right field and dropped into the Red Sox bullpen for a game-winning, two-run home run. The Red Sox poured out of their dugout to celebrate. The reaction would have been appropriate for a team that had just won a spot in the playoffs instead of a midseason day game against a division rival. It was as if the players knew that, one day down the line, they'd be able to draw inspiration from their comeback against the best reliever in baseball.

Theo Epstein's parents, Leslie and Ilene, were at Fenway that day. They'd been warned by their son not to embarrass him in public. (Following his installation as the youngest general manager in baseball history, Theo had to explain to his parents why giving out baby pictures to the media was not going to make it any easier to convince people to take him seriously.) The Epsteins almost always steered clear of Theo at the ballpark, waiting until they saw him alone to talk about this or that game or play. But, on this day, Theo's parents had to congratulate their son. They went down to the waiting room outside of the Red Sox clubhouse to share in the joy of the day.

Even Epstein himself, known for his steely demeanor and distrust of hyperbole, seemed a bit overwhelmed. "What can you say? The game was a classic," he said afterward. "It was a cataclysmic event. This win, the way it happened, should prove to be very important to us. It's hard to have a more meaningful regular season victory."

## CHAPTER 32

# *Trading an Icon*

JULY 31 is one of the most tension-filled days of the baseball season. A little less than two-thirds of the games have been played, and teams looking to make a playoff run have just two more months in which to prove their mettle. The All-Star game is in the past, pitching rotations have been settled on, and unlikely stars have emerged. It's also Major League Baseball's annual nonwaiver trade deadline.* Teams that have fallen out of the playoff race look to unload a high-priced star in return for young, cheap talent that can help the team rebuild. Teams convinced they have a shot at making the play-

---

* The rules and regulations governing baseball can be comically complex. July 31 is the nonwaiver trade deadline, which means that up until that date teams can freely trade any player on their rosters so long as that player doesn't have a no-trade clause in his contract and doesn't have what are referred to as "10-5 rights," which means he has at least 10 years of major league service time, the last five of which have been with the same team. Players that fall into either of those categories must give their permission to be traded. From August 1 through August 31, a player can be traded so long as he's cleared waivers, meaning his team put him on waivers and no other team claimed the player for nothing more than the remaining money due on his contract. (Players placed on waivers in August are placed on conditional waivers, which give the team the right to pull the player back if he's claimed.) The most recent big-name waiver trade occurred in 2004, when the Colorado Rockies traded outfielder Larry Walker to the St. Louis Cardinals.

offs try to find that one missing part, a consistent middle reliever, say, or a potent bat off the bench. And teams like the 2004 Boston Red Sox—well-paid, talent-laden clubs saddled with the attendant high expectations—try to figure out what they can do to save their seasons.

Since John Henry and Tom Werner had bought the team, the trade-deadline move had become a staple of life in Boston. On July 30, 2002, the Red Sox traded barely used pitcher Sun-Woo Kim to the Montreal Expos for outfielder Cliff Floyd. In 2003, the team picked up two pitchers—Scott Williamson and Jeff Suppan—in the last two days before the deadline. A July trade, explained Larry Lucchino, helped show the players that management was as committed to winning as the players were.

As the calendar moved toward July 31, 2004, there were plenty of rumors swirling around the Red Sox clubhouse. Despite a remarkably healthy starting rotation—the fivesome of Schilling, Martinez, Lowe, Wakefield, and Arroyo hadn't missed a start all year—and a prolific offense, had the season ended on July 29, the Sox would have missed the playoffs, with the Yankees winning the American League East in a cakewalk and the Texas Rangers snatching the American League's wild-card spot. Lowe was perhaps the most-discussed trade chip. The tall right-hander's record wasn't atrocious—he was 9-9—but he had an earned run average over 5.00 and, on many days, was the worst starting pitcher in all of baseball. One frequently discussed rumor had Lowe heading to Florida in return for Marlins pitcher Brad Penny.

Behind the scenes, it was Nomar Garciaparra who was being discussed most intently at the Red Sox's Fenway offices. On July 24, the same day as the Sox's 11–10 walk-off win against the Yankees, Henry, Lucchino, and Theo Epstein met with Garciaparra and his agent, Arn Tellem. Both sides agreed the meeting would be a good way to clear the air. "The meeting was, 'We want to know why you are unhappy,' " says Garciaparra. "And I go, *'Et tu, Brute?'* Because that is all I've been hearing for the last couple of years: I'm unhappy, I'm unhappy. I go, 'Where are you getting this? What am I unhappy about?' I said, 'Is my performance a problem?' And they are like, 'No.' "

The meeting did not improve the relationship between Garciaparra and the Red Sox executives. "By that point, there was a high degree of alienation on Nomar's part from the franchise and from the city," says Lucchino. "After the meeting, there was, to me, a near certainty that he would leave at the end of the year. He didn't say it outright, but it seemed clear." Tellem later told the Red Sox he had to talk Garciaparra out of demanding a trade that day, although Garciaparra insists he never told Tellem he wanted out. "Wanting to be traded out of Boston has never, ever come out of my mouth, publicly or privately," he says.

A couple of days later, while the team was in Baltimore, Red Sox officials say Garciaparra told members of the team's training staff and Terry Francona that he'd need to miss considerable time in August and September because he was still injured. One of the team's trainers says Garciaparra also said his top priority was not playing, but getting healthy for November, when he'd be a free agent. Alarmed, Francona called Epstein to tell him about his conversations with Garciaparra. The Red Sox had already begun exploring potential moves, and this revelation only firmed Epstein's resolve to deal with the situation. "After that conversation," Henry says, "Theo, Larry, and I met, and Theo said . . . that we needed somebody to play shortstop."

On Friday, July 30, the Red Sox opened up a three-game set in Minnesota against the Twins. Garciaparra, who'd played in the previous five games, was given the night off. With Pokey Reese out with a strained rib cage, Ricky Gutierrez, already playing on his third team in 2004, got the start at shortstop. The next day, players began arriving at the clubhouse at around two thirty in the afternoon, four-and-a-half hours before game time. The trade deadline is at 4:00 P.M. Eastern Standard Time, or 3:00 P.M. in Minnesota. Derek Lowe, easily excitable in the best of circumstances, was particularly geeked out that day—he was scheduled to start that night's game, but knew he could, in fact, end up on a plane headed to another team before the day was out. When 3:00 P.M. finally came, the rumors began flying. Word was the Red Sox and the Cubs had made a trade—it was Lowe, apparently, who was being sent to Chicago for pitcher Matt Clement. As Lowe waited nervously by his locker to get official word, Terry Francona called Garciaparra into the visiting manager's office and closed the door. He handed Garciaparra the phone. Theo Epstein was on the other end, telling one of the most popular players ever to play for the Boston Red Sox that he'd just been traded to the Chicago Cubs.

"I just felt empty," says Garciaparra. "Just like, 'No way.'" He hung up the phone and walked out of Francona's office. "I go to my locker and I see D-Lowe there and I go, 'Don't worry, it's not you, it's me. See ya, bro.' And word starts spreading around and I'm just trying not to cry." Garciaparra packed his stuff, left Minnesota, and got on a plane to Chicago. (The trade of Lowe for Clement had, in fact, nearly happened, but the Red Sox decided it would be too disruptive to trade Lowe and Garciaparra on the same day; better to perform a simple extraction of one veteran player.)

The full details of the Garciaparra trade shocked everyone. In the multi-team deal, Boston had sent Garciaparra and minor league outfielder Matt Murton to the Chicago Cubs and gotten Montreal shortstop Orlando Cabrera and Minnesota first baseman Doug Mientkiewicz in return. Cabrera and Mientkiewicz were both Gold Glove winners, and their defensive prowess would, Epstein thought, help Boston shore up its infield. But neither had ever appeared in an All-Star game, and the two players combined had hit only 109 home runs and batted over .300 twice. Garciaparra, as everyone in Boston knew, had a lifetime average over .320, and as recently as 2003 seemed like a sure Hall of Famer. Minutes after the deal had been announced, Epstein's cell phone rang. It was his twin brother, Paul.

"That's all you guys got for Nomar?" Paul asked. As Epstein explained that it would end up being a good trade for the team, his brother told him about the reaction on talk radio. "You're getting killed," Paul said. "People are furious that Nomar was traded for a couple of .240 hitters."

The trade would test's Epstein's mettle like no other since he'd become general manager. In the post-trade press conference, Epstein, sporting several days' worth of stubble and looking haggard, patiently explained how the move would improve the team's defense. He went on to tell WEEI, Boston's sports-radio station, that, "given what we know from prior negotiations that we weren't going to sign [Garciaparra] . . . we were looking forward to the next two months and said, 'Well, what do we have here?' " Since Reese was injured, Epstein said, the Red Sox would be faced with "a situation where we're likely to have Nomar Garciaparra and Ricky Gutierrez playing short and we don't think that's going to be enough. We haven't been playing well, and Nomar's likely to play less over the next month than he's played the last month." If they wanted to make a run at the playoffs, Epstein said, Boston needed to upgrade, even if that meant trading a franchise icon.

Privately, Epstein wasn't nearly so self-assured. A couple of hours after the trade, he wandered back into his office in the basement of Fenway. The baseball operations offices are three floors below the team's executive offices, and the rest of Epstein's crew had headed home for the night, leaving Epstein secluded. As he flicked through the stations on a flat-screen television mounted to the wall across from his desk, he passed by ESPN, which had a picture of Garciaparra in a Cubs hat. "It hit me for the first time, emotionally, that there would be real consequences to the organization and to me personally if it didn't work out [well]," Epstein said later.

That evening, Epstein spoke to John Henry on the phone. "It was the right trade, but no one likes it," said Epstein. "You must feel like the loneliest man in America," Henry replied. The next morning's papers couldn't have consoled him any. The *Globe*'s Gordon Edes wrote, "What the Sox lost was a role model for an entire generation of Little Leaguers. . . . From Amesbury to Bangor, there were certain to be tears last night." Later that day, the Red Sox lost to the Twins, and Cabrera, despite hitting a home run in his first game with Boston, committed an error that led to Minnesota's winning run. That night, for the first time in his life, a restless Theo Epstein took a sleeping pill.

The trade also introduced new tension into the already strained relationship between Epstein and Larry Lucchino. Boston fans were upset, and they reflexively looked for someone to blame. Epstein was the golden boy, the hard-working, selfless Brookline native who felt, somehow, like one of them. Lucchino, whom the *Herald* said "often played the role of the Sox enforcer," already had a reputation for being an overeager tough guy. He'd been blamed for screwing up the A-Rod trade, for inciting George Steinbrenner with his "Evil Empire" comment, for being the adversary of agents like Scott Boras and Arn Tellem. "No matter what happens, Larry's the one who gets blamed," says John Henry. "A lot of the time, it's Theo and I who are in favor of the unpopular moves, and Larry wants to be more conservative. He doesn't like it when people get upset. But people think I'm this nice guy and he's this thug, so he gets blamed."

Behind the scenes, Charles Steinberg, the Red Sox PR chief, was quietly trying to do some quick damage control for the only man he'd ever really worked for. Steinberg stressed to reporters—on background—that Lucchino had been plenty conflicted about the deal. "Larry believes in marquee players staying with their clubs," Steinberg says. "He believes in the old-fashioned, illustrated by [the Orioles'] Brooks Robinson being a one-franchise player, [the Red Sox's] Carl Yastrzemski being a one-franchise player, [the Orioles'] Cal Ripken [Jr.] being a one-franchise player, [the Padres'] Tony Gwynn being a one-franchise player. Now, Brooks occurred before Larry was in the business, but [Ripken and Gwynn] he was involved in." It is Lucchino's preference, says Steinberg, "as a true old-fashioned baseball fan, to keep your star players," while it's Epstein, Steinberg says, who "is aggressive and is going to seek to make the changes he sees fit." But, Steinberg says, at the end of the day, it's Lucchino who feels obligated to take the heat off his bosses. "When it comes to being the ultimate tough guy on the other side of a table . . . he's your man," Steinberg says. "Maybe it's because he wants to, maybe it's because he's instructed to, but either way, he's the SOB. Now that's a reputation that is a part of the job when you're protecting the ownership."

It didn't take long for what Steinberg was saying sotto voce to reporters to reach Theo Epstein and his colleagues in the Red Sox baseball operations department. Because this message was being conveyed second- and third-hand instead of directly by the people involved, it became amplified and distorted. Although there was no concrete evidence that Lucchino knew anything of what Steinberg was saying, it felt to Epstein as if Lucchino had hung him out to dry.

It was almost an exact mirroring of the situation that had occurred in the aftermath of the failed A-Rod trade. "After the Nomar trade, we get the opposite thing going on," says a high-ranking Red Sox executive. "Now Theo believes Larry's throwing him under the bus." At least, Epstein thought, he had Henry's full support.

Ironically, it was Henry, if anyone, who seemed to suggest he was conflicted about the Garciaparra trade. A *Globe* article that ran four days after the trade began, "Red Sox principal owner John W. Henry placed full responsibility for the Nomar Garciaparra trade on general manager Theo Epstein yesterday." It then quoted Henry as saying the trade was "extremely difficult—he was the face of the franchise." Lucchino, meanwhile, seemed to be giving Epstein credit for the move. "Congratulations to Theo for diagnosing the problem and acting boldly to correct it," he said, putting what seemed to be a positive spin on the "bottom-up" message that had been conveyed to reporters. But no matter. Just as Lucchino had decided, seven months earlier, that Epstein had betrayed him by blaming him for the A-Rod trade, now Epstein felt that Lucchino was no longer someone he could fully trust. He began to pull away from Lucchino, and became even more isolated from the rest of the Red Sox employees, choosing to surround himself almost solely with his colleagues in baseball operations. "We're literally in the basement, far away from everybody else," Epstein says, speaking of his Fenway Park offices. "And figuratively we came to rely upon each other even more. It was sort of like, 'You say it was a bottom-up trade? Well how do you like us now?' mentality, although we probably didn't realize it at the time."

CHAPTER 33

# "We're Gonna Kick Fucking Ass Starting Today"

**IN THE TWO WEEKS AFTER THE TRADE,** the Red Sox played much as they had all year—winning a couple of games, then losing a couple. After an August 15 loss to the Chicago White Sox, the team's record on the month was 8-6, for a winning percentage just a shade better than their mark on the season. Right around this time, Henry, Werner, and Lucchino convened one of the player roundtables they held periodically throughout the season. Henry asked the players if there was anything else management could do to help them out for the remainder of the season.

"You guys have done everything you can do," Jason Varitek said. "It's up to us now." Then Kevin Millar began to speak. "We're gonna go on a run," he said. "We're gonna win, and we're gonna kick fucking ass starting today." It was good to see the team had so much confidence, but for months, there hadn't been much to support that notion.

On August 16, the Sox beat the Toronto Blue Jays, 8–4, behind a decent outing from Derek Lowe. The next night, Orlando Cabrera won the game for Boston with a one-out double in the bottom of the ninth. On the 18th, Boston completed its sweep of Toronto, before taking the next three from the Chicago White Sox. Facing Toronto for another series, the Sox took two out of three, before sweeping the Detroit Tigers in a four-game series. The Red Sox, after stumbling through so much of the season, had suddenly won 12 of their last 13 games. Still, the sternest test seemed just ahead: The next nine games were against the Los Angeles Angels of Anaheim, the Texas Rangers, and the Oakland A's, three teams all riding hot streaks— the A's had won 12 of 13, the Angels 10 of 11, and the Rangers 12 of 16—and fighting for playoff spots.

The Red Sox ripped through their American League West opponents like a buzzsaw, sweeping the Angels and the A's and taking two out of three from the Rangers. All of a sudden, Boston had won 20 of its last 22 games. On August 15, the Red Sox were 10.5 games behind the Yankees. On the morning of September 9, they were just two back. "The Red Sox are now the hottest property in baseball," *Sports Illustrated* proclaimed in a September 13 cover story. "With a 16-1 burst through Friday, Boston remade itself into a pitching-and-defense juggernaut . . . and outdid itself producing melodramatic script material." John Henry couldn't help but think back to Millar's speech a few weeks earlier. "From that point on," Henry says, "we were basically unbeatable."

The Yankees, meanwhile, seemed to be imploding. They were humiliated to the tune of 22–0 by the Cleveland Indians, at Yankee Stadium no less. With Schilling dominating the league, Kevin Brown and Javier Vazquez, two of New York's offseason pickups, were pitching poorly, when they were pitching at all: In early September, Brown punched a wall in the Yankees clubhouse and broke two bones in his left hand. And, while Orlando Cabrera had energized Boston with both his defense and his playful personality, the Yankees' trade-deadline acquisition, pitcher Esteban Loaiza, had gone 0-2 with an earned run average of more than 8.00.*

---

* Loaiza was such a bust he was called on to pitch mop-up duty in the Yankees' 22–0 loss, a fact he protested by grooving eminently hittable fastballs to the Indians. Watching the game in the Boston clubhouse, the Red Sox couldn't

The Red Sox and the Yankees split their remaining six games, and Boston never did overtake New York, finishing the regular season at 98-64. But their record, good only for second place in the American League East, was the third-best mark in all of baseball (only the 101-61 Yankees and the 105-57 St. Louis Cardinals were better), and for the second year in a row, the Red Sox made the playoffs as the American League wild-card team. They'd face the Anaheim Angels in the first round. The first two games, beginning October 5, would be out in California.

Of course, the regular season didn't end without its share of Bostonian melodrama. About a week before the playoffs were set to open, Pedro Martinez announced to reporters that Curt Schilling had been tapped to begin the postseason, meaning he was the pitcher Boston wanted to ensure got the maximum number of starts.

"Without a doubt, he deserves to be the number-one starter," Martinez said. "He's been better than Pedro Martinez and better than anyone on our team." It was true. While Martinez lost his last four starts to finish the year at 16-9 with a 3.90 earned run average, the highest of his career, Schilling went 21-6 with a 3.26 ERA. Remarkably, the Red Sox were actually worse on days in which Martinez—the active pitcher with the best winning percentage in baseball and the player with the third highest winning percentage in history—was the team's starting pitcher than they were the rest of the year: Boston went 19-14 in Martinez's 33 starts* for a .576 winning percentage, while putting together a 79-50 record the rest of the time, good for a .612 clip. When Schilling took the mound, the team was 25-7. In games after a Red Sox loss, when a victory would halt a potential losing streak, the team was 12-3 in Schilling's

---

help but laugh. "They trade for Loaiza, then pitch him in a 16–goose egg game," said Derek Lowe, splayed on a clubhouse couch. "Wow."

* A starting pitcher can get credit for a win only if he pitches five full innings and leaves with a lead his team doesn't relinquish. A pitcher can be credited with a loss whenever he leaves a game with his team behind and his team doesn't rally to win. If a starting pitcher leaves a tie game, or if he leaves with his team trailing in a game they go on to win, or leaves with his team in the lead but before completing five full innings of work, he doesn't get a decision.

starts, 7-7 in Martinez's. If Martinez had been wounded by Schilling's acquisition, even he had to admit that in 2004 the beefy, verbose right-hander had been the better performer on the mound.

There was also the question of what to do about Derek Lowe. Lowe had finished the year with an adequate 14-12 record, but with a frightening 5.42 ERA. In his last four regular season starts, Lowe had averaged only about two-and-a-half innings per game. On several of those occasions, Red Sox officials wondered if Lowe's penchant for late-night socializing might have contributed to his poor performances, as he looked bleary-eyed and gave up runs by the fistful. At least once, Lowe himself felt compelled to respond to the rumors that he'd been out partying. "To say . . . I didn't come to play because of the night before is using an excuse that wasn't really there," he told reporters after one game late in September.

Whatever had been the cause of Lowe's poor performances, Theo Epstein and Terry Francona decided not to use him as one of the team's four postseason starting pitchers, instead choosing a rotation of Schilling, Martinez, Bronson Arroyo, and Tim Wakefield. Francona insisted Lowe, who just two seasons earlier had finished third in the league's Cy Young voting, could still be a playoff asset coming out of the bullpen. "Lowe has some experience in big games, getting some big outs," Francona said. "I guess my point is, we don't need to hide him." In the next day's *Herald,* Steve Buckley responded by writing, "That's complete nonsense, and the only real surprise was that Francona was able to speak the words with a straight face. See, hiding Lowe is PRECISELY what the Red Sox are doing."

Despite all this, Boston entered into the playoffs the favorites to capture the American League pennant. The team had a deep bench, healthy starters, and a strong bullpen. "We're just the idiots this year," said Johnny Damon before Boston's first round series with the Angels. "We feel like we can win every game. We feel like we have to have fun—and I think that's why this team is liked by so many people out there."

Damon's statement wasn't just hyperbole. This Red Sox team seemed to be as beloved as any in the history of the city. Damon, with his long hair and mangy beard, had embraced his cult status as

Boston's personal Jesus. Upon arriving in Boston, Orlando Cabrera crafted comically intricate, individually tailored handshakes for every member of the team; when Cabrera came back into the dugout after a hit or a good play, the Red Sox looked as if they were communicating in some sort of goofy sign language that involved lots of fist-thumping and pointing at the sky.

And then, of course, there was Schilling, who sometimes seemed to so crave the fans' adoration he came off like an overeager teenager. All year long, he would post on the Sons of Sam Horn website, and the night before the playoffs began, he began a thread in the area of the site in which members dissect every pitch of every game in real time.

"Why not us?" Schilling wrote. "There is no reason the last team standing can't be us, you know it, we know it. Now is the time to go and prove to ourselves, the fans, the game, how good of a team we are. If 25 guys believe that what we are after is the most important thing in their lives for 4 weeks, there is <u>nothing</u> that can't be done. Figured I may as well start one game thread this year, considering that coming in here and reading them is sometimes more entertaining than any movie you could see, and often times more entertaining than the game itself." It seemed as if everyone connected with the team, from the players to the front office to the fans, was convinced 2004 might really be the magical year that Boston banished its demons for good. The Yankees, meanwhile, seemed more than ever like a bunch of stiff, well-paid mercenaries. Gary Sheffield and Alex Rodriguez might be potent offensive forces, but they didn't look like they'd be much fun to hang out with.

The Red Sox and their fans certainly enjoyed themselves in the first round. They beat the Angels handily on October 5 and 6, taking a two-game lead in the best of five series back to Fenway for Game 3 on Friday, October 8. That afternoon, the Red Sox squandered a late five-run lead to send the game into extra innings with the score tied at six. In the bottom of the 10th inning, with a man on first and two out, David Ortiz came to the plate.

Before Ortiz could dig into the batter's box, Angels manager Mike Scioscia popped out of the visitor's dugout and walked to the mound. His best reliever, right-hander Francisco Rodriguez, had been pitching since the eighth, and Scioscia wanted a lefty to come in to face Ortiz. He summoned Jarrod Washburn.

"Washburn is a guy I've faced a lot," Ortiz later told the *Globe*'s Chris Snow. "Pretty much the last couple of games he's trying a lot of sliders because I'm driving his fastball pretty good. As soon as I saw him coming out of the bullpen I thought, 'Here comes my slider.' . . . I thought, 'First pitch, he's going to throw me this, and I'm going to look for it. Give it to me.'" Washburn came in and threw Ortiz the slider. Ortiz smashed it over the Green Monster for a game-ending, series-clinching home run.

Afterward, as the Red Sox sprayed champagne on their fans, the Angels seemed oddly accepting of the methodical dispatching they'd been subjected to. "Those boys are winning the World Series," first baseman Darin Erstad said. "That's the deepest team I've ever seen. They have every piece of the puzzle. I don't see anybody beating them." Shortstop David Eckstein nodded. "As long as they can get the Yankees out of their heads," he said.

## CHAPTER 34

# "Can You Believe It?"

**THE RED SOX AND THE YANKEES** began their second straight American League Championship Series on Tuesday, October 12. For the first time ever, it was Boston, not New York, that was the clear favorite of the sportswriters and oddsmakers around the country. Boston was the sentimental choice of the rest of the country as well. Two-thousand three's dramatic Game 7 loss to the Yankees had solidified the Red Sox's reputation as perpetual underdogs, and the team's shaggy-dog charm threw the Yankees' businesslike façade into sharp relief.* The lineup, anchored by David Ortiz and Manny Ramirez, didn't have an easy out in it—batting ninth was Bill Mueller, the 2003 American League batting champion. Schilling and Martinez appeared strong and the relievers were well rested and confident. The Yankees, on the other hand, looked like a poorly constructed fantasy league team. The top of their order was ferocious, with Derek Jeter, Alex Rodriguez, Gary Sheffield, and Hideki Matsui batting in a row. After that, the batters were mostly a collection of castoffs and once-great players well past their prime. How could a team with a $182 million payroll have the depleted 36-

---

* More than one opposing general manager quipped that only the $182 million, George Steinbrenner–owned Yankees could make the $127 million Red Sox look like lovable rebels.

year-old Bernie Williams batting fifth and playing center field, or career utility man Miguel Cairo hitting eighth and playing second, or Kenny Lofton—who averaged about 10 home runs a year—as the designated hitter? New York's pitching looked bad, too, with the starting rotation decimated by age and injuries and the bullpen having been worked into the ground during the regular season. "Going into the series, I thought, looking at the matchups, that we looked pretty good," Henry says. His players agreed. On the afternoon of October 12, a couple of hours before game time, relievers Mike Timlin and Alan Embree were fielding grounders on the infield grass at Yankee Stadium. "I liked our chances last year," Timlin said. "I really like [our chances this year]."

The only real concern for Boston was Curt Schilling's right ankle. Throughout the season, Schilling had struggled with a deep bone bruise in his right ankle joint—an injury the Red Sox had tried to keep under wraps until Schilling wrote about it on Sons of Sam Horn. From early May through mid-July, Schilling had received an injection of marcaine—a novocaine-like local anesthetic—before every game he pitched, and had frequently been spotted wearing a removable cast-like boot. On September 26, Schilling's final regular season start, he tweaked his right ankle again, but for the first five innings of Game 1 versus the Angels, he seemed fine. Then, with one out in the sixth inning of that game, Schilling aggravated his ankle injury covering first base. The next inning, with Boston leading 8–1, Schilling was sent to the mound to pitch again, and was obviously uncomfortable while running off the mound to field a lazy ground ball. (Schilling ended up forcing an off-balance, wild throw to first and was charged with an error on the play.) When the next Angels batter hit a run-scoring double, Schilling was finally removed from the game.

This time, the Red Sox said, Schilling's ankle injury was not a bone bruise but a tendon injury. It didn't sound severe—"I don't know if you'd call it tendinitis. It's a tendon problem," said Terry Francona—and Boston's team doctors assured the press Schilling would be in top form in New York.

It was clear from the first inning of Game 1 that this was not the case. Schilling began the game by retiring Jeter and Rodriguez, but not before both hit balls hard to right field. The next three batters reached base, and before the inning was over, New York was leading, 2–0. They picked up four more runs off Schilling in the third before the Red Sox's best pitcher was taken out of the game to a cascade of catcalls and jeers. After six innings, Mike Mussina had retired every Red Sox batter he'd faced and Boston was trailing 8–0. While the Red Sox salvaged some dignity before the end of the night—the final score was 10–7—the loss of Game 1 felt less important than the potential loss of Curt Schilling for the rest of the postseason.

After the game, the Red Sox finally acknowledged that Schilling was hobbled not by tendinitis, but something far more serious: a ruptured sheath that caused a dislocated tendon behind his right ankle. Tendons are bands of tissues that connect muscle to bone, giving muscles the ability to move the bones. The tendons that connect the shoulder muscles to the upper arm, for instance, allow a pitcher to use those shoulder muscles to propel his arm overhead while throwing a ball to the plate. The rear ankle tendon is positioned in a groove in the fibula, the thinner of the two calf bones that connect the knee with the ankle. For a power pitcher like Schilling, who generates much of his velocity by pushing off his right leg, this tendon is crucial both for balance and for harnessing the leg power he uses to drive off the pitching mound. Schilling had ripped the sheath that holds the tendon in place, and when he tried to pitch, the tendon would snap back and forth across the bone, causing extraordinary pain. Before Game 1 of the Yankees series, the Red Sox had outfitted Schilling with a customized brace and shot him up with painkillers, to no avail. There was no question he'd need surgery as soon as the postseason was over; the only question was whether he'd be able to pitch again that October. At that point, it looked very unlikely. The Red Sox had finally managed to enter the playoffs better positioned than the Yankees, and now, with Schilling sidelined, they went from being favorites to being underdogs once again.

As if that wasn't bad enough, the next night Pedro Martinez lost a taut pitcher's duel to Jon Lieber, whose sheer averageness was reflected in his career statistics: 100-91 with a 4.20 ERA. Boston's bats, so powerful all season long, had been silenced. In the first two games, Johnny Damon had gone 0-for-8 with five strikeouts. Manny Ramirez was just 2-for-8 with no runs batted in, while Kevin Millar and Bill Mueller were a combined 2-for-15. As bad as that was, it was about to get worse. In Game 3, played at Fenway Park, the Red Sox were embarrassed, 19–8, putting themselves into a three-game hole in the best of seven series. A season that had once seemed so full of hope had become numbingly depressing. "The Red Sox have been beaten senseless by those damn Yankees again, and the psychological toll threatens to shake the faith of a long-suffering Nation," Dan Shaughnessy wrote in the next day's *Globe*. "The Yankees stripped the Red Sox of all dignity last night. . . . So there. For the 86th consecutive autumn, the Red Sox are not going to win the World Series. No baseball team in history has recovered from a 3-0 deficit and this most-promising Sox season in 18 years could be officially over tonight. Mercy."

Everyone, it seemed, expected the Red Sox to lose. And why not? Their two best pitchers had been beaten. Bronson Arroyo, their Game 3 starter, had been abused, and Tim Wakefield, scheduled to start Game 4, had selflessly offered to pitch mop-up duty in Game 3 to protect the other bullpen arms. Now, the season was thrust into the hands of Derek Lowe, a pitcher so maddeningly inconsistent that Boston had bounced him out of the starting rotation. Three days earlier, scalpers were selling tickets for Sunday's Game 4 for thousands of dollars. After Saturday night, they were available for less than face value.

But in the Boston clubhouse, there was a sense not of resignation, but of grim determination. "Don't let us win one," Kevin Millar kept saying. It became a mantra that night, as player after player repeated it, sometimes to teammates, sometimes to themselves. "I mean, why not us?" asked Keith Foulke, repeating a slogan Curt Schilling had printed on T-shirts he'd made for the team. "Maybe we'll be the first team to come back from 3-0. We'll find out. We have to use every bullet we can to fight and get to tomorrow, and then tomorrow's no different. We'll do what we need to do to try to win a ballgame."

After the Sox's Game 3 loss, Theo Epstein downed vodka-and-tonics late into the night with some friends. "I just thought, you know, we need a miracle in Game 4," he says. At that point, Epstein wasn't even thinking about coming back to win the series; he was just hoping not to get swept. "I really didn't want us to lose [Game 4]," he says, "and have our whole season be remembered for getting slapped by the Yankees and for the colossal defeat in Game 3. Our players had been through a lot of adversity, and I really believed in their spirit. I thought it would be inappropriate to be remembered for a loss, or a sweep, rather than for what they had accomplished."

On Sunday, just after eleven thirty at night, it seemed that an ignoble sweep was precisely what the 2004 Boston Red Sox would be remembered for. October 17 was a windy night, with temperatures just below 50 degrees. Lowe had pitched admirably in his first postseason start of 2004, allowing just three runs in 5⅓ innings. But in the bottom of the eighth Boston was trailing, 4–3, when Yankees manager Joe Torre called on Mariano Rivera, the best postseason reliever in history, to pitch the game's final two innings. By this point, even the 35,000 fans that had packed their way into Fenway, not to mention the team's owners, were bracing themselves for another defeat, another humiliation.

Suite L1, the first luxury box along the third base line, is Larry Lucchino's box, and he, along with John Henry, Tom Werner, and Charles Steinberg, stared glumly at the field. George Mitrovich, the president of the City Club of San Diego and a guest of Steinberg's, was talking and gesticulating loudly, and after Rivera pitched his way around a leadoff hit to Manny Ramirez in the eighth, Steinberg decided he had better keep Mitrovich occupied lest he inflame Lucchino. He suggested Mitrovich park himself at a computer and work on preparing some remarks for the postgame press conference the Red Sox would be forced to endure following their unceremonious dismantling.

Meanwhile, Sox closer Keith Foulke came out of Boston's dugout to pitch what surely would be the last inning of baseball for the Red Sox in 2004. It was his third inning of work, and Foulke was tiring. He began the inning by walking Derek Jeter, the Yankees leadoff hitter, on six pitches. Jason Varitek threw the ball back to Foulke, who snapped at it in the air, yelled "Fuck" to himself, and turned to stare vacantly at the outfield. Foulke had already thrown

37 pitches. In 72 regular-season appearances, he had thrown more than 30 pitches in a game only four times; he had gone over 40 pitches only once. What's more, he would now have to face the Yankees' three most fearsome hitters—Alex Rodriguez, Gary Sheffield, and Hideki Matsui—a trio that was hitting better than .500 for the series. On television, Fox was preparing for its postgame show, and its "Plays of the Game"—a couple of infield squibbers in the sixth inning that scored a pair of runs and gave the Yankees the lead—flashed on television screens around the country.

After the Jeter walk, Lucchino and Steinberg joined Mitrovich and began hammering out statements for the press. Lucchino scribbled away on a yellow legal pad, while Steinberg shared the computer with Mitrovich. "We were concerned we might say something inappropriate or intemperate," says Lucchino.

"After the acute pain of this wound subsides, we'll look back on so many remarkable aspects of this season," Lucchino wrote. "The most remarkable was the passion of Red Sox Nation, of these fans." As they were writing, Foulke successfully escaped from the ninth inning, striking out Matsui with his 50th pitch of the game. The Red Sox had one last chance.

As the Sox prepared to bat, Fenway's PA system blared Eminem's "Lose Yourself," the motivational song that had become the team's unofficial anthem. "Look," Eminem drawled, "if you had one shot, or one opportunity to seize everything you ever wanted— one moment—would you capture it? Or just let it slip?" A week ago, this song seemed to mean something, and it had riled the Fenway crowd in the bottom of the 10th inning of the final game of the Angels series, right before David Ortiz's game-winning homer. But now the crowd was lifeless, waiting only for the string to play itself out. At that moment, the lyrics felt like a mockery: "You better lose yourself in the music, the moment / You own it, you better never let it go / You only get one shot, do not miss your chance to blow / This opportunity comes once in a lifetime, yo."

Lucchino kept writing as Rivera took his warmup tosses, now just scratching down phrases: "deeply disappointed," "bitter taste of defeat," "lost to an exceptional baseball team." He thought once again of the fans: "The R.S. fans gave their undying loyalty. We will give our relentless effort, redoubled, next year." And then he turned to the passion for a victory: "This loss in the A.L.C.S. only intensifies our resolve to win. We will be back." Due up in the last half of the ninth was the bottom third of the Red Sox batting order: Kevin Millar, Bill Mueller, and Mark Bellhorn. Henry was, he says, "utterly distressed." "We thought we had done everything we could to get back to the point [we were at] last year when it didn't happen," he says. "You always ask: What went wrong?"

The first pitch to Millar was a ball, inside: 1-0. Rivera's strength is his cut fastball, a pitch thrown more than 90 miles per hour that explodes in on a left-hander's hands or back over the inside part of the plate against a right-hander. It is considered one of the most uniquely unhittable pitches in the history of the game, but Millar is an excellent fastball hitter, and he was waiting for his pitch. The second pitch was one Millar could handle, and he hammered it, but foul, into the left-field stands. The third pitch, thrown just after the clock turned midnight, was inside again: two balls, one strike. The fourth pitch was also inside. And on the fifth pitch of the at-bat, Mariano Rivera, the most dependable reliever in all of baseball, walked Kevin Millar. It was the first postseason walk Rivera had issued in three years.

Up in L1, Henry glanced down at the diamond and began running numbers in his head. "When Millar walked at the top of that inning, I knew the chances of him scoring had gone to about 55 percent," says Henry. "I'm the math guy. If he makes an out, our chances of scoring drop to about 15 percent." Still, logic often seemed to have no place when it came to the Red Sox and the Yankees; after all, Manny Ramirez had opened the eighth inning with a hit but never came around to score. Nonetheless, Lucchino and Steinberg abandoned their concession statements to walk to the edge of the suite, where they looked down at the field.

As Millar trotted to first, outfielder Dave Roberts stepped out of the Sox dugout. Roberts had been another trade-deadline pickup for the Red Sox, sent to Boston from the Los Angeles Dodgers in exchange for a minor leaguer. One of the best base-stealers in the game, Roberts was exactly the type of player it seemed the Red Sox wouldn't be interested in: He had little power, a weak throwing arm, and didn't hit for very good average. But Epstein knew that just because stealing a base isn't a smart idea most of the time didn't mean it couldn't be a crucially important weapon in very specific situations. Now was just such a situation. The Red Sox had one inning left to manufacture a single run. If they couldn't, their season was over. Before he was called on to pinch-run, Roberts had been hunkered down in the video room of the Red Sox clubhouse, studying Rivera's pickoff moves to first base. This was his first appearance in the Yankees series.

Roberts and Millar knocked fists, and Millar jogged back to the dugout. His night was over. Roberts, who was 38-for-41 in steal attempts in 2004, glanced back. From the dugout, Terry Francona winked, a single bat of the eyelid that meant Roberts had the green light to try to steal second base.

As Rivera prepared to pitch with Bill Mueller at the plate, Roberts shuffled down the base path, stretching his lead to five, six, 10 feet. He was poised on the edge of movement, his left leg almost straight, his right leg bent, his arms twitching between his knees. Every time Rivera made a move on the mound, Roberts's entire body would tense as he decided whether to dive back to first or take off for second. Rivera threw to first; Roberts dove back in safely. Rivera threw to first again; again Roberts dove back, safe. When Rivera threw over to first one last time, the Fenway crowd began to boo. The throw was close, and as the first base umpire signaled safe, Roberts pursed his lips into an O. "When everyone in the ballpark knows you're going to steal against Rivera, it's pretty tough," Roberts would say later. After three pickoff throws, Rivera was ready to pitch. As he made his move to the plate, Roberts took off. Yankees catcher Jorge Posada's throw to Derek Jeter was slightly to the left of the second base bag, and Robert's left hand slid in just ahead of Jeter's sweeping tag. Safe.

That first pitch to Mueller had been a ball, so now the count was one ball, no strikes, no outs, a man on second. Fenway Park, depressingly subdued for most of the night, suddenly came to life. The switch-hitting Mueller was batting left-handed—just as he had been on July 24 when his ninth-inning home run had beaten Rivera and the Yankees—and he stepped out of the batter's box and peered down at Dale Sveum, the team's third base coach. The Red Sox, a team that hated to sacrifice the batter in order to move a runner over a base because it meant wasting an out, were going to bunt. Rivera squared to throw again, and Mueller leveled his bat before letting the ball land squarely in Posada's catcher's mitt, a cutter thrown right over the plate. Strike one.

Mueller stepped back and once again looked down to third. With Fenway now at a fever pitch, everyone, seemingly, knew what Mueller would do: try again to lay down the bunt to move Roberts over to third. Rivera, likely concentrating on getting in position to field the ball, grooved a pitch down the middle of the plate.

Except the bunt sign was called off. "Dave's at second base with no one out," explains Epstein. "The crowd's murmuring, 'Bunt— you don't have anyone out.' But the bunt is not the right play there. With a guy like Rivera throwing 94-mile-per-hour cutters in on Mueller's hands, the most likely outcome of that at-bat [if he swings away instead of bunting] is a ground ball to second base, which gets [Roberts] over [to third base] anyway. [Without the bunt] you have a shot of getting a base hit."

True to the script, Mueller lashed Rivera's eighth pitch of the inning straight up the diamond, sending the Yankees pitcher sprawling and Roberts sprinting in from second base. As Roberts rounded third, Bernie Williams, the Yankees weak-armed center fielder, threw the ball in, and Rivera caught it near the mound without even bothering to throw home. The score was now 4–4. Tie game. "You know the analogy 'Get up off the canvas'?" asks Epstein. "We had been kind of down and out after Game 3, and that was sort of the start of a rising. The crowd finally got into it."

The Red Sox had their chance to win it in the ninth. An error and a walk loaded the bases with two outs, sending Ortiz to bat. His two-year tenure as the Sox designated hitter had already been filled with dramatic, game-winning hits. But Ortiz popped out. As he came back to the Sox dugout, he was inconsolable, and the game remained tied at 4–4.

"You can't do it every time," Jason Varitek told Ortiz. "It's not humanly possible to get a hit in every single time in these situations." Varitek's words were well-intentioned, but Ortiz probably found no comfort in them: Ortiz, after all, *does* feel he can do it every time. Three innings later, at 1:22 A.M., he proved it. With no outs in the bottom of the 12th, Ortiz hit his second game-ending home run of the postseason, smashing an offering from Paul Quantrill into the Yankees' right-field bullpen. Fenway Park erupted as Ortiz and the Red Sox danced around home plate. As the Standells' 1960s garage-rock classic "Dirty Water," with its moaning talk of frustrated women, lovers, fuggers, and thieves, played from Fenway's loud-speakers, one of the uniformed policemen ringing the field nodded to a reporter and said out of the side of his mouth, "Oh, we're gonna win this thing. No doubt about it. We're gonna win." Curt Schilling agreed. "I believed we felt like we had them when we won Game 4. Whether we did or not, I don't think was relevant. I think we believed it. Which was all that really mattered."

Game 5, which began less than 16 hours after the end of Game 4, already had special significance. With Pedro Martinez set to become a free agent once the postseason ended, this was, as everyone knew, potentially the last game he'd ever pitch as a member of the Red Sox. "I just want to treat my fans, if this is my last outing, to the best I can give them for today and let's see what happens at the end of these playoffs," he said. Martinez was matched up, as he had been so many times over the last several years, with the Yankees' Mike Mussina. Both pitchers lasted six innings, but when Martinez walked off the mound, the Red Sox were trailing, 4–2. The score remained there until the bottom of the eighth, when Ortiz brought Boston to within a run with yet another homer and Jason Varitek tied the score at four with a sacrifice fly off Mariano Rivera. And there the score stayed, through the ninth inning, then the 10th, then finally the 11th and 12th. By the 13th, the Red Sox were on their seventh pitcher, Tim Wakefield, who once again had been called upon for emergency relief duty. The good news was that his knuckleball was dancing so effectively it was confounding the Yankees. The bad news was that it was also confounding Varitek—three passed balls put runners on second and third, despite the fact that the Yankees hadn't collected a hit in the inning. Finally, on the fifth batter of the inning, Wakefield struck out Ruben Sierra. After Varitek looked down at his glove to make sure he'd actually caught the ball, he sprinted into the dugout to refuel with some Gatorade and apple-sauce.

In the bottom of the 14th, Yankees pitcher Esteban Loaiza came out for his fourth inning of work. A bust during the regular season, Loaiza had been unhittable in this game, with a devastating sinker falling off one side of the plate and a wicked cut fastball collapsing on the other. His last three innings of work may have been the best pitched innings of the series thus far. Since entering the game in the 11th with runners on first and second and one out, he'd allowed just one walk. Now, Loaiza struck out Mark Bellhorn to begin the inning, and a pair of walks sandwiched around another strikeout put Johnny Damon on second base and Manny Ramirez on first with two outs. David Ortiz was due up at the plate. A base hit would likely win the game.

As Ortiz walked to the plate, he spit into his batting gloves and then smashed his hands together. As he dug into the batter's box, he tried to drown out the serenading cries of "PAPI, PAPI," to ignore the adulatory signs that freckled the Fenway stands. "You want to shut everything down," he later told the *Globe*'s Chris Snow. "After you shut down all the noise and everything around you, that's when your concentration comes. That's when you focus on what you want to do."

Ortiz is often described as a hitting genius, as if his talent is purely God-given. He's more comfortable than many other players talking with and teasing reporters, but English is not his first language, and he often plays the part of the friendly jokester. However, Ortiz works on his hitting as much as anyone in baseball. While his teammates are in the field, Ortiz often retreats to the Red Sox clubhouse to study his previous at-bats against that night's pitcher. Ortiz had been preparing for Loaiza ever since he'd taken the mound. "I wasn't trying to go too crazy with him," Ortiz said later. Because of the late movement of Loaiza's pitches, Ortiz said, he "just wanted to stay on the ball longer."

Loaiza's first pitch looked hittable, and Ortiz took a monstrous cut, but at the last moment the ball dove down and away, and Ortiz missed. Strike one. A ball and a foul made it 1-2. The Yankees were one strike away from sending the game, which had already taken longer than any postseason game in baseball history, into the 15th inning. The fourth pitch was outside but not by enough for Ortiz to take, and he punched it foul. He hit the next pitch deep enough to be a home run, but it hooked foul into the right-field stands. Loaiza followed with another ball, bringing the count even, to 2-2. Ortiz stepped out of the batter's box.

As Ortiz and Loaiza battled, Fenway was in a complete frenzy. A group of young men just behind home plate had been pounding on the dividing wall that separated the field from the stands since the eighth inning. Down the third base line, ESPN's Peter Gammons stood, poised by the entrance to the field, as he waited for the game to end so he could run out and collect a few quick on-camera quotes. He'd been standing there for a couple of hours already, ever since the bottom of the eighth, when the Yankees looked as if they were about to put away the game, and the series. Gammons, who'd seen the Red Sox beat the Cincinnati Reds in extra innings in Game 6 of the 1975 World Series, couldn't seem to erase the grin from his face. "Unbelievable," he occasionally murmured, shaking his head.

Ortiz knew a walk would load the bases, and with Doug Mientkiewicz on deck, he also knew the Yankees would much prefer to pitch to the light-hitting defensive specialist than to the man whose postseason highlight reel seemed to grow with each passing day. At this point, the difference between men on first and second and men on every base was negligible: With two outs, the lead runner would be off on contact in either case, and a base hit would likely win the game regardless of whether Damon was on second or third. Even with two strikes, Ortiz knew Loaiza wasn't going to give him anything on the fat part of the plate, and the way Loaiza was pitching, he could keep on painting the corners forever. Ortiz dug in, determined to foul off as many pitches as it took until there was one he could handle.

And so Ortiz fouled off the seventh pitch of the at-bat, and then the eighth and the ninth. As he stepped out of the batter's box again, he examined his bat before seizing it by the barrel and smacking it, handle first, into the ground to make sure one of Loaiza's cutters hadn't splintered it. Satisfied, he tucked it under his arm, spat into his gloves once more, smacked his hands together again, and settled back in to hit. On the 10th pitch of David Ortiz's seventh plate appearance of the night, Loaiza threw a cut fastball in on Ortiz's hands. Ortiz, no longer swinging for the fences, fisted the ball over Derek Jeter's head, where it fell in front of center fielder Bernie Williams. On national television, commentator Joe Buck exclaimed, "Damon coming to the plate, he can keep on running to New York. Game 6, tomorrow night!" As Loaiza walked dejectedly off the mound, he spit out his gum and took a swat at it with his glove. This had been the best he'd pitched all year, and still Ortiz had beaten him.

It was Ortiz's second walk-off hit of the series and his third of the postseason; no other player in history had hit more than two in his entire career. Afterward, Theo Epstein said, "It might be the greatest game ever played. I'd like to hear other nominations. . . . That might have been one of the greatest at-bats to end the greatest game ever played." Pedro Martinez, who'd made headlines in September after referring to the Yankees as "my daddy" after a tough loss to New York, said simply, "The Yankees need to think about who's their Big Papi."

In less than 48 hours, the Red Sox had crawled from a three-game hole to bring the series to 3-2. The next two games were in the Bronx, but even with the Yankees returning to their home turf, the entire tenor of the series had shifted. Curt Schilling, perhaps the best postseason pitcher of his generation, was slated to pitch Game 6, just days after it looked like he was finished for the season. And if Schilling won Game 6, anything could happen in a winner-take-all Game 7.

The fact that Schilling looked prepared to take the mound at all was nothing short of a minor medical miracle. The Sox had been desperately casting about for some short-term solution to Schilling's dislocated tendon. "Everyone was thinking, 'Well, is there some way to strap [the tendon] down?' " Epstein explained. "Can we just screw that freakin' tendon to bone? What can we do here?" Red Sox medical director Bill Morgan and the Boston training staff had another idea: How about suturing the skin around the injured tendon down to the deep tissue, creating what was essentially an artificial sheath to hold the tendon in place? Epstein was willing to consider it as a last-ditch scenario. But, as far as they could tell, the procedure had never been attempted before, so Morgan had no other surgeons to consult. He decided to do what med school students did when first learning surgery: practice on human cadavers. After a couple of tries, he was convinced it could work, and Morgan, Epstein, and Schilling decided the big right-hander would go under the knife. On Monday, a couple of hours before Boston's Game 5 victory, team doctors cut into Schilling's ankle. The doctors were actually making the injury worse—they were suturing the tendon out of place—but they hoped that by immobilizing it they could stop the tendon from snapping back and forth across Schilling's anklebone.

It was clear from early in Game 6 that this was a different pitcher than the one who had taken the mound in Yankee Stadium a week earlier. Schilling retired nine out of the first 10 batters he faced, and then, after letting up a pair of back-to-back singles to start the fourth inning, retired 10 more in a row, even as blood seeped out of one of his newly opened stitches and into his sanitary hose. The only blow against him was Bernie Williams's seventh-inning home run. Amazingly, Schilling lasted seven full innings, and left with a 4–1 lead. This gave the Boston bullpen a crucial break: Over the previous 48 hours, Alan Embree, Keith Foulke, and Mike Timlin had each thrown more than two innings, every one of them in high-pressure situations. Game 3 starter Bronson Arroyo came in to pitch the eighth. A one-out Miguel Cairo double and a Derek Jeter single scored New York's second run and brought Alex Rodriguez to the plate. After going 6-for-14 in New York's three victories, Rodriguez was only 2-for-12 in Games 4, 5, and 6. Now, facing Arroyo, the pitcher who'd nailed him in the elbow in July, Rodriguez hit a meek dribbler up the first base line. Arroyo fielded the ball and went to tag Rodriguez, but Rodriguez took an odd, uncoordinated, open-handed swipe at Arroyo's arm, knocking the ball loose and sending it rolling into right field. The first base umpire called Rodriguez safe, and Jeter scrambled around to score. But, after convening as a group and discussing the play, the umpires reversed the call. Rodriguez was out and Jeter was sent back to second base.

It was the second time that night the umpires had overruled a decision in the Red Sox's favor: In the fourth inning, with two out and two men on, Mark Bellhorn had hit a home run to left field that a fan had caught and dropped back onto the field. The hit was initially ruled a ground-rule double before the umpires got together and correctly called it a homer. This second call was too much for the New York fans to handle. A couple of days earlier they'd been pounding their chests and preparing for another satisfying victory at the hands of their Boston rivals. Now, the Yankees looked poised to suffer the worst postseason collapse in baseball history. Fans began throwing baseballs onto the field, which were quickly followed by bottles and debris. Before play resumed, riot police were called out to ring the infield. Once they were in place, Gary Sheffield popped out to end the inning.

In the ninth, Keith Foulke was called upon for the third straight game. Out of everyone in Boston's bullpen, Foulke was likely the most spent. He'd thrown 50 pitches two nights earlier in Boston's Game 4 victory, and followed that up with 22 more pitches in Game 5. Before that, the most pitches Foulke had thrown in a game that year was 41, and the most he'd thrown in any three-day stretch was 62. When he came to the mound in Game 6, he'd thrown 72 pitches in the previous 48 hours.

Foulke's best pitch is his changeup. Changeups are thrown with the same pitching motion as a fastball, but come in with less speed; because the hitter can't tell what's coming, the reduced speed leaves him off-balance. In order for a changeup to be effective, a pitcher must have a decent enough fastball to keep the hitter honest. Foulke's fastball had never been overpowering, but at 90 or 91 miles per hour it was respectable enough to adequately set up his change.

It was clear from the first batter Foulke faced in Game 6 that he wouldn't be throwing in the low 90s. His fastball was topping out at 88 or 89 miles per hour, which didn't provide as much deception for his mid-70-mile-per-hour, knee-buckling changeup. What's more, home plate umpire Joe West had a tight strike zone: anything the slightest bit off the plate was going to be called a ball. Hideki Matsui, the first man up in the inning, walked, bringing the tying run to the plate. After Bernie Williams struck out and Jorge Posada popped up, Ruben Sierra came to bat. Like Matsui, Sierra—who'd been 0-for-3 with three strikeouts against Schilling—battled his way on base via a seven-pitch walk. He was followed by first baseman Tony Clark, and as Clark prepared to hit, the angry and frustrated fans in Yankee Stadium came to life. This was how it was supposed to work in New York. A walk-off home run by one of the Yankees role players would make up for the anguish of the last several days.

"That at-bat, for me, was the most nerve-wracking moment of the series," says Epstein. "Foulke has nothing, he's getting squeezed, and a Clark home run ends it all." At home, at least the Red Sox would get a chance to bat last—in Yankee Stadium, there would be no more chances. As Clark settled into the batter's box, the Boston outfielders moved back about 10 feet. They'd gladly sacrifice a single in order to save a game-tying double from getting over their heads.

When Foulke pitches, he looks a bit like a cobra striking: He has a compact delivery and jerks the ball out of his glove before exploding toward the plate. He wound up and threw in to Clark. Ball one. Seconds later, he tried it again. Ball two. In the Red Sox dugout, Terry Francona bowed his head and began rocking back and forth. Foulke's third pitch was eminently hittable, but Clark held off, bringing the count to 2-1, and a fourth pitch foul evened it up. The fifth pitch of the at-bat was in the dirt. With a full count, the Yankees runners would be off with the pitch, meaning they'd be even more likely to score on a single. Foulke took a deep breath, walked around the mound, and started his windup. He threw an 88-mile-per-hour fastball, which Clark swung through to end the game. As Foulke ran off the field, his voice hoarse, he pounded Bronson Arroyo on the back. "Gotta make it interesting," he shouted before heading to the showers.

In the 25 previous Major League Baseball best-of-seven series in which one team had gone up three games to none, not a single series had been forced to a seventh game. "We just did something that has never been done," Schilling said afterward. "It's not over yet by any stretch." The Red Sox had already made history. Now the pressure would really be on New York.

After all the drama of the previous three days, Game 7 was almost anticlimactic. With Derek Lowe pitching one of the best games of his career, the Red Sox annihilated the Yankees. It was 2–0 after one, courtesy of a David Ortiz home run. It was 6–0 after two, courtesy of a Johnny Damon grand slam, and 8–1 after four, after another Damon homer. The final score: Red Sox 10, Yankees 3. By the end of the night, the loudest sound in Yankee Stadium came from the Boston fans in the stands chanting "Let's go Red Sox!"

"How many times can you honestly say you have a chance to shock the world?" Kevin Millar asked afterward in the champagne-drenched Red Sox clubhouse. "It might happen once in your life or it may never happen. But we had that chance, and we did it." Epstein, mindful of Boston's history, nodded to the Red Sox's long-time tormenters. "There have been so many great Red Sox teams and players who would have tasted World Series champagne if it wasn't for the Yankees," he said. "Guys in '49, '78, and us last year. Now that we've won, this is for them. We can put that behind us and move on to the World Series and take care of that." Then, once the cameras were off, he embraced John Henry. "We did it," Epstein shouted. "We did it in their fucking house."

There was lots of talk about how beating the Yankees and winning the American League Championship Series was only the first stop on the Sox's march into the history books. The Red Sox insisted that they still had to win the World Series, where they'd face the mighty St. Louis Cardinals, the winningest team in the major leagues and one stocked with prodigious sluggers and slick fielders.

But this matchup would have none of the drama of the Yankees series, Boston won in four straight games as a World Series that can only be called anticlimactic. The first game was the only one that featured any real excitement, when the Red Sox won 11–9 following Mark Bellhorn's eighth-inning, two-run home run. Schilling shut down the Cardinals in the second game, 6–2, and two days later Pedro Martinez won the first World Series game he'd ever pitched, 4–1.

Derek Lowe took the mound for Game 4 and, once again, he pitched brilliantly. "Basically, for the last 13 innings he pitched, no one hit a ball hard," says baseball operations executive Jed Hoyer, referring to the final game of the Yankees series and the clinching

World Series victory. "It was remarkable." In the ninth inning, Boston was leading 3–0 with Keith Foulke once again on the mound. With two out and a man on base, Cardinals shortstop Edgar Renteria came to the plate. Henry, Werner, and Lucchino fidgeted nervously in their seats near the Red Sox dugout. A Red Sox staff photographer was located nearby, ready to take their picture at the moment of victory.

In the visiting team's radio booth in St. Louis's Busch Stadium, Joe Castiglione surveyed the field. Castiglione, a Connecticut native, had been broadcasting Red Sox games since 1983, and his high-pitched, nasal voice has introduced thousands of fans to the team. Back in 1986, he had missed one of the most iconic plays in baseball history: When Mookie Wilson's ground ball rolled through Bill Buckner's legs, Castiglione had been in the bowels of Shea Stadium, camped out in the Red Sox clubhouse so he would be on hand to cover the victory celebration.

Foulke's first pitch to Renteria was a ball, and Albert Pujols, who'd led off the inning with a single, swiped second base without drawing a throw. Foulke set to pitch once again, and this time, Castiglione was ready, the words coming out in a rush. "Swing and a ground ball, stabbed by Foulke. He has it. He underhands to first, and the Boston Red Sox are the World Champions! For the first time in 86 years, the Red Sox have won baseball's world championship! Can you believe it?"

# PART VI

# Feeding the Monster: 2005

## CHAPTER 35

# *The Morning After*

**THE DRAMA AND EXCITEMENT** of the Yankees series had, in some ways, dulled observers to how completely Boston had annihilated its ultimate opponent. The 2004 St. Louis Cardinals won 105 games, a total only five other teams in the previous 30 years—the 1975 Cincinnati Reds, the 1986 New York Mets, the 1998 New York Yankees, the 1998 Atlanta Braves, and the 2001 Seattle Mariners—have managed to reach.* The Cardinals's offense had been almost as dominant as the Red Sox's during the regular season, leading the National League in average runs per game, total hits, batting average, and slugging percentage. Not to be outdone, the team's pitchers had allowed the fewest runs per game and were virtually tied with the Braves for the league's lowest earned run average.

The Red Sox transformed the mighty Cardinals into a collection of overmatched Little Leaguers. During the regular season, center fielder Jim Edmonds, first baseman Albert Pujols, and third baseman Scott Rolen had been the most prolific offensive trio in baseball, collectively hitting .316 with an average of 41 home runs and 119 runs batted in. In their four World Series games against Boston,

---

* In Boston's two previous World Series appearances—in 1975 and 1986—the Red Sox played the winningest National League team of the decade. As of the beginning of the 2006 season, the 2004 Cardinals were the winningest National League team of the '00s.

Edmonds, Pujols, and Rolen were a combined 6-for-45, for a measly .133 average, with no home runs and just one RBI. Boston didn't just sweep St. Louis, it did so without ever trailing, the fourth team on record to accomplish such a feat.* In so doing, the Red Sox became the first team in the history of Major League Baseball to end the season by winning eight straight playoff games.†

After so many decades of agonizing defeats, the Red Sox World Series victory functioned as a kind of exorcism and, as such, seemed rich in coincidences of the sort that inevitably came to feel deeply symbolic. Two-thousand four's clincher was played on the 18th anniversary of the final game of the Red Sox–Mets World Series in 1986, the loss that had inspired the first stories about the Curse of the Bambino. The final out of the Series had been made by Edgar Renteria, whose uniform bore the number 3—the same number Babe Ruth had worn with the Yankees.‡ After that out was recorded, the first two Red Sox players to embrace were right fielder Gabe Kapler and center fielder Johnny Damon, who wore the numbers 19 and 18, respectively, which combined to represent the year in which the Red Sox had last been champions. The Cardinals, in addition to being the second-most successful organization in baseball history, had been the team that had dashed the Red Sox's championship hopes in both 1946 and 1967. Best of all, Boston's march to the World Series had involved not just a mere defeat of New York, but its abject humiliation. Although nothing would ever erase the demoralizing losses the Red Sox had suffered at the hands of their archrivals, this came close. Not even the Red Sox had ever managed to blow a 3-0 lead in a best-of-seven series.

On the night of the final game against the Cardinals, October 27,

---

* The Red Sox scored in the first inning of every game, and were tied with the Cardinals for a total of only two-and-a-half innings during the 36 innings of World Series play: for two innings of Game 1 and for the first half-inning of Game 2.

† In 2005, the Chicago White Sox became the fifth team on record never to trail in the World Series when they swept the Houston Astros. The White Sox also finished the postseason with eight straight victories.

‡ Players didn't wear numbers when Ruth was with the Red Sox.

2004, at 9:14 P.M. Eastern Daylight Time, the full moon slowly faded out of sight as it settled into the earth's shadow, the first full lunar eclipse to occur during a World Series. The mythologies of many ancient cultures, from the Chinese to the Serrano Indians to the Vikings, explain lunar eclipses as the moon being swallowed by a malevolent force. In all these cultures, the people of earth had to make as much noise as possible to scare off the evildoer and restore the moon to its rightful place in the sky.

Red Sox fans certainly did their part. At 11:40 P.M., after the final out was made, church bells rang throughout New England. In Boston itself, the streets were filled with honking cars and delirious Red Sox loyalists. In St. Louis, hundreds of Boston fans gathered behind the Red Sox dugout,* screaming themselves satisfyingly hoarse as they waited for each one of their sweat- and champagne-soaked heroes to emerge from the clubhouse. Dave Roberts, who hadn't appeared in a game since he pinch-ran for Kevin Millar in the eighth inning of Game 5 of the Yankees series, hoisted the championship trophy above his head and paraded it around the field. Derek Lowe lit up a victory cigar and surveyed the frenzy. Even the hundreds of assembled reporters got into the act, surreptitiously grabbing handfuls of infield dirt or anything with a 2004 WORLD SERIES logo on it.

The players spent more than an hour celebrating on the field before riding the team bus the few short blocks to their hotel, where the festivities continued. Just after two in the morning, the team, by now blissed out on a combination of alcohol and exhaustion, piled back into their buses, which were immediately engulfed by scores of screaming fans too wired even to consider sleep. The Red Sox flew back to Boston early that morning, and by the time the team charter landed at Logan Airport, the roads into the city were lined with fans and adulatory banners. It was clear this was a celebration that was not going to end anytime soon. Within hours, Larry Lucchino was

---

* Late in the game, the staff at St. Louis's Busch Stadium opened the main stadium gates to allow hundreds of ticketless Red Sox fans to see the team finally win a championship.

meeting with Boston mayor Tom Menino, planning the details of the team's victory parade, which, they decided, would occur that very weekend. Saturday brought a chilly drizzle, but no matter: As the Red Sox rode the city's iconic duck boats through downtown Boston and eventually onto the Charles River, throngs of fervent fans lined the streets to shout their thanks.

The coming months served as a testament to how epic and all-encompassing the Red Sox's wild ride had been. It wasn't only Boston that was swept up in the team's victory, or just Massa-chusetts or even New England—it was the whole country. *The Washington Post*'s Thomas Boswell asked of the Red Sox's victory over the Yankees, "Is it possible to weigh the sports equivalent of a miracle?" He went on to call the American League Champion-ship Series "the most fun—the most unadultered, disbelieving, decades-overdue fun—that baseball has experienced in our time." The week of November 1, 2004—a week that featured a presiden-tial election—*Time* magazine put a picture of Jason Varitek leaping into Keith Foulke's arms on its cover. "The Joy of Sox!" read the headline; nothing else had to be said. *Sports Illustrated* named the entire Red Sox team its Sportsmen of the Year. In his cover arti-cle, *SI*'s Tom Verducci explained that "the most emotionally power-ful words in the English language are monosyllabic: love, hate, born, live, die, sex, kill, laugh, cry, want, need, give, take, Sawx." ESPN named the Sox the team of the year, Game 5 of the Yankees series the game of the year, and Curt Schilling the championship performer of the year. Throughout New England, the Red Sox were as ubiquitous as Michael Jackson during the *Thriller* era or the Bea-tles in 1964. There didn't seem to be a gas station or a convenience store that wasn't selling commemorative World Series memorabilia, and it often appeared as if those people on the street not wearing Red Sox caps had missed the memo about the regionwide dress code.

By Monday, November 1, Larry Lucchino was already looking for ways to build on the team's victory. "Some would think when you get to some level of success you stop and enjoy it," says Lucchino. "Fans are pouring into games, things are going well.

But from our point of view that's the moment of maximum opportunity to capture other people, to deepen the relationship with existing fans. We need to proactively exploit the moment and not just passively celebrate it." To that end, Lucchino launched the World Series trophy tour, vowing to bring the Red Sox's trophy to every one of the 351 cities and towns in Massachusetts, as well as scores more cities throughout New England and the rest of the country.

With this type of effort, Lucchino hoped, the Red Sox could mirror their on-field success with accomplishments on the business side. Every year since John Henry and Tom Werner had bought the team, the Red Sox had added new seats to Fenway Park, starting with the two rows of dugout seats, then the seats atop the Green Monster and on the right-field roof. New luxury boxes had been built, and there were plans to renovate the .406 Club. (In four years, the team had spent almost $100 million improving Fenway—the ballpark John Harrington had insisted couldn't be saved.) Instead of simply figuring the Sox would sell out most of their games and that that was good enough, the team had assembled 10-game packs of tickets that went on sale months before the season began. These packs all included a handful of highly desirable games (there was a pack that featured several Yankees games, as well as an Opening Day pack and a weekend pack) as well as some April and May midweek games that usually didn't sell as well. The team's creative efforts paid off, and in 2004 and 2005, the Red Sox sold out their entire 81-game home schedule, becoming only the second team in baseball history to do so.*

Although these marketing and promotional efforts led to increased revenues, they did not translate into profits for the Red Sox. Baseball's revenue-sharing system meant the Sox were handing

---

* The Red Sox's sell-out streak began on May 15, 2003. At the end of the 2005 season, the Sox had sold out 226 consecutive regular-season games at Fenway, the second-longest streak in Major League Baseball history. By the time spring training began in 2006, the Sox had essentially sold out the entire '06 season as well. From 1995 to 2001, the Cleveland Indians sold out 455 consecutive games.

over 34 percent of all their taxable local revenue (about $50 million in 2004*) to less financially successful teams.† The theory behind revenue sharing made sense—Henry, Werner, and Lucchino had all advocated for it when they owned or ran the Padres and the Marlins—but the practice, they felt, had gone too far.

Instead of leveling the playing field, baseball was squashing innovation on the part of the most successful clubs and discouraging creative efforts among the least successful ones. The Red Sox, in baseball's sixth largest market, were effectively being punished for running their business so effectively that they generated the second-most revenue in baseball. Instead of rewarding innovation, baseball discouraged it: The Sox, by 2005, had to generate $2 in pre-Major League Baseball taxed revenue in order to justify every $1 investment because of the combined effect of revenue sharing, income tax, and inflation. On the other hand, teams like the Philadelphia Phillies, the Baltimore Orioles, and the Toronto Blue Jays knew that if they generated more income, they wouldn't be adding to their bottom line but would simply be getting less of their competitors' money.‡

Even when the Sox came up with new money-generating plans that would produce taxable revenue, Bud Selig often rejected

---

* In 2005, the Yankees paid about $77 million into the revenue-sharing pool, while the Red Sox paid about $51 million. The Devil Rays received $33 million from the revenue-sharing pool and $34.5 million from baseball's central fund. Their entire payroll was $26.5 million.

† With Bud Selig doling out money disproportionately from baseball's central fund, Boston's marginal tax rate ended up closer to 40 percent. Baseball's central fund is seeded by revenue that goes to Major League Baseball instead of individual clubs; this money comes from things like national television contracts and apparel sales. Since teams like the Red Sox are more of a television draw and sell more merchandise than less popular teams, the Sox simultaneously contribute more to, and get less from, the central fund. In 2005, $72.7 million from the central fund went into the revenue-sharing pool.

‡ Economist Andrew Zimbalist estimates that the effect of revenue sharing on teams with low revenues is an implicit marginal tax rate of 47 percent: for every dollar in revenue they generate, those teams will get 47 cents less from Major League Baseball.

them—his goal, more and more baseball owners were coming to feel, was not to increase competitiveness but to completely flatten the playing field. At one point, the Red Sox and Yankees had discussed selling local sponsorships for their regular season series, a deal that could have brought in millions of dollars. Major League Baseball nixed the idea. The Sox had proposed opening Red Sox Taverns around New England and selling Red Sox lager; Selig said no.

"It's frustrating," says Henry. "It's easier to depress the entrepreneurship of the upper clubs and try to reduce their revenues as much as possible than to increase lower clubs' revenues. Teams like the Red Sox, the Yankees, the Dodgers—we should be allowed to compete in the global entertainment marketplace, and also against football and basketball and hockey. But we're not allowed to do that." By this point, even the terms of the Red Sox's deal with NESN had become a source of conflict, as baseball's revenue-sharing committee tried to force the team to charge above-market rates for the right to broadcast the team's games.* The result of that, of course, would be more shared revenue.

When the owners of successful baseball clubs like the Red Sox and the Yankees say they're not making money, the public's reaction is usually one of disbelief. But it's true. In 2004, a year in which the Red Sox raised ticket prices, set attendance records, sold more merchandise than any year in their history, and won the World Se-

---

* Situations in which a team's ownership also owns other entities that do business with the team are known as "related party transactions." If a team disagrees with the revenue-sharing committee's decision about the value of such a transaction, the team can eventually appeal to the commissioner. If the team disagrees with the commissioner, the next step is a lawsuit. In 2005, baseball's revenue-sharing committee was made up of Indians president Paul Dolan, the son of Larry Dolan and the cousin of losing Red Sox bidder Charles Dolan; former Padres president Dick Freeman, who worked for John Moores, with whom Larry Lucchino had parted so acrimoniously; and Mariners president Chuck Armstrong. None of the three teams represented on the revenue-sharing committee owned its own regional sports network, and none was considered a large-market team.

ries, the team lost money.* (The Yankees, under the burden of their bloated payroll, lost around $37 million.) Instead of paring back payroll or cutting down on marketing, Henry, Werner, and Lucchino had looked for ways to generate profit that didn't have to be shared with other teams. Since 2003, Fenway Park had hosted midsummer rock concerts, and there had been discussions about opening up the park to ice-skating in the winter.† The previous March, New England Sports Ventures—the name of the company Henry and Werner had formed to buy the Red Sox—had launched a wholly owned subsidiary called the Fenway Sports Group for the express purpose of building an asset that diversified the business. What's more, the money FSG earned that wasn't related to baseball couldn't be touched by Major League Baseball.‡

These restrictions were frustrating, but even dealing with the business challenges they created were invigorating. The Red Sox were imbued with a sense of purpose, and now that they'd won the World Series, they could continue transforming the rest of the organization into a textbook example of how a smart and unified leadership team could make anything happen. "Almost every part of this experience has exceeded my expectations," Henry says. His partnership with Werner and Lucchino, two men he'd never worked with before buying the team, had proven astoundingly successful. "It's been a perfect relationship," he says. "You have three guys who really like each other, and we're surrounded by people that are just brilliant." It felt almost too good to be true. "Deals don't work out that way, you know," he says. "You put a deal together and hope for

---

* This does not mean that Henry, Werner, and the Red Sox's minority partners failed to make money, because other divisions of the company, such as NESN and non-baseball events at Fenway Park, turned a profit. In *Forbes* magazine's 2006 "Business of Baseball" package, the Yankees were listed as losing $50 million and the Red Sox $18.5 million in 2005 before interest, income taxes, and depreciation.

† While NESN's deal with the Red Sox is a related party transaction, since a concert at Fenway is not dependent in any way on the team itself, money earned through such events is not subject to revenue sharing.

‡ The Fenway Sports Group initially focused on finding ways to outsource the Red Sox's marketing acumen; in early 2005, FSG announced it would handle Boston College's athletic marketing and media.

the best but it never works out. Well, in this case, it turns out you have three guys who love each other, who work so well together, who have so much fun together. We were the outsiders who came in and won the World Series. It just doesn't happen like that."

Just as rewarding, thought Henry, was how the harmony and effectiveness of his three-way partnership had trickled down through the ranks, creating an organization in which everyone was working together toward common goals. Lucchino's lieutenants were creative, tireless, smart, and ultra-competitive, and looked to be in Boston for years to come. Mike Dee, who'd first met Lucchino in Baltimore, was running the Fenway Sports Group, while Theo Epstein had transformed the team's baseball operations department into the envy of the major leagues. In March, Dee had been persuaded to remain in Boston as the chief operating officer of the Red Sox even after the owner of the Los Angeles Dodgers offered to make him the president of the team. And while Epstein's initial three-year contract would expire at the end of the 2005 season, Henry assumed re-signing him would be a mere formality. Lucchino's close relationships with his various department heads and executives, from architect Janet Marie Smith to public relations guru Charles Steinberg and Red Sox Foundation head Meg Vaillancourt, gave Henry and Werner the freedom to involve themselves mainly in issues about which they were most passionate. They were confident that the day-to-day operation of the team was in their CEO's capable hands.

Only rarely did anything interrupt the idyll, and it was hard to take the interruptions seriously. When Bob Kraft, the owner of the defending Super Bowl champion New England Patriots, warned Henry about the infighting and unhappiness that often follows victory, Henry wasn't sure this applied to the Red Sox. But after everyone had worked together so brilliantly to achieve the Holy Grail, what could possibly derail the team's plans?

## CHAPTER 36

# Goodbye to No. 45

**NO SOONER HAD THE WORLD SERIES PARADE ENDED** than Theo Epstein and the team's baseball operations crew dove back into their work. Despite his masterful pitching in the playoffs, there was little doubt that Derek Lowe would go elsewhere in 2005; after his erratic performances of the past two years, the Red Sox weren't even expected to make him an offer. Orlando Cabrera, the replacement for Nomar Garciaparra, would likely switch teams as well. (Even on the morning of the parade, Cabrera, a free agent, was telling people he doubted he'd be back in Boston.) And both Pokey Reese and Dave Roberts hoped either to sign with or be traded to teams with which they could land starting jobs.

That left Pedro Martinez and Jason Varitek as the team's big free agent question marks. Both were, in their own ways, crucial to the performance and personality of the team. In a clubhouse full of clowns and cutups, no one worked harder than Varitek, who spent hours preparing with the team's pitchers and had become a true of-fensive threat. His agent, the notoriously tough Scott Boras, was seeking a five-year, $55 million deal for his client. But Varitek was already 32 years old, and there are very few catchers in the history of the game who have remained productive past that age. By the time he was 33, the legendary Johnny Bench had all but hung up his mask and chest protector and became an infielder. After hitting .300

or above every single year from the time he broke into the league, Mike Piazza began his sorry decline at precisely age 33, slipping from .280 to a woeful .251 in just four seasons.

Martinez, meanwhile, had cemented his stature as one of the most dominant pitchers in the history of baseball. What he'd accomplished during the previous seven years with the Red Sox was astounding. His record since arriving in Boston was 117-37, good for a .760 winning percentage; the best career winning percentage since the beginning of the twentieth century for a pitcher with at least 100 decisions was .717. Despite numerous stints on the disabled list, he had amassed 1,683 strikeouts, for an average of 240 a season. His aggregate earned run average in Boston was 2.52, which would have been good enough to lead the American League every year since 1998. (He won the American League's ERA title in 1999, 2000, 2002, and 2003 with ERAs of 2.07, 1.74, 2.26, and 2.22, respectively.) The pitcher to whom he was most often compared was the incomparable Dodger great, Sandy Koufax.* He was the most popular Latino athlete in the history of Boston, and one of the most beloved and recognizable people in New England.

To be sure, he did have his downsides. Manager Terry Francona had been clashing with Martinez since Opening Day, when the pitcher took off from the ballpark before the end of a game he had started. The next day, Martinez and Francona had a fierce argument, and as the season wore on, Francona grew increasingly frustrated with Martinez's ceaseless desire for special treatment.

That in itself wouldn't have meant much one way or another. In modern-day baseball, the wishes of a superstar almost always trump

---

* Martinez's two best seasons were, in fact, superior to Koufax's two best years. In 1999 and 2000, when Martinez was 27 and 28, Martinez went 41-10 with 597 strikeouts and a combined 1.90 ERA. Koufax, during 1963 and 1964, arguably his finest two seasons, was 44-10 with 529 strikeouts and a 1.82 ERA. But Koufax pitched on a higher mound during an era of decreased offense, and his home park, Dodger Stadium, tended to suppress scoring. Martinez was pitching during an era of much greater offensive production. In those years, Martinez's ERA+, a figure that compares a pitcher's ERA to that of the league, averaged out to 265. Koufax's averaged to 174. Martinez's 2000 ERA+ of 285 is the best of the modern era, and his 2000 WHIP, or walks+hits per inning pitched, is the lowest ever, at .7373.

those of a manager, and Lucchino saw Francona's insistence on treating all of the team's players equally as unrealistic, even foolish. "Pedro is a unique talent," Lucchino says. "When you're dealing with superstars, they're different than the rest of us, and you've got to treat them accordingly."

More than Martinez's petulance, there were also questions about his durability. While there had been times during 2004 when he'd performed extremely well, he'd also had extended periods of mediocre play. In September, Martinez was 2-4 with a 4.95 ERA, and gave up a hit per inning. As the season wore on, he looked increasingly like a pitcher who would need to be coddled for the rest of his career. In 2004, he had a 4.77 ERA while working on four days', or normal, rest, and a 2.98 ERA with five or more days' rest. And for the sixth season in a row, he'd thrown fewer than 220 innings; over that time span, Martinez averaged just 192 innings per year.

Perhaps most worrisome was the fact that Martinez's arm slot* was considerably lower than it had been in years past, which led to a decrease in velocity—Martinez's fastball now topped out in the low 90s, markedly lower than its peak of over 95 miles per hour—and raised questions about the strength of his shoulder. Was Martinez not throwing all out in order to ensure he'd be healthy when the time came to sign a contract at the end of the year? Or was he masking an injury?

To Martinez, all these issues were inconsequential. The great and proud pitcher didn't look at the arc of his career and see the risks a club would incur by laying out tens of millions of dollars for him, nor did he see his performance in 2004 as indicative of a once-elite player beginning his inevitable decline. He'd watched as the team he'd led for the past seven years had gone out and wooed an older, less successful pitcher, and then watched as that pitcher had supplanted him as the team's ace. Now it was time for the Red Sox to show *him* the love. Martinez and his agent, Fernando Cuza, ar-

---

* A pitcher's arm slot is where he brings his arm over his shoulder before releasing the ball. For a full overhead arm slot, the pitcher's arm would be, at full extension, pointing straight up to the sky and be perpendicular to the ground. When a pitcher lowers his arm slot, the angle formed between his arm and the ground gets smaller, and less pressure is exerted on the shoulder.

gued that, at 33, Martinez was younger than many of the game's other highly paid hurlers, and should be paid accordingly. After all, Curt Schilling was five years older than Martinez, Randy Johnson eight, and Roger Clemens nine, and all three men had contracts that would pay them more than $14 million in 2005. What neither Martinez nor Cuza acknowledged was that Schilling, Johnson, and Clemens were all at least five inches taller and 30 pounds heavier than the slight Martinez, and that none had experienced the kind of shoulder problems that had plagued him.

By the end of the 2004 playoffs, the Red Sox's on-and-off negotiations with Martinez were almost at the two-year mark. In the spring of 2003, the two sides had begun discussing an extension to Martinez's contract. Since his club option in 2004 was worth $17.5 million, Martinez took the position at the time that any movement down from that figure would be a major concession on his part. In addition to having the Red Sox pick up his option year, Martinez wanted a three-year deal worth about $15 million per year. When this was turned down, he told the press they'd be "shocked" if they knew how little he was willing to play for. He then refused to take a team physical until after the team exercised his '04 option, thereby asking the team to guarantee him the most money ever paid to a pitcher before they knew whether he was healthy.

Now Martinez wanted a contract that, at minimum, would pay him as much as Schilling was scheduled to make. Instead, the Red Sox offered Martinez a two-year deal worth $25.5 million with a $13 million option for 2007 and various performance bonuses. This was very similar to the initial deal the Red Sox had agreed to with Schilling: a contract worth $12.5 million a year, with a $13 million club option. But Schilling's base salary for the remaining years of his contract was increased by $2 million per year and his option year became guaranteed with Boston's World Series win. Martinez wanted a deal in which his base equaled what Schilling was set to make after this increase. "If they don't get me," he said after his victory in St. Louis, "it's probably because they didn't try hard enough. My heart is with Boston."

By early November, Martinez had begun wooing the New York Yankees, an unusual move for a player—generally, the pursuit is in the opposite direction. Martinez asked Cuza to set up a meeting with Yankees owner George Steinbrenner at Steinbrenner's Tampa home base. Martinez also arranged to eat dinner with Alex Rodriguez.

The Yankees weren't the only baseball team in New York Martinez was trying to interest in his services. Astoundingly, he'd begun reaching out to the New York Mets before the World Series had even concluded. Before the second game of the Series, with Curt Schilling preparing to pitch against the Cardinals,* Martinez had run into Jay Horwitz, the longtime New York Mets director of public relations, outside of the Red Sox clubhouse. "Say hello to Omar," Martinez told Horwitz, referring to Omar Minaya, who'd been named the Mets general manager less than a month earlier. Later that night, Martinez repeated his greeting. "When you're [about to be] a free agent, that's a pretty clear coded message: 'Hey, keep me in mind,' " Minaya said later. "The timing of it tells me, this isn't Pedro being polite; this guy's interested."

By the end of November, it was clear Steinbrenner and the Yankees were going to pass on Martinez's services. The Mets, meanwhile, were conflicted. The team's statistics guru told Minaya that Martinez wasn't a smart long-term investment; he was already exhibiting an increasing walk rate and a declining strikeout rate. The better option, Minaya was told, would be free agent Matt Clement. But Minaya, eager to make his mark on his new team, decided to make a run at his fellow Dominican. By the end of November, the bidding for Martinez was essentially limited to the Mets and the Red Sox. Minaya put the Mets in the lead by offering Martinez a guaranteed three-year deal for $38 million with an option for a fourth year.

The Red Sox's own internal debate was similar to the Mets', except the Red Sox had even more specific medical data about Mar-

---

*Even though Martinez had started Game 5 and Schilling Game 6 of the American League Championship Series, the Red Sox wanted Schilling to start Game 2 of the World Series at Fenway so he wouldn't need to bat when the Series traveled to St. Louis for Game 3, which would be played under National League rules. The decision meant Martinez didn't get a chance to pitch a World Series game at Fenway.

tinez's rotator cuff. To varying degrees, the people in the team's baseball operations office, from Theo Epstein to Bill James to assistant general manager Josh Byrnes, didn't think it was wise to guarantee Martinez more than two years. His shoulder was too questionable, his decline too suggestive of what was to come. Ownership and top management were more conflicted—Larry Lucchino, for one, wanted to do whatever the team could to bring Martinez back. "I was Pedro's biggest supporter," says Lucchino.

On December 8, Henry and Lucchino flew down to the Dominican Republic and met Martinez under a tent on an airport tarmac. Once there, the two executives made their pitch. Martinez, they said, should be with the Red Sox for the rest of his career. He'd go down as the best pitcher in the history of the club. He had a comfortable situation with his teammates and a fan base that already embraced him, quirks and all. The Red Sox, they said, might even be willing to go to three guaranteed years, but wanted a provision that allowed for some relief should Martinez seriously injure his shoulder.

Martinez and his agent nixed any deal that would allow any part of the contract to be voided, but both sides agreed they'd moved closer to a deal. Still, both Henry and Lucchino returned to the United States feeling confused. On the one hand, it seemed as if they were closing in on a deal; on the other, both men sensed that Martinez wasn't excited about returning.

"I never had the feeling that he wanted to re-sign," says Henry. "That's just my perception, which could be totally flawed. And it didn't matter—we were going to try to sign him. But I didn't think he wanted to come back." Lucchino wondered how much Schilling's success was weighing on Martinez's mind. "He's certainly a very proud person," Lucchino says, "and he's earned a whole lot of self-confidence. His performance justifies that . . . but I do think there were personality issues involved. I don't know if it was so much wanting equal status, but there were some issues at the end of the year [in 2004], and that may have been a factor. I do think the Mets approach to him—'You'll be the rock on which we'll build this church'—had to have a lot of appeal."

By Saturday, December 11, Martinez's agent told the Red Sox

that if they offered three guaranteed years, with a fourth year as a club option, the pitcher would return to Boston. Amid much debate, the team agreed to Martinez's demands, topping the Mets with an offer of a guaranteed $40.5 million for three years, with a $13.5 million option for the 2008 season. That, Lucchino thought, settled the issue: the Red Sox would start 2005 with Martinez once again wearing No. 45.

"I was led to believe that if we did a third year, we would have a deal," says Lucchino. "So we went to a third year." All that was left was working out some final details, which would be handled by Epstein and Cuza, both of whom were in Anaheim for baseball's annual winter meetings. But at some point on Sunday, December 12, Cuza told the Mets about Boston's latest offer and gave Omar Minaya another chance to increase his bid. Minaya did just that, offering Martinez a guaranteed four-year, $54 million contract. By Monday morning, the news that Martinez would sign with the Mets had been leaked to New York papers.

For the Red Sox, Martinez's departure meant losing their second franchise icon in less than six months. Behind the scenes, the failure to re-sign the pitcher widened the already sizable rift between Theo Epstein and Larry Lucchino. In some ways, Pedro Martinez represented exactly the kind of player Theo Epstein thought the Red Sox *shouldn't* be over-committing to: a difficult, expensive superstar on the downside of his career. The only way the Red Sox could consistently compete with the Yankees, Epstein thought, was by avoiding these costly mistakes. Falling irrationally in love with a superstar was fine for the fans, but it wouldn't lead to long-term success. Lucchino, on the other hand, was more sentimental. "I'm often the guy who's in favor of making a less seismic change," he says.

Lucchino knew Epstein had been conflicted about re-signing Martinez, and at times it sounded as if he suspected his general manager had not done everything he could to see that Martinez's contract was signed. "We thought we had [come to terms]," Lucchino says. "Theo was [in Anaheim] doing the day-to-day. . . . I think if we had gotten to that point earlier in the process, it would've gotten done." At least one of Lucchino's allies on the club told reporters in background conversations that Epstein had purposefully dragged his feet with Cuza because of the general manager's loyalty to Terry Francona—a shocking (and false) accusation. As had been the case in the aftermath of the Alex Rodriguez negotiations, Lucchino didn't approach Epstein about his concerns. And to everyone except Lucchino's and Epstein's closest confidants on the club, it seemed as if the Red Sox were a well-oiled machine, preparing to do battle once again.

# CHAPTER 37

# *Theo Epstein Looks to the Future*

**WITH MARTINEZ GONE** and the Red Sox not interested in re-signing Derek Lowe, Epstein set about trying to remake the pitching rotation. He pursued Randy Johnson, Curt Schilling's former teammate in Arizona, whom the Diamondbacks were looking to trade, and also went after 28-year-old Carl Pavano, a free agent who had gone 18-8 with a 3.00 earned run average for the Florida Marlins in 2004. Since both pitchers seemed more inclined to sign with the Yankees, Epstein also looked elsewhere. Within a week of Pedro Martinez's departure, the Red Sox had added two new pitchers to Boston's starting rotation: 41-year-old David Wells and 30-year-old Matt Clement.

Wells and Clement could not have been more different. The left-handed Wells was known as much for his off-field rabble-rousing as his on-field performances. He was overweight and loud, and bragged in his autobiography that he'd pitched a perfect game while still half-drunk from the night before. (He later admitted this was an exaggeration.) A curveball specialist, Wells was one of the best control pitchers in the game, and often posted one of the lowest walk totals in baseball. He was also incredibly durable: Since 1996, he'd made fewer than 30 starts only once.* His brash—some would say obnoxious—personality rubbed many people the wrong way, and, Epstein believed, caused some teams to overlook his talent. As far as Epstein was concerned, he was one of the most underrated pitchers in the game, and in an out-of-control market for starting pitchers, Wells at a guaranteed $8 million over two years was much more attractive to the team than some of the pitchers demanding $30 million for three years.

Clement, on the other hand, was a skinny right-hander who featured a great slider and a sinking fastball. A onetime San Diego Padres prospect, Clement had frustrated team after team with his inability to put together a full season's worth of performances indicative of his talent. He had control problems—since 1999, he'd averaged 90 walks a season, compared to 33 for Wells—and a reputation for becoming too easily intimidated. The Red Sox hoped that Clement's 2004 season, in which he'd held opposing batters to a .229 average and posted a 3.68 ERA, was a sign that the pitcher had finally turned a corner. They signed him to a three-year, $25.5 million deal.

Wells and Clement did not, at first glance, seem like adequate replacements for Martinez and Lowe. Whereas the departing Red Sox pitchers had gone 30-21 in 2004, the new additions had posted only a 21-21 record. But in 2004, Wells and Clement had thrown almost as many innings as their predecessors, 377 compared to 400, and had a significantly better combined earned run average, 3.71 compared to 4.59. Martinez and Lowe together would have likely cost the Red Sox somewhere between $23 and $25 million per year; Wells and Clement required shorter commitments and would cost only between $10 and $17 million a year, depending on how many of his incentives Wells reached. For a savings of anywhere from $6 to $15 million, there was a good chance the Red Sox had just made their 2005 rotation better.

---

*During this same stretch, Pedro Martinez, despite being eight-and-a-half years younger, failed to make 30 starts in a season on four separate occasions.

Before the end of the month, Epstein also picked up a pair of pitchers whose careers had been sidetracked by injuries. At 31, Matt Mantei should have been looking at another four or five years of productive relief work. As recently as 2003, he'd notched 29 saves as the Arizona Diamondbacks closer, but elbow and shoulder surgeries had sidelined the pitcher. The 28-year-old Wade Miller had been one of the best young pitchers in the National League just a year earlier, but had badly injured his rotator cuff in 2004. The Red Sox signed Mantei for $750,000 and Miller for $1.5 million, while giving both pitchers appearance and performance incentives that could triple their salaries.

Two years earlier, in Epstein's first offseason as general manager, Boston had picked up Todd Walker, Jeremy Giambi, Kevin Millar, Bill Mueller, and David Ortiz for a combined $10.85 million. If the Red Sox had believed that midlevel offensive players with a penchant for getting on base had been undervalued in 2002, the team was now indicating that there was a crop of pitchers that could be had for low risk and the possibility of high return: Wells, Mantei, and Miller—two quality starters and a solid reliever—had cost a total of just $6.25 million in guaranteed money.

Before the end of the year, Boston had filled its other two major remaining holes. Convinced Jason Varitek could be the rare catcher who remained productive into his mid-thirties, the Red Sox decided he was worth overpaying, and re-signed him to a four-year, $40 million deal. For the same price, they also nabbed free agent shortstop Edgar Renteria. Renteria, a four-time All-Star and two-time Gold Glove winner, was just 29, had an excellent defensive reputation, was a strong hitter, and had been relatively injury free. All that remained was the annual Manny Ramirez sweepstakes. At one point, the Red Sox came very close to a deal that would have sent Ramirez and Byung-Hyun Kim to the New York Mets for outfielder Cliff Floyd and minor league prospects, including the promising Venezuelan pitcher Yusmeiro Petit. Boston then would have used the money Ramirez's departure had freed up to go after another big bat, such as free agent J. D. Drew. (Drew ended up signing a five-year deal with the Los Angeles Dodgers for $55 million.) But at the last minute, Mets general manager Omar Minaya asked for between

$4 and $5 million a year to offset Ramirez's salary, killing the proposed trade.*

With Ramirez seemingly on board for another season, spring training in 2005 brought a Red Sox team that looked quite similar to the one from 2004. Eight of the team's nine everyday starting players had returned, with Renteria the only addition. Three-fifths of the starting rotation were also holdovers, as were the three men at the back end of the Red Sox bullpen—Keith Foulke, Alan Embree, and Mike Timlin.

But the clubhouse felt like a much different place. For the first time since 1997, there was no Nomar Garciaparra—not that he would be missed.† In the first half of 2004, he had, as one player put it, "sat by himself in a corner, mad at the whole world." "People didn't notice Nomar in the clubhouse," says pitcher Bronson Arroyo. "If Nomar had been a very vocal guy, like a Millar, and was voicing the negativity, then maybe it would've affected the clubhouse. But it never did." Still, Garciaparra was one of the most iconic players in the history of the club. Having him gone felt, at the very least, odd.

Pedro Martinez and Derek Lowe, on the other hand, had been active presences. Even when Martinez didn't show up at the park everyday, his quirky sense of humor and impish enthusiasm pervaded Boston's clubhouse.‡ When Orlando Cabrera had arrived

---

* After signing a two-year, $10 million deal following the 2003 season, Kim was maddeningly ineffective in 2004. On March 30, 2005, the Sox essentially gave Kim to the Colorado Rockies, while effectively agreeing to pay about $5.7 million of the $6 million he was still owed. Speaking of Kim's difficulties in Boston, Epstein said, "This is a disappointing end to the saga. It remains to this day a mystery for us."

† Early in the 2005 season, the following hand-written sign was tacked on a bulletin board in the Red Sox clubhouse: "1918 + 24 Manny + 34 Ortiz + 33 Varitek - 5 Nomar = 2004."

‡ In 2001, the *Herald*'s Jeff Horrigan was doing an interview with Martinez for *Sports Illustrated for Kids*. Horrigan asked Martinez his favorite color. "Green." Favorite book? "Whatever." Favorite actress? "Sandra Bullock." Secret ambition? "I would like to fuck Sandra Bullock," Martinez replied with a grin. Horrigan explained that likely wasn't an appropriate response for a children's magazine and asked the question again. Martinez dutifully amended his answer: "I would like to sleep with Sandra Bullock."

in Boston, Martinez had presented him with a STOP SMOKING poster the pitcher had posed for several years earlier. "I'm a flamin' mullion with a big pecker and a big bank account," Martinez had scrawled, before signing the poster with a flourish: "Pedro Martinez, #45." He'd famously brought Nelson de la Rosa, a 28-inch Dominican dwarf, into the Red Sox clubhouse the previous September as a good luck charm. (De la Rosa's previous claim to fame was a role alongside Marlon Brando in *The Island of Dr. Moreau.*) There was the time Martinez wore a Yoda mask in the Boston dugout during a game, the times he did a chicken dance at opposing batters who took walks from Red Sox pitchers, the time he did wobbly cartwheels along the infield grass or allowed himself to be duct-taped to a dugout pole like a hazed high-school freshman.

Lowe was just as animated, if more tortured, a presence. He'd shout across the team's cramped clubhouse to anyone who happened to be in his field of vision, offering opinions on football or beer or babes or anything else that was on his mind. For seven seasons, these two pitchers had helped set the tone for the team. "Both of those guys brought a lot of personality to the [team]," says Arroyo. Two-thousand five would be different. Curt Schilling was an outsized personality, but he didn't have Martinez's infectious joie de vivre. Jason Varitek, who'd been appointed the team's captain after re-upping with Boston in December, was more comfortable leading by example than actively setting the mood for the team. There were plenty of self-proclaimed "idiots" still around, guys like Johnny Damon and Kevin Millar, but the freewheeling, anything goes ethos that had defined the Red Sox for the previous two seasons was undeniably changing.

As far as Theo Epstein was concerned, that was a good thing. When he was named general manager in 2002, he set three immediate goals for himself: winning a World Series, rebuilding the team's minor league system, and managing the transition away from the team dominated by the 2004 free agent class. Two-thousand five would be the second year of that transition, and it was going well. This year, instead of the prospect of Garciaparra, Lowe, Martinez,

Trot Nixon, and Varitek all reaching free agency at once, the Red Sox had only two players in the last year of their contracts whom they'd likely try to retain, Damon and knuckleballer Tim Wakefield, along with two they'd likely let sign elsewhere, Millar and third baseman Bill Mueller.

There was, of course, still one significant contract issue the Red Sox still had to deal with: Epstein's initial three-year deal was set to expire on October 31, 2005. The young general manager's popularity had only grown in the wake of the Red Sox's World Series victory. *The Boston Globe*'s Sunday magazine had recently named him Bostonian of the year, and he was arguably as recognizable a star as any of the team's players. Epstein's contract negotiations were not expected to be as contentious as those of Garciaparra or Martinez. For one thing, there would be no agents mucking up the negotiations, since the team had a policy of not allowing its front office personnel to use agents. More important, both Epstein and the team's owners had expressed their strong desire to continue their working relationship.

Going into spring training, Epstein was hopeful he'd be able to work out a deal before the season began. There was certainly precedent for re-signing an executive before his deal expired. Larry Lucchino's initial eight-year deal had been scheduled to conclude before the 2009 season, but in January 2004, John Henry and Tom Werner signed the team's CEO to a four-year extension that would run through February 2012.* Surely Epstein could expect similar treatment.

At spring training, Henry and Epstein had a brief discussion about the future. The two men had an unusually close relationship. In Epstein, Henry had found the rare general manager who was open to fresh ideas and not obsessed with fan reaction. The Garciaparra trade, Henry says, was "one of the bravest moves anyone could make in baseball. It shows how incredibly special and selfless Theo

---

* Part of the impetus for that deal, Lucchino admitted, was that there were rumors he was on his way out of town in the wake of the Red Sox's failed pursuit of Alex Rodriguez. "That's why this makes sense," Lucchino had said at the time. "I hope this puts to rest that notion."

is and was to do that for the club." In Henry, Epstein found an owner who agreed with him about the proper way to put together winning ball clubs. They would, they both thought, work together for years to come.

But John Henry isn't the Red Sox CEO, and Henry and Epstein felt it would be more appropriate for Epstein to work out the specifics of his new deal with Larry Lucchino, the man who'd helped bring Epstein into baseball. Before the season began, Epstein sent an email to Lucchino in which he expressed his desire to stay with the team and said he was amenable to beginning discussions anytime. What Henry didn't know at the time, and what perhaps neither Epstein nor Lucchino fully realized, was the extent to which the unspoken bitterness of the previous years had affected both the general manager and the chief executive officer.

By the end of spring training, Epstein felt confident that the 2005 Red Sox team had more depth than the '04 team had had. The Sox had traded Dave Roberts to the San Diego Padres for outfielder Jay Payton, who didn't have Roberts's speed but was a much better hitter. Kevin Youkilis was ready to spell Bill Mueller in the field, which would give the 34-year-old Mueller's knees some much-needed rest. Doug Mientkiewicz was gone, but there was a low-cost option as a potential first base backup in 34-year-old Roberto Petagine, who'd been a star in Japan for the previous six years. Getting all of these players adequate time on the field didn't look like it would be a problem; the team's average age was almost 32, and plenty of players would need rest before the season was over. Even the news that Curt Schilling hadn't fully recovered from his offseason ankle surgery and would start the season on the disabled list wasn't too worrisome. The Red Sox rotation was deep enough to withstand a couple of weeks without its ace.

The regular season began on April 3, a cold and wet New York night at Yankee Stadium. Randy Johnson, New York's left-handed pickup, handily outpitched David Wells, Boston's left-handed pickup, and the Red Sox began the season with a 9–2 loss. They lost the next day, too, before winning a pair, then losing two more. The season was only a week old, but the Olde Towne Team's disappointing 2-4 record would have been, in many years, reasons enough for the locals to begin to panic. (The *Boston Herald* once famously ran "Wait Till Next Year" as a headline after an Opening Day loss.) But in 2005, everyone remained calm. After all, the Red Sox were the World Series champions, and this was only the start of a very long season. This year, of all years, would be different.

## CHAPTER 38

# *The Defending Champs*

APRIL 11, 2005, marked three years and 10 days since John Henry had greeted fans as they entered Fenway Park on Opening Day of his first season as the Red Sox principal owner. And although this year he wouldn't personally welcome the 33,702 ticketed fans who made their way into the park for Boston's 2005 home opener, no one minded. On this day, for the first time since World War I, the Red Sox would be officially crowned baseball's champions.

That day's ceremony began around two fifteen, as members of the Boston Symphony Orchestra and the Boston Pops played the opening fanfare of Richard Strauss's symphonic poem, "Thus Spake Zarathustra," made famous by Stanley Kubrick's *2001: A Space Odyssey*. With each resounding chord, a pennant was unfurled vertically down the Green Monster, until there were five in all, one for each of the Red Sox's World Series victories: 1903, 1912, 1915, 1916, and 1918. Then, with the final, climactic flourish, an enormous, Wall-encompassing banner flapped down over the other five. It read, simply, 2004 WORLD SERIES CHAMPIONS.

Across the field, the Red Sox dugout was as full as it had ever been. The 2005 team was all there, as were some returning members of the '04 squad, including playoff heroes Derek Lowe and Dave Roberts. Theo Epstein sat off to one side, trying to avoid the cameras. As Lowe looked out onto the field he'd called home for so many years, he turned to his old teammate, catcher Jason Varitek. "You're lucky," said Lowe, now a member of the Los Angeles Dodgers. "You get to play here for the next four years. There's nothing like it." Trot Nixon, the second-longest tenured player on the team, said, "I was just taking it all in—as slow as possible." Johnny Pesky, who's spent more hours in the Red Sox clubhouse than any person, ever, fought back tears.

The rest of the ceremony was heavy on signature Charles Steinberg–orchestrated moments. As New England's James Taylor sang "America the Beautiful," 19 Army and Marine soldiers who'd been injured in the war in Iraq marched from the left field wall to the Red Sox dugout. Before the ring ceremony began, an impressive assemblage of Red Sox players from the decades past formed a greeting line. Hall of Fame second baseman Bobby Doerr, who last played a game on the Fenway grass in 1951, was there, as was everyone from Dom DiMaggio and Jim Lonborg to Fred Lynn, Oil Can Boyd, and Carl Yastrzemski. The retired players formed a column through which the 2004 team would pass on the way to accept their rings. Lowe and Roberts received some of the loudest cheers of the day.

Then, just before three o'clock, the 85-year-old Pesky and the 65-year-old Yastrzemski made their way to the center-field flagpole, surrounded by members of the '04 team. The two men had played a combined 4,337 regular-season games during their 31 years as uniformed members of the Boston Red Sox. Together, they raised Boston's official World Series banner. Celtics great Bill Russell, Bruins legend Bobby Orr, and New England Patriots Tedy Bruschi and Richard Seymour threw out the ceremonial first pitches. Bruschi was making his first public appearance since suffering an offseason stroke; he hugged fellow University of Arizona alum Terry Francona for almost a full minute before skipping off the field.

The ring ceremony and the raising of the World Series banner would have been enough to satisfy almost every Red Sox fan, but still to come was that day's matchup with the Yankees. Tim Wakefield, appropriately, was pitching. It was Wakefield's 200th Fenway appearance, the second highest total for a pitcher in team history, and he'd turned in dominant performances against New York for several years. (His 2004 record against New York was 1-0 with a 1.83 earned run average over three starts.) On this day, he continued his mastery of the Red Sox's rivals, pitching seven innings of five-hit ball. The Red Sox had no such trouble with Mike Mussina, and at the end of the day, Boston had won, 8–1. In his box above home plate, John Henry looked at Tom Werner and Larry Lucchino. "Can't ask for much more than this," Henry said. "It's gonna be a fun year."

The next two months didn't feel like much fun. On June 11, the Red Sox were a mediocre 32-29, four games behind the Baltimore Orioles, who were surprising everyone. After joining the team in mid-April, Schilling had been put back on the disabled list following three awful starts. Keith Foulke had also been struggling, and the Boston bullpen, meant to be one of the team's strengths, was a mess. What's more, the Sox were just five games into an 18-game stretch during which 15 of their matches would be against National League opponents, and the team had historically done badly in interleague play. The fact that the Yankees were doing even worse—at 30-31, they were off to their poorest start of the Joe Torre era—provided some consolation, but then the Yankees were soon to play seven straight games against last place teams: four versus Tampa Bay and three versus the Mets.

Instead of faltering, the Red Sox reeled off 12 wins in their next 13 games, sweeping series from Philadelphia, Cleveland, and Cincinnati, while the Yankees dropped six of their seven games versus the Devil Rays and Mets. On June 26, the 44-30 Sox had vaulted over the Orioles and were six-and-a-half games in front of the 38-37 Yankees. The New York tabloids began excoriating the "bumbling Bombers" and wondering whom owner George Steinbrenner would fire. In Boston, Dan Shaughnessy began his June 26 *Boston Globe* column with these words: "It's OK to say it. Don't worry about jinxing them. The 2005 Red Sox are going to win the American League East. By a landslide. . . . Stop worrying about the Yankees, Orioles, and Jays. It's not even going to be close." In the mid-July All-Star Game, the Red Sox featured four of the American League's nine starting players: center fielder Johnny Damon, designated hitter David Ortiz, left fielder Manny Ramirez, and catcher Jason Varitek.

Despite, or perhaps because of, the team's success, the all-for-one ethos that had been so contagious in 2004 had been replaced with a me-first attitude that seemed to pervade every aspect of the club. First baseman Kevin Millar and third baseman Bill Mueller had begun complaining whenever there was the slightest hint that they might be rested for one of the team's bench players, while Jay Payton moaned about serving as a backup. (At different points, all three players' agents had asked the club to explore possible trades.) Members of the team blamed manager Terry Francona when pitchers Mike Timlin and Matt Clement were initially left off the American League's All-Star roster despite the fact that Francona had no control over the selections.* After Keith Foulke went on the disabled list and Curt Schilling was named the team's closer, Johnny Damon blasted the move in the press. "Mike Timlin definitely deserves that spot," Damon said, while another player, speaking anonymously, said it was a "slap in the face" to the rest of the pitching staff that Schilling was made the closer. And in early July, Payton, frustrated over his lack of playing time, planned an in-game tirade against Francona in an effort to secure a trade. By the middle of the season, Francona, who'd enthusiastically told John Henry during spring training that he was more excited about working with this club than any in his career, became so dispirited by the constant whining and complaining that Theo Epstein asked Henry to give the manager a pep talk.

"They became the biggest bunch of prima donnas ever assembled," says one Red Sox executive. "It's a problem with a veteran team, especially one that's had some success. And winning the World Series makes it worse." In America, professional athletes are constantly taught they don't need to obey the rules that apply to the rest of society. The team takes care of travel arrangements. Business managers and agents deal with money and investments. Restau-

---

* Francona, as the manager of the American League pennant winner, got to coach the All-Star Game; however, unlike managers in years past, Francona had almost no latitude to choose players. This change was put into effect after Yankees manager Joe Torre larded the All-Star team with his players during the Yankees' late-1990s run. Clement was eventually given a spot on the team when Toronto Blue Jays starter Roy Halladay dropped out due to an injury.

rants and stores lobby for the right to give away free products. And, of course, women are available virtually around the clock. After the Red Sox won the World Series, the special treatment accorded to members of the team became even more pronounced. Everyone, from Schilling to the rarely used Kevin Youkilis to laidback pitcher Bronson Arroyo, was treated like a god. For some, this provided all the impetus needed to indulge their more selfish natures.

Take the case of Kevin Millar. In mid-December, Millar—in the midst of doing his personal victory tour of paid mall appearances and signings—had announced that he was unwilling to platoon with Doug Mientkiewicz in 2005. "Can't have us both back," Millar said. "I've already expressed that to Theo. . . . I'm not going to platoon behind Doug Mientkiewicz, to be honest with you. I've proven myself here." Millar had been, to be sure, a solid addition to the Red Sox's offense, hitting 25 home runs in 2003 and batting almost .300 in 2004. However, he was atrocious defensively, and just two years earlier had been on his way to Japan. Among American League first basemen who qualified for the batting title* in 2004, he'd had the second fewest home runs and runs batted in. Still, Millar got his wish, if only because none of the teams Boston contacted were interested in trading for him, and before the season started, Mientkiewicz was shipped to the New York Mets. None of this stopped Millar from rolling into camp overweight and out of shape.

Throughout the first half of the season, as Millar went from being a solid addition to the team to one of the worst players in all of baseball to hold onto his starting job, he became ever-more truculent and entitled. When, on May 1, the Sox offered a minor league contract to 36-year-old John Olerud, a veteran first baseman known for his strong fielding, Millar took it as an affront. Because he was such an integral part of the social fabric of the club, his unhappiness affected a disproportionate number of people on the team. As Terry Francona had pithily put it in the offseason, "Millar is a great team player—as long as he's playing."

* To qualify for the batting title, a player must have an average of 3.1 plate appearances for every one of the team's games. Over the course of a normal 162-game season, that comes out to just over 500 plate appearances.

"For most of the nights for the past two years, Millar has been the worst guy [out on the field]," says one member of the team's front office. "Worse than [second baseman Mark] Bellhorn, who's incredibly underrated defensively. But for all his talk about 'Cowboy Up,' you know, team first, he bitches and moans when it looks like 'team first' might mean he needs to ride the pine." Indeed, from late May, when John Olerud was first promoted to the Red Sox, through mid-July, Olerud had gotten only 53 at-bats, while Millar had gotten 104. In addition to being far superior defensively, by July 15, Olerud had a higher batting average (.321 to .273), a higher on base percentage (.383 to .355), and a higher slugging percentage (.472 to .386). Yet it was Millar who needed to be coddled and Olerud who was philosophical about the situation. "You want to do as good a job as best you can," he said on June 27, "and hopefully . . . you'll be a starter. I think you try to make the best of the opportunities you have, given the role that you have."

For players like Millar—and Mueller and Payton—the anxiety over playing time wasn't only about ego or recognition; it was also about money. The 33-year-old Millar, 34-year-old Mueller, and 32-year-old Payton all had guaranteed contracts that expired at the end of the 2005 season. All three had been made wealthy by baseball, but they'd earned nowhere near the amount of money players like Garciaparra and Martinez had made when they headed into the last years of their contracts. At the conclusion of the 2004 season. Garciaparra had earned $45 million from baseball contracts. Martinez had made $95 million. In contrast, Payton's baseball earnings would total around $8 million at the end of the 2005 season, Millar's around $11 million, Mueller's around $15 million. That is, without a doubt, a lot of money. But to a baseball player whose employment opportunities and earning power shrink dramatically after his playing days are over, it might feel not quite enough to guarantee a lifetime of comfortable living. If Payton was perceived by other teams as nothing more than a role player or if Millar spent half the year on the bench, how much could they reasonably expect to make in their next contract?

Money and playing time weren't the team's only distractions. Early in the season, a series of snapshots in which a Red Sox pitcher was shown snuggling with a Northeastern University student were posted on several Red Sox fansites. In one of the more widely circulated pictures, the buxom blond, in a revealing sleeveless top and tight jeans, is curled in the married pitcher's lap. A pair of bunk beds is visible in the background; the picture was taken in one of Northeastern's freshman dormitories. A teammate of the featured pitcher soon called the girl and asked her to remove the pictures from her online photo album, which she did.* But the player's brief spell of online infamy was a sign of what was to come. For the rest of the season, snapshots of Red Sox players showing off their World Series rings, or hugging a half-dozen girls at once, or licking a young coed's face, made regular appearances in various online scrapbooks.†

The Red Sox still managed to enter the last week of July in first place, with a one-and-a-half game lead over the Yankees. In spite of these mini soap operas and the pitching woes of both Schilling and Foulke, the team seemed to be cruising, and was poised to lead the American League in offense for the third straight year. Dan Shaughnessy, it seemed, had been right. What could sidetrack them now?

---

* In early 2006, the pictures were again posted in the girl's online photo album.
† Later in the season, Derek Lowe received some unwanted attention when news of his affair with a TV sports reporter broke. One day when the Red Sox pitcher who'd been in the widely disseminated online photographs came to the ballpark, a teammate had left at the player's locker a copy of the *Herald*, opened to the same gossip column that had written anonymously about the pitcher's online photos. This time, there was a full item about Lowe, his paramour, and his wife's reaction. "Come on D-Lowe," the pitcher muttered. "You got to keep yourself out of the gossip columns."

## CHAPTER 39

# The Manny Sagas, Part 2

ON TUESDAY, JULY 26, *Sports Illustrated*'s Tom Verducci published a two-paragraph, 142-word piece in his weekly baseball roundup. "Manny Ramirez wants out of Boston," Verducci wrote. "Again. The Red Sox left fielder has asked to be traded for at least the third time in the past four seasons." Verducci, who didn't attribute his scoop to any particular source, stated that Ramirez was upset with "his lack of privacy off the field" but that the Sox "have no intention of trading Ramirez . . . not during the season, anyway." The story, which was published five days before the annual trade deadline, generated some attention, but a late-July, unsourced story about an often-unhappy All-Star requesting a move didn't qualify as earth-shattering news. After all of the various trade rumors involving Ramirez over the past several years, it made sense there'd be at least some discussion of his status while he could still be freely swapped.*

---

*The 2005 trade deadline was, for all intents and purposes, the last time Ramirez could be traded by the Red Sox without his permission. Ramirez doesn't have a no-trade clause in his contract, but he'd become a "10-5" player at the conclusion of the 2005 season, with at least 10 years of service time in the major leagues, of which the last five were with the same team.

It had been a peculiar season for Ramirez. A year earlier, he had appeared as outgoing and happy as he had been at any point in his career, and he'd made a concerted effort to be available to the media. After winning the World Series MVP award, he giddily told the press, "I never thought I'd get to be part of a World Series winner, but it's fun, let me tell you. Before we went to spring training, I told my wife . . . I'm going to be the MVP of something. And I did." Two-thousand five had not been nearly as upbeat. Before the season began, he skipped the team's congratulatory trip to the White House because, he said, his grandmother was sick. (He later said this was not the same grandmother whose illness had caused him to be late to the 2001 All-Star Game.) In early April, he announced he'd retire at 36, after his contract ran out following the 2008 season. *"No más,"* he said. "I'm gone. I'm tired." He was certainly playing like it: After entering the season with a career .316 batting average, he dipped as low as .224 on May 27. And it wasn't mere slumping, something that happens to even the very best hitters. Ramirez seemed to be sleepwalking through games. Speaking on ESPN Radio, Peter Gammons said he found Ramirez "as distracted as any time I can remember him. He just doesn't seem to be into the games at all. There was a time when he was a dominant offensive force at the end of games." That time, it seemed, was gone.

On May 14, Ramirez, who had resumed his habit of avoiding the media, granted a rare interview to *The Boston Globe*'s Chris Snow as the Red Sox were getting ready to take batting practice at Seattle's Safeco Field. There was a reason, Ramirez told Snow, he'd been slumping. "My mom's been real sick," Ramirez said. "I've been thinking a lot about that. She's now getting better. Like, what's the name of the disease? She's got a disease. She can't move with her legs. It's a weird name. She's getting better. She's got to get a lot of massages." Is it arthritis? Snow asked. "Yeah, yeah, arthritis," Ramirez answered. As for the grandmother whose illness caused him to skip out on the White House trip, Ramirez explained, "They've got to change her blood, stuff like that. She's like 90 years old."

Ramirez's unburdening did not appreciably change his performance on the field. In mid-June, he was still hitting only around

.250. On June 20, the North Andover *Eagle-Tribune*'s John Tomase wrote what many in the Red Sox front office were privately think-ing: "The free pass Ramirez has received this season from the fans, the media, and his teammates is mystifying. . . . Manny Ramirez does not care this season." With three-and-a-half years left on Ramirez's $160 million contract, Boston's front office was worried it could be saddled with an immature, expensive albatross for years to come. Then, suddenly, and for no discernible reason, Ramirez seemed to awaken from his stupor. By July 26, he'd raised his bat-ting average to .275, and was on pace to hit 44 home runs and 147 runs batted in on the season. In just the previous 36 games, he'd hit 16 home runs—almost one every other game.

On the night of the 26th, Ramirez came to bat in the top of the 10th inning of what was by then a 9–8 game in Tampa Bay. Ramirez had some history in Tampa. Three years earlier, it had been here that Ramirez failed even to leave the batter's box after hitting a ground ball. It had been one of Ramirez's most criticized moves as a member of the Red Sox, and led to a confrontation with then-manager Grady Little. Surely, there would be no repeats on this night. He'd already hit one home run, and the game was shaping up to be one that would have far-reaching consequences for the Red Sox season. In the top of the third inning, right fielder Trot Nixon clutched at his side after taking a vicious swing; he'd strained his oblique muscle and would be out for several weeks. The loss of Nixon, along with the absence of Jay Payton, who'd successfully bullied his way out of town (he had been traded to the Oakland A's for pitcher Chad Bradford), meant that the Red Sox's once-deep bench was suddenly looking perilously thin.

Then, in the bottom of the third, a Carl Crawford line drive hit Red Sox pitcher Matt Clement on the right side of the head. The ball was moving so fast, the sound of it striking Clement's skull was clearly audible on the television replays, and it ricocheted with such force that it ended up in shallow left field. Clement, one of the bright spots on Boston's beleaguered pitching staff, crumpled to the ground, where he lay for more than five minutes. While he never lost consciousness, he was eventually ushered off the field on a stretcher and taken to a local hospital.

By Ramirez's at-bat in the 10th inning, the game had already seesawed back and forth many times. A loss, the Red Sox knew, would push the team into second place. With Edgar Renteria on first with one out, Ramirez tapped a ball to second base for what looked to be an inning-ending double play. And, while he didn't stand in the batter's box, his lackadaisical jog down to first base was less than inspiring. At the time, the play received little notice; an error by the Devil Rays second baseman meant Ramirez made it safely to first base in any case. Compared to everything else that had transpired that night, Ramirez's lack of hustle hardly seemed worth special attention.

For the team executives and the members of the Sox baseball operations office, however, it was an ominous sight. Tom Verducci's report had indeed been accurate: Less than a week earlier, before a game at Fenway, Ramirez had, once again, asked the Red Sox for a trade. That night, Theo Epstein, Larry Lucchino, and Tom Werner met with Ramirez in a private room off of the Red Sox clubhouse. Ramirez, still dressed in his baseball pants, began by praising the owners. "You guys are awesome," he said. "The whole time I've been here, you guys have been awesome to me. But I can't take Boston anymore. I can't even take my kid to the park without being bothered. I need to get out of here." Ramirez said there were a handful of teams he was willing to play for, and rattled off the Texas Rangers, the Toronto Blue Jays, the Cleveland Indians, the Florida Marlins, the Los Angeles Angels of Anaheim, the Seattle Mariners, and, possibly, the New York Mets.

By that time, one of Ramirez's representatives had already told the Red Sox there was a chance that, if Ramirez wasn't traded, he'd simply "shut it down." "The threat [of refusing to play] was always implicit," says Lucchino, speaking of Ramirez's previous trade demands. "But this was a little more specific. We were obviously concerned." That night, Epstein, Lucchino, and Werner agreed they would explore the issue. "There's always been some interest on the part of Theo and the baseball ops people in particular to have greater payroll flexibility going forward," says Lucchino. "So the issue of trading Manny has been debated. And [our coaching staff] at this point was . . . frustrated by Manny, so we felt we had to seriously examine it."

Lucchino was most in favor of holding onto the star, as he had been during the Pedro Martinez negotiations. "I've always been the most reluctant and most conservative on this issue," he says, but even he was worried by Ramirez's lollygagging. "I thought, 'What the heck was that?' " Lucchino says of Ramirez's performance in Tampa Bay. The team had begun documenting the various ways in which they'd bent over backward to try to accommodate Ramirez. If at some point he did flat-out refuse to play, the Sox wanted to be able to demonstrate their efforts during a possible suspension hearing.

On Wednesday, July 27, the Red Sox's worst fears seemed to be realized. With the team battling for first place and Trot Nixon unable to play, Ramirez, according to Terry Francona, said he needed the night off. Before Tuesday's game, Francona acknowledged, he'd told Ramirez he'd be rested the next day. But, Francona said, Nixon's injury changed the situation. "[Tuesday] night after the game I kind of went to him and said, 'How do you feel? Because we've got obvious issues,' " Francona later told the press. "He said, 'I still need it.' So we're giving it to him."

On July 26, the Red Sox fielded a team whose outfield had hit a cumulative 669 home runs and appeared in 11 All-Star games. The next night, the Sox were forced to rely on an outfield that had slugged 433 fewer home runs and appeared in nine fewer All-Star games. In right field, rookie Adam Stern would be making the second start of his career. Ramirez's mercurial behavior was, by this point, even causing strife between him and his teammates. That afternoon before the game, according to the *Globe*'s Chris Snow, Curt Schilling and Ramirez got into such a heated confrontation they had to be separated by David Ortiz.*

*The *Herald*'s Michael Silverman reported several days later that the confrontation began when Ortiz said, of that day's Tampa Bay pitcher, "Man, that guy's got some nasty stuff," to which Schilling responded, "Yeah, that's why Manny took the day off." According to Silverman's article, Ramirez then said to Schilling, "Screw you, I can hit anyone in baseball, including your ass."

The next day, Thursday, July 28, was a travel day for the Red Sox, as the team returned to Boston to prepare for a three-game series against the Minnesota Twins, but the absence of a game didn't mean the team wasn't generating headlines. That morning, Larry Lucchino confirmed on his weekly radio appearance on WEEI that Ramirez had asked for a trade. "Our general response was, 'It's that time of year,' and we'll explore it as we explore other trades," he said. Lucchino's acknowledgment, confirmed later that day by Charles Steinberg, stood in contrast to what Theo Epstein was telling reporters: "It would be wise for us to refrain from talking to the media until Sunday night," after the trade deadline had passed.

Lucchino's statements to WEEI, coupled with what Ramirez saw as Francona's unfair characterization of their interaction, only exacerbated the situation. It was true that Ramirez and Francona had previously agreed that Ramirez would get Wednesday night off. What was not true, however, was Francona's implication that he had *personally* appealed to Ramirez to play after Nixon had gotten injured. In fact, it was Francona's bench coach, Brad Mills, who had asked Ramirez following Tuesday's game if he still wanted Wednesday night off. Ramirez, apparently not realizing Nixon's injury would keep him out of the lineup, said yes. If he'd been told Nixon was unavailable, Ramirez said, he would have agreed to play. Ramirez now told Red Sox officials he wouldn't play again until he received a public apology from Francona. On Thursday night and for much of Friday, Epstein and other Red Sox executives were in near-constant contact with Ramirez and his representatives. At one point, Epstein even went over to Ramirez's apartment to lobby the petulant slugger.

By Friday, July 29, with a game scheduled for that night at Fenway, the Red Sox still weren't sure what Ramirez would—or wouldn't—do. "Manny's going to come to the ballpark," Lucchino remembers thinking. "Are we going to have an incident? Are we going to have an episode?" In fact, Ramirez had changed his mind again, and had sent word to Epstein that he did not, in fact, want to play for the Mets, the Red Sox's most likely trade partner. Now he said he would prefer to stay with the Red Sox.

• • •

Of the four major North American professional sports leagues, Major League Baseball gives its fans the greatest illusion of intimacy with its players. Baseball's 162-game regular season is almost twice as long as basketball's and hockey's 82-game seasons, while football players suit up for a mere 16 non-playoff games a year. The rhythms of the game and the all-encompassing nature of its coverage help foster this sense of closeness between fans and players. When a pitcher steps off the mound with the bases loaded in the bottom of the ninth, you can watch as he takes a deep breath, screws up his courage, and enters back into the fray. Every player on the diamond spends much of every game standing on the field waiting for something to happen. These are times in which he can be observed, times in which small quirks of his personality come through. Depending on the length of a team's playoff run, a committed fan could spend eight months of every year watching their favorite players perform for several hours a day, no fewer than five times a week. It's not unheard of for a baseball fan to spend more hours each year watching his team play than interacting with his family.

The perception of ubiquitous accessibility has become an integral part of both the game's marketing and its appeal. In baseball, even preseason exhibition workouts are an attraction. Every year, a couple of weeks before spring training games begin, thousands of fans head to Florida and Arizona to watch their preferred teams go through hour after hour of throwing, catching, and hitting drills. Baseball, fighting to compete with flashier (and less time-consuming) entertainment options, has become dependent on feeding this intimacy as a way of highlighting its uniqueness.

That's where the media comes into play. In addition to a seat in the press box, accredited reporters get access to the home and visiting teams' clubhouses. Fenway's clubhouse is notoriously cramped. The manager's office is on one side, and the showers and trainer's room on the other; locker stalls line the walls. In a given year, the average Red Sox player will spend anywhere from 650 to 900 hours during the regular season in a baseball clubhouse, with a little less than half of those hours at Fenway and the rest divided among spring training sites and other ballparks. On a typical game day, with a scheduled 7:05 P.M. first pitch, players arrive anywhere from noon to three. Some make the clubhouse a virtual second home: They eat there, they watch television there, they do crosswords and Sudokus and talk on cell phones there. Others scramble in just in time to shower, change, and get out on the field for batting practice.

For around 500 of those hours—for three hours during every one of the 162 regular season games a year—dozens of reporters are there as well. In Boston, a handful of reporters are usually waiting outside the clubhouse doors for 3:30 P.M., when they're officially allowed in. By that time, NESN broadcaster Jerry Remy, a former Red Sox second baseman, has already been hanging out for a half-hour or so. From three thirty to four, the crowd slowly grows, until anywhere from 10 to 25 scribes are waiting expectantly as baseball players shower and change around them. During this time, there's an unwritten set of rules that dictates behavior. Don't approach a player if he's naked. Don't approach a player if he's eating or on the couch watching television. If a reporter working on a feature or a scoop approaches a player whom other reporters have no special reason to speak with, keep your distance. If a reporter approaches a player who is in the news for some reason—a recent injury, a particularly good (or bad) performance—then he's fair game, and everyone is allowed to join in the fun.

Much of the time, the reporters are playing a defensive game:* They're there because they want to make sure their competitors don't get an exclusive by witnessing a juicy scene,† even though many of the juiciest will never see print. Ballplayers will occasion-

---

* Considering the eagerness for material, it's confusing that no media outlet has seen it fit to assign a Spanish-speaking reporter to the team. In 2005, not a single regular Red Sox beat reporter spoke Spanish, the native language of a third of the Red Sox regular starting lineup: David Ortiz, Manny Ramirez, and Edgar Renteria. Former *Boston Herald* columnist Howard Bryant, who often wrote about the Sox, is fluent in Spanish.

† On September 21, 2000, many reporters missed Carl Everett's violent tirade at teammate Darren Lewis because it occurred before the first game of a rare weekday doubleheader. Expecting upward of 10 hours at the ballpark, a number of the Red Sox beat reporters opted to skip the normal pregame clubhouse ritual.

ally joke about needing to figure out a way to get tickets to that day's game for both a wife and a mistress, or openly mock former teammates (and supposed friends) who have the misfortune of having a blunder broadcast on the clubhouse's flat-screen television, or speculate about this or that player's reliance on steroids. None of this sees the light of day. If a beat reporter were ever to print any truly salacious detail, he would be frozen out and would find it almost impossible to continue to cover the team.

At 4:00 P.M. the reporters are herded into Terry Francona's office, where they ask a handful of rote questions, ranging from "what are you expecting tonight" to "were you happy with how the team performed yesterday." At 4:35, the media is shooed out of the clubhouse, only to reassemble on the field as the team takes batting practice. An hour later, they're allowed back inside until 6:15, and then are allowed in again for an hour after the night's game is done.

On July 29, the mood in the Red Sox clubhouse was as tense as it had been all year. In addition to the speculation about Ramirez, there were rumors that Boston was on the verge of trading Bill Mueller to the Twins, that weekend's opponent, for a left-handed pitcher. According to scuttlebutt, Kevin Millar was also being shopped around. That afternoon, Millar came out of the showers, looked at the throng of reporters, and bellowed at the top of his lungs, "GET OUT! GET OUT! GET YOUR STORIES AND GET OUT!"

At first, it was hard to tell if Millar was joking or not. Since arriving at the Red Sox, Millar had been a media magnet, helping draw the spotlight away from those players, like Ramirez, who didn't want the attention. Even when the press wasn't around, his natural disposition helped keep the clubhouse loose. But now, watching him rant, even his teammates seemed a bit tired of his act. "You are the story," Mike Timlin muttered beneath his breath.

And then, as quickly as his outburst had begun, it was over. Millar quickly flashed a smile at the quizzical group of reporters and headed over to his locker. Still, when one writer approached him a couple of minutes later, he begged off for perhaps the first time since arriving in Boston. "I'm not talking today," he explained. "I'm taking a day off." He soon canceled most of his previously scheduled interviews for the weekend.

After three days of hearing accounts of how Ramirez didn't like playing in Boston and had refused to play in a game a few days earlier, after watching countless replays of his July 26 stroll down to first base, the fans weren't in the best of moods, either. That night, during an 8–5 Boston victory, Ramirez was heartily booed for the first time in his career with the Red Sox.

Ramirez may have decided that he'd rather stay in Boston, but unfortunately, it wasn't that easy. For the past several days, Epstein had been hard at work on a three-team trade with the Devil Rays and the New York Mets. Boston would send Ramirez to New York and some prospects to Tampa, and would receive in return outfielder Mike Cameron and prospect Lastings Milledge from the Mets, and the Devil Rays left-handed slugger, Aubrey Huff.

"At that point . . . we told [Ramirez] to take a couple of days off to clear his head," says John Henry. They decided Ramirez should take both the Saturday and Sunday games off. Since Monday was an off day, that meant Ramirez would play in only one game between Wednesday, July 27, and Monday, August 1. If a trade didn't work out and Ramirez was going to be sticking around, the team wanted to do what it could to try to soothe the situation. "Once we knew he [might be] staying, we sort of had this issue," says Lucchino. "Would Manny be upset? Would he be a problem?" The time off, the team hoped, would show Ramirez they were willing to do whatever they could for him.

The media, of course, were told none of this. When, just before game time on Saturday, July 30, the Fenway Park public address announcer gave the game's lineups, Ramirez was announced as playing left field and batting cleanup. But when the players took the field a couple of minutes later, it was Millar who jogged out to left and John Olerud who was playing first base and batting fourth. Naturally, Ramirez's absence fueled rumors that a trade was imminent —why else wouldn't he be playing? After the game, as the Red Sox celebrated their 6–2 victory, Ramirez unexpectedly emerged from the Boston dugout to congratulate his teammates. The Fenway crowd, now seemingly worried they were on the verge of losing one of the premier hitters in the game, serenaded Ramirez on a night he didn't play a day after booing him in a game in which he did.

The next morning, the day of the trade deadline, Terry Francona met with the press for his daily pregame briefing. Francona's Fenway office is a cramped, characterless place, with hardly enough room for a desk, a shower stall, a small couch, and a couple of chairs, not to mention the dozen or so reporters who squeeze in for these daily sessions. After the print reporters are finished asking their questions, the TV and radio crews file in and Francona does the whole thing all over again. It's a tedious process.

That Sunday, at least twice as many reporters as usual had crammed into Francona's office, all anticipating a possible repeat of 2004's last-minute Garciaparra trade. The local papers had doubled their representatives, and many of the national and New York–based media outlets had sent people as well. As Francona surveyed the scene, he couldn't help himself. "Holy shit," he muttered. "Fuck. I think the best I can hope for is one of you bumps each other and gets into a fight."

The questions, and the day's routine, began as usual. A promising Red Sox rookie, Jonathan Papelbon, would be making his first big-league appearance as that day's starting pitcher. Francona had last seen Papelbon pitch during spring training, where the pitcher made a memorable debut. In his first game with major league players, Papelbon threw a fastball up and in on the Orioles' Sammy Sosa in retaliation for Orioles pitcher Daniel Cabrera hitting Jay Payton earlier in the exhibition game. "I'm trying to get him out," Papelbon insisted at the time.

"Your first impression of somebody, you know how it is," Francona said that morning in his office. "You have to be careful in spring training of doing that . . . but his first impression was really good." Francona was about to continue when suddenly Kevin Millar and Manny Ramirez materialized in the doorway.

"I'm translating," Millar shouted to the astonished reporters before bursting into his high-pitched, giggly laugh. "I want to introduce you to Manny Ramirez." Ramirez, who was wearing an All-Star game T-shirt and clutching a bat, grinned his crooked grin and said simply, "I'm back." Francona gamely played along.

"Manny kind of wanted to have an opportunity where me and him were together so people didn't think we'd want to kill each other," he explained to the assembled reporters.

Millar pointed to Ian Browne, a reporter from the Red Sox website, and told him to ask the first question. Browne complied. "Manny, are you still happy with the Red Sox and how do you feel about probably playing the rest of the season?"

"I want to stay here," Ramirez said. "I want to help the team win a World Series."

"That's Manny being Manny," Millar cut in, before shouting out some gibberish in Spanish. "Manny being Manny. There he goes again."

The *Globe*'s Gordon Edes went next. "Manny, there was a story in the *Boston Herald* that you're unhappy with the manager, that he doesn't talk to you, that you're not his kind of player." Edes was referring to a story in that morning's *Herald* by Michael Silverman, who was sitting a few feet away, in which "a source close to Ramirez, authorized to speak for the slugger" said that Francona and Ramirez "don't talk" and that the Red Sox manager "had it [in] for Manny for a while. . . . Francona has one way of thinking and there's one type of player he wants on his team and that's not Manny."

"Nah, I never said that," Ramirez said. "My situation with Terry's perfect, man. I never had no problem. The thing that happened, you know, I was supposed to get Sunday off in Chicago, and I told Tito [Francona], 'No Tito, I was going to play on Sunday. Why don't you give me Wednesday off . . . ?' So, OK, when Trot got hurt, one of the coaches came up to me and said, 'Do you still want Wednesday off?' and I said, 'Yeah.' If they came up to me and said, 'We want you to play Wednesday,' I'd say, 'Yeah.' I'm here to play. I'm here to play. I'm a player. That's what happens. I'm not here because I don't want to play or whatever. I'm not that kind of guy."

Now the questions came more quickly. Did all the trade talk bother him? "No way, man. I'm strong. I'm just here to play, win. I'm a gangsta." ("You bet your ass you are," Francona said.) "I've always played the game and have fun. That's the way I deal with things. . . . I'm still here. I'm here to win. I'm here to help this team."

Millar announced that Ramirez would take one more question. He was asked if the booing on Friday night had bothered him. "It doesn't bother me, man. This is not my first time, you know, getting booed. The fans, I don't care about that. I'm just going to go out there and play the game." With that, Millar announced the interview was over. "We gotta go," he said. "Thank you guys. *Gracias.*"

When Millar and Ramirez left, the assembled reporters looked around the room at one another, utterly confounded. Over the years, there had been no shortage of bizarre scenes in the manager's office. Once, when asked why he hadn't been called on to close the first game of Joe Kerrigan's tenure, Derek Lowe told reporters to "go ask that motherfucker in there." There was Joe Morgan's odd repetition of "Six, two, and even," a nonsense phrase from *The Maltese Falcon*, and Jimy Williams's vituperative blasting of his boss, general manager Dan Duquette, during one pregame media session.

This one, though, might have been the strangest of them all. First there was Ramirez acting as if he wanted to do nothing more than hang out and shoot the breeze with the press. There was Millar, who was constantly reminding reporters of the intangibles he brought to the team during his abysmal first half; this incident almost seemed as if he was trying to show people he was needed to help soothe the moody Ramirez. And even in a sport in which the players were pretty much expected to flat-out lie to the media whenever it suited their needs, the juxtaposition of Ramirez asking one of his confidants to tell a reporter that he and Terry Francona didn't get along and then refuting the resulting story the very next day was a bit much to take. ("He wasn't lying," a reporter said later that day. "He just changed his mind.")

Francona did an impressive job acting as if this was nothing out of the ordinary. "Actually, when I was talking to Manny this morning," he began, subtly referring back to, and refuting, Silverman's story without actually addressing its content, "he really wants to speak to you guys with me. I think my concern was—first of all, I thought it was pretty cool that he wanted to—but people are going to think, 'OK, he's fucking dragging him out there.' " That, Francona said, was definitely not the case. "I'm not mad at [Ramirez,]" he said. "We get through these things. But he really wanted to do that, and that's OK." So would Ramirez be playing that day? "I'll see how the day progresses," Francona said. "I'm not sure I want [Twins manager Ron] Gardenhire to know."

When the lineup for that day's game was posted, Ramirez's name was missing. Once again John Olerud would bat cleanup behind David Ortiz, with Kevin Millar in left field and Gabe Kapler getting the nod in right. It was, by any measure, an exciting game. Papelbon, the 6-foot-4-inch right-hander the Red Sox had drafted two years earlier, was already drawing comparisons to a young Roger Clemens.* He opened the game by striking out Shannon Stewart with a 95-mile-per-hour fastball; after three shutout innings, he had five strikeouts.

Still, most of the attention in Fenway was not focused on the field, but on one of the players not in the game. R9 and R10 are the two luxury boxes designated for use by the team's minority partners. The suites sit down the first base line, just over the Red Sox dugout. From there, one can see across the diamond into L1, Larry Lucchino's suite, and into the glassed-in owner's box where John Henry often spends the game. The team's minority partners knew nothing more than the fans in the park, and when Henry appeared in his box, the partners strained to see if they could learn anything from his appearance. Was he smiling? Did he appear grim? At one point, Theo Epstein walked in and the two men had a brief conversation. Had a deal been made?

A couple of hundred yards away from the partners suite is the Fenway Park press box, which sits directly behind home plate, above the grandstand and the .406 Club. The front row is reserved for local writers, with preference going to members of the Baseball

---

* Papelbon is unquestionably a poised, dynamic pitcher, but the comparisons to Clemens say more about how the local press invariably hypes players than it does about his actual ability. At this point in his career, Papelbon's only truly outstanding pitch is his fastball, though his split-fingered fastball has shown marked improvement; in 2005, his breaking pitches were still very much works in progress. A pitcher might be a successful reliever with only one plus pitch, but it's unlikely he'll be a dominant starter, never mind one of the best pitchers to play the game.

Writers Association of America* and print reporters who cover the Red Sox for daily papers. The second row seats the overflow local scribes as well as visiting media. The obstructed view rows above are usually first-come, first-served, and generally seat TV and radio reporters. Space is tight even under normal circumstances, and on July 31, the press box was bursting. Most of the reporters were not watching the game; instead, they were emailing sources or ducking out to take cell-phone calls from league officials, all in an effort to glean some intelligence about what to expect. At one point, a rumor began circulating: Bill Mueller would be traded for the Twins' J. C. Romero. Later, this rumor shifted: It was Kevin Youkilis who was going to be traded. All the while, the latest permutation of this or that Manny Ramirez deal was floated up and batted down.

Four o'clock came and went. If a trade had been made, it would have to have been completed by then. Mueller remained in the field, meaning he definitely wasn't going anywhere—a player can't play for his old team after a trade has been finalized. But Ramirez still hadn't made an appearance, and everyone remembered how, the year before, the announcement concerning Garciaparra's trade hadn't been made until around four thirty.

By the eighth inning, the score was tied, three all. With the Twins' Juan Rincon now on the mound, Gabe Kapler led off the inning with a strikeout. That brought up the top of the order, and Johnny Damon grounded out to third base. With two outs and nobody on, Edgar Renteria doubled into center field. David Ortiz was up next, followed by Adam Stern, who'd entered the game as a defensive replacement in the top of the inning.

---

* The BBWAA was founded in 1908 as a way for writers to guarantee themselves access to press boxes and clubhouses. Membership is limited to daily print reporters who cover baseball as a beat writer, columnist, features writer, or editor, although members who leave the daily print world to cover baseball for the Internet or a magazine can retain membership. BBWAA members vote on most of baseball's major awards, including the MVP, Cy Young, Rookie of the Year, and Manager of the Year, and writers who've had membership for 10 years are eligible to vote on whether players should be elected to the Hall of Fame.

When Renteria reached base, Ramirez began prowling around the Red Sox dugout, eventually walking toward the rack of bats. He picked up a batting helmet, then sat back down, grinning. As Ortiz strode to the plate, Stern came out and settled into the on-deck circle. With first base open and two men out, Twins manager Ron Gardenhire ordered Rincon to intentionally walk Ortiz. There wasn't a manager in baseball who wouldn't prefer to face the rookie Stern with the game on the line.

At 4:49 P.M. after the first two intentional balls had been thrown to Ortiz, Ramirez popped out of the dugout, summoning Stern back inside. The cheers in Fenway Park were deafening. "I was confused," Ortiz said later. Why were the fans suddenly cheering his intentional pass? "I looked back [toward the dugout]. I saw my man."

When Ramirez comes to the plate, he's impassive. Often, he'll stare vacantly into the crowd, and it's hard to tell if he's even fully aware of what's going on around him. As he walked to the plate, the fans surrounding home plate began maniacally screaming his name. The Fenway Park PA system blasted a couple of chords from "Superman." If Ramirez noticed any of this, he gave no indication.

In the Boston dugout, Terry Francona couldn't help but smile. Despite all his problems with Ramirez, he knew this was a special moment. "You get chills when that stuff's happening," he said. "Our dugout was alive. The stadium was alive. That's as electric as you'll see." Papelbon, just a couple of hours removed from his big-league debut, turned to Manny Delcarmen, another rookie pitcher whose first big-league appearance had come just five days earlier. "Man, I got goosebumps," Papelbon said. Delcarmen laughed. "They're going up your neck," Delcarmen said. After the game, Papelbon, a Louisiana native, told a group of reporters about that moment. "Man, I tell you what, he had goosebumps, too," Papelbon said in his Cajun drawl. "I think, to be honest with you, I bet you everybody on the bench did."

Ramirez wears his jersey loose on his frame, and as he walked up to the plate, he shrugged his arms, as if trying to get comfortable. Once in the batter's box, he squinted at Rincon, as if he couldn't quite make him out. Rincon, a fastball specialist, reared back and threw one over the plate. Ramirez didn't lift the bat off his shoulder.

Strike one. The next pitch was a bit outside, and Rincon followed that with another fastball for strike two. Three pitches into the at-bat, Ramirez still hadn't taken a swing.

Ramirez fouled off the next pitch. In L1, an anxious Larry Lucchino turned to his wife. "Life is not good enough for him to get a hit here," he said. And then, on Rincon's fifth pitch to the man often regarded as the best right-handed hitter in the American League, Ramirez stroked another fastball right up the middle. The ball wasn't hit particularly hard, but it snaked its way over the pitcher's mound and into center field. On this day, there was no loafing out of the batter's box. Ramirez took off for first like a man possessed. Renteria, running from second base on contact, scored easily, giving the Red Sox a 4–3 lead. As Ramirez settled onto first, he began clapping, as if congratulating himself for his performance. He took his helmet off, scrunched up his face, and gave his signature doubled-handed point into the Boston dugout. Fenway Park erupted. An inning later, the Sox had won, with Ramirez's hit providing the deciding edge. After the game, NESN reporter Eric Frede caught up with Ramirez as he walked into the clubhouse. "This is the place to be," Ramirez said, a huge grin on his face. "Manny being Manny. It's great, man."

In the end, the Mets' insistence on extra money to offset Ramirez's salary and the Red Sox's unwillingness to provide it had been the key factor that killed the most discussed proposed trade. But the money hadn't been the only consideration. Just as they'd done the year before with Nomar Garciaparra, team officials had quietly polled the other players as to Ramirez's impact on the club-house. Garciaparra had been so bitter and upset that almost everyone agreed he had to go. (His trade had also made the Red Sox a better team.) Ramirez was sometimes frustrating, but he certainly wasn't poisoning the team.

Instead of sulking, he was more likely to put his cell-phone camera down his pants, take a picture, and interrupt other players' interviews to show them the image.* Ramirez may have been in-

---

* Kevin Millar, apparently, was not impressed. Once, he walked over to a naked Ramirez, pointed at his groin and exclaimed, "Forty home runs and 140 RBIs, and with this penis!"

scrutable and sometimes obtuse, but he wasn't so significant a distraction to his teammates that trading him became imperative. What's more, a Ramirez trade might have made the Red Sox better in 2007 and 2008, and maybe even in 2006, but it would have almost certainly made the team worse in 2005.

Another factor impeding potential trades was the issue of Major League Baseball's new steroid policy. Earlier in the year, baseball and the players association reached an agreement that would allow for random tests during the course of the season and penalties ranging from a 10-day suspension to a year-long ban for those who tested positive. After just a half-season of the new policy, it was clear there were, as one high-ranking official in baseball said, "a lot of players not going on the field with the same support system they once had." That made searching for artificially undervalued players considerably more difficult. Since Theo Epstein, Josh Byrnes, and Bill James had joined forces two-and-a-half years earlier, they'd been relentless about searching for ways to add impact players at below-market rates. One way they did so was by searching for players who'd had a half-season's or a season's worth of performances that were worse than what could be expected from looking at their career trajectories.

Now, every prolonged slump raised a red flag. If a player averaged more than 30 home runs a year in 2003 and 2004, but hit only a handful before the All-Star break in 2005, was that the result of a tweaked back muscle? Or was it because the player was no longer on steroids? "If you're looking at a player whose production has dropped suddenly . . . you have to be concerned about the possibility that there may have been some steroid use involved," says James.* The Red Sox front office could only guess what was going

---

* Out of everyone in the Red Sox front office, James was perhaps the wariest of ascribing too much weight to the effects of baseball's testing program. "The new steroid policy is more of a media focus than a looming factor in analyzing what has happened or is likely to happen," he says. Teams need to worry about the possibility that players are taking steroids, but "you have to worry about 500 other things, too," James says. "Stan Musial had an off season in '59 and attributed it later, in a biography, to the fact that [the Musials] had a newborn baby who wasn't a good sleeper and was keeping him awake nights. . . .

on among its own players. How could it know what was going on in other clubhouses?*

In a press conference after the game, Theo Epstein tried to be philosophical about the fact that, for the first time since he'd become general manager, the team had not made a significant trade-deadline deal. "I think it was the ultimate sellers' market," he said. "If you're a buyer and you're in the ultimate sellers' market, it's hard to make a fair deal. It's hard to make a deal that doesn't hurt you more than helps you. I kind of liken it to if you need a carton of milk and put five bucks in your pocket and go to the store . . . and all of a sudden milk is $100, you may walk out of that store without some milk. That's what we did." Soon, Epstein's colleagues had fashioned a sign that read MILK—$100 and put it in the window of his office. It would remain there for the rest of the season.

It's not that steroids aren't a legitimate factor, it's just that there are a very wide range of legitimate factors, so adding one more doesn't change anything very much."

* By the second half of the season, the consensus among a Major League Baseball official and executives on several teams I spoke with was that players quickly figured out ways around the testing program. Human growth hormone, or HGH, was assumed to be the new drug of choice among many players since it is undetectable by urine tests, which is currently all that is allowed by baseball's collective bargaining agreement. Some players—like the slugger who went from fewer than 10 first-half home runs to more than 25 in the season's second half—were so widely assumed to be using that this is discussed openly around the game.

## CHAPTER 40

# *The Rift Widens*

**AS CONSUMING** as the Ramirez trade-deadline saga was, the Red Sox seemed unaffected on the field. From July 26 through July 31, the team won all five of its games. The Sox would eventually win eight straight and 14 out of 16, sweeping series with the Kansas City Royals, the Texas Rangers, and the Chicago White Sox, and Ramirez would hit home runs in the first two games after the trade deadline.

Even if things seemed to work out for the team, the saga still ended up having an adverse effect on the organization. The relationship between Larry Lucchino and Theo Epstein, already tense, deteriorated even further. Epstein and his colleagues felt that Lucchino's acknowledgment of Ramirez's trade request on WEEI had made it harder for the organization to stay focused on its goals. "Larry's radio appearances often have a bit of, 'Let's get the fire extinguishers ready,'" says one team employee. "[In any given year], there's the strong, strong likelihood these guys will not be traded. Given that, why not work at trying to repair the relationship in advance instead of fanning the flames? What's the point? The extra publicity?"* Another staffer wondered, "Why is it the only guy in

---

*Ironically, much of the press corps was also questioning Lucchino's judgment and wondering why Lucchino had confirmed Ramirez's trade

the front office who can't keep things in-house is our CEO?" Already, Epstein had spent 2005 increasingly isolated from the rest of the organization. Now his coworkers were also growing resentful of the man with whom Epstein had had an unspoken battle for much of the season.

The days immediately following the trade deadline only inflamed the situation. On Tuesday, August 2, the *Globe*'s Chris Snow reported that "Sox ownership" blocked an agreed-upon trade with the Colorado Rockies in which the Red Sox would give up Adam Stern and a minor league prospect and get outfielder Larry Bigbie and a prospect in return. In order to complete the trade, the Rockies had to first trade for Bigbie, who was a member of the Baltimore Orioles. They completed that trade, only to have the Red Sox back out of their deal at the last minute.

In Snow's story, Lucchino laid blame for this mishap at the feet of assistant general manager Josh Byrnes, Epstein's right-hand man. "Byrnes, according to Sox CEO Larry Lucchino, did most of the work on the Bigbie deal because GM Theo Epstein's attention was focused on Ramirez," Snow wrote. And after all the time spent soothing Ramirez's jangled nerves, Lucchino also said the team had been discussing deals for the left fielder until 4:00 P.M. on Sunday. (Epstein, in his press conference after the deadline, took pains not to discuss who on the team, if anyone, had been available as a trading chip.) Finally, he implied that Epstein had been so distracted by

request. Charles Steinberg made the situation worse when he tried to argue to a couple of reporters that Lucchino might not have actually been talking about a current trade demand. "I don't know still when the most recent time was that he asked to be traded," Steinberg said in early August in an effort to defend Lucchino against criticism that his comments had made the situation harder to deal with. "What Larry says is, 'My goodness, he has asked to be traded since a week before we took over as owners, it's been an annual occurrence.' He says, 'So the short answer is yes.'" Reporters have a finely honed sense of outrage, and when they feel they're being lied to, they're likely to decide the source is incapable of being honest with them in the future. This was an obvious falsehood.

the Ramirez negotiations that it hindered the team's ability to make other moves.

Lucchino, for his part, thought that some of the previous week's drama could have been avoided if only Epstein had taken his suggestions. "I independently talked to Theo on [the] Wednesday [before the trade deadline] and stressed to him that we needed a direct conversation, a direct request from Francona to Manny to play if we were going to consider . . . some kind of disciplinary action if he refused to play in the future," Lucchino says. "Theo discouraged that idea. He thought it might make too much of an issue right before the game, and that it would be disruptive."

Even more damagingly, Lucchino felt that once again Epstein might have contributed to criticism Lucchino had received in the press after the trade deadline. On August 3, Peter Gammons laced into Lucchino in Gammons's first ESPN.com column since his election several days earlier to the writers wing of the Baseball Hall of Fame. Gammons derisively referred to Lucchino as ownership's "assistant." Red Sox management had, Gammons wrote, "agreed to keep quiet" about Ramirez's trade request, but on Thursday, "Lucchino did just the opposite, and Ramirez felt that he'd been lied to." It was Epstein, Gammons said, who "fortunately . . . had repaired much of the damage." Finally, Gammons wrote that Lucchino had been the one to nix the Bigbie deal, which "rightly" incensed the Rockies. Instead of "accept[ing] responsibility," Gammons wrote, Lucchino "threw Byrnes under the bus."

Lucchino was already convinced that Epstein and Gammons's close relationship meant the general manager was feeding the reporter stories. "By this time," John Henry told me in January 2006, "every time the needles came out, from [Lucchino's] standpoint, it came from Theo."

Not until the end of 2005 would Henry learn of the deep antipathy between Epstein and Lucchino. In early August, virtually everyone in Red Sox Nation, from John Henry to the media to the fans, was in the dark about the situation. Accordingly, there was almost no concern about the fact that it was Lucchino who was responsible for negotiating Theo Epstein's contract, which would expire in just three months.* Sure, there were those journalists who'd noticed that Epstein seemed oddly truculent—one reporter said watching Epstein in 2005 reminded him of watching Nomar Garciaparra in 2004. And several of Epstein's colleagues in the baseball operations department were worried that the stress and isolation of his job were becoming overwhelming. But there were enough day-to-day things to focus on without digging into a subject everyone assumed wouldn't be an issue. In July, when Henry was asked by the *Globe* about Epstein's contract situation, he said, "It just is not an issue with Theo, Tito, Larry, or myself." Henry wasn't spinning; he really thought that was the case. When Charles Steinberg was asked the same question, he replied by saying it would actually be rude for Epstein to ask about his contract during the season. "One can see why two collaborative colleagues, albeit in a vertical relationship, shouldn't take time in the delicious, speedy, luge of a season to square off," Steinberg told me at the time. "It would seem disrespectful . . . to go in to Larry and say, 'By the way, let's talk about how much I'm going to get next year.'" Warming up to the role-playing, Steinberg continued. "'Now? Why now?' 'The media's asking, Larry.'"

But for Epstein, his contract was becoming more of an issue with each day. After his spring training email to Lucchino, Epstein says he didn't hear back from the Red Sox CEO for months. By the time he did, his frustration had grown. When Lucchino made an opening offer of around $750,000 a year—considerably less than Epstein felt he was worth—it was Epstein who said the two men should wait until the season was over to work things out. The offer was so low, Epstein said, "there was sort of no way to counter it, especially while we were still playing." What should have been a relatively simple process now looked like it would be a drawn-out negotiation. "I didn't want to focus on it and be pissed off," Epstein says. His bitter-

---

* Because of the team's policy of not allowing front-office personnel to use agents, Epstein and Lucchino would have to negotiate Epstein's deal without the benefit of intermediaries, putting the two already frustrated executives into an adversarial position in which Epstein was forced to justify his worth and Lucchino had to argue against his value.

ness over his contract, combined with his frustration over the aggressive PR approach of the team and the suffocating nature of life in Boston, made him increasingly disenchanted. "For me personally, if this organizational approach keeps up, I think I have one or two more years here and that's it," Epstein said in August. "I don't care for it and it makes it impossible for me to have a life that's tolerable, by my standards."

Epstein, to be sure, wasn't the only person who felt suffocated by the effects of the Red Sox's ubiquity in 2005. Lack of privacy was the main reason Manny Ramirez gave for his most recent trade request. David Wells, the burly, hard-living, spotlight-loving lefty, complained that the overbearing Boston fans made playing for the Red Sox actually unpleasant. "In New York, you can hide, you can go anywhere you want," Wells says. "In Boston, you can't go anywhere. We're all hermits because of the fact that if we try to go out, we just get bombarded with fans. . . . When the game's over, you've got to let us breathe. I mean, look at Manny." Boston, Wells says, is far worse than any of the other cities he's played in, including New York, Baltimore, Detroit, and Chicago. "It's a no-brainer. It's hard for an athlete in this town because you don't have a life. . . . I feel bad for my kids, because they like to get out there. They love Boston. They say, 'Dad, this is a cool city,' but I can't take them out. We've watched a lot of movies [at home] this year."

Wells is renowned throughout baseball for saying practically anything that pops into his head, but his frustration was far from unique. A year after riding his bike to home games at the Chicago Cubs' Wrigley Field, Matt Clement practically had to wear a disguise to drive to Fenway without his car being mobbed at stoplights. Even the usually diplomatic Terry Francona acknowledges that playing in a city where the fans and the media are so intense can be exhausting. "I'll give you a good example," he says. "We were in Toronto, and their catcher said something about their closer, just hammered him. And it got about a four-inch article in the paper. If that had happened in Boston? It would've been World War III."

## CHAPTER 41

# The End of an Era

ON AUGUST 15, 2004, the Red Sox were 64-52, 10.5 games behind the Yankees in the American League East and tied with the Texas Rangers for the wild-card lead. It was at precisely that point that the team went on its season-defining run, winning 20 of its next 22 contests and closing the gap with the Yankees to just two games.

A year later, the team's record was 68-48, a full four games better, and Boston had a three-and-a-half game lead over New York in the American League East. The Sox had opened the month by winning nine of their first 12 games. Perhaps this year, instead of closing the gap with the Yankees, the Red Sox could build on their lead. Certainly there was reason to be optimistic. Curt Schilling was getting ready to return to the team's starting rotation, Jonathan Papelbon had shown promise in his start against the Twins, and Trot Nixon was about to return after a stint on the disabled list due to his strained oblique.

But, unlike the year before, when the Red Sox were a hugely talented and healthy team that struggled for much of the season to get into a groove, the 2005 club seemed, if anything, to be overachieving. The team's bullpen had been, as assistant general manager Josh Byrnes put it, "atrocious." There was the total collapse of Keith Foulke, the disintegration of formerly reliable set-up man Alan

Embree, and the physical breakdown of Matt Mantei.* Only the Red Sox's offense—which often made the league's other elite relievers look as bad as its own—had kept Boston in contention. The Orioles' B. J. Ryan, who finished the year with a 2.43 earned run average, was 0-2 with a 5.87 ERA against the Sox. The Angels' Scott Shields, who posted a 2.75 ERA on the season, was 0-3 with a 10.80 mark versus Boston. Even the great Mariano Rivera, who successfully converted 91 percent of his saves overall in 2005, blew two out of eight, or 25 percent, of his save opportunities when facing Boston.

If the Red Sox were going to put some distance between themselves and the Yankees during the season's final seven weeks, they would need to work hard. On the 15th, the Sox began a 10-game road trip, during which they'd travel to Detroit, Anaheim, and Kansas City. From August 23 through September 21, Boston would play a remarkable 30 games in 30 days, the longest stretch of consecutive games in all of baseball.†

The Red Sox went 3-4 on the first two legs of their road trip. The last-place Royals, with one of the worst offenses in the league, seemed like the perfect antidote for the team's mini-slump. Far from being a normal late-August visit to an American League cellar

---

* Mantei, in 34 appearances from the beginning of the season through July 1, posted a 6.49 ERA, although that figure is a bit deceptive: Mantei added more than a run and a half to his ERA in his final appearance of the year, a third-of-an-inning outing in which he gave up five runs in a 15–2 Red Sox loss. On July 21, Mantei underwent season-ending ligament surgery on his left ankle. Embree, after being so valuable to the Red Sox in 2003 and 2004, completely fell apart in 2005, posting a 7.65 ERA in 43 games with Boston before being cut by the team in late July. After telling the Red Sox he wanted to play closer to his home on the West Coast, Embree signed with the Yankees. He was almost as bad in New York, putting up a 7.53 ERA in 23 appearances with the Yankees, and he was soon being booed by his new home fans. "Sometimes it seems like they still think I'm wearing a No. 43 Red Sox jersey," he said of Yankees fans when Boston visited New York in September.

† Normally, baseball teams are not required to play more than 20 games in a row without a day off. The Red Sox's stretch was necessitated because of the rainout of an August 14 game versus the White Sox, which was rescheduled for September 5.

dweller, this would be one of the most anticipated series of the summer, because it would feature the return of Curt Schilling to the team's starting rotation.

Since returning to the team as a closer in mid-July, Schilling had alternated periods of effectiveness with seeming incompetence. In his 21 relief appearances, from July 14* through August 21, he went 4-3 with 9 saves and a 5.17 ERA. He still did not, as the Red Sox would readily admit, have his usual great stuff, and his move back to the starting rotation was more a reflection of the general disarray of the team's pitching than it was a testament to the faith the Sox had in him. A year earlier, when Schilling and the Red Sox had agreed to suture his ankle tendon out of place so that he'd be able to pitch in the playoffs, they did so knowing they were taking a huge risk. Since the procedure had never been done before, there was no guarantee he'd ever fully recover. His track record thus far in 2005 didn't inspire confidence. "It would be harder to move him out of the bullpen if his time there had been really successful," a member of the team's baseball operations staff told me in late August. "And it would be harder to put him in the rotation if the rotation was doing well."

Schilling's return was scheduled for August 25, the final game of the road trip. It had already been a tense couple of days. After winning the first game of the Royals series two nights earlier, the Sox had lost the next game by a score of 4–3, and once again, Manny Ramirez's half-hearted effort had potentially been the difference in the game. In the fifth inning, with Boston leading 3–1, Ramirez came to the plate with the bases loaded and one out. He hit a ball to

---

* Schilling's inaugural appearance as the Red Sox closer came in a home game against the Yankees in the Red Sox's first game after the All-Star break. Schilling, who spent the previous night in California receiving an award from ESPN honoring his 2004 playoff performance, had to take a redeye flight back to Boston to make it to the park on time. He entered the game in the top of the ninth inning to the strains of Guns N' Roses' "Welcome to the Jungle" and Aerosmith's "Back in the Saddle" with the score tied at six. Gary Sheffield laced Schilling's sixth pitch against the left field wall for a double, and Alex Rodriguez hit the first pitch he saw to straightaway center field for a game-winning, two-run home run. "That," said one writer in Fenway's pressbox, "was the most effortlessly crushed ball I've ever seen in my life."

short, and began one of his customary jogs down the first base line. David Ortiz, who'd walked ahead of Ramirez, barreled into second base in an effort to break up a double play, but Ramirez was still out at first.* (Ortiz ended up injuring his hand on the play.)

By this point in the year, Terry Francona was physically and mentally exhausted. The 2005 season, which he'd been so optimistic about in spring training, had become torturous. He had been hospitalized before the third game of the season with tightness in his chest, which was eventually diagnosed as a viral infection. His balky knees—he'd already had 18 knee operations—were bothering him, and when the season ended, he planned on having his right knee replaced. If the day-to-day requirements of leading the Red Sox weren't difficult enough, the selfish demands of his veteran team made coming to the park sometimes seem like a chore. "I felt myself getting a little edgy at times and losing my patience," Francona admitted after the season ended. Even his daily sessions with the Sox beat reporters were growing tense and occasionally combative.

On August 25, in just such a session, the *Hartford Courant*'s Dave Heuschkel pushed Francona close to the edge. Heuschkel can be acerbic at times, and he prides himself on asking questions other reporters avoid. "Old school!" he's been known to shout, in reference to his reporting style. "I'm old school, baby!"

"Did you happen to see that ball Manny hit last night with the bases loaded in the fifth?" Heuschkel asked.

Francona, already tired of coddling Ramirez, was in no mood. "No, I wasn't watching," he shot back.

"Did you see him jog?" Heuschkel asked.

"I don't think he jogged," Francona said. "I don't think that is correct."

"It wasn't hit that hard though," Heuschkel countered.

"Well, if you're going to make a statement, make it right," Fran-

---

* Bill James, who traveled to the Royals games from his home in nearby Kansas, said the play would have been designated as a "failure to hustle" in his 2003 study "because there was at the least the possibility there would have been a different outcome" had Ramirez put in more of an effort.

cona replied. Now Francona's back was up, but Heuschkel wasn't about to give in: "He jogged. I saw it."

"I don't agree with that," Francona said. "I don't agree with that." As the rest of the reporters in the room shifted uncomfortably, Heuschkel tried again. "Was he going hard?"

"I don't agree with that. I think when you're trying to make a point, you've got to be correct," Francona said, now staring directly at the reporter. He ended the conversation without ever answering what he knew was Heuschkel's real question: Does it bother you that the team's $20 million a year left fielder can't be troubled to run out a bases-loaded grounder in the middle of a pennant race? Francona, who made about $600,000 in 2005, couldn't answer, because if he had, the answer would have to have been yes.

August 25's game began well, with Schilling notching two strikeouts in the first inning. But, in the second inning, five singles led to three Kansas City runs, and the Royals weren't just making contact, they were hitting the ball with authority. Schilling let in another run in the third and two more in the fourth, and his final line on the night was actually worse than his first start of the year: five innings pitched, nine hits, six earned runs.

"If that start had been on March 10 [in spring training], we would have said, 'We're doing okay,' " says Josh Byrnes. "He had some nice splitters, and he reached back for a 95-mile-per-hour fastball on one of the strikeouts. But it wasn't [spring training]. Baseball is all about repetition, doing the same thing 90 or 100 times and getting the same results every time." That night in Kansas City, Schilling's split-fingered fastball would sometimes dive out of the strike zone as it had done in years past, but other times it would stay over the meaty part of the plate. Schilling himself often seemed to be surprised to see where his pitches ended up.

Still, with seven more starts before the end of the year, both Schilling and the Red Sox were hopeful the big right-hander could regain his form before the start of the playoffs. This was, after all, the pitcher who had carried the team to a world championship the year before, the pitcher who gutted his way through a pair of postseason starts on just one good ankle and his fierce pride.

Schilling's next start came on August 30, back at Fenway Park, when he took the mound for a game against Tampa Bay. From the second pitch of the game, it was clear that this would not be the night in which Schilling morphed back into his 2004 self. After taking stock of Schilling's first offering, the Devil Rays' Julio Lugo squared off on the next pitch and smacked a double into left field. Two batters later, Tampa had a 1–0 lead. Schilling escaped the first inning without incurring any more damage, but in the second he let in four more runs on a single, three doubles, and a triple. It seemed at times as if he were throwing batting practice.

After the game, Francona met with reporters in the Fenway Park interview room, located directly above the team's clubhouse. The manager tried to put a positive spin on his pitcher's outing. Schilling, Francona said, "looked more confident" as the game went on. "I think his velocity is fine, [he's just having trouble] executing it."

After Francona left, Schilling came in, already showered and in his street clothes. He wouldn't turn 39 for another two-and-a-half months, but on that night he looked considerably older. Schilling is known as being a good interview, and he tries to be thoughtful and articulate when he speaks to the press. Now, speaking softly and deliberately, he sounded like a shell of the bravado-filled athlete who'd said before a Yankee Stadium start in the 2004 playoffs, "I'm not sure I can think of any scenario more enjoyable than making 55,000 people from New York shut up."

"I think after that second inning [I] was probably as down as I've been in a long, long time," he said. "Emotionally, [I was] just frustrated. [I was] at a point where I was at a crossroads mentally and it was either continue to either, to keep beating myself down or to make some adjustments. I tried to make some adjustments." Schilling had rarely, if ever, shown this level of self-doubt. It sounded as if he wondered if he'd ever be able to pitch effectively again.

"I'm sitting there after the second inning and we're down 5–0, and I'm showing no signs of being able to get them out. You know, I've always taken a lot of pride in being the guy that took the ball, the eight guys that go out there with me, we're going to win," he said. That was no longer the case. "It's hard to be confident when you're not successful, and it's been going on since spring training—seven months now. It wears on you. . . . You start to find yourself throwing personal pity parties, and you get nothing accomplished."

Schilling was merely vocalizing what everyone associated with the Red Sox was already thinking. Still, it was a sobering press conference. Ten months ago, on October 19 and 24, 2004, he'd pitched a total of 13 innings against the Yankees and the Cardinals, letting in just one earned run while striking out eight. He hardly seemed like the same person. Now even Schilling, who was signed through 2007 and still owed almost $30 million, had to wonder: Would he ever be able to pitch that well again?

In early September, Kevin Millar, the self-fashioned team mascot, handed out to his teammates T-shirts he'd had printed up. FUCK 'EM ALL, the shirts read. 2005 SOX—ALL WE HAVE IS EACH OTHER. Even some of his teammates found this new us-against-the-world stance a bit odd. The Red Sox, after all, were in first place and were arguably the most beloved team in baseball. The average salary of the players on the roster was over $4 million. What were these unnamed forces against which the Red Sox had to band together?

For Millar, the FUCK 'EM ALL shirts came to represent a kind of sorry coda to his career in Boston. After energizing the team and helping push it toward its successes in 2003 and 2004, both the press and Millar's teammates had begun to tire of his antics. Trot Nixon, whose locker was next to Millar's, found himself barking at his teammate to quit aping for the cameras so he could get to his clothes. Millar had even lost his starting job, and was now platooning at first base with John Olerud. The fans at Fenway booed his feeble at-bats, and his prospects for the future seemed limited.

Toward the end of the month, he finally found an outlet for his frustrations. On September 21, Howard Bryant, in his *Boston Herald* column, quoted an anonymous teammate of Curt Schilling's slamming the pitcher. "When he comes into the game people cheer him like he's the Pope," the player said, complaining that Schilling wasn't confronted with the jeers the rest of the team faced when they struggled. "You think they'd let Pedro get away with this? Why does he get the pass?" That Millar was Bryant's source was no secret to the team. Millar, while palling around with Schilling in the clubhouse—the two had even dyed their hair similar shades of platinum blond not long before Bryant's column came out—had been overheard several times making these exact same comments. To those who knew him, it was clear Millar wasn't asking why Schilling didn't get booed; Millar wanted to know why he did.*

The Schilling-Millar spat bubbled up in the local newspapers and on sports radio during the season's final week, although only *The Eagle-Tribune* publicly hinted that Millar was the source of the comments. Millar responded by saying, "I 100 percent deny it. You can write whatever you want about anything and it'd become a story for no reason. That's why we deal with it." In the end, no one really cared—which may have been Millar's worst nightmare.

On September 30, the Red Sox began the final series of the year, a three-game set at Fenway Park versus, naturally, the New York Yankees. After leading their division for most of the season, Boston had slipped into second place on September 20, and for the last 10 days, the two teams had been circling each other in the rankings. Now Boston was one game back. A sweep would give them the division, while winning two out of three would leave the teams tied, but even that wouldn't guarantee a playoff spot for the Red Sox. The Cleveland Indians were tied with Boston and just one game behind New York. If Cleveland won two of its final three games and the Red Sox took two out of three from the Yankees, all three teams would end the year with identical records, forcing one-game playoffs to determine who would win the American League East and the wild-card slot.

That weekend's series was, as always, hyped to no end, and there was much talk of how these two teams would likely face each other again in the American League Championship Series. However,

* Earlier in the year, Millar had been overheard complaining to Mark Bellhorn that, "We're getting killed [by the fans], but we're not the guys making $20 million a year."

there was also a definite sense—among the press, among the team executives, and even among the players—that enough was enough. Heading into the weekend, the Red Sox and Yankees had already played each other 68 times since the beginning of 2003. For all the pronouncements about how perfect it would be for there to be a third straight Red Sox–Yankees series to determine the American League pennant winner, the overheated atmosphere and the incessant teasing out of this or that storyline began to feel contrived and suffocating. "We had 26 heavyweight fights a year for two years," John Henry says. "Fifty-two fights. Then another 19 [games during the 2005 regular season]. We needed a break. We needed a rest from the Yankees–Red Sox."

The Red Sox won Friday night's game, bringing the two teams even, before dropping Saturday's match. On Sunday, the last day of the regular season, Curt Schilling pitched Boston to a 10–1 win, and the Red Sox and Yankees finished the year with identical 95-67 records, tied atop the American League East. Or so it seemed. Because the Indians had lost their three final games of the season, and because the Yankees had won the season's head-to-head matchup with the Red Sox, 10 games to nine, New York was named the winner of the division. For the third year in a row, Boston would enter the playoffs via the wild card.

The final weekend of the Red Sox season felt, in a weird way, like the end of the era. "The whole weekend had a little bit of an odd feel," Theo Epstein said at the time. "It was supposed to be the most hyped regular season series in history, but I don't think the ballpark had the same intensity everyone was expecting." Everyone knew what a Red Sox–Yankees series was supposed to mean: baseball's ultimate winners against the game's ultimate losers. But the Yankees were no longer invincible, and the Red Sox were no longer cursed. Now they were just two division rivals, battling it out at the end of an exhausting year.

After Boston lost the first two games of its playoff series in Chicago, there was talk of how staring elimination in the face was nothing new for this team. Epstein even joked that the Sox didn't even start trying until they were trailing 2-0. But this year really was different. There would be no miraculous last-second escapes, no coming together as a team. Unlike 1999 versus Cleveland, or 2003 versus Oakland, or 2004 versus the Yankees, the 2005 Red Sox did what most teams do when facing elimination: They were eliminated.

# CHAPTER 42

# *Apocalypse Now, Redux*

ON SATURDAY, OCTOBER 8, 2005, about 15 hours after the end of the Red Sox season, Theo Epstein dragged himself out of bed and into his Fenway Park office. On weekends, Epstein traded his pressed, button-down shirt and dress pants for the uniform of the average, thirtysomething bachelor: a loose-fitting flannel shirt, a Pearl Jam baseball cap, a stubbly goatee.

The previous night's playoff loss had been disappointing, but Epstein didn't feel the sense of bitter frustration he'd experienced after Boston's 2003 defeat at the hands of the Yankees. This year's team, he knew, had been lucky to make it as far as it had. At the beginning of the season, he'd predicted the Sox would win 95 games. They'd done exactly that, but it had been a messy, exhausting, and occasionally ugly journey. "This was the best we've ever done," Bill James said immediately after the conclusion of the 2005 season. "Our problems this year were huge: an accumulation of age at many positions, several players coming off of peak seasons, injuries essentially robbing us of our closer and our number-one starter. . . . We have more to be proud of this year than any other since I've been here."

In 2006, the Red Sox would field a dramatically different team, and Epstein and his staff were energized by the chance to remake the organization. "We've been on the cusp of being an aging team

*375*

for two or three years," James said. "We can't push it anymore." Almost every position on the team was up for grabs, or at least held the possibility of change. Kevin Millar, who'd gone from being a clubhouse catalyst to an annoying distraction, wouldn't be offered a new contract. If either Alex Cora or Tony Graffanino, the two second basemen the team had picked up in 2005, returned, it would likely be in a part-time role. With any luck the team would even be able to trade Edgar Renteria,* who, since arriving in Boston at the beginning of the year, had appeared physically incapable of playing shortstop in the big leagues. Third baseman Bill Mueller, one of the players Epstein, and the team's owners, respected most, would likely seek a two-year contract on the West Coast, closer to his Arizona home.

The team's outfield was in just as much flux. The Sox would, once again, need to deal with Manny Ramirez's trade demands. Center fielder Johnny Damon was a free agent, and while the team hoped to re-sign him, Epstein didn't think it smart to offer Damon, who'd turn 32 in November, the five- or six-year contract agent Scott Boras would likely demand. Right fielder Trot Nixon had been hobbled by injuries for the previous two years. In fact, only the team's designated hitter and catcher—David Ortiz and Jason Varitek, respectively—were sure things for 2006.

The opportunities all this change presented invigorated Epstein. The team had already considered trading Nixon to the Chicago White Sox for Aaron Rowand, perhaps the best defensive center fielder in the game.† The Sox had also been debating how much of Renteria's $10 million per year contract they'd be willing to eat in order to get rid of the shortstop, who still had three years left on his deal. If Boston essentially gave Renteria to another team and agreed to pay, say, $4 million annually of his salary, could the team use the remaining $6 million a year to land a better

---

*As far back as June, the Red Sox had been in discussions with the Atlanta Braves about sending Renteria to Atlanta and bringing Chipper Jones to Boston.

† In November, Rowand would be traded for another injury-prone slugger, albeit one with better credentials than Nixon: Philadelphia Phillies first baseman Jim Thome.

player?* Finally, the Sox were counting on 2006 as the year that the carefully cultivated minor league system would yield dividends. After a discouraging season spent shuttling back and forth between the Red Sox and the minor leagues, third baseman Kevin Youkilis would finally get a chance to play regularly, while, over at second, 22-year-old Dustin Pedroia would likely begin his transition to the majors. The Sox pitching staff would go from being one of the oldest in baseball to one well-stocked with young arms. Twenty-four-year-old Jonathan Papelbon had already had some success in Boston, and there were high expectations for Craig Hansen and Jon Lester, a pair of hard-throwing 21-year-olds. Epstein and director of player development Ben Cherington had been monitoring and working with some of these players for years. This was Epstein and Cherington's chance to create a team that learned how to work selflessly with one another from early in their careers. Here, finally, was their opportunity to assemble an exciting young club, one that would define Red Sox baseball for years to come.

Despite this, Epstein didn't feel unequivocally excited about the coming year. In fact, he hadn't even made up his mind whether he'd return after his contract expired on October 31. His discomfort with Larry Lucchino and Charles Steinberg was weighing ever more heavily on his mind, and the stifling lack of privacy he felt in Boston was becoming a greater and greater burden. "When we suffer the inevitable off season or downturn in performance, however brief, things could get really ugly around here," Epstein said late in the 2005 season, referring to the fan and media reaction. "If I'm going to commit to staying, I need to know we're all in this together. I need to know the first time I make a controversial trade or something's not going right, I'm not going to be undercut and thrown out there as chum."

At this point, after two years of mounting tension, Epstein and Lucchino had still never discussed their frustration with each other.

---

* In December, the Red Sox did manage to get rid of Edgar Renteria, trading him to the Braves for third base prospect Andy Marte, one of the most highly rated minor league players in baseball. The Red Sox agreed to pay $8 million of the $26 million remaining on Renteria's contract, as well as the $3 million he'd be owed if his 2009 option weren't picked up.

Instead of having an open dialogue, the two executives transferred their mutual distrust into the negotiations over Epstein's contract. After first approaching Lucchino in spring training, Epstein hadn't gotten an offer from the team's CEO until well into the year. The offer he did get—for around $750,000 a year, conveyed to him one night in a hurried phone call—would keep his salary in the lower tier of baseball general managers. Epstein eventually asked for $2.5 million a year, a figure that would make him the highest paid GM in the game. Resentful of the sacrifices he had to make in his personal life and convinced that Lucchino didn't properly appreciate or respect him, Epstein decided to use money as the barometer of his worth to the organization.

On the afternoon of October 8, John Henry came down to Epstein's office. For months, Henry had been worried about Epstein. He seemed, Henry thought, unhappy and exhausted. "I could see in his expression that he wasn't having a good time," Henry says. "He stopped sitting in the stands [during games]. I really began to be concerned." Henry knew that for many people in the organization, the past year had been incredibly strenuous. "There were some people, especially the manager and the general manager, who had a hard time coping with it," he says. Henry was now realizing what Patriots owner Bob Kraft had warned him about before the season began. "Success doesn't necessarily make people happy," Henry says. "People get a sense of entitlement, and it was Theo and Tito who mainly had to deal with that."

Over the time that Epstein had been the team's general manager, Epstein and Henry had grown close. Epstein would frequently call Henry in advance of a big series simply to shoot the breeze about this or that pitcher or what the team's scouting reports indicated. The two shared a passion for searching out new ways to understand the game, and their conversations sounded as much like two friends talking as they did an employee speaking to his company's owner. But they had never, out of respect for the hierarchy of the organization, discussed Epstein's disintegrating relationship with Larry Lucchino.

That day, Epstein at last told Henry of his months of anxiety and frustration. He explained how he'd felt left out to dry after the Garciaparra trade, how he felt increasingly isolated from much of the organization, how he felt that the team's obsession with generating more and more press coverage actually made it more difficult to focus on what he thought should be the team's primary goal: winning baseball games.

Lucchino had also opened up to Henry about how he felt that the criticism he received from the press originated, at least in part, from within the organization. During the 2005 season, Lucchino had become more agitated in the face of Peter Gammons's pointed barbs. "A lot of the whole PR tension began over the A-Rod situation," Lucchino says. "I look back to that as a time where there was a lot of pillorying going on, and I really started to be the preferred target." Lucchino says he doesn't know what caused this, but that "certain of those writers—like Peter [Gammons]" have been historically close to the team's baseball operations department. "[Gammons] does have the ability to sort of protect young people for future jobs," he says.

Only now did Henry begin to appreciate the severity of the rift between Epstein and Lucchino. "With Larry, there was the A-Rod stuff and the Gammons stuff, so you had this situation as far back as before we won the World Series where both [Epstein and Lucchino] felt the other was throwing him under a bus with the media, that they were out to get the other," Henry says. "Until then, I never realized it. I didn't realize it was a big deal." Instead of letting the situation fester, Henry told Epstein he had to speak with Lucchino. "You need to lay it on the line and have a difficult conversation," Henry told Epstein. "You guys need to trust each other. You have to have each other's back. Tom and Larry and I, we have each other's backs. We've always felt that way, from day one." Henry says he told Lucchino the same thing.

And so, at Henry's urging, Epstein and Lucchino met on Tuesday, October 11. But Henry had underestimated the calcified rancor and bitterness that existed between the two men. Instead of helping to clear the air, their recitation of grievances only further poisoned the atmosphere. "It didn't work," Henry says. "It blew things up. It drove them further apart as opposed to bringing them together." With just less than three weeks left before Epstein's contract expired, it seemed less likely than ever that the boy-hero GM would stay with the Red Sox.

Over the next several weeks, the Boston media, after largely ignoring the issue during the season, began to focus on Epstein's future. Even as the New England Patriots geared up for a run at their third straight Super Bowl title, Boston's sports pages and airwaves were dominated by debates concerning Epstein and his contract and endless speculation about the possibility of a rift between Epstein and Lucchino. For the first time, the new-era, feel-good Red Sox were being compared to the dysfunctional clubs of old. "Epstein is young, smart, and 31—and he isn't signed yet?" asked the *Herald*'s Tony Massarotti. "How in the name of John Harrington does that happen, particularly to an organization that has otherwise taken so many strides in the last 3½ years? Not so long ago, the Red Sox front office was perceived as being badly out of touch. . . . [T]o be in this position, now, reminds all of the old days."

As the press coverage intensified during these final weeks of October, Epstein's salary demands were leaked to the media. Even as Epstein considered the leaks further evidence he couldn't trust certain people in the organization, Henry, who'd first learned of Epstein's salary request through a newspaper report, found himself angry with his general manager. Epstein was asking to be the highest-paid GM in the game, double what most other general managers were making. Henry, who'd talked often with Epstein about their determination to accurately read the market, was confused. "How can that be the market?" Henry asked. One of the ways Henry deals with his displeasure is by simply ignoring a person. "Theo and I had been very close," says Henry. "But when money became the issue, we basically stopped communicating. At that point, I was mainly on Larry's side."

Despite Epstein and Lucchino's strained relationship and despite John Henry's newfound anger, Epstein and the Red Sox began to inch slowly toward an agreement. By late October, the main stumbling block seemed to be Epstein's bitterness over the continual leaks about the negotiations. Early in the week of October 24,

Epstein, while turning down a three-year offer worth $1.2 million annually, gave Henry, Werner, and Lucchino what he considered his bottom line: He wouldn't come back for less than $1.5 million a year. By Thursday, October 27, Epstein and the team had come to terms for precisely that amount. "We pretty much had a deal," says Henry. "All of the [outstanding] issues had been laid to rest," says Henry, "except these ongoing leak issues." But instead of signing the deal before the end of the week, Lucchino recommended they wait until Monday, October 31, the last day Epstein was still under contract. Henry was confused. "I said, 'Why are you pushing it back to Monday?' " Henry says. "And Larry said, 'To give him three extra days to think about it. It's a big decision.' I wasn't in favor of waiting, but I said fine."

Epstein did think about it, and by the time he woke up on the morning of Sunday, October 30, he was at peace with his decision. He would remain with the Boston Red Sox. He'd reconciled himself to a lack of privacy for as long as he stayed in the job. He'd promised John Henry he would no longer isolate himself in the baseball operations basement fortress, and now, after more than a year of resenting and blaming Lucchino, he realized he shared responsibility for their damaged relationship.

Then he got a phone call alerting him to an article in that day's newspaper. On the front page of the *Globe*'s sports section was a Dan Shaughnessy column entitled, "Let's iron out some of this dirty laundry." When Epstein began reading, he felt his stomach drop. After weeks during which he'd talked with Henry, Werner, and Lucchino about his unease about the organization, here was confirmation of his worst fears. In his column, Shaughnessy, who'd known Lucchino and Charles Steinberg since the 1980s, when all three men worked in Baltimore, chided and belittled Epstein for not properly respecting his superiors. After all, Shaughnessy wrote, it was Lucchino and Steinberg who'd "discovered" Epstein and "held his hand" during his first years in baseball. Now, Shaughnessy wrote, Epstein was exhibiting an "alarming . . . need to distance himself from those who helped him rise to his position of power." Epstein, according to Shaughnessy, didn't even know all that much about baseball. "[I]t's a mistake to say [Epstein] knows more about baseball than Lucchino or anyone else in the Red Sox baseball operation," he wrote. Lucchino, after all, "was a good high school baseball player" and started working in the game "as an executive . . . when Theo was 5 years old." Finally, Shaughnessy gave Lucchino credit for "fall[ing] on" Epstein's sword by taking the blame for the aborted Larry Bigbie trade with the Colorado Rockies —presumably because Epstein was too much of a coward to do so himself—and implied that Epstein had recently been spurring Peter Gammons into "trashing the Sox CEO."

Either Lucchino or Steinberg, Epstein felt sure, had prompted the column. The two men were, after all, the heroes of the piece, and both had said lines almost identical to some Shaughnessy had used.* Where else could Shaughnessy have gotten the incorrect notion—repeated in the column as fact, without any attribution— that Epstein had asked Lucchino to shoulder the blame for the Bigbie trade?† It was actually Henry and Epstein who had decided to nix the deal; Lucchino had never been a part of the conversation.

After reading Shaugnessy's column, Epstein sat down and wrote John Henry an email. The next day, Epstein wrote, he would resign as general manager of the Boston Red Sox. "I have a huge pit in my stomach," Epstein wrote. "But it's nowhere near as big a pit as I'd have if I'd already signed a contract."

"I love baseball," Epstein said two weeks earlier while discussing his future plans. "It dominates my life because I'm a part of it so much. But the big picture is, there's so much fucking more out

---

* About a week earlier, several sources confirm that Charles Steinberg had a conversation with Dan Shaughnessy and another reporter in which he said many of the things that ended up in Shaughnessy's column. Steinberg says he never "spoke ill against Theo." "Nor would I," he says, "because that's inconsistent with how I've felt about him all these years, and I still know with the grace of God he's destined for more greatness."

† Over the next several months, Dan Shaughnessy repeatedly insisted that neither Lucchino nor his allies within the organization had urged him to write his October 30 column. But, on November 1, Shaughnessy wrote that the version of the Bigbie trade he wrote as fact was "the version held by Lucchino's camp (three sources)." Wherever he got the information, it simply wasn't true. "I vetoed the trade," says Henry. "It was me, after Theo and I talked about it. It was never Larry. He had nothing to do with it."

there. You become such a prisoner of the game, because there's 162 games. . . . The best thing [any baseball executive] might be able to do is, in between teams, take a year and do other things. That might be the single most valuable thing you can do." Now, Epstein would have just that opportunity.

CHAPTER 43

# *Putting It All Back Together Again*

ON MONDAY, OCTOBER 31, there was, fittingly, one final leak, as *The Boston Globe* announced that Epstein and the Red Sox had agreed on a three-year contract extension worth $1.5 million a year. A press conference announcing the deal, the *Globe* said, would be held "either today or tomorrow at Fenway Park." In fact, there would be no celebratory press conference at Fenway Park. Even as the *Globe* was being read across New England, the Red Sox offices were in a state of chaos. At one point, Lucchino charged down into the baseball operations department's basement offices and shouted at Epstein to get ready to clean up the public-relations mess his resignation would create. By midafternoon, the *Herald* had broken the news of Epstein's departure on its website. Epstein released his own statement soon after. "In my time as General Manager, I gave my entire heart and soul to the organization," the statement read. "During the process leading up to today's decision, I came to the conclusion that I can no longer do so. In the end, my choice is the right one not only for me but for the Red Sox." If the strained relationship between Epstein and Lucchino had received intermittent coverage in the weeks before, it was about to become the region's central story.

"I think it caught everyone by surprise," says Terry Francona. "I

guess everybody, myself included, figured, you know, it will play itself out and there will be a nice press conference. It'll be a hugfest
and he'll sign a three- or four-year contract, because Theo *is* the Red
Sox. In the end, it didn't work out that way. It was tough to watch."
That night, in order to evade the assembled media hordes, Epstein
was forced to exit Fenway Park in a borrowed gorilla suit a Red Sox
employee had brought in to work as a Halloween joke.* After another day and a half of trying to avoid the media camped outside his
house, Epstein returned to Fenway Park for a November 2 press
conference. John Henry was in attendance; Larry Lucchino and
Charles Steinberg,† conspicuously, were not. After Epstein spoke,
Henry came to the microphone. He appeared shaken and at times
near tears. "This is a great, great loss," Henry said. "I feel responsible. What could I have done? There's plenty I could have done. . . . I
have to ask myself, Maybe I'm not fit to be the principal owner of
the Boston Red Sox. . . . Did I blow it? Yeah, I feel that way." Both
Epstein and Henry stressed that Epstein's departure had not been a
result of tension in his relationship with Lucchino. "I can tell you,"
Henry said, "that one of the problems in this process was the media
did not have access to what was going on, so they had to rely upon
unnamed sources. . . . I don't blame the media, but there were
things that were said that were inaccurate."

Even as Epstein and Henry were giving their tortuous explana-
tions for Epstein's departure, Henry had begun a campaign to secure his return. He began by asking Epstein outright to come back.
When Epstein said no, Henry tried a different approach. How,
Henry asked Epstein, would he recommend running the team's
baseball operations department in his absence?‡ As much as he
didn't want to discuss his own future with the team, Epstein

---

* The gorilla suit was auctioned off for $11,000 in January 2006. The proceeds
went to charity.
† It was the first time in memory that Steinberg hadn't parked himself front
and center during a major Red Sox announcement.
‡ This was a smart move on Henry's part. Before his resignation, Epstein, during a long conversation with me about his future and the future of the team,
had said, "Now you've gotten me fired up talking about the [2006] season, I'm
going to end up taking a horseshit deal to stay here."

couldn't help but get excited when discussing the Red Sox and how they could best achieve their goals. The team, Epstein told Henry, had to be less concerned with the next day's headlines. "The reason the Red Sox never win the World Series is because they're always concerned with what the newspapers are saying," he said. "There's a sort of extreme short-term thinking, always trying to build a super-team that wins the World Series that year. They're way too concerned with the Yankees, the fans, and the media. And now that we've won the World Series, it's a great opportunity to do what's right: ignore all that and build something that will last, something for the long haul." Henry agreed wholeheartedly, and over the next several weeks, the two men spoke in more detail and with more passion than they had in months. "The experience of us doing that, of having these conversations, definitely brought us closer together," says Henry. As they kept talking, "it became clear that he and I were completely on the same page with respect to our long-term vision for the organization," says Epstein.

Here, Epstein realized, was what he had been craving for much of the last year: more direct involvement from John Henry. The reason the Red Sox were such a good opportunity for him wasn't because he'd grown up rooting for the team, or because his family still lived in Boston. If anything, those were the very factors that made working for the Red Sox difficult. The reason the Sox presented a uniquely appealing environment was because John Henry and Tom Werner were perhaps the only owners in all of baseball with whom Epstein felt truly simpatico.

By mid-November, Epstein was already getting job offers from around the league—Frank McCourt, the native Bostonian who now owned the Los Angeles Dodgers, offered Epstein an ownership stake in the team if he'd sign on as the team's new GM.* Toward the

* McCourt, who'd failed in his bid to buy the Red Sox, looks determined to assemble as much of Boston's recent teams as possible. In the past two years, the Dodgers signed two Red Sox free agents—Derek Lowe and Bill Mueller— then signed Nomar Garciaparra to play first base. They also hired Grady Little as the team's new manager, former Red Sox scout and coach Dave Jauss as the team's bench coach, and former baseball operations executive Bill Lajoie as a senior advisor to the Dodgers general manager.

end of November, Henry again broached the subject: Would Epstein consider returning to the team? After a month of conversations, Epstein's stance had softened. "If [Henry] does [become more involved]," Epstein remembers thinking, "and we pledge mutual commitment for a certain ideal, then does it go from being a bad situation that was ripe for leaving to possibly one of the best situations I could imagine? Yes, it does." By the time of baseball's winter meetings in early December, Epstein, Henry, and Werner had agreed Epstein would return to the team in some capacity. "I guess some people might take this as a slap at Larry," says Henry, "but it's not. But the one thing we agreed to was that I would be more in baseball operations."

As Henry and Epstein were talking, it was Lucchino who was taking the hit in the press and in popular opinion. Now, he seemed determined both to shift attention away from Epstein's absence and to offer proof that his former protégé was not as vital as the press believed. In late November, Lucchino pushed through a deal that sent two of the Red Sox's top minor league prospects, shortstop Hanley Ramirez and pitcher Anibal Sanchez, along with two lesser prospects, to the Florida Marlins for pitcher Josh Beckett, third baseman Mike Lowell, and reliever Guillermo Mota. The 25-year-old Beckett is one of the best young pitchers in baseball, with a wicked fastball and a tremendous curve. Two years earlier, he'd shut down the Yankees in the midst of being named the MVP of the 2003 World Series.

The Beckett trade appeared to be a fantastic one—young, proven arms are rare commodities in baseball—and the local media reacted accordingly. After calling the trade "one of the most significant deals in recent team history," the *Globe*'s Nick Cafardo noted how it was "CEO Larry Lucchino" who had "sealed the deal with the Marlins." It didn't take long before details about the trade began to emerge that made it seem less of an obvious steal. An MRI of the oft-injured Beckett's shoulder—he'd been on the disabled list nine times in the previous four years—raised serious concerns about his rotator cuff. Assistant to the general manager Jed Hoyer, in constant consultation with Epstein, had been wary about making the trade, but Lucchino had been eager to get it done. "It was so clear what was going on," says someone with an ownership stake in the team. "You had the people who were looking out for the long-term interests of the club advising to hold off, and the people who wanted to get the focus off of the front-office fiasco pushing to make the deal."

There were other, more active ways in which some Sox executives felt Lucchino was rushing to turn the page. By mid-November, Lucchino had begun interviewing GM candidates, including former Montreal Expos and Baltimore Orioles executive Jim Beattie and the Washington Nationals' Jim Bowden. While it was obviously necessary to prepare for a scenario in which Epstein didn't return, Lucchino repeatedly, and publicly, met with Beattie, creating an awkward situation in which it appeared as if Beattie was being actively rejected by Red Sox ownership despite Lucchino's recommendation. By late November, Jeremy Kapstein, best known as the man in the blue windbreaker who sat directly behind home plate during Red Sox home games, began loudly promoting himself as a GM candidate. Kapstein, who had been the CEO of the San Diego Padres in 1989 and 1990, was one of several Lucchino cronies to land nebulous positions with the Red Sox.* His official title with the organization was "senior advisor/baseball projects," but he was almost never involved with baseball-related decisions. To the extent he was thought of at all, it was as the somewhat odd, sour-faced man who squirreled away catered sandwiches and brought bags of raw sweet corn to people's offices as gifts.

Despite Lucchino's recommendations, Henry and Werner did not hire Beattie, and never seriously considered Kapstein. With Henry in constant contact with Epstein, Werner focused on reconciling Epstein and Lucchino. "I spent more time on this than on anything else since I've been here," Werner says. "It was crucial we made this work. These were the best people out there." By early December, Epstein's return was all but assured. As he began working

---

* Another was Ken Nigro, a former Padres employee whom Lucchino hired to run the Red Sox cruises and fantasy camps. Nigro and Dan Shaughnessy both worked at Baltimore's *Sun* in the early 1980s, and both Nigro and Kapstein have reputations within the Red Sox as sources for Shaughnessy.

behind the scenes with the team's front office, the Red Sox set out about planning for his return, which would officially occur some time before the season began. In the meantime, the Sox decided to appoint Jed Hoyer and director of player development Ben Cherington the team's interim general managers; that way the team could have some short-term stability in its front office. Hoyer and Cherington had both worked closely with Epstein, and Hoyer had been in daily contact with the former GM since he'd left on Halloween night.

Even this seemingly straightforward plan somehow went awry. With Henry out of town and Lucchino helping to coordinate the announcement, the CEO told Hoyer and Cherington that they would simply be named co-general managers. For simplicity's sake, there wouldn't be any "interim" title attached. There were those within the Red Sox who viewed this as one more way of placing a hurdle in front of Epstein: Now, when he returned, he would appear to be pushing aside two allies who had loyally worked beneath him for years. At the press conference announcing Hoyer and Cherington's appointment, Lucchino was forced to answer a barrage of questions about Epstein, who was by this time known to be making calls about possible trades on behalf of the organization. Lucchino acknowledged there was a chance the former GM would return. "I think it's premature to discuss exactly what role, if any, Theo would have," he said. "All we're saying is we'll keep the light on at the window, the door ajar. If there's a fit, we'd love to see it happen." He was more circumspect in private. "All human relationships have to change over time," he told me in January, speaking of himself and Epstein. "He's getting older and I'm getting older. There is a dynamic between us that necessarily must change. But I . . . that's about all I have to say on that. I don't feel any . . . it happens to lots of relationships. You hope that people are flexible enough and sensible enough to adjust to the new dynamic that's developed."

With Beckett on board and Hoyer and Cherington in place, Lucchino and the Red Sox next turned their attention toward re-signing Johnny Damon. Two-thousand five had been, in many ways, a career-defining year for Damon. His cult status in Boston had been solidified, and his relaxed good looks and high comfort level with the media made him one of the most accessible and popular players on the team. He had spent much of the season leading the American League in batting average, and had had several impressive hitting streaks. And notably, during a year in which much of the team seemed fixated on individual statistics, Damon eagerly suited up even when hurt, despite the fact that his injuries likely contributed to poorer numbers, as he slumped from a .340 average on August 9 to .316 by the season's end. In mid-September, Henry, while watching Damon grimace after taking an awkward swing, remarked, "This is a guy you want on your club. Look at what he's going through right now. He's in all this pain, he's a free agent, his batting average has dropped. He could say he needs to shut it down. But not this guy."

Still, despite Damon's durability and popularity, the Red Sox knew there was a good chance they'd lose him. The team was prepared to offer Damon a contract similar to the four-year, $40 million deal they gave Jason Varitek a year earlier, but Damon's agent, Scott Boras, said he was looking for a seven-year deal worth around $12 million a year. In preparation for the likely loss of Damon, the team's baseball operations staff had been quietly exploring deals that would bring a young outfielder to the team. Even if the Red Sox were able to re-sign Damon, they figured, there were enough question marks in the outfield, from Manny Ramirez's uncertain status to Trot Nixon's health, to make it prudent to have a surfeit of healthy outfielders when the season began. At one point, the team had negotiated the terms of a trade of pitcher Bronson Arroyo to the Seattle Mariners for the up-and-coming 24-year-old Jeremy Reed. Later, there was a preliminary deal that would send Arroyo and newly acquired reliever Guillermo Mota to the Cleveland Indians for 26-year-old Coco Crisp and pitcher David Riske. Both times, the deals got put on the back burner. Lucchino wanted to stay focused on re-signing Damon.

In early December, the Red Sox began for the first time to feel optimistic about bringing back their star center fielder. Despite Boras's claims of multiple teams being interested, there seemed to be very few suitors for Damon, and it was clear that no team was willing to commit seven years to a player who was already showing decreased range. "By then, we began to think that there really isn't anyone out there," says Henry. Boston made its offer official—four years at $10 million a year—and told Boras they'd like to have things settled one way or another by Christmas. Boras responded by telling the Red Sox that Damon was already fielding offers of up to $70 million. "You aren't even in the game," the agent said.

Once again, it was Lucchino who favored taking a more aggressive approach. "I certainly saw his value to the club for the next few years," he says. "Of course, part of my job is to look at the image of the club and the marketing of the club, the star quality of players on the club, and I knew what an asset we had in him in that regard. In fact, we'd helped make [Damon a star]." But the Red Sox didn't want to raise their offer and start bidding against themselves without any real indication there were other suitors. "We all reached a consensus about how five years was just too much [to offer Damon]," says Lucchino.

The situation remained stalled through much of December. By December 20, John Henry and Boras were in direct communication. Now Boras said Damon had a six-year deal "on the table," but was willing to stay with the Red Sox if they offered him five years because he loved the city and the team so much. Then, later that evening, Boras told both Henry and Jed Hoyer that there was another "hot" deal on the table, this one for $13 million a year for five years, totaling $65 million. The Sox had already agreed among themselves that they'd be willing to go up to at least $11 million a year for four years, but even that figure totaled some $21 million less than what Boras told the team Damon was being offered. We can't, Henry told Boras, go *that* high.

That night, word began to trickle out that Damon was signing with the Yankees. This had been a scenario the Red Sox had been prepared for—back in September, Henry, Epstein, and assistant general manager Josh Byrnes* had discussed how Damon could

* On October 28, 2005, Byrnes was named the general manager of the Arizona Diamondbacks.

very well end up in the Bronx because of New York's desperate need for a reliable center fielder. The Yankees, it seemed, were the mystery team who had offered the five-year, $65 million contract. But when the details of the deal finally emerged, the Red Sox were shocked to learn that Damon had signed only a four-year deal worth $13 million a year, for a total of $52 million.

Henry, furious, confronted Boras. What of the five- and six-year deals? Henry asked. Why did you tell us not to bother bidding if we weren't going to go to $65 million? There had been a five-year deal, Boras insisted. But in the end, Boras said, Damon decided he actually *wanted* to play in New York, and when the Yankees "stepped up to the plate," Boras accepted their offer without giving the Red Sox a chance to raise their bid.*

It turns out that Johnny Damon never had a firm six-year offer from any team, as Scott Boras had repeatedly told the Red Sox. A high-ranking official in Major League Baseball's central office, who spoke on condition of anonymity, said that as far as officials who'd been in contact with every team in baseball could tell, Damon had never even received a solid five-year offer. To Boras, any effort to weaken the bonds of loyalty a player felt to his old team would mean the possibility of more lucrative contracts. Players had traditionally been hesitant to cross the Rubicon from Boston to New York; even Damon had said just seven months earlier that there was "no way" he could play for the Yankees even though he knew they were "going to come after [him] hard." If Boras could orchestrate it so that Johnny Damon, one of the most popular players on one of the most popular Red Sox teams in history, switched sides, what other players might be willing to do so in the future? And how much higher might player salaries go if agents could regularly get the Yankees to bid for Red Sox free agents, and vice versa?

---

* In March 2006, Damon said he would have been willing to go back to Boston for $11.5 million a year, just $500,000 more annually than the Red Sox had already agreed to offer him. Of course, he also said he was hurt that the Red Sox didn't want him back and implied that he felt disrespected by the team's $40 million offer. "I even bought a home [in Boston] because they'd told me I'd be there a long time," he said early in the 2006 season.

## CHAPTER 44

# *Reversing the Curse*

BY JANUARY 19, 2006, much of the turmoil and drama that had defined the winter months at Fenway Park had passed. Down in the team's baseball operations department, Epstein's office remained unoccupied, the sign advertising $100 cartons of milk still taped to the window. Jed Hoyer and Ben Cherington were ready and waiting for their once and future boss to come back to work. Epstein and Hoyer spoke several times that day, as they prepared for an announcement regarding Epstein's return that was scheduled to occur within the week. The rest of the department's staffers joked about how they hoped Epstein was resting up. Once he officially returned to work, they knew he'd be back on the same relentless schedule.

Three floors up, the team's public-relations office seemed uncharacteristically calm. During the season, the department would be a frenetic whirlwind of staffers dealing with credential requests, culling clips, and preparing pre- and postgame informational packets. Now, a handful of staffers were flipping through one of the team's page-a-day calendars and playing a lighthearted game of "name that Red Sox player." Everyone seemed relaxed.

Everyone, that is, except for Charles Steinberg. In the wake of Dan Shaughnessy's October 30 column, there was a vigorous effort within the organization to determine if Steinberg, the most commonly mentioned suspect, had actually been one of the sources for the piece. Steinberg resolutely insisted he'd had nothing to do with it, but he'd still been muzzled, and had remained uncharacteristically quiet for much of the winter.

About a month earlier, Steinberg had taken his annual trip to Aruba. Every year, he buys the same type of lined notebook, lies down on the beach, and "tries to get in the mind frame of the 10-year-old fan" in order to brainstorm new ways to promote the team. This year, he'd filled page after page with ideas for in-game video shorts to be aired on the stadium's JumboTron: a day in the life of a ballboy; a day in the life of a clubhouse attendant; a day in the life of a groundskeeper. But on that beach in Aruba, Steinberg had other things on his mind as well, and at one point he wrote down some questions to which he did not have an answer. "Will this be my last year working with the Red Sox? With Larry?"

Late in the afternoon on January 19, Steinberg paused to reflect about everything that had occurred during the previous months. He tried to deflect attention away from himself, explaining why he'd been less visible than usual by saying, "This has been a difficult time for Larry." He went on: "I would imagine it's been a difficult challenge that he is proud to have met. He doesn't seek any pity."

At almost the precise moment that Steinberg was speaking, Dan Shaughnessy was talking to John Henry on his cell phone. Not long after Epstein left the team, Shaughnessy had written a column titled, "Time to kiss and make up: Sox search should look back at Epstein." Now, Shaughnessy said, he was preparing to write a piece that said Epstein was selfishly holding the club "hostage," and that Henry should either "fire Lucchino or tell Epstein to get lost."

Henry, who was with Tom Werner in Phoenix at the annual baseball owners meeting, explained to Shaughnessy that Epstein was not holding the club hostage. In fact, Henry said, all of the key people in the organization already knew of his impending return. Since the team's limited partners were meeting that weekend, Henry said, he wanted to wait to make an official announcement until he had had a chance to speak with all of them.

Tough luck, Shaughnessy replied. His column was running the next day. "He was going to write things that were nasty," says Tom Werner. "And false." After all that had transpired in the wake of

Shaughnessy's October 30 column, Henry and Werner did not want to deal with the fallout from another broadside. That night, they rushed out a statement: Epstein would be returning to the club, and the details of the arrangement would be announced soon.

Shaughnessy seemed to take the announcement as a personal affront. In his next day's column, he wrote, "The white knight is riding back to Fenway on his high horse." Calling Epstein "at best, immature and at worst, duplicitous," he said the entire situation was "embarrassing." Shaughnessy then went on to imagine the scene at the Red Sox offices: "The people in baseball operations were working hard as usual late Thursday night, trying to plug the team's holes in center field and shortstop, when Epstein called them and told them there was going to be an announcement that he's coming back next week. No one knew quite what to say to their former boss. There's been no discussion about who will report to whom. No one knows how this is going to work, and Theo has burned some bridges with his own people."

It is true that there were those in the Red Sox baseball operations department who felt frustrated and even a little betrayed by Epstein. His decision to walk out was seen as peevish, his need to see the world in black-and-white unrealistic. There were, after all, plenty of people who worked for difficult bosses, and most of them managed to find a way to deal with the situation. While Epstein had been off chilling with Pearl Jam in Argentina and vacationing in Hawaii, his mostly unheralded former colleagues had to deal with the turmoil that resulted from his absence. But these were the minor gripes of people who felt close and loyal to Epstein. The notion that his return wasn't anticipated was comical, as was the charge that there were chain of command issues that remained unsettled.

In the years since John Henry and Tom Werner had bought the Red Sox in 2002, the team had made remarkably few missteps. The new owners quickly overcame the skepticism and distrust of the local media and were embraced by the fans. They ushered the Red Sox to the playoffs for three straight years for the first time in team history, and brought a World Series title to Boston for the first time in 86 years. For a while, it seemed as if they could do no wrong.

Then, in one cataclysmic two-month span, the Red Sox lost their lionized general manager due to interoffice dysfunction, traded away two top prospects for a possibly injured pitcher, and appeared flatfooted as their most recognizable star waltzed off to join their hated rival. To the Boston media, this was an occasion for a paroxysm of overheated coverage. Smooth-running success was compelling for only so long. In the winter of 2005 and 2006, reporter after reporter remarked excitedly, the Henry-Werner Red Sox took on the ugly, unpredictable, and endlessly entertaining sheen of teams from years gone by.

"We had a very good year last year," Tom Werner said on January 20 as he ate breakfast in the living room of his apartment overlooking Boston Common. "Because of the regrettable manner in which the Theo decision was made—and I think everybody admitted that they made some mistakes—our standing has taken a big hit . . . but we've taken more bashing than is warranted. OK, so we went on a general manager search, but we've come to a very clean conclusion at the end of it. Even this recent period has come to, hopefully, a positive ending."

The narrative of the Red Sox's 2004 World Series win begins with the appointment of Theo Epstein as the team's general manager in the winter of 2002 and ends with their loss to the Chicago White Sox in the first round of the 2005 playoffs, an almost three-year stretch in which the Red Sox became the biggest news story in Boston's history. The events of those years forever altered the core identity of the club. The desperate, yearning edge that had been associated with the team for so long disappeared. The devotional aspect of being a Red Sox fan dissolved, the sense of purpose and the promise of redemption implicit in each new season was no more.

Larry Lucchino realized the challenges this transformation would create sooner than most. In the short term, the team's world championship brought more fans and the Red Sox became more popular than at any point in their history. Even if Fenway in 2005 rarely felt as electric as it did in '03 and '04, the Red Sox remained the hottest ticket in town. It was Lucchino who intuitively recognized that without a larger-than-life storyline binding fans to the team, the Sox would have to work even harder to hold onto New England's attention in the future. A couple of middling seasons would no longer serve as further proof of the Red Sox's Sisyphian fate; instead, they'd likely transform the team into nothing more than another mediocre ball club fighting for people's already sparse time and attention and money. Everything from the team's exhausting World Series trophy tour to Lucchino's fretful desire to see the Red Sox remain an elite team in the years immediately following the 2004 championship were part of his efforts to make sure the Red Sox did not crash and burn after soaring so high.

What Lucchino didn't realize was that while he was aggressively pushing for more, 2005 was, as John Henry says, a "hangover year" for much of the rest of the organization. "You've been focusing on something, you accomplish your goal, and you say, 'Now what?' . . . Human beings really thrive when they have a cause or a goal regarding something larger than themselves," Henry says. And if one of Lucchino's biggest strengths as a CEO is his inability to rest on his laurels, his most glaring weakness is the sense of unease he instills in many of the people who serve underneath him. When the Red Sox were united in their effort to win a World Series, Lucchino's management style wasn't an overriding concern. After the Red Sox had won and Lucchino appeared to be the dominant personality at the head of the organization, it became more of an issue.

Lucchino is as dedicated to Edward Bennett Williams's philosophy of "contest living" as ever, and the combative edge that transforms so many of his daily interactions into inimical negotiations remains—a lifetime's worth of habits cannot, after all, be shorn away in a couple of months. But even Lucchino seems to have a new appreciation that more is not always better. "I realized [after 2005] that we need to slow down," he says. In the offseason, Lucchino usually comes up with new ways for the Red Sox to promote their brand or new business ventures the organization can embark on. This year he did the opposite, drawing up an "86 list," named for the shorthand restaurants use when a dish is no longer available. "We're going to 86 the players' picnic in Fenway in September," says Lucchino. "We're going to 86 excess [Red Sox] Foundation events. . . . They're small things, but they all get to the big picture, which is that we're first and foremost a baseball team and we've got to sort of keep our eyes on the prize."

Cataclysmic events can cause great destruction or fundamental change, and for the last several months of 2005, it looked as if the aftershocks of winning the World Series had wreaked havoc on the Red Sox. Theo Epstein's departure and the roiling drama that preceded his return threw the organization into a frenzied panic, and the Boston media, smelling blood in the water, dove in for the kill. Now Epstein has returned, and there's a sense throughout the organization that a new narrative is emerging both on and off the field.

The Red Sox teams of 2003, 2004, and 2005 featured historic offenses that will be fully appreciated only with the passage of time. For three years in a row, the Red Sox led all of baseball in runs scored. They averaged 940 runs a year during a span in which only one other team managed to top 900 runs even once* and averaged 5.80 runs per game while the rest of baseball was scoring at a rate of just 4.69 runs a night.

By early 2006, many of the players on these teams had been replaced. The Red Sox had plugged their holes in center field and shortstop, completing deals Epstein, Cherington, and Hoyer had been working on for weeks. They replaced Johnny Damon by trading Andy Marte, Guillermo Mota, and minor league catcher Kelly Shoppach to the Indians for Coco Crisp, reliever David Riske, and catcher Josh Bard, and signed former Marlins shortstop Alex Gonzalez to a one-year deal worth $3 million.

While the starting players that remain from the previous years—Trot Nixon, David Ortiz, Manny Ramirez, and Jason Varitek—are still offensive threats, they're all on the wrong side of 30, and outside of Ortiz, none is likely to duplicate his recent performances. The team's newly acquired starters, from Gonzalez to second baseman Mark Loretta and third baseman Mike Lowell, are known

---

* Combined, the 30 Major League Baseball teams scored more than 900 runs in a season four times in 2003, 2004, and 2005, meaning four out of 90 teams scored more than 900 runs: the 2003 Boston Red Sox (961), the 2004 Boston Red Sox (949), the 2005 Boston Red Sox (910), and the 2003 Atlanta Braves (907).

more for their defensive prowess. Even Crisp, whom the Red Sox hope will come close to duplicating Johnny Damon's offensive production, is well known for his range in the outfield.

This is no accident. For several years, the team's baseball operations crew has been searching for new ways in which to understand and analyze players' defensive contributions, and have oftentimes used their own data instead of relying on that provided by either Major League Baseball or Stats, Inc., the main third-party statistics clearinghouse.* "Eventually, there will be a new way to measure defensive value," says Epstein. "We need to first find a new way of thinking about it, a new paradigm shift."

The 2006 Red Sox have a chance at being one of the best-fielding teams Boston has ever produced.† They will also, much to Epstein's delight, be a more poised and professional group of ballplayers. The personality of this year's team will likely bear little resemblance to the Cowboy Up, Idiot, Fuck 'Em All Red Sox that held Boston in

---

* Unlike offense or pitching, fielding statistics are maddeningly imprecise. Both fielding percentage (the percentage of plays a fielder makes without committing an error) and range factor (a measure of how many plays a fielder is involved in per game, compared to other players at his position) are dependent on a number of circumstances outside a player's control. Zone rating, a measure of the percentage of the balls a fielder reaches in a prescribed zone of the field, is enormously dependent on observers' analyses, and these observers—sometimes poorly trained college kids—can spit out bad information. Since teams almost never gather their own defensive statistics, faulty defensive data can lead to trades that might otherwise have worked out differently. Before the 2005 season, the Oakland A's traded pitcher Tim Hudson to the Atlanta Braves for minor league left fielder Charles Thomas and pitchers Dan Meyer and Juan Cruz. The A's viewed Thomas, who had a reputation for being a defensive whiz in left, as a prize catch. In fact, Thomas's defensive numbers were vastly inflated because of improper zone rating calculations. Bad data can skew even the most sophisticated analyses. For example, John Dewan's *The Fielding Bible,* published in 2006, is a fascinating addition to the study of defensive prowess; however, some baseball executives feel some of the data Dewan used were collected improperly.

† In addition to Lowell, a Gold Glove winner in 2005, and Gonzalez, considered one of the best defensive shortstops in baseball, the Red Sox added J. T. Snow as a backup first basemen. From 1995 through 2000, Snow won six straight Gold Glove awards.

thrall. What's more, the Sox, at the end of what was supposed to be a lost offseason, look exceedingly well positioned for the future. After devising four different methods of ranking teams' minor league nonpitching prospects and averaging the results, Bill James concluded the Sox had the 10th best minor league system in baseball even after trading hotshot prospects Hanley Ramirez and Andy Marte. "We are," as James wrote in a 30-page report he delivered to the team in early 2006, "doing fairly well." And the Red Sox have plenty of money to sign up free agents in the years to come. In 2009 and 2010, years in which the Yankees have more than $120 million in contract commitments, the Red Sox are on the hook for just $31 million.*

Behind the scenes, Theo Epstein and Larry Lucchino found their working relationship, while not necessarily harmonious, was better than it had been at any point since 2003. Not long after Epstein's return, Lucchino suggested that, in order to cut down on confusion, Epstein should be the person from whom the media got their information about the team's baseball operations, and the general manager began parceling out news as he saw fit instead of eagerly feeding the baseball press's always voracious appetite.† Epstein made a commitment to integrate his staff more with the rest of the organization, and both men realized they had allowed

---

* In 2008, the Sox have committed $48 million to five players: $20 million to Manny Ramirez, $12.5 million to David Ortiz, $10 million to Jason Varitek, $4.75 million to Coco Crisp, and $700,000 to reliever Craig Hansen. That year, the Yankees have $111 million in salary commitments divided among seven players. In 2009, the Yankees have $73 million committed to four players, all of whom will be 34 or older by the end of the year, and in 2010, the Yankees have $48 million committed to Alex Rodriguez and Derek Jeter alone, who will turn 35 and 36, respectively, during the season. In 2009, the Sox will owe Ortiz, who will be 34 at the end of the year, $12.5 million, and Crisp, who will be 30, $5.75 million. For 2010, the only player the Sox have under contract is Ortiz, at $12.5 million.

† Epstein has often professed admiration for the Bill Belichick–led New England Patriots, who seem to treat even the most benign information as being available on a need-to-know basis. The media, needless to say, doesn't need to know much of anything in Belichick's view.

several years' worth of resentments and unspoken recriminations to fester unnecessarily.

"You know how it is in relationships," says Henry. "You refuse to say something to your wife or girlfriend, and it builds up until you finally talk about it. So we had some things build up, and now that we've gotten them out, it's much better. It's good."

At the beginning of spring training in 2006, John Henry and Tom Werner were talking about one of Werner's nascent television projects called *Twenty Years*. The show focuses on two older men—Werner wants Danny DeVito and John Lithgow—who realize they have approximately 20 good years left and spend each episode deciding how they want to spend that time. Henry says he and Werner could not help but see the parallels to their own lives. "Tom and I have been having conversations over the last several weeks," he says, "and we've realized again how much we love what we're doing. And how we're lucky.

"The World Series, that was just the beginning. You know how hectic that beginning was. We had no idea. It's sort of like when you're expecting a baby. You have the baby and it's a great moment, and you take pictures and look back at it and show all your friends. That's what you focus on: the moment you had the baby. But that's nothing. You wake up 10 months later and you have a small child. And 10 years later . . . who knows what's in store?"

# *Epilogue*

**ON APRIL 10, 2006,** the Red Sox announced they had signed David Ortiz to a four-year, $52 million extension that would keep the slugging designated hitter in Boston through 2010. The deal made official what everyone already knew: Ortiz, in his three years with the team, had become the face of the franchise. Since joining the Red Sox, Ortiz had 120 home runs, and his 392 RBIs were tops in the majors over that span. He'd collected 13 walk-off hits, eight of which were game-ending homers, and was the only person in history with more than two postseason walk-off hits to his name, as well as the only player with more than one in a single year.

At the press conference announcing the deal, Ortiz, clutching an unlit cigar and sporting a black fedora and a pair of gaudy diamond earrings, told reporters he signed the extension because of his commitment to Boston. "This is my house," he said of Fenway. "I've got to protect this house." With his father watching from the back of the room, Ortiz went on. "This is not all about David Ortiz. This is about the group of guys that play together day by day. Whenever something happens to any of these guys, the whole [Red Sox] Nation feels that. I can feel that. I can see that. . . . I'm pretty sure New England is going to take this as the good news. I want to finish my career as a Red Sox player." John Henry, Tom Werner, Larry Lucchino, and Theo Epstein flanked Ortiz on the podium, and their mood was appropriately upbeat. The Sox, at 5-1, were tied for the best record in baseball. An ambitious set of offseason improvements to Fenway had been completed to glorious effect, as Lucchino and architect Janet Marie Smith worked their ballpark magic once again. The glass in front of the luxury club behind home plate had been removed, and a two-tiered, open-air section was put in its place. Elsewhere, the concourses were widened, new bathrooms were built, and concession stands were added.

In many ways, the rest of the organization felt as rejuvenated as Fenway Park. A year before, the Sox had opened the season with an aging lineup, tension festering in the front office, and players and staffers alike worn out from the exhausting effects of Boston's first World Series celebration in 86 years. By Opening Day in 2006, only nine out of 25 players—Keith Foulke, Trot Nixon, David Ortiz, Manny Ramirez, Curt Schilling, Mike Timlin, Jason Varitek, Tim Wakefield, and Kevin Youkilis—remained from the team's 2004 World Series roster. Lucchino and Epstein were working together more closely and seamlessly than they had in years, and the team's new strategy of keeping their planned moves out of the press seemed to be working: When, on April 12, the Sox announced they'd signed Coco Crisp to a three-year contract extension, the news caught Boston sportswriters by surprise.

In the first month of the season, even as the Sox tinkered with their roster and dealt with an injury to Crisp that would keep him out of the lineup until mid-May, the team was buoyed by the rebirth of Schilling as an elite starter and the emergence of Jonathan Papelbon as a dominant closer. Schilling started the year 4-1 and led the league with 40 strikeouts in April, while Papelbon set a rookie record with 10 saves while putting up a 0.00 ERA and striking out 14 in 13 appearances. On May 1, the Yankees traveled to Boston for the first Red Sox–Yankees game of the year. The intensity of the rivalry was undiminished, but the storylines had clearly changed. Johnny Damon was booed lustily during every one of his at-bats, and it was Mark Loretta who provided the game-winning RBI for the Red Sox in the bottom of the eighth inning. In the top of the ninth, Papelbon retired the side to seal the victory. The young right-hander hadn't let up a run since September 2005, and he opened the inning by blowing away Alex Rodriguez on three pitches. "I knew in the bullpen I was coming in to face him," Papelbon, who'd warmed to his role as one of the public faces of the Sox, said later. "I wanted to set the tone." John Henry, Tom Werner, Larry Lucchino, and Theo Epstein hoped Papelbon and his teammates on these new-look Red Sox would be setting just such a tone for years to come.

# A Note on Sources
# and Methodology

I've been a Red Sox fan since 1977, when my family moved to the Boston suburb of Newton. I was at Fenway on October 2, 1983, for Carl Yastrzemski's final game, and sank into a depression following Boston's Game 6 loss to the Mets in the 1986 World Series. My mom used to clip out box scores and standings from the *Globe* and send them to me at summer camp. I was sitting in the upper deck of Yankee Stadium on September 10, 1999, when Pedro had 17 strikeouts in a complete game one-hitter, and sank into another depression after the Sox's Game 7 loss to the Yankees in 2003. After following the team for 27 years, I finally succeeded in finding a way to combine my love for the team with my work life when, in the fall of 2004, I wangled an assignment from *Vanity Fair* to cover the team's playoff run. It was the chance of a lifetime.

This book grew out of that assignment, and is the product of a unique arrangement I had with the Red Sox. In the months following the Red Sox's World Series victory, the team's executives and management were deluged with book proposals. By that time, I had gotten to know John Henry, who was familiar with *Hard News*, my book on *The New York Times*. (The Times Company is the largest minority partner in the Sox.) While the book proposals poured in,

John and I had a general conversation about the publishing industry, and at the end of that conversation, I told him I'd love the chance to write about the team. I also told him that the book I was interested in writing was a very different one from those that had been suggested to him—projects in which he'd share royalties with the author or dictate what material the book included. The book I wanted to write was not an official or sanctioned history of the team, and I wasn't willing to grant John (or the team) any editorial control over the final product. There was a sprawling story to be covered, from the sale of the team in 2001 to the aftermath of the World Series victory, and in order to do it justice I wanted to treat the Red Sox as I'd treat any other journalistic subject, with the freedom to ask about anything and write about everything.

John almost immediately agreed. I was surprised, although I've since learned this level of openness and transparency is totally consistent with how he does business. I was granted access to all levels of the organization, from John and his partner, Tom Werner, to top management, baseball operations, and the team's coaching staff and players. Larry Lucchino set me up with a desk at Fenway and an electronic passkey that opened almost every door in the park. I sat in on meetings and traveled with the team, and no subject was off limits. (There was only one caveat to my arrangement: as a result of having access to Fenway's offices and free run of the organization, I had to clear any proprietary financial documents I came across. Everything else was fair game.) While there have been behind-the-scenes books about major league sports teams and tell-alls written by current and former players, *Feeding the Monster* is, to the best of my knowledge, the first book in which a writer was given unfettered access to every level of a club.

The openness with which John greeted me with was replicated by almost everyone within the Red Sox. As a result, this book is informed by more than 100 hours of exclusive interviews with past and present employees of the team. In addition to those one-on-one meetings, I attended more than half of the Red Sox's 162 games during the 2005 season. My routine on game-day usually went something like this: After spending the morning in the Sox offices, I'd retreat to the team's clubhouse at three thirty and spend the next several hours masquerading as a beat reporter. At six, I'd either head up to the press box or over to the partners' or the principal owner's suite. I also interviewed dozens of people not directly associated with the Red Sox, from Boston businessmen to people involved in the sale of the team, as well as journalists, baseball officials, agents, and players from other teams. In general, any quotes that result from an exclusive interview are designated by a present-tense verb: *says, asks,* etc.

For recent history, I relied heavily on coverage in *The Boston Globe,* the *Boston Herald, The Providence Journal,* and the *Hartford Courant.* When quoting from a particularly impressive scoop, I tried to give that reporter credit. When re-creating box scores or computing pitching or batting statistics, I strove to use as many independent sources as possible. Still, there's always the possibility the data I relied on may be off. ESPN.com's website contains detailed game logs; however, these are occasionally faulty, especially when it comes to pitching lines. In a sport with so many numbers floating around, other vagaries abound. As I discovered, sometimes reputable sources will have different numbers for a particular pitcher's splits as the result of a switch-hitting batter choosing to hit the "wrong" way: batting lefty against a left-handed pitcher, for instance, when a scorer assumes he'll bat righty. Even figures from Major League Baseball and Stats, Inc., sometimes differ because of mistakes such as this.

I consulted a handful of the many books written about the Red Sox, including Baseball Prospectus's *Mind Game,* Howard Bryant's *Shut Out,* Johnny Damon's *Idiot,* Peter Gammons's *Beyond the Sixth Game,* Peter Golenbock's *Red Sox Nation,* David Halberstam's *The Teammates,* Richard A. Johnson and Glenn Stout's *Red Sox Century,* Tony Massarotti and John Harper's *A Tale of Two Cities,* Leigh Montville's *Ted Williams,* and Dan Shaughnessy's *The Curse of the Bambino* and *Reversing the Curse.* Robert K. Adair's *The Physics of Baseball,* Michael Lewis's *Moneyball,* Daniel Okrent's *9 Innings,* Okrent and Harris Lewine's *The Ultimate Baseball Book,* Alan Schwarz's *The Numbers Game,* and Andrew Zimbalist's *In the Best*

*Interests of Baseball?* were also much-used references. Bill James's and Roger Angell's articles and books, the annual Baseball Prospectus guides, Ben McGrath's *New Yorker* articles on Bill James and the knuckleball, and the websites Baseball Prospectus, Baseball Reference, ESPN.com, Retrosheet, and Sons of Sam Horn were valuable resources as well.

# *Acknowledgments*

For the past 20 years, my mother has been teaching me how to write. As I've moved from high-school essays to a college thesis to newspaper and magazine stories to books, the biggest change in our working relationship has been the demands I've made on her time. In the month before this manuscript was due, she was available around the clock. I could send her 10,000 words two hours after asking her to read through the first half of the book for the 10th time and her only question would be, "How soon do you need it back?" (Since my mother deserves credit for any of the felicitous writing contained herein, those who enjoyed this book should check out—and buy—her poetry, which you can find at www.wendymnookin.com.) During those same frantic final weeks, my father would call in comments from airports around the country, and on more than one occasion he asked for entire chapters to be sent to him via BlackBerry. In my periods of greatest exhaustion, he helped boost my flagging spirits as only a father can.

Hanya Yanagihara, Karen Olsson, and Jonathan Mahler gave me invaluable insight and feedback. Hanya, in the middle of editing features and redesigning portions of *Condé Nast Traveller,* listened to my complaints, tightened my prose, and indulged me during several semi-coherent fits. Karen, fresh off of the publication of her amazing novel, *Waterloo,* responded to my panic by suggesting a cross-country exchange. Her daily queries and encouragements both sharpened the book and helped me to keep on keeping on. Jon, whose *Ladies and Gentlemen, The Bronx Is Burning* is the model for literary nonfiction that combines social history with baseball, helped sort out what seemed to be intractable structural problems.

I met Tim Mennell when he was hired to do a blind read of *Hard News*. A year and a half later, I was still in awe of how spot-on his comments, suggestions, and fixes were. Despite being asked to help on this book at the last moment, Tim—the self-appointed "vice president of the Upper Midwest branch of the Denny Doyle Appreciation Society"—signed on. He caught clumsy errors, stupid errors, and completely understandable errors. He offered elegant fixes for thorny problems and humorous solutions for daily dilemmas.

I first encountered John Tomase during the Red Sox's 2005 home opener, the beginning of my season with the team. John, then the Sox reporter for the North Andover *Eagle-Tribune*, was warm and welcoming from the start. More important, he was exceedingly funny and one of the smartest writers working the beat. (One of the perpetual frustrations of 2005 was slogging through the *Trib*'s user-repellent website in order to read John's articles.) At the end of the 2005 baseball season, when the *Boston Herald* hired John to cover the Patriots, it was bad news for fans of great baseball writing and reporting. It was a boon for me in that it freed up John to read and make suggestions on my manuscript without being tempted to poach my best material. He offered insightful suggestions and helped with some particularly troublesome sections. And he kept me laughing, even after I'd spent the previous 18 hours staring at a computer screen.

This project grew out of a story I wrote for *Vanity Fair,* where I've been lucky enough to have Anne Fulenwider as an editor and Graydon Carter as an editor in chief. Not many editors of a glossy magazine known for combining high society and celebrity coverage with hard-hitting political and investigative stories would set a writer loose on a baseball team, but Anne and Graydon did just that. At *Vanity Fair,* I was paired with Sarah Czeladnicki and John Huba, a photo editor and photographer who are both rabid Yankees fans. (I believe Huba's first words to me were, "I can't fucking believe this is the assignment I got.") It's a testament to the incredible talents of both that they produced a spread that contained some of the best sports photojournalism I've ever seen. I was so taken with Huba's photographs (and Sarah's photo editing) I asked them both to help out on this project. Despite the fact that it meant they'd once again have to pore over images of David Ortiz and Curt Schilling, they readily agreed. (Even Yankees fans, it seems, can be generous.) Many of the other photographs contained in this book come from the pages of *The Boston Globe*. Kathleen Cable, from the *Globe*'s photo research department, helped me select those pictures. When she sent me the initial packet of shots she'd put together without the benefit of having read any of the book, they so perfectly illustrated my text that I was convinced she'd found some way to tap into my hard drive.

Rebecca Seesel and David Fellows transcribed so many hours of interviews I'm sure the sound of my voice makes them cringe. They both did an admirable job, often turning around tapes in record time.

At Simon & Schuster, Bob Bender (another Yankees fan—they apparently breed like mice) constantly amazed me with his encyclopedic knowledge of baseball and his willingness to edit as many thousands of words as I could spit out. He's one of the deftest and gentlest editors I've encountered. Thank God for that: When Bob suggested we trim my section on the history of the Red Sox by half—half!—it was his mellifluous tones that made me realize he was right. David Rosenthal has been in and out of my life for the better part of a decade, and I'm lucky to finally get the chance to work with him. He's an almost perfect publisher: smart, funny, savvy, and aggressive with a huge set of balls. My agent, David McCormick, immediately saw the incredible opportunity this book afforded me and was a forceful and convincing advocate from the day I told him I wanted to spend the next year of my life following the Red Sox.

I spent much of the spring and summer in Boston where Judith and Sean Palfrey, the housemasters of Harvard's Adams House, gave me refuge. More than a decade after she thought she'd gotten rid of me, Victoria Macy helped deal with all my little problems, from figuring out how to gain access to the gym to securing a working air conditioner.

I could not have completed this book without a place to actually write. For three straight months, I essentially moved into Paragraph, a workspace for writers in downtown Manhattan. It saved me. Anyone looking for a quiet place to work should visit www.paragraphy.com. (Just don't steal the perch.)

Finally, the men and women who work for the Boston Red Sox were remarkably warm, accommodating, and gracious. Naming everyone who was helpful would require listing almost every last person on the team's payroll, from the clubhouse attendants to the PR interns to John Henry, Tom Werner, and Larry Lucchino. I thank them all.

# *Index*